THE NEXT ARAB DECADE

Published in cooperation with the
Center for Contemporary Arab Studies,
Georgetown University

مركز الدراسات العربيّة المعاصرة ـ جَامعـة جُورجـتاون

THE NEXT ARAB DECADE
Alternative Futures

EDITED BY
Hisham Sharabi

WESTVIEW PRESS
Boulder, Colorado

MANSELL PUBLISHING LIMITED
London, England

All rights reserved. No part of this publication may be reproduced or transmitted in any form or by any means, electronic or mechanical, including photocopy, recording, or any information storage and retrieval system, without permission in writing from Westview Press.

Copyright © 1988 by the Center for Contemporary Arab Studies, Georgetown University

Published in 1988 in the United States of America by Westview Press, Inc.; Frederick A. Praeger, Publisher; 5500 Central Avenue, Boulder, Colorado 80301

Published in 1988 in Great Britain by Mansell Publishing Limited, 6 All Saints Street, London N1 9RL

Library of Congress Cataloging-in-Publication Data
The Next Arab decade.
  Includes index.
  1. Arab countries—Forecasting. I. Sharabi,
Hisham, 1927–
DS39.N49 1988   303.4'9174924   87-10674
ISBN 0-8133-7440-5

British Library Cataloguing in Publication Data
The Next Arab decade: alternative futures.
  1. Arab countries—Social conditions
I. Sharabi, Hisham
303.4'9174927   HN766.A85
ISBN 0-7201-1957-X

Printed and bound in the United States of America

∞ The paper used in this publication meets the requirements of the American National Standard for Permanence of Paper for Printed Library Materials Z39.48-1984.

10   9   8   7   6   5   4   3   2   1

Contents

List of Tables and Figures ix
Preface xi

Introduction: Patriarchy and Dependency and
the Future of Arab Society, *Hisham Sharabi* 1

Part One
The State, Democracy, and Human Rights

1 Forecast for the Future: State and Society in Egypt,
Sudan, and Libya in 1995, *Ibrahim Ibrahim* 11

2 State, Society, and Legitimacy: An Essay on Arab
Political Prospects in the 1990s, *Michael C. Hudson* 22

3 The Future of Human Rights in the Arab World,
Saad Eddin Ibrahim 38

4 Democracy, Development, and Human Rights:
Can Women Achieve Change Without Conflict?
Nadia Hijab 45

Part Two
The Political Economy of Arab International Relations

5 The Shape of Inter-Arab Politics in 1995,
Rashid I. Khalidi 55

6 Unwelcome Guests: The Political Economy of Arab
Relations with the Superpowers, *Bahgat Korany* 64

Part Three
The Economy: Breakthrough or Breakdown?

7 The Lean Years: The Political Economy of Arab Oil
   in the Coming Decade, *George T. Abed*   91

8 Arab Agriculture in 1995: Apocalypse or Muddling
   Through? *Alan Richards*   107

9 The Prospects of Technological Growth in Arab
   Societies: An Analysis of the Potential for Progress
   Toward Technological Autonomy in the Arab World,
   1985–95, *Michael J. Simpson*   129

Part Four
Cultural Change, Creativity, and Authenticity

10 Challenges to Arab Cultural Authenticity,
   Issa J. Boullata   147

11 Cultural Creation in a Fragmented Society,
   Kamal Abu-Deeb   160

Part Five
Social Transformations

12 Future Arab Economic-Demographic Potential:
   Whither Policy? *Ismail A. Sirageldin*   185

13 Arab Women: 1995, *Leila Ahmed*   208

14 Class Structure and Social Change in the Arab
   World: 1995, *Samih K. Farsoun*   221

Part Six
The Arab-Israeli Conflict

15 Israel: The Political Economy of a Garrison State
   and Its Future, *Joel Beinin*   241

16 Palestinian Impasse: Constraints and Opportunities,
   Naseer H. Aruri   255

17 The Implications of Current Trends in the Arab-Israeli
   Military Balance, *Anthony H. Cordesman*   279

Part Seven
Priorities for Arab Studies

18 Social Science Research and Arab Studies in the
    Coming Decade, *John Waterbury* — 293

19 In Search of a New Identity of the Social Sciences
    in the Arab World: Discourse, Paradigm, and Strategy
    El Sayed Yassin — 303

20 Middle East Studies in the United States:
    The Coming Decade, *Judith E. Tucker* — 312

21 Futurology and the Study of the Arab World,
    Elia T. Zureik — 322

About the Contributors — 329
Index — 334

Tables and Figures

Tables

6.1	Evolution of balance of payments deficits of agricultural products	81
6.2	Arab countries' exports	81
6.3	Origins of Arab countries' imports	82
6.4	Destination of Arab countries' exports	82
6.5	Soviet bloc military technicians in selected countries, 1979	83
6.6	Middle Eastern military personnel trained in Soviet bloc countries, 1955–79	83
6.7	Defense expenditures of Gulf and some other Arab countries, 1969–81	84
6.8	Public foreign debt of Arab countries	86
6.9	Projected public debt service of Arab countries, 1986–91	87
6.10	Students abroad from Arab countries	87
7.1	Projection of world oil market, 1995	98
8.1	Selected agricultural indicators, Middle East and North Africa, 1970–82	110
8.2	Gini coefficients of farm size	114
8.3	Food self-sufficiency ratios for selected foods and countries, 1970 and 1981	119
8.4	Proportion of total agricultural imports coming from the United States, 1983	120
8.5	Share of agriculture in public investment, according to development plans, 1975–80	121
9.1	Commitments to scientific and technological research and experimental development in different world regions, 1970–80	133
9.2	Students graduating in scientific subjects at the university and equivalent levels within the Arab world, c. 1981 and 1971	138
12.1	Demographic change in Arab countries, 1960–2000	187
12.2	Economic indicators, selected Arab countries, 1970–82	200

15.1	Israeli military expenditures as a percentage of GNP	244
15.2	Israel's military exports, 1972–83	246
15.3	Average number of Knesset members	249
15.4	Distribution of the 1984 Knesset vote	250

Figures

12.1	Demographic transition(s) in the Arab world, 1960–2000	188
12.2	Socio-demographic transitions: A new international revenue system	196
17.1	The Israeli-Syrian balance, 1987	281
17.2	Israeli vs. Syrian defense effort, 1985	282

Preface

In putting together these proceedings of the 1985 annual symposium of the Center for Contemporary Arab Studies at Georgetown University, we have tried to preserve such coherence and continuity as would give this book a unity and focus that are often lacking in collections of conference papers. The central concern of the symposium was the deepening crisis of the Arab world—as seen from the political and economic points of view, in terms of social and cultural life, and from the standpoint of internal and international relations. The questions raised in these papers are primarily concerned with defining the nature of the crisis, with tracing its possible development, and with charting the conditions of its possible outcomes. One central question raised in the panel discussions and many of the papers is, what will the Arab world look like in the mid-1990s, less than ten years from now?

The first panel focused on the question of human and democratic rights, the central and most explosive issue of Arab political life in the coming decade. The subject of the second panel was political economy and international relations; it dealt with inter-Arab relations and superpower relations with the Arab world. The third panel focused on the economy—and especially on oil, agriculture, and technology transfer, the most sensitive aspects of Arab economic life. The fourth panel concentrated on the cultural aspects and tackled the problems of creativity and authenticity in their relation to change and modernity. The fifth panel dealt with social transformation, with emphasis on demographic change and the status of women. The discussion of the sixth panel centered on the Arab-Israeli conflict and its impact on regional developments in the next few years. A roundtable discussion of the priorities of Arab studies in terms of methodology and research issues brought the symposium to a close.

All the writers of papers printed here were given the opportunity to revise and update their analyses. Thus, the time lag between the actual date of the symposium and the publication of this book was adequately covered: These papers address the next decade from the vantage of 1986 rather than that of 1985.

This book appeared in an Arabic translation, published in Beirut by the Centre for Arab Unity Studies in early 1987.

Many individuals have contributed to the organization of the symposium and the publication of these proceedings. I should like in particular to thank the members of the Symposium Steering Committee, Halim Barakat, Michael

C. Hudson, and Judith Tucker, for the time and effort they put into refining the topics and structuring the program. Special thanks go to Zeina Azzam Seikaly and Michael Baker, without whose diligent and ever-present assistance the symposium and the publication of proceedings would not have been possible. I also wish to express my thanks to Jane Power for a sensitive copyediting of the final text, to John D. Lawrence and Eileen Rogers Orfalea, who served as publications assistants, and to Norma Sharara and Sally Ann Ethelston for an excellent typing of the final draft.

Hisham Sharabi

Introduction: Patriarchy and Dependency and the Future of Arab Society

Hisham Sharabi

Sitting in a bedouin tent one crisp afternoon last January, I sought to formulate some appropriate thoughts with which to open my remarks. We had just watched color television (a panel discussion from Egyptian television on the interpretation of some obscure religious texts, and an American program with Robert Wagner and Stephanie Powers); and as I sat there trying to frame my thoughts, several cars, including some station wagons and large campers, sped past the tent's entrance; in the distance I could see a busy highway, and beyond it a large satellite station. All around the desert was alive with people and cars, with not a bedouin or a camel in sight. This was Kuwait's northern desert, not far from the Iraqi border at the head of the Gulf, where two major oil-producing countries were at that moment doing their best to sink oil tankers carrying their own oil to the world market. In any event, no appropriate thoughts came to me that afternoon.

It was not until a week later, while attending a conference of Arab sociologists in Tunis, that I came upon the appropriate formulation. This was in the form of two theses advanced by the distinguished Egyptian economist Samir Amin, who happened to be a member of the panel I was chairing.

The first thesis held that the age of Arab awakening (*nahda*), which in the nineteenth century launched the movement of enlightenment, was now over and a new historical stage was beginning. The second thesis stated that with the end of the age of awakening the leadership of the national bourgeoisie has come to an end with no new leadership to take its place. As Amin put it, the next phase presents a vacuum which religious fundamentalism, being nothing more than a populist movement lacking a strategy and a direction, cannot fill.

To try, as we shall do at this symposium, to project an image of the politics, economics, society, and culture of the Arab world in the next decade may seem somewhat ambitious. But our goal is not simply to make predictions about the future, but to try to give an interpretation of it. Such an interpretation would not take the future as an independent category of analysis but as part of a larger concept articulating the other two temporal dimensions. Thus past, present, and future would constitute a single category defining a unified horizon in which the future is but the far extension.

From this position, looking ahead is no longer a passive practice, but one shaped by our understanding of the past and the present; and the way we see the future becomes a factor determining that same future.

In my own remarks I shall confine myself to defining what I think is an essential interpretive framework, and then to making some suggestions regarding the conditions that are likely to determine developments in the next decade.

The current crisis becomes clearer when we view it in its Third World context. Over thirty years after decolonization and independence most Third World countries have failed to build strong and stable social systems, whether in the image of Western European democracies or of Eastern European socialism. Most of them have dictatorial, autocratic, or theocratic governments, based on tribal or ethnic or religious foundations. It is interesting from this standpoint that while among the exceptions, China and India—two of the three largest literate cultures of the Third World—have succeeded in developing viable socialist and liberal systems, the Arab world—the third major literate culture in the underdeveloped world—has failed to achieve lasting development in either direction. For instance, how can we account for the outcome of the three great revolutions of the post-independence era (1950–80): the Nasserist revolution (to realize Arab unity), the Palestinian revolution (to achieve liberation), and the oil revolution (to bring about radical economic transformation)?

I find it difficult to deal analytically with this and other related questions without using two broad analytical categories, the categories of *patriarchy* and *dependency*. Here let me briefly touch upon these two categories and their significance for our analysis.

The systems of patriarchy and dependency, when joined together (as they have been in Arab society in the course of the last century), give rise to a particular sociopolitical structure which may be described as *neopatriarchal*. Strictly speaking this neopatriarchal structure is neither traditional nor modern; it is unique in that it has its own particular patterns of doing and thinking, its own ways of valuing and behaving, its own manner of dealing with reality and the world. Projected in social terms, neopatriarchy may be characterized by the following attributes:

1. *Social fragmentation*—i.e., the family, clan, religion, or ethnic group (rather than the nation or civic society) constitute the basis of social relations and corresponding social organization.

2. *Authoritarian organization*—i.e., domination, coercion, and paternalism (rather than cooperation, mutual recognition, and equality) govern all relations from the microstructure of the family to the macrostructures of the state.
3. *Absolutist paradigms*—i.e., a closed, absolutist consciousness (in theoretical practice, in politics, and everyday life) grounded in transcendence, metaphysics, revelation, and closure (rather than in difference, plurality, diffusion, openness, etc.).
4. *Ritualistic practice*—i.e., behavior governed by ceremony, custom, and ritual (rather than by spontaneity, creativity, and innovation). And so on.

The uniqueness of neopatriarchy is perhaps nowhere more clearly revealed than when contrasted with modernity. (By modernity here I do not refer just to the Western type, but to a diffuse, general type.)

Thus if we take, for example, the category of "knowledge," which in the context of modernity would correspond to the concepts of "thought"/"reason," we find that in neopatriarchy the corresponding concepts would be "myth"/"faith." Similarly, in the category of "truth," where the concepts in modernity would be "scientific"/"ironic," in neopatriarchy the concepts would be "religious"/"metaphoric." For the category of "language," we have in modernity the concept "analytical," in neopatriarchy the concept "rhetorical"; for the category of "government," we have in modernity the concepts "democratic"/"socialist," in neopatriarchy that of "sultanate" or of "neosultanate"; for the category of "social relations," in modernity we have the counterpoised concepts of *"gesellschaft"/"gemeinschaft,"* in neopatriarchy the single concept of *"ra'iya"*/"flock"; and for the category of "social stratification" in modernity we have "social class," and in neopatriarchy, "family"/"clan"/"sect"; and so on.

It is possible to say that patriarchy is converted into neopatriarchy at the moment it is absorbed into dependency, and that neopatriarchy as a social formation is nothing else than corrupted patriarchy wedded to distorted modernity. But the corruptive factor in this relationship is not patriarchy (traditionality) as such, but dependency whose historical expression and agency is Western imperialism. It is important, however, to stress that dependency is the product of more than just crude aggression, domination, expropriation, and oppression—more, that is, than the direct economic and military overpowering of the periphery by the center. In the Arab world, dependency presents itself in all these forms but additionally and crucially in the form of an *inner* cultural relation, one sustained in the shadow of the dominant Other. In this sense, besides being a political, economic, and military *outside*, the relation of dependency is also a cultural *inside*. This is the essential character of the socio-psychological structure we call neopatriarchy.

In this light, the failure, indeed the entire behavior, of the neopatriarchal bourgeoisie cannot be understood merely in terms of its external context—

imperialism and Zionism, corruption and ignorance, chance and conspiracy, and so on—but must be interpreted in terms of the dynamics of neopatriarchy itself. As a social and psychological system it is not enough to talk about the failure of a specific social class, even though it may be the dominant class. The category "class" here is too narrow and too vague to account for all the relevant phenomena. Hence the necessity, at least for the neopatriarchal moment, of featuring structure over agency, and culture over social class.

In support of this position I shall quote Lukacs, who argued that the essence of a historical period may be grasped by understanding its cultural gist as by its forms of production.

> The development of society is a unified process. This means that a certain phase of development cannot take place in any area of social life without exerting an impact on all other areas. Through this writing and coherence of social development it is possible to grasp and achieve an understanding of the same process from the standpoint of one social phenomenon or another. Thus one can speak of culture in its apparent isolation from other social phenomena, for when we correctly grasp the culture of any period, we grasp with it the root of the whole development of the period, just as we do when we begin with an analysis of economic relations.[1]

In any case, the question has more than methodological interest. The point is that the kind of view we form of the possibilities of the future largely depends on whether we limit our perspective to received doctrine or, which amounts to the same thing, to immediate pragmatics, or whether we admit a mode of analysis that transcends the prevailing abstractions and platitudes and allow ourselves to look at the future in a new light.

The future would appear quite different if we were to make a basic assumption: the possibility of alternative action by the Arab ruling class. This small group of individuals controls virtually all the power and most of the wealth of society, not so much by virtue of their subjects' love or free consent expressed at the ballot box (indeed, every now and then some ruler or other tries to act out his electoral fantasies by carrying out elections that usually result in his obtaining 99.9 percent of the vote), but rather by means of a ruthless small group of servants and state officials, perhaps not exceeding a few thousand in number for the entire Arab world, consisting of military and security police officers, leaders of the party militia or special forces, bureaucratic chiefs, special advisors, and top technocrats. Given this situation, how possible is alternative action by the ruling elite? I do not suggest an expansive, ideal program, but one which would be quite feasible in terms of the socially available resources. The status quo would survive for a long time if only those in power were to carry out some version of such a program. For example, the following objectives are certainly not beyond reach, even for leaders with the most limited vision:

1. *On the political level*: To dismantle the system of internal oppression as cruel and counterproductive (without necessarily having to change

the political system), to end violation of human and civil rights, and to acknowledge basic political rights.
2. *On the economic level*: To introduce rationality into economic behavior by treating national wealth as a social and not as a family or a clan possession, to prohibit arbitrary appropriation and expenditure, and to end corrupt practices.
3. *On the national level*: To establish a minimum basis of inter-Arab cooperation, based on pan-Arab interest, by ending inter-state rivalries, by resolving current differences through negotiations and compromise, and by setting Arab collective security as the dominant goal of Arab collective action.
4. *On the level of international relations*: To maintain a common Arab front in all international dealings by, for example, reinvesting the League of Arab States with its original powers and by maintaining close consultations and cooperation among its members on political, economic, and military matters affecting any member of the League, and by taking collective action when collective decisions have been taken.
5. *On the level of the Palestine question and the Iran–Iraq war*: To act collectively on a common strategy, policy, or approach to end the Iran–Iraq war and to resolve the Palestine question.

These objectives, and many others, can be successfully achieved by a forward-looking, intelligent ruling elite. Sometimes, however, it is difficult to avoid the impression that this elite is neither strikingly intelligent nor exactly forward-looking. Most of these rulers, in any event, seem to have chosen to act in ways that are not always easy to explain. So let us now turn from speculation to the description of some of the hard realities that are likely to determine concrete developments in the next decade.

In the first place, the prospects of a revolutionary change in the intermediate future, on the Iranian or the South Yemeni model, seem rather limited, given the state of the forces of radicalism, whether of the ideological left or the fundamentalist right. This, however, does not eliminate the possibilities of internal upheaval and social instability in some Arab countries where Islamic sentiment runs deep and where economic conditions may deteriorate beyond the threshold of present tolerance.

This much is clear, however; whatever form change might take, it will necessarily be determined by the structure of the individual regimes. These regimes may be classified according to three types: the quasi-liberal, the conservative, and the personalized leadership type. Excluding the possibility of external intervention (which, however, should not be excluded in concrete political analysis), one may assume that, politically, the first and second types of regime have a better chance of absorbing change and surviving into 1995 than does the personalized leadership type with its personal, rigid concentration of power. Thus both the quasi-liberal and the conservative structures will probably weather qualitative incremental (i.e., non-radical) change without undergoing structural transformation, while the personalized type of structure is more likely to undergo radical transformations and collapse.

For all three types of regimes, however, economic stagnation and demographic pressure, combined with external threats and continued humiliation (by Israel and the United States), might in the next ten years create conditions of high vulnerability. At present, obviously, the two major factors affecting all developments on the internal scene are the Iran–Iraq war and the Palestinian question, which contain an unpredictable and explosive potential for the future of all the states of the Arab East. By the same token, Israel's hegemonic ambitions, if not somehow checked, will increase the feelings of impotence and frustration and thus further contribute to the destabilization of the status quo.

Let us return to the question of revolution. Why is revolution unlikely to occur, at least in the near future? The answer to this question must necessarily be ambivalent. In the first place, revolutions are historical opportunities, openings in the historical process which, once missed, close up and do not soon recur. Recent history in the Arab world is strewn with skewed, unfinished, or failed revolutions. The revolutionary aims with which 10 or 15 years ago the educated youth scared their teachers and members of the older generation are no longer plausible, even for those who still mouth them.

Nor is the other kind of revolution, the revolution from above by the man on horseback, any more likely to happen. One reason for this is the consolidation of political power and the development of practically invincible internal security systems, by far the best example of modernization in neopatriarchal society. But even if a coup d'état were to take place, it would change little in most countries, for it would have little effect on the way power is applied and organized.

This is not to say that the status quo will not change in the next decade. The question is, what form is such change likely to take?

The worst case scenario would be a fulfillment of the familiar remark: "The worse things get, the better," that is to say, things will get better only by getting worse. But how much worse can things get before getting better?

On this view, things might really go bad—hence become better—if a leading country in the eastern Arab world were to collapse in the Iranian fashion. Presumably this could occur in the wake of a grassroots fundamentalist upheaval, which would then spread to other countries. From this standpoint, a worst-case scenario would envisage not only a chain reaction throughout the Arab world, but the progressive transformation of many countries into closed, fanatical, backward-looking societies.

Strangely enough, a best-case scenario also would assume some kind of disintegration of the status quo occurring from within, but not necessarily as a result of violent upheaval. To begin with, the progressive, anti-fundamentalist forces within Arab society today are not so negligible as some might think; they include significant social strata drawn into the body politic over the last two or three decades through the advances made in education, public health, and communications. The movement of enlightenment and secularization spearheaded by a significant segment of the rising generation seems irreversible and will in the years ahead have a profound, transformative effect on the structure of neopatriarchal society. More significant perhaps is the emergence of a new critical consciousness in the progressive secularized intelligentsia. Those of you familiar with recent Arabic writing, particularly in the Maghrib, know the kind of consciousness I am referring to; it is one based on a different vision of self and history, providing the makings of a new intellectual sensibility.

A concrete expression of the direction this movement is taking is the current effort by Arab scholars and intellectuals to organize professionally on a national (Arab) level, in itself a form of political defiance by nonpolitical means and a way of loosening the grip of official political and ideological control. Already in existence are the Arab Association of Sociologists and the Arab Association of Political Scientists, and very shortly the Association of Arab Economists and the Arab Women's Association will be organized. In 1984 the first pan-Arab organization of human rights was formed in Cairo; it is already engaged in the defense of human rights in the Arab world. If the next decade indeed represents a transitional phase, a period between two epochs, leading to a new, higher, stage of development, then we might be able to point to some specific possibilities of change.

Some of the main forces of change would probably operate outside the direct political field, but they will have profound significance for future political development. If these forces, expressed in social, ideological, intellectual forms, succeed in breaking through, they will be difficult to stop; neopatriarchal society is typically incapable of repressing new awareness once it penetrates the existing ideological barriers. Social and ideological change in the context of neopatriarchy will inevitably lead to some form of structural disintegration, as we saw happening, for example, in the late Ottoman Empire. The question is, if Samir Amin is right in his thesis that *classical* revolutionary change in the next phase is not likely to occur, is a cultural revolution possible?

If the answer is yes, then a best case scenario would envisage a kind of positive development taking place in the next decade, with the status quo being able, internally, to absorb the pressure of fundamentalism without succumbing to it and at the same time to respond to social and political demands, particularly regarding political rights and basic freedoms, and, externally, to withstand Israeli belligerence.

I know that this may not be quite consistent with what I said earlier about the self-defeating behavior of the existing ruling class. But the point I am trying to make is based on possible alternatives governing the struggle in the next decade, which will be primarily a cultural struggle, with decisive social and political consequences, between the forces of religious conservatism and the forces of secular critical modernity.

From this conclusion you will see that I make allowance, with Antonio Gramsci, for the pessimism of intellect without giving up the optimism of will.

Notes

1. George Lukacs, "The Old Culture and the New Culture," in Bart Grahl and Paul Piccone, eds., *Towards a New Marxism* (St. Louis, MO: Dell, 1973), p. 21.

PART ONE

The State, Democracy, and Human Rights

1

Forecast for the Future: State and Society in Egypt, Sudan, and Libya in 1995

Ibrahim Ibrahim

The purpose of this paper is to discuss Egypt's prospects for the mid-1990s and the future of its immediate, and important, Arab neighbors, Sudan and Libya.

As with all projections into an uncertain future, many arbitrary elements come into play, along with occasional moments of wishful thinking on the part of the speculator. Nevertheless, this exercise of forecasting the future can be deemed worthwhile, despite the risk of error, simply because the problems of state and society in the Middle East are mirrored throughout the Third World.

By the turn of the century, there will be more than 200 million people living in the Arab world. Indeed, the enormous material and manpower wealth the region already contains requires each of us to summon forth any degree of prescience he has to attempt to sort out the most promising avenues for political and social development in the years to come.

Therefore, one must begin with Egypt—the largest, most advanced, most powerful country—and, until recently, the undisputed leader among the Arab states. Today, the bright promise that Egypt holds has been greatly dimmed by a complex web of social and economic ills that threaten the very existence of society. If these conditions are left to fester, it can be expected that the society will eventually explode.

Before proposing a way out of this unfortunate predicament, let us first examine the dimensions of Egypt's problems today. It is weakened by a tremendous crisis propelled by a spiralling demographic explosion: the population, even by conservative estimates, will reach 60 million by 1995. This burden will exacerbate existing dilemmas—such as the shortage of food, housing, land, and water—and further strain an already sorely tested infrastructure.

The decaying infrastructure and the housing crisis may be Egypt's most pressing problems: one-third of the population is without adequate accommodation, sanitation facilities, drinking water, or electricity.[1]

Given the fact that Egypt's budget is strapped with a deepening international deficit—currently debt repayment absorbs 25 percent of its revenues, and this condition will become more critical in the next decade if no solution is found—Mubarak, or his successor, must continue Egypt's dependence on American and international aid.

It is estimated that Egypt is dependent upon foreign aid for nearly 60 percent of its basic needs and upon Washington alone for 70 percent of the economic aid destined for food, military equipment, oil drilling and refining, and infrastructure modernization. Egypt's debt is particularly on the increase in the military field, as President Mubarak recently indicated. "The military debt is creating problems for our economic plan. I need the help of the U.S. not to put me in a difficult position."[2]

But, if one presumes a detente can be reached between the two superpowers within the next decade, Egypt will then find itself faced with a new dilemma: in an age of detente, an American Congress will be far less inclined to raise, or perhaps even maintain, its current high level of aid to Egypt. That congressional reluctance may be reinforced in the future by a softened Egyptian stance toward Communism in the Afro-Arab world.

It should not be overlooked that American aid to Egypt today is linked to that given Israel, and it can be expected that the U.S. administration(s) and Congress will continue to monitor Egypt's relations with Israel and ensure that Egypt remains within U.S.–Israeli strategic designs. Indeed, unlike Egypt, Israel already enjoys preferential treatment in terms of aid as well as trade, a favoritism that will be institutionally reinforced by 1995: on April 23, 1985, the United States signed an agreement with Israel that will eliminate all trade barriers between the two countries within ten years, a move hailed by President Ronald Reagan as adding "a new dimension to the special relationship between our countries."[3]

Like many Third World countries, Egypt's fortune—or misfortune—depends in large measure on relations between the two superpowers. To be sure, Egypt's geopolitical importance has given her the privilege of living, although not thriving, on international largesse. But such a state of dependency is dangerous, especially when rivalry between the two superpowers comes to an end, as happened in the early 1970s; when detente was reached between the United States and the Soviet Union in 1972, it foreclosed some opportunities for Egypt to exploit superpower rivalries to her material advantage. Detente's impact was in both domestic and foreign policy fields: it brought about *infitah*, the economic "open-door" policy; a break with the Soviet Union; and alignment with the conservative Gulf states and the United States.[4]

Given the likelihood of a Washington–Moscow reconciliation by 1995, Egypt—again, unlike Israel—will be left out in the cold. Cairo has little choice, therefore: it must undertake a plan designed to result in self-sufficiency by the year 2000. And it must achieve that self-sufficiency by itself. To do this, it must reclaim an area equivalent to virtually all of its current arable land in order to be able to feed its burgeoning masses. But pursuit of this policy has been shown to be both very costly and economically unsound in the long term.

Since the answer to this dual problem cannot be found within its own borders, Egypt must look outside, to its closest Arab neighbors, Sudan and Libya, for each is endowed with unique possibilities. In combination, at a propitious political moment, the three Arab states could become a self-reliant unit, able not only to escape the pressing social and political quandary each faces, but also to generate a vibrant and lasting economic order which could carry all three states well into the twenty-first century. It is, perhaps, a familiar idea, but one which has added urgency—and possibility—today.

Sudan, a massive country one-third the size of the United States, is a tremendous untapped agricultural reservoir, with more than 200 million acres of arable land. Its animal wealth includes tens of millions of heads of livestock, with additional resources that are beginning to surface, notably promising oil reserves and mineral wealth. Yet this exceptionally well endowed and potentially thriving country will continue to face dire economic and institutional maladies in the next ten years unless it can seek a solution outside its borders.

With a population of only 23 million, Sudan today ranks among the 25 poorest nations of the world; despite the fact that, apart from Egypt, it is the second largest recipient of American aid on the African continent, it remains, nevertheless, one of the most indebted nations. It lacks both a sufficient body of advanced manpower, with many of its best minds at work outside of the country, and a minimum of the infrastructural prerequisites for development.

There is also justifiable concern about tribal and associational differences, as well as regional and sectarian cleavages. Like most African countries, Sudan suffers from its ethnic, religious, and cultural diversity. When it obtained independence, the Muslim North and the animist–Christian South were almost alien parts of the country; soon after independence a civil war ensued, lasting 17 years. However, on March 3, 1972, a peaceful settlement was reached between the two regions and a formal agreement was signed, according to which a regional government and regional institutions were created. In the mid-1980s, the peace broke down and a second revolt erupted in the South when Numayri extended his "Islamicization" policy and dictatorship to that region: the Sudanese People's Liberation Army, led by Colonel John Garang, is fighting now not only against the application of the *shari'a* but also for regional self-government and the restoration of the Addis Ababa agreement.

The recent successful revolution against Numayri's regime might bring about a second reconciliation with the South; this is not impossible in view of the fact that North and South alike are cognizant of their Sudanese identity. Today, more than ever, secession is anathema to the two sides.

Apart from the fact that borders have become sacrosanct in the African idiom, neither South nor North alone can escape the hardships that Sudan as a whole must confront; difficult as it may seem at present, then, unity will continue to be imperative.

As Sudan's ambassador to Canada, the respected Southerner Francis M. Deng, so eloquently put it in 1981:

> One of the most challenging intellectual and diplomatic tasks in Africa is how to reconcile principles that now appear to be in conflict. In particular, the principle of maintaining the inherited boundaries needs to be reconciled with the right of self-determination by balancing national unity with the aspirations of minority groups for recognition and effective participation in their own government. While it is not easy to achieve a satisfactory balance, *I know it can be done because it has been done*. . . .[5] (my italics)

Obviously the ambassador was referring to the 1972 peaceful settlement of the civil war between North and South, an achievement which brought reconciliation and participation of the South in the national government. For more than ten years, reconciliation and unity have freed national resources for development and have opened up possibilities for better relations with Sudan's African neighbors.[6]

One of Sudan's eight neighbors is Libya, which, too, is a precarious entity: despite its oil wealth, it suffers from a scarcity of population and a lack of trained manpower. The unstable character of Muammar Qadhafi's Libya is obvious in view of his numerous attempts at various unions, including ones with Egypt, Syria, Tunisia, and Sudan, and the more recent one with his purported arch-enemy, Morocco.

This instability stems from the fact that Libya has never had the sense of surety and confidence that comes with the status of statehood. To be sure, the Sanusi king transformed the Sufi order into a monarchical one, but he failed to create a political community. Qadhafi inherited this rather precarious polity: using modern techniques and the advice and assistance of hired hands, he has been laboring to integrate the countryside with the city and to centralize the government.

To be sure, Qadhafi's social and economic policies were in line with the wishes of the majority: free housing, medical care, education, and transportation for any needy Libyan. More than Nasser's Egypt, Libya under Qadhafi has radically overturned the old order. His commitment to egalitarian values brought about a total nationalization of the economy: private enterprises were turned over to employees in workers' committees; rental properties were seized; retail trade was abolished; and, to guarantee that all Libyans had equal assets, bank accounts were frozen. Indeed, Libyan society in the late 1970s had been radically restructured, especially since a substantial part of the population had grown into adulthood with the revolution.[7]

But despite social and economic reforms, the state under Qadhafi has remained omnipotent: the state takes precedence over society. It has been estimated that by 1981 as many as 100,000 Libyans had left the country to join the six or seven major opposition groups operating in exile.[8] Both the middle class and the growing intelligentsia are challenging the authoritarian nature of the state and its repressive policy. At the same time, state oppression and the counter-assassination attempts it has engendered not only reveal the dichotomy between the people and their government, but also betray a sort of civil war raging beneath the surface.

Libya's present behavior mirrors the lack of cohesion in its contemporary society. It suffers from ecological divisions between an urban minority in Tripoli, on the one hand, and hinterland tribal and rural populations, on the other. One should remember that Libya became a unitary state only in 1963. During the monarchy it had been much more of a loose federal state composed of three *wilayat* (Tripolitania, Cyrenaica, and Fezzan).

The unification of the state was achieved with the expansion of bureaucracy and the armed forces under Qadhafi. But—notwithstanding Qadhafi's *schwärmerei* for and total devotion to Nasser and the idea of pan-Arabism—it was the lack of a well-defined Libyan identity that propelled him to look beyond Libya's borders, to seek a wider entity in Arab unity.[9]

Thus, Qadhafi's numerous attempts at establishing Arab unity can be likened to the pan-Arab ideology of the Ba'th in Syria, which, conscious of the absence of a well-defined Syrian national identity, attempted to transcend the partition of Greater Syria through unity. A post-Qadhafi Libya will continue to seek unity as a means of securing its identity.

Today, in Libya, Sudan, and Egypt, as in the Arab East in general, the authoritarian, bureaucratic state has exhausted itself. Even Nasser, the architect and master of the bureaucratic, authoritarian Egyptian state, could see—alas, belatedly—his own failures in this regard:

> The stage of revolutionary administrative measures is in fact outmoded. The time has come for us to rely upon the popular conscience of the people and not upon government intervention. . . . The only path that will allow us to meet the challenge of reaction and imperialism, the only way that will enable us to accomplish the transformation from capitalism to socialism is that of political and not governmental action.[10]

It is true that in the past two or three decades the bureaucratic authoritarian state was able to suppress society at will, depoliticizing the population in the process. Its rationale was a convenient alibi—that internal state security was a prerequisite to true independence, Arab unity, socialism, development, and, most importantly, victory over Israel.

But now it has become obvious that the state has failed on all of these fronts. Economic disarray and dependence on foreign aid underscore the failure of Arab socialism; even the idea of pan-Arabism has been relegated to the back burner.

Having thus failed to deliver, the state in each of the three countries has betrayed its impotence. Today, a state of immobilization, rather than one of stability, prevails. Indeed, the state is cracking under the stress; like the Iranian state under the Shah, it too will fall apart.[11] Government by the sheer force of coercion and repression will no longer be tolerated by a society reaching for emancipation and maturity. This is seen most vividly in the recent popular uprising against Numayri, who, it should be remembered, was last reelected with 99.6 percent of the vote.

Socioeconomic change and the natural erosion of power at the end of each and every generation, coupled with the aspirations of the masses for freedom, social justice, and economic welfare, all contribute to ripen the conditions for change in the state. I predict, therefore, that the regime in each of these three countries will be replaced within the next decade by freely-elected governments, thereby setting the stage for true human liberation.

This change, particularly in the case of Egypt, will be fueled by the demographic explosion, accelerated by the rise of millions of students and graduates from secondary schools and universities. With 43 percent of its people under the age of 15, and with a student population of more than ten million—a staggering number, larger than the entire population of many Arab states,[12] Egypt's crisis cannot be resolved by doses, no matter their size, of international assistance. Furthermore, revenues from oil exports, emigrant remittances, the Suez Canal, and tourism also are dependent on regional and international factors beyond Egypt's control.[13]

Rather, Egypt's internal chaos will be heightened by a drop in workers' remittances, as the infrastructure is completed in the Gulf. That in turn will prompt the return of many unskilled workers, who will be consigned, like so many millions of others in Egypt today, to unemployment or underemployment.

It can be expected that millions of workers, trade unionists, and new urban dwellers will coalesce with students to hasten the rise of resistance in many forms, including militant Islamic and leftist groups. In this setting, mass and continuing unrest, and perhaps violence, will result.

In such a state of anarchy, there can be no viable alternative to parliamentary rule: it will become a *prima facie* imperative—and the only one—to reintroduce order and placate the competing groups, institutionalizing a more sophisticated form of representative government in the process.

Indeed, Egypt is more fit than most countries in the Third World to return to the multi-party system (and parliamentary government). Compared to other societies in the Afro–Asian world, Egypt has a cohesive society and a long history of secular institutions, a large body of modern, educated men and women, but, above all, a long tradition of tolerance and participation. As far back as the 1860s, Egypt, under Khedive Ismail, was experimenting with parliamentary activities. One hundred years ago, in replying to the Khedive's opening speech on January 27, 1879, to the assembly, one member expressed himself as follows:

> We, the representatives of the Egyptian nation and defenders of its rights and interests, which are at the same time those of the government, thank H.E. the Khedive for his goodness in assembling this chamber of delegates which is

the foundation-stone of all progress and the turning-point in the achievement of our liberty without which no equality of rights is possible, equality which is the essence of justice.[14]

In the interwar period there was also a genuine and serious "liberal experiment":[15] most intellectuals and political leaders adhered to and fought with vigor for the establishment of a freely elected parliament to which government would be accountable. "The Ruler has become the people themselves, who choose their representative to conduct their affairs," wrote the eminent historian and essayist Ahmad Amin in 1937. "And if any government hopes to survive, it must then embody the will of the people, provided that they, in their turn, are aware of their rights."[16]

Of course, under Nasser's authoritarian government the multi-party system was destroyed and parliamentary rule was overthrown; nevertheless, Nasser's Egypt could not be described as a "police state," or likened to some of her "radical" Arab sister states. There was a large element of consent, discussion, and persuasion involved, and most of the aims of the regime were in line with a broad national consensus. There was critical comment both publicly within the Arab Socialist Union and in the National Assembly. In this respect, Egypt remained a much more "open society" than many other Arab societies.[17]

This is not difficult to explain: Egypt's history of modernization is the longest in the Arab East, and its educational and cultural institutions are the most prolific. Not only is social mobilization further advanced there than elsewhere in the region, but the political structure is more differentiated as well. As Michael Hudson writes:

> Nowhere else in the Arab countries . . . could one find such a diversity of opinions and political organizations: Islamic fundamentalists, liberal constitutionalists, varieties of Marxists, influential intellectual circles concerned with politics . . . [and] labor and student organizations.[18]

Currently, opportunities to criticize the government, to unmask corruption, and to formulate policy alternatives exist in Egypt to an extent not enjoyed by the people in most Arab countries. There are also serious opposition parties with press organs, such as *Al-Sha'b* of the Socialist Party, led by Ibrahim Shukri, and *Al-Ahali*, a radical weekly of the left, which is said to have reached a circulation of about 100,000, with actual readership estimated at a quarter of a million people.[19] Muhammad Sid Ahmed, political columnist for *Al-Ahali*, says Egypt's press today is "freer than at any time since Farouk."[20]

With such a multiplicity of organizations and structures, and with a large educated elite, trained manpower, and concerned public opinion, the public eventually will wrest from the government the right to participate in the political process; neither Mubarak nor his successor can reverse this trend without a serious and costly battle.

In Egypt, the new government will have to be truly representative, formed as a national bloc comprised of Nasserites, Wafdists, leftists, and, if need be, the Muslim Brothers. Any attempt by militant Muslim groups to seize power from the newly established regime is bound to fail, not only because the new government will enjoy a broad social base, but also because of the absence of strong, cohesive, and autonomous religious institutions that could assume popular leadership: neither the *'ulama* nor the Azhar can perform this role, since each has long since been brought under the firm control of the secular state. But, above all, the professional officer corps will militate against and abort if necessary any attempted takeover by the Muslim Brothers or other militant Muslim groups.

Thus, a parliamentary system will be established first in Egypt, as it will later in Sudan and Libya, with a strong presidency able to check and balance competing political groups and parties. But the state will be a *Rechtstaat*, in which the government will be held accountable to parliament, with a guarantee of individual rights, including freedom of speech and political association. In sum, the rule of law will prevail and civil society will assert itself *vis-à-vis* the state.

While parliamentary rule will not, in and of itself, provide the solution to the host of problems that beset Egypt, Sudan, and Libya, it will provide the foundation for what I ultimately envision—namely, a voluntary confederation of the three states. This will not be a union, but instead will be a formalized configuration of three natural partners, an arrangement which would preserve the sovereignty and independence of each within a pragmatic alliance.

Practically speaking, how could a confederation so seemingly unattainable—from today's perspective at least—be reached? Initially, a common market would be created among the three, one in which free movement of labor and capital would be guaranteed. Sudan and Egypt have already taken a step in this direction with the Joint Integration Charter of October 12, 1982, underlining interdependency between the two countries. The rationale behind the Charter was explained in terms of historical ties and Arab brotherhood, but the real reasons are to be found in economic circumstances and political necessity. The elimination of passports between them is a step toward integration. In the second phase of the common market, the three countries would establish a formal political confederation, allowing for free trade, the integration of production, and technical integration.

Only then can the three embark on a systematic, long-term plan of investment for the twenty-first century. Unlike current attempts at expensive development projects, this strategic design would be part of a government-to-government relationship of development and mutual security, with a horizontal relationship of equals much more likely than today's endeavors, or those previously considered, to succeed in its undertakings.

Egypt, with its abundant labor and technical expertise, can join with an inherent Arab ingenuity to turn Sudan of the year 2000 into the breadbasket which it was to have become in the 1970s—an achievement which would be of immense significance not only to the almost 100 million citizens of the confederation but also to the citizens of a number of other Arab countries.

The key to achievement of the confederation will be its purely voluntary and flexible nature: Nasser's bitter experience with Syria should not be forgotten. Before embarking on such a grand design for the future, Sudan must first focus on its current domestic discontent; it must restore the unity of its own fragmented nation. Here, one must not overlook the fact that while some Sudanese groups are justifiably skeptical of unity schemes, only a freely-elected Sudanese government can take such a decision and implement it with success. Again, both Sudan and Libya must come to the conclusion—voluntarily—that it is in their own best interests to confederate with Egypt and with each other.

Sudan in particular may be close to this realization, since its economy at present is moribund; in September 1984 its national debt reached $8 billion, up $2 billion from its level when the International Monetary Fund intervened in 1978. Today the national debt is more than $9 billion. That debt, unfortunately, is only the tip of the iceberg: the Sudanese people face famine, hastened by massive influxes of more than one million refugees permeating its multiple borders. In short, the state is falling apart. Above and beyond this domestic instability, however, the threat of neighboring countries hostile to Sudan will prompt a search for a new solution. A confederation will offer a shield against potential aggressors as well as a haven from bankruptcy and starvation.

It is in the interests of Libya, too, to join the confederation as a means of alleviating its vulnerability. The grouping will reinforce its stability, give it a sense of belonging, and enhance its status within the Arab world and on the international scene as well. Such a tripartite agreement would ensure that Libya is not abandoned to the wiles of history.

Thus, in a more mature stage of statehood some ten years hence, both Libya and Sudan can be expected to realize that in the long run it is to their own advantage to confederate with an advanced country such as Egypt, which, after all, offers the largest pool of talent in the Arab world. Egypt must also take cognizance of the fact that her own security will be enhanced through the confederation. Egypt's security is tied to that of Sudan because both share the blessings of the waters of the Nile, while to confederate with Libya also will add to Egypt's security along the long, exposed border between them: a Libyan state allied to a country (or a superpower) hostile to Egypt could pose a threat of destabilization to Cairo. But, most important, confederation will give Egypt the opportunity to regain its natural leadership within the Arab world. Moreover, a confederation of Egypt, Sudan, and Libya, with almost 100 million people by 1995, in such a strategically important location, will enhance Egypt's status and power in the Arab East. Such an arrangement will not only give Egypt the opportunity to reassert itself against Israeli hegemony in the region, but will also vastly increase Egypt's bargaining power *vis-à-vis* the superpowers. Finally, the formidable Egyptian military might and its incipient arms industry will guarantee the permanence and security of the confederation, both within the inter-Arab state system and in Africa.

Lastly, let me point out that the rise of parliamentary government (an event likely to occur in Egypt first, as mentioned above) and the establishment of the tripartite confederation will capture the imagination of 200 million Arabs in the year 2000, and may well motivate them to act, just as Egypt's leadership in the 1950s and 1960s pointed the way to the overthrow of an oppressive past. Once again, it can be expected that such a neo-revolutionary evolution of relations among Egypt, Sudan, and Libya might promote similar associations with long-term development goals and lasting political content in both the Mashriq and the Maghrib. Certainly Saudi Arabia and the Gulf Cooperation Council countries, the confederation's neighbors to the east, will seek close cooperation with the confederation; they will be eager to participate in its development plans, but above all will seek cooperation for the comfort it offers in security matters. For them, the confederation's armed forces will offer the only reliable protection against external threats.

Of course, skeptics may label such a scheme as this a futile intellectual exercise. To them I would respond that the confederation is not a work of art but a work of necessity. The economic and security interdependence of the three countries is such that the choice is either to sink alone or swim together. Indeed, self-interest alone dictates the need for such a confederation.

Like the Hobbesian Leviathan, it has to rise so that the people may escape violent death. There is no alternative.

Notes

1. Eric Rouleau, "Egypt's Identity Crisis: Struggling to Surmount Economic Ills and Islamic Extremism," *World Press Review* (November 1984): 26–28.
2. *The Washington Post*, February 28, 1985, p. A5.
3. *The Washington Post*, April 23, 1985, p. C4.
4. John Waterbury, *The Egypt of Nasser and Sadat: The Political Economy of Two Regimes* (Princeton, NJ: Princeton University Press, 1983), pp. 123ff.
5. Francis M. Deng, "Security Problems: An African Predicament," Thirteenth Annual Hans Wolff Memorial Lecture, delivered at the African Studies Association Conference, Bloomington, Indiana, October 1981.
6. See Michael C. Hudson, *Arab Politics: The Search for Legitimacy* (New Haven, CT: Yale University Press, 1977), p. 355.
7. Jacques Roumani, "From Republic to Jamahiriya: Libya's Search for Political Community," *Middle East Journal* 27, no. 2 (Spring 1983): 168.
8. Lisa Anderson, "Assessing Libya's Qaddafi," *Current History* 84, no. 502 (May 1985): 200.
9. Marius K. Deeb and Mary Jane Deeb, *Libya Since the Revolution: Aspects of Social and Political Development* (New York: Praeger Publishers, 1982), p. 127.
10. Gamal Abdel-Nasser, November 12, 1964, cited in John Waterbury, *The Egypt of Nasser and Sadat*, p. 3.
11. Eric Rouleau, "Instability and New Leadership," in Thomas Naff, ed., *The Middle East Challenge, 1980–1985* (Carbondale: Southern Illinois University Press, 1981), p. 33.

12. Mary McDavid, "Egyptian Education and the Developmental Process: A Case Study," (unpublished paper), Washington, DC, 1985.

13. See Friedemann Buettner, "A Country Scenario Analysis of Egypt," *Vierteljahresberichte* 96 (June 1984): 163–79.

14. Cited in Jamal M. Ahmed, *The Intellectual Origins of Egyptian Nationalism* (Oxford: Oxford University Press, 1960), p. 23.

15. Afaf Lutfi al-Sayyid Marsot, *Egypt's Liberal Experiment* (Berkeley, CA: University of California Press, 1977).

16. "Fann al-hukm," *Al-Risala* 5, no. 218 (September 6, 1937), p. 1442.

17. Robert Stephens, *Nasser: A Political Biography* (London: 1971), pp. 566–77.

18. *Cf.* Michael C. Hudson, *Arab Politics*, p. 234.

19. See Friedemann Buettner, "A Country Scenario Analysis of Egypt."

20. Cited in Judith Miller, "The Embattled Arab Intellectual," *New York Times Magazine*, June 8, 1985.

2

State, Society, and Legitimacy: An Essay on Arab Political Prospects in the 1990s

Michael C. Hudson

In analyzing Arab politics, it is easier to predict the past than the future. Neither the positivist, empirical approaches that were predominant two decades ago nor the historicist, neo-Marxist, and dependency approaches that emerged in the 1970s offer the analyst much security against the surprises which the future always has in store. In recent years, however, there has been a continuing and fruitful dialogue between political scientists and historians focusing on the changing relationships between state and society. Fundamental issues such as authority, political community, and legitimacy are being reexamined from a perspective that emphasizes historical political culture formation, social stratification, political economy, and the phenomenon of the state itself. With this new perspective in mind, I would like to speculate cautiously about Arab domestic politics in the 1990s.

I would like to propose three different scenarios for the decade ahead. Each depends on a different assessment of certain internal and external factors. The first is a continuation of the present status quo; a second is an era of turbulence, marked both by severe authoritarian rule and by breakdowns of order; and the third is the development of more legitimate political systems—characterized by more authoritative government, greater significant popular participation, and greater effectiveness. This third scenario might encompass various structural and ideological forms in different countries: liberal-pluralist, constitutional monarchist, single party-socialist, corporatist-nationalist, or Islamic. Whatever the form, the outcome of the third scenario (unlike those of the first two) would be a state whose rulers have a broad social constituency and whose institutions have the capability for orderly power transfers, consensus-building, and conflict regulation in the divided, changing Arab societies of the 1990s.

Three Scenarios

The Status Quo

The Arab political order today is essentially authoritarian. To be sure, there are significant variations from country to country, but there is no denying this core characteristic. Rulers rule; people obey; there is little accountability of the rulers to the ruled. Furthermore, the trend since the beginning of the 1970s has been toward more authoritarian rule. Spontaneous demonstrations and protests have declined; dynasties and regimes once thought to be unlikely to survive are still with us; genuinely independent opposition parties, movements, and groupings have declined in importance; and political freedoms are more or less repressed in what has become almost a permanent "state of emergency." The bureaucracies of the state—civil, military, security—have grown bigger and more pervasive.

The political formula of the status quo varies significantly across the Arab world. There are regions, such as the Maghrib, in which the identity and historical roots of the state are more firmly established than in others, such as the Mashriq. There are rich states and poor; and among the rich there are the oil-exporting rentier states whose bureaucratic growth has been directly fed by huge revenue inflows. There are those that have been thoroughly penetrated by Western influences and those that have been comparatively isolated. One of the most important distinctions for political analysts is simply size. Those states with small populations, small cities, small industrial sectors, small middle classes, and oil-exporting economies have experienced a relatively smooth assertion of state control over the society, and it has been possible for traditional hereditary families to strengthen their control over the state. Compared to the big Arab states with more complex societies, these states would seem to offer the best case for maintenance of the status quo. But as I shall suggest below, the coming decade may prove rougher for them than the last.

These Arab states with large populations have presented the greatest challenges to their rulers. Traditional legitimizing formulas like hereditary kingship have been insufficient in themselves to provide security. Rulers have had to resort to three additional strategies: ideologies and symbols that both mobilize and pacify "the masses"; reliance on externally located potential political "assets," such as big power security and diplomatic assistance and Western commercial and financial linkages to accommodate the interests of important strata and elites; and the growth of loyal constituencies, either themselves part of the expanding state's bureaucracy or else dependent on the state and the regime that controls it. Nevertheless, each of these strategies has its weaknesses, and in the next decade the problems of maintaining the status quo in the large Arab states may well be even more serious than those in the small ones.

In the large Arab states as well as the small ones, the growth of the state and its control capabilities by the mid-1980s seems to have contained the changes in society that generate political demands. From a social class perspective, the dominant element, the bourgeoisie, is too weak and divided fully to control the state and thus impose its narrow interests; at the same time, however, the dominated elements, the urban and rural poor, are too fragmented to express serious protest. Many scholars, then, would be prepared to predict that the status quo will persist. Even though a serious case can be made for this position, there are reasons to be skeptical, as I shall argue below.

If, however, the status quo continues, what might a commentator on Arab politics around 1995 be observing? In the small hereditary states the same ruling families would remain, peaceful transitions to brothers or sons having been made in Saudi Arabia, Abu Dhabi, Dubai, and Bahrain. The monarchs who were middle-aged in the mid-1980s—in Morocco, Qatar, Jordan, Kuwait, and Oman—would continue in power by virtue of their personal skills and authority, their usage of the control instruments of the state, and the continuing passivity of their societies. In the large states such as Egypt, Syria, and Iraq the leaders of the 1980s would have followed a similar course, but in addition they would have learned both to use the enlarged state apparatus to cultivate and appease key clienteles with the greater patronage available and at the same time to develop and control a personal network (under the guise of "the Party") to maintain their grip on the state itself. The transfers of executive power that occurred in the non-hereditary systems would sometimes be orderly (as in Algeria) and more often irregular (as in Libya, Tunisia, the Yemens, and Sudan), but never revolutionary. Politics (and conflict) in Lebanon and the Palestinian community continue as in the mid-1980s—chaotic but contained. In general, discontent and frustration would remain endemic because of unsolved regional political issues and domestic economic conditions, but a judicious combination of "tame" opposition activity and a strong security presence would be sufficient to permit the rulers to ride out the rough political weather.

An Era of Turbulence

To believe that the second scenario, the "era of turbulence," is the emerging Arab political reality, it is necessary to accept the assumption that the "growth of the state" hypothesis is, at best, incomplete. It means accepting the proposition that while the state may be bigger, it is not necessarily stronger. It means doubting whether the state is developing the moral authority commensurate with its enhanced technologies of control. It means expecting that society is not so incoherent as to be indefinitely manipulable by the state and that social forces are emerging that can support significant opposition movements. While sociopolitical ferment is predicted, however, it is not expected that coherent and effective alternatives will emerge; in this respect, the assumptions underlying the second scenario differ from those that support the third one, the "era of legitimacy" described below.

It is important, for theoretical clarity, to emphasize the difference between the assumptions underlying the first and the second scenarios. The status quo scenario assumes that the growth of the state is the dominant and stabilizing feature of the political scene and will remain so. The stronger state vastly enhances the social control of the ruling class so that even a small, narrowly-based ruling class is now more capable of maintaining its position. Syria and Iraq come to mind as examples. The dependency theory variation asserts further that the external factors enhance stability. The "era of turbulence" scenario, on the other hand, assumes that the enlarged state is or can be relatively autonomous; it is "up for grabs," so to speak. Moreover, society is becoming too complex and volatile to be completely controlled. The second scenario therefore postulates a greater degree of indeterminacy in the Arab political situation than the first one does. The Arab state today may be bigger than it was, but it is still unable to confer legitimacy on those elements that happen to control it at any given time. Technically, it may be harder now for an opposition to wrest control of the state from a given regime, but at the same time the incentives for oppositions to try and do so increase with the value of the "prize" to be won. This is particularly true in situations where incumbent regimes must resort increasingly to threat and coercion, even terror, to maintain their grip on the state.

The key characteristic of the "era of turbulence" scenario is the failure of the state to acquire legitimacy in the eyes of society. Indeed, the growth of the state itself, in its bureaucratic dimension, is responsible for a growing estrangement. Burgeoning bureaucracy breeds frustration; lack of access breeds resentment; ubiquitous repression breeds subversion; ineffective policy exacerbates discontent, bruises interests, and generates protest. Politicized elements in a society increasingly educated and yet excluded from access to power incessantly challenge the *right* of regimes to rule. Morever, the extent to which incumbent regimes are perceived as "clients" of external powers pursuing "neo-imperialist" policies will also weaken their legitimacy. Thus, the incipient Leviathan creates a renaissance of opposition, but the opposition is not sufficiently universal and coherent to achieve a new social contract, or synthesis.

If the "era of turbulence" scenario comes to characterize Arab politics in the 1990s, what governmental forms might it take? I can envisage a variety of types, ranging from quasi-totalitarianism to anarchy. For historical examples, the era of the 1950s and 1960s might be suggestive. In the smaller, more traditional states, "monarchy by *mukhabarat*" may become more prevalent as hereditary ruling families rely increasingly on the security and intelligence services to ensure stability. In the larger polities that have already experienced some form of "popular" rule through nominally presidential or parliamentary systems, models borrowed from the Latin American experience may become relevant to the Arab world. For example, following the terminology of G. O'Donnell, one can easily imagine a kind of "bureaucratic-authoritarianism" (with an emphasis on the authoritarian) taking root in states like Syria, Iraq, Algeria, and Egypt. In these countries the state itself is so large that it can not only regulate, it can also generate and maintain a kind of self-serving constituency of interests through the manipulation of patronage. The only significant arena of politics is within the state itself, not in society at large—at least until "outsiders" wrest control of the state from incumbents. Unlike in the first scenario, however, the politics of bureaucratic-authoritarianism (either intra-state or intra-societal) will not be stable.

Another model suggested by O'Donnell, "populist authoritarianism," is distinguished by the attempt on the part of the ruler(s) to create popular legitimacy through a mobilizing ideology. Political Islam, in some form or other, is likely to figure prominently in the legitimizing formula of Arab populist-authoritarian systems in the years ahead, just as Arabism did in the 1950s and 1960s. In the intense competition of regimes and oppositions for popular legitimacy, one should not rule out the return of Arabism, as well as other familiar populist symbols—among them democracy, socialism, and anti-Westernism. Arab populist authoritarianism is usually associated with a charismatic leader who is cast as the living embodiment of the given symbolic code. The archetypical Arab example of this model is Nasserism. Today, perhaps Qadhafi's Libya is the most prominent case. In the future, one can envisage an Arab Khomeini-figure emerging in a populous, poor, religious political culture such as Egypt, Tunisia, or Morocco. One can envisage as well such a figure employing a fascistic or corporatist strategy to secure his power.

A third model is what Samuel Huntington calls "praetorianism." Here one is confronted with rule by a succession of military juntas, each seizing power by force of arms and ruling essentially by force. Such regimes do not last long enough to generate an effective legitimizing formula or to establish a protective constituency of interest groups. Syria of the 1950s and 1960s is the prototype. Some would argue that the growth of the Arab state makes this type of rule most unlikely, but this is true only to the extent that the enlarged state makes it "technically" difficult for oppositions to dislodge incumbents. It is quite possible for praetorianism to reassert itself in a state such as Syria if (for some reason) the stable bureaucratic-authoritarian regime is overturned: then intra-state and extra-state factions, acting "rationally" to win high stakes, none with a superior claim to legitimacy, will fight each other just as states in international politics will fight to fill a power vacuum that is too important to ignore. Furthermore, in states where incumbent regimes of other kinds (such as hereditary monarchs or populist presidents) come to an end, the tendency to praetorianism may be all too strong, especially since armies and officer corps have grown so large.

Finally, there is the Lebanese model—chaotic anarchy. Is the Lebanese experience a preview of things to come elsewhere in the Arab world, or was Lebanon a *sui generis* case? At first glance at least, it appears to be a fundamental deviation from the general trend toward the growth of the state; whatever else it may be, its central feature would seem to be the withering away of the Lebanese state. Compared to the other so-called "artificial" states in the region (a reference to their creation by European imperialism), was the Lebanese state uniquely underdeveloped bureaucratically? Was it uniquely underdeveloped in terms of its authority and legitimacy? Or was Lebanese society uniquely fragmented, thus rendering impossible any kind of social contract? Many would argue in the affirmative. But it is at least arguable that the differences in Lebanon were a matter of degree and not of kind, and therefore that something similar could happen elsewhere in the area. Then too, Lebanon's collapse itself could be a factor (setting an example, as it were) promoting similar disintegration in neighboring places. A well-known orientalist perspective argues that the fundamental sociocultural units in the Middle East are familial, tribal, and sectarian; the superimposition of modern states across these boundaries is in a sense "unnatural"; therefore, there is a significant possibility that the political map eventually could be redrawn along these more "natural" lines. States imposed on "divided" societies like Syria, Iraq, Sudan, the Yemens, and others might thus be vulnerable to disintegration in an era of turbulence. The bloody upheaval in South Yemen in early 1986 suggests that even a Marxist one-party state may not be immune to "Lebanonization."

What precisely might happen to various Arab states in the 1990s in an "era of turbulence" scenario is, of course, difficult to forecast with confidence. But among Middle East observers there is no shortage of the following kinds of speculation: the disintegration of Saudi Arabia into its historic geographic components of Najd, Hijaz, and Al-Hasa; the emergence of a "Shi'i arc of crisis," embracing Iran, Iraq, eastern Saudi Arabia, northern Syria, and Lebanon; the establishment of an Islamic republic in Egypt; the splitting of Sudan into two separate states; the dismemberment of Libya; creation of a Palestinian state in Jordan and perhaps southern Syria; the appearance of communal conflict in Algeria; and the collapse of traditional regimes in Morocco, Tunisia, and several small Gulf states. An increasingly beleaguered and divided Israel presumably views all these upheavals with a mixture of satisfaction and nervousness from behind its nuclear shield.

An Era of Legitimacy

The third scenario, "an era of legitimacy," differs from the first in that it forecasts significant political change; it differs from the second in that it envisions change leading to a new, more authoritative political order rather than intensified tension and turbulence. In light of the Arab world's current political conditions, any analyst who proposes such a scenario must consider whether he has committed the error of wishful thinking. The third scenario is not necessarily a liberal scenario, although it could be; nor is it necessarily secular or Western. It is not presented as a "best case" as opposed to "worst case" scenarios of turbulence or status quo. It is, however, akin to what Western political scientists and philosophers have in mind when they speak of "political development" or "legitimate government."

Many scholars now question the political development paradigms of the 1960s insofar as some of them postulated a unilinear path toward such development. Such tendencies as there may have been in this direction more often than not were overridden by factors mentioned above in the discussion of the status quo scenario. In the face of "realistic" analyses of class conflict, hegemonic behavior, exploitation, and the priority of material interests over "idealistic" drives, the liberal propositions about the social beneficence of the educated middle class, the possibility of technical solutions to political problems, and the "norm" of social harmony sound naïve indeed. Throughout the Third World, the application of liberal-democratic formulas usually seemed to rationalize the self-interest behavior of bourgeois or feudal elites. Masses were either apathetic or easily manipulable with demagogic slogans. In the Arab world, too, as we have seen, the state, even though controlled by narrowly-based elites, came to dominate society and politics; independent opposition parties and organizations more often than not were either suppressed or co-opted. Human and political rights generally accepted as universal norms increasingly were abused. The social science paradigms that have become so influential since the 1970s make it difficult to believe that this situation will change, even though (ironically) many of their advocates expect major change (in the long run) and usually favor it on ideological grounds as well.

Considering the widespread rejection by many students of the political development paradigm in favor of political economy, neo-Marxist, and dependency theory, is there any justification for continuing to talk about the emergence of broadly-based government transcending particular class interests, the possibility of the ethically neutral state, or the relevance of institutions and strategies for regulating or even solving conflict within divided societies and between regimes and oppositions?

There is, if one is willing to believe in the primacy and partial autonomy of politics—that is, that the political behavior of individuals and groups can be understood in terms not limited to their socioeconomic situation, and that calculation based on a rationality that transcends class interests can be important in explaining political decision-making. If such assumptions can be entertained, then it makes sense to consider the possibility of achieving the basic features of the third scenario. These, it will be recalled, include a ruling elite with a broad social base, structures for social conflict regulation and for nonviolent regime-opposition relations, popular recognition of the authority—not just the coercive power—of the state, some limitations on the tendencies of the enlarged state toward absolutism and arbitrariness, and some minimal degree of effective policy making (or, to use the old-fashioned term, "good government"). Anybody involved with Arab politics on a day-to-day basis perceives that actors have *some* freedom of action; that choices can be and are made; that within the constraints of society, the economy, culture, and the international order, there is a zone of indeterminacy in which "idiosyncratic" factors like leadership, intelligence, rationality, and cooperative behavior—even altruism—*may* sometimes significantly affect political outcomes.

Furthermore, the very enlargement of the state would seem to make possible its relative emancipation from the control of narrowly-based social groups. Under such circumstances the political arena falls increasingly within the structures of the state, and bargaining and negotiation—i.e., politics—become not just possible but necessary. Liberal modernization theory was correct in arguing that the state in a modernizing society may develop the capabilities to engineer social cohesion, mitigate class conflict, and create consensus. This idea is echoed in a way in the neo-Marxist and political economy literature, but from a perspective that insists that such consensus masks the domination of state and society by a hegemonic social stratum rather than represents a legitimate expression of society and the political community as a whole. Here is the core assumption of the "era of legitimacy" scenario: the growth and autonomy of the state, on the one hand, and the increasing complexity of society, on the other, facilitate the development of a political process in which public opinion, bargaining, and negotiation within the terms of a social contract or constitution—rather than absolutism or anarchy—are the principal structures. This is because social modernization gradually but inexorably fosters both subjective norms favorable to such a process and cognitive perceptions of the heavy costs of the alternatives.

Such a relatively benign scenario may be possible to conceive of in the abstract, but what of its applicability to Arab political systems in the decade ahead? The notion of an era of legitimacy in Arab politics is not inconceivable, even though it may (in general) be unlikely. For evidence, one should examine aspects of the recent past that our discussion has not emphasized. The stability of the past decade and a half may be due in large part to the new Leviathan with its formidable bureaucracies for administration and the suppression of opposition. But, with some notable exceptions, Arab states have been less oppressive than other Third World states, including neighbors like Iran, Turkey, Pakistan, and Ethiopia. A certain national solidarity is often observed in most of the African Arab states and in parts of the Arabian peninsula. Regimes such as those in Egypt, Morocco, Algeria, Tunisia, Kuwait, and the Palestinian community appear to enjoy a degree of authority that cannot be ascribed mainly to fear. While considerable social and communal fragmentation has been evident, especially in the Fertile Crescent, the social transformation has not been entirely negative in terms of political integration: increasingly educated populations may diminish particularism under certain conditions. The emergence of regime toleration for suitably constrained opposition groups in the appearance of limited electoral and consultative activity in Egypt, Tunisia, Kuwait, Iraq, Morocco, Jordan, and North Yemen probably should not be dismissed out of hand.

Some Trends and Their Political Implications

Of the three scenarios outlined here, which is most likely to describe the decade ahead in Arab politics? Such a judgment requires identifying a number of factors, some of which would seem to promote the status quo and others significant transformations toward either turbulence or legitimacy.

Whether one can usefully generalize about the Arab world as a whole is, of course, debatable. Regional particularisms, local circumstances, historical and cultural diversity in a vast area ruled by 21 states, each jealous of its sovereignty, suggest some of the problems involved. Nevertheless, there do seem to be some factors common throughout the region that promote the political status quo and others that promote change. The first task is to identify and, if possible, compare the importance of the status quo factors and the change factors; the second is to subdivide the change factors into those favoring "turbulence" and those favoring "legitimacy." This exercise can be exploratory and speculative only; empirical research would be necessary to establish concretely the dimensions and significance of the trends discussed.

Status Quo Factors

I can think of five trends that will support the maintenance of the Arab political order as we know it in the mid-1980s into the decade ahead. Three are internal to Arab societies; two are external. The internal trends are (a) the continuing growth of the state security organizations, (b) the interest in a stable order held by increasingly influential and cosmopolitan technocratic elites, and (c) the organizational and ideological weaknesses of opposition groups. The external trends are (d) the regional and international balance of power and (e) the international economic order, which generates both security for Arab elites and constraints on their political decision-making.

Of all the transfers of technology that have taken place in the Arab world, probably none have been as effective as those in the political security field. New electronic means of surveillance, the computerization of lists of security suspects, and technical assistance from the security services of big-power patrons will raise the threshold of technical competence necessary to disturb regimes. One may expect that governments will continue to spend freely to develop the efficacy and pervasiveness of their security bureaucracies as well. Even the mosque, and the segment of society symbolized by it, will become more vulnerable to regime monitoring—especially after the Islamic upheavals of recent times. Regimes, for this technical reason at least, will perhaps feel more empowered to enact "unpopular" policies, foreign and domestic, and withstand the pressures of public opinion and opposition groups. Within the region geography, topography, and demography will enhance or diminish these technical security benefits: the larger, denser, more mountainous, more urban, and poorer states will remain harder for regimes to secure.

As government bureaucracies grow and government economic intervention remains high (notwithstanding some decline in direct state control), and as educational stock grows, the role of the educated middle classes, already much analyzed, also is likely to continue to grow. The intriguing question is whether its political tendency can be forecast. Recent Arab experience as well as a large body of theory about the role of the bourgeoisie lead one to suppose that this stratum may become the chief social supporter of the status quo. The age of the Arab technocrat may be dawning, and the technocrat of the 1990s probably will be closer to the model of the Ph.D.-holding pragmatist, believer in moderate, evolutionary, incremental change, than to the discontented, morally-indignant activist intellectual who, excluded from power in the 1950s and 1960s by the "aristocrats," led the protest movements of those times. By contrast, the coming decade should see the elevation of the technocrats and their new expertise to the commanding heights of economics, finance, development planning, politics, and military affairs. Rules and procedures for a far more complex society will impose a stability of their own, and the new makers and arbiters of these rules and procedures—a different group from the traditional lawyers—will develop their own stake in an orderly system. On the other hand, it is also possible that the new technocrats may embrace radical protest ideologies, feeling more alienated than their predecessors because of the relative austerity and dearth of opportunities available in the decade ahead. If so, they may come to question the status quo.

A third trend is the continuing organizational and ideological weakness of opposition political groups. Although it will be argued below that new technologies will become increasingly available to the opposition, the failures of the opposition in recent years suggest persistent structural problems. Much has been made of the failure of the pan-Arab nationalist parties and movements, and rightly so. Similarly, Communist parties have suffered one setback after another. Even the current Islamic movements, though probably expressing deep-rooted social discontents, have not demonstrated remarkable organizational successes in the Arab world. As for "permitted" opposition, its impact on politics and policy is hard to discover. While there are many reasons for the weakness of opposition in the recent past that are "external" to the opposition groups themselves, one cannot but wonder whether there are also explanations of an internal kind. For example, do the socialization process and the particularist structure of society themselves make it difficult for effective political organizers to emerge and to function? Are management skills, cooperative behavior, and loyalty to the group and its goals systematically weakened by pervasive values and habits? If so, even the rapid socioeconomic change that is taking place is not likely to generate more positive basic behavior patterns in the *near* future.

The structure of the regional state system—multipolar, polycentric—also exerts a stabilizing effect on the political systems of the member states. Despite several ongoing regional conflicts—so ongoing, indeed, that they too are part of the status quo—the regional system appears resistant to fundamental revision on the part of any member or foreseeable coalition of members. There is no powerful, destabilizing core state any longer. Almost every regime is committed to respecting the integrity of other states. Within the states there seems to be widespread agreement among elites about giving priority to national security concerns, a factor which engenders internal solidarity. The uncertainty of the regional environment promotes domestic cohesion. To be sure, there are destabilizing aspects of the regional situation which will be discussed below; yet one must emphasize how the combination of the uncertainty which flows from ongoing conflicts plus the structural diffusion of power facilitates maintenance of the established internal order.

The fifth status quo factor is the support for Arab elites and regimes that flows from the major financial and industrial countries. To the extent that the dependency perspective is valid, the linkages that exist between local political and economic establishments and the centers of the international system must be seen as enhancing the monopoly of resources of those establishments. These resources are not just financial but political, technological, and cultural as well. The expressions of "world center" support include tangible instruments like foreign economic and military aid, international loans and investment, technical assistance, and security and intelligence information. It also includes intangible assets like prestige and cultural access on an international level. It cannot but enhance the position of Arab ruling elites to have influential international constituencies and networks behind them.

Even without further research on these five trends it is clear that each of them is rooted in a sociopolitical context that is changing only slowly. One would be surprised, therefore, to observe any of them weakening or disappearing in the decade ahead.

Change Factors

Against these formidable conditions favoring the political status quo, it is necessary to juxtapose another set of trends whose political implications facilitate change and transformation. Whether these trends tend to favor the "era of turbulence" or the "era of legitimacy" scenarios will require further discussion. I identify eight such trends, the first three of which are social or external in origin: (a) the decline of oil revenues, (b) the growth of change-oriented social elements, and (c) the delegitimizing aspects of the "American connection." The other five trends arise out of the domestic political system and include (d) weakening leadership and ineffective policy-making, (e) the inadequacy of institutionalized participation, (f) the probable weakening of control over the security bureaucracies, (g) the beginnings of technological development in the opposition, and (h) ideological revivals.

Scholars from Aristotle to a host of modern social scientists have argued that when affluence begins to taper off and relative deprivation sets in, then discontent, protest, and even revolution can be expected. Some oil industry experts expect that the world oil glut of the 1980s may dry up in the 1990s. Even if this relatively optimistic forecast is correct, the oil-rich societies and their dependent neighbors face at least several years of relative austerity. Perhaps Saudi Arabia can absorb a 40 percent drop in revenues without severe internal repercussions, but its less rich neighbors are less well placed to do so. The first of the "post-oil" oil states, Bahrain, already has experienced unrest. The effects on the Yemens, Egypt, Sudan, Jordan,

Lebanon, Tunisia, and the Palestinians may be significant. Most of those who argue that the oil recession is a "healthy" thing are wealthy enough not to feel the pain.

Arab regimes in general are narrowly based. Economic growth since the 1970s has favored the wealthy business and professional classes. Agriculture has been stagnant and industrial growth modest, while population growth and urban migration have been strong. The proportion of the population that is semi-educated or educated and youthful is large and growing. The place of women in society is being undermined by socioeconomic and ideological trends. Social tensions appear to stimulate ethnic and sectarian identifications at the expense of civic commitments. All this leads one to suspect that certain social elements—"pockets of protest"—are likely to emerge: rural poor, an increasingly squeezed lower middle class, urban unemployed and slum dwellers, students and intellectuals, educated women. Members of the ruling elite itself have been known to express a loss of self-confidence and morale. Will the control and legitimizing instruments of the regime and the state be able to contain these tensions? Can corporatist, patron-client, ideological strategies do the trick?

While it has been suggested above that the international system supplies a sort of stabilizing cement for Arab political incumbents, there is another aspect of the external connection. To the extent that the Arab world of the mid-1980s is dominated by a "Pax Americana," regimes with a special American connection are blessed, but they are also cursed by the hostility in Arab public opinion to U.S. policy on the Palestinian issue and the Arab–Israeli conflict. Regimes in Saudi Arabia, Egypt, Jordan, Tunisia, and Morocco are especially vulnerable to charges of subservience to Washington. Militant opposition from the religious right to the secular left finds this an effective charge and rallying cry. Little wonder that "pro-American" Arab elites worry so much about U.S. policy.

The strength of leadership will become an issue in the coming decade if certain trends that are already evident are not curbed. The staying power of several Arab regimes in the recent past may have been due in part to able leadership on the part of the head of state. One thinks immediately of a Nasser, a Bourguiba, a Faysal bin 'Abd al-'Aziz, a Hussein, an Asad, whose intelligence and force of personality contributed to regime longevity. The successor generation of kings and presidents, to the extent that it can now be discerned, does not indicate the same level of strength and skill. Disenchantment with ongoing policy failures may also sap the authority of leaders and their governments. Arab policy making weakness is most evident in regional matters: the protracted Arab–Israeli conflict represents failure on both the ideological and national security levels; and this of course is not the only poorly managed regional conflict issue. In domestic policy, certain regimes may be called to account for inability to manage development or stave off economic and financial crises. The eruptions triggered by financial reforms (often demanded by the International Monetary Fund) are by now predictable. Recent examples have occurred in Egypt, Morocco, Tunisia, and

Sudan. In the face of various policy failures, members of ruling elites themselves sometimes express a loss of esteem and confidence in their ability (and right) to rule.

The fifth trend is the failure of Arab political systems to develop institutionalized participation beyond the tokenism indicated by 99.9 percent election victories for incumbents. It was noted above that there has been a certain loosening of constraints on opposition activity in some countries, although such liberalization is quite limited. On the whole, authoritarianism of one type or another prevails almost everywhere. Is the reluctance of most regimes, hereditary or republican, to allow free political activity to be considered a factor supporting the status quo or supporting change? On its face, it can hardly be anything but the former; but if social ferment has the potential for unseating the regimes in even very strong states, then the lack of "safety valves" may be a powerful agent of change.

Modernization theorists such as Huntington and Manfred Halpern argued long ago that the growth of the military and security bureaucracies would ultimately threaten the traditional regimes. The non-hereditary regimes as well have indicated their concern about this threat by building multiple and competitive praetorian guards, intelligence services, and the like in the hope that one would counteract another's rebellion. Numbers and logic alone might suggest the growing probability of subversive challenges. In the absence of genuinely legitimate regimes and commitment to lawful procedures, is it feasible for regimes to secure the loyalty of their guards mainly through good pay, perquisites, and rival security organizations? There were fewer coups, successful or abortive, in the last decade and a half than in earlier decades, but the assassination of Anwar al-Sadat by army conspirators suggests that the proposition is still worth considering. Presumably the leaders of Morocco, Iraq, Syria, the two Yemens, Saudi Arabia, Sudan, and Libya, as well as Egypt, would think so.

There is a time lag in technological development between regimes and oppositions in the Third World. Governments, especially the security services, are the first to get the computers and other high-technology capabilities. While the *mukhabarat* has the cameras, eavesdropping devices, and information resources, the militant pan-Arab, Communist, or Islamic circle is limited to the mimeograph machine and a far more labor-intensive mode of "production." This was true, at least, in the 1960s. In the 1990s the picture may be quite different. What the transistor did to create a mass constituency for pan-Arabism, the copying machine and cassette tape recorder did for the Islamic movement in Iran—successfully—and may be doing in many Arab countries. High-technology inventions in the communications field, such as these, may gradually be closing the technological gap between regimes and oppositions. No less important are "low-tech" but effective inventions like the truck-bomb. Guided not by electronics but by highly motivated human beings ready for martyrdom, it proves more powerful politically than renovated battleships or late-model jet fighter aircraft.

The last of the trends that promote change is the ideological revival, represented in recent years by movements of Islamic political militancy. In this domain, contradictory images compete for attention. Some see virtually an end of ideology in the Arab world and in its place a pragmatist, incrementalist, instrumentalist world view. Others, however, foresee a revival of high-intensity symbolic politics. Regimes, on the one hand, will be driven to this legitimizing strategy to cope with rising social unrest and political protest. The masses, on the other, will take solace in the promises and the sense of belonging that neo-fascist, corporatist slogans offer. The serious challenge to existing regimes posed by ideological revivalism lies mainly in its moral purity and rectitude and its promise to strike back against the hostility of the outside world and the corruption of the existing order. In the mid-1980s some students of the Middle East are arguing that the Islamic wave set in motion by the Iranian revolution has crested: setbacks in Kuwait, Sudan, and Egypt and in the Iran–Iraq war support this thesis. Others, however, dispute this assessment, pointing out that the objective conditions that underlay the Islamic revival still exist. They maintain that even more extreme forms will displace the flagging "moderate" Islamic organizations.

Conclusions

Which of the three scenarios posed at the beginning of this essay is likely to be truest, in general, to emerging political realities in the Arab world in the next decade or so? To answer that question requires first weighing the "status quo" and "change" factors and judging which seem to be the strongest. If in general the prediction is for change, what kind of change is it to be: toward "an era of turbulence" or "an era of legitimacy?" Unfortunately, in the absence of valid and reliable indicators of the relative weight of these factors, one cannot answer the question except in an impressionistic and tentative way.

Recognizing (again) that conditions vary from country to country, one is persuaded to predict change of some sort rather than the status quo. This judgment rests, first, on a theoretical perception of state and society in the Arab world that sees society as capable of nurturing significant political forces independent of the state, notwithstanding the structural growth of the state. This perspective views the Arab state as a powerful instrument which is not irrevocably or permanently the possession of a particular class or stratum. The control of particular regimes over the state is not necessarily or permanently unchallengeable. Furthermore, the growth of state bureaucracies increases the possibility of subversion from within. One should not underestimate the extent to which external dependencies, financial and political, cement the established Arab order; and yet one should not forget the double-edged political impact of these dependencies, especially in the Arab world: "neo-imperialism" remains a potent rallying point for the advocates of change.

Second, from observation of contemporary Arab politics, one is prompted to suppose that, on the whole, the factors supporting the status quo are not so powerful as those which generate change. "Technical" trends like the development of internal security services are not likely to be decisive because of the limitations imposed by "underdeveloped" administration, communications, and the like. The prevalence of technocrats and professionals, who yearn for stability, cannot in itself support predictions that they can actually engineer it; they may be far more likely to adjust, with supine flexibility, to continuing upheavals in leadership and ideology. The "underdevelopment" of opposition groups is certainly an impediment, but they may be now at a state in which their "learning curve" (their ability to absorb technical and organizational innovation) is ascending, while that of regimes and their security bureaucracies remains flatter. Perhaps the most important supports of the present Arab order are external, emanating especially from the United States in the form of military-strategic, security, economic development, and political-diplomatic assistance. However, as noted above, American patronage also exerts a "kiss of death" effect on friendly Arab regimes by virtue of the United States' larger Middle East policy concerns.

The processes likely to disturb the status quo are numerous and profound. In addition, they may be cumulative. Relative economic austerity, social imbalances, and the moral burden of domestic and external policy failures, among other things, suggest that incumbent rulers and elites in the Arab world will have to work hard to maintain their position. Although the long-term process of state formation deserves attention, the processes whereby regimes and ruling elites maintain their control of the state in the Arab world may not be so strong. I suggested above that "internal political system factors" centering around the relationships between state and society and between regime and opposition are fraught with problems. If observations of these trends toward stagnation and incoherence in Arab political systems are correct, then change of some kind may be in the offing. But what kind of change?

The "era of turbulence" scenario sketched above foresaw an Arab political scene marked by instability and incoherence. Unable to solve a pervasive crisis of authority, Arab governments would oscillate between various forms of absolutism and chaos; but even the absolutist episodes—whether bureaucratic, populist, or praetorian—would be short-lived. The "era of legitimacy" scenario, in contrast, envisioned a broadening of the constituencies of ruling elites, the development of authoritative procedures for settling disputes and making policy decisions, the growth of accepted guarantees for oppositions and rules for non-violent regime-opposition relations. The logic of this scenario emphasized the primacy of politics, rationality, and the public interest; and the scenario provides a variety of "legitimate" forms including constitutional monarchy, liberal-pluralism, single-party socialism, corporatist-nationalism, and theocracy.

Regional variations within the Arab world and the problem of comparing the significances of the several factors I have identified makes it difficult to forecast whether the "turbulence" or the "legitimacy" scenario will best describe Arab politics in the decade ahead. On balance, should one expect the growth of community, social consensus, "rules of the game," and the public interest in Arab societies? Should we be encouraged to expect established regimes to experiment with new forms of representation or to allow a more open political life? While there are a few examples of this tendency, as noted above, one can also plausibly anticipate—in light of the new austerity, social ferment, and regional tensions—a trend toward absolutism and illegitimacy which, contrary to the expectations of "growth of the state" theorists, may result in significant political turmoil. There may be some legitimization success stories to be told in the Arab countries in the years ahead, but there are also powerful tendencies that may generate an "era of turbulence." The issue of political legitimacy, with all its conceptual difficulties, will have to remain the central issue for analytic attention.

Selected Bibliography

Anderson, P. *Images of the Absolutist State*. London: NLB–Humanities Press, 1974.
Batatu, H. *The Old Social Classes and the Revolutionary Movements of Iraq*. Princeton, NJ: Princeton University Press, 1979.
Binder, L. *In a Moment of Enthusiasm*. Chicago, IL: University of Chicago Press, 1978.
Brinton, C. *The Anatomy of Revolution*. New York: Norton, 1938.
Carnoy, M. *The State and Political Theory*. Princeton, NJ: Princeton University Press, 1984.
Evans, P. *Dependent Development*. Princeton, NJ: Princeton University Press, 1979.
Gurr, Ted Robert. *Why Men Rebel*. Princeton, NJ: Princeton University Press, 1970.
Halpern. M. *The Politics of Social Change in the Middle East and North Africa*. Princeton, NJ: Princeton University Press, 1964.
Hudson, M. "Social Mobilization Theory and Arab Politics," in R. Merritt and B. Russett, eds. *From National Development to Global Community: Essays in Honor of Karl W. Deutsch*. London: Allen and Unwin, 1981, pp. 46–69.
Huntington, S. *Political Order in Changing Societies*. New Haven, CT: Yale University Press, 1978.
Ibrahim, S. *The New Arab Social Order*. Boulder, CO: Westview Press, 1982.
Linz, J. and A. Steppan, eds. *The Breakdown of Democratic Regimes*. Baltimore, MD: The Johns Hopkins University Press, 1978.
Kerr, M. and S. Yassin, eds. *Rich and Poor States in the Middle East*. Boulder, CO: Westview Press, 1982.
O'Donnell, G. *Modernization and Bureaucratic-Authoritarianism*. Berkeley, CA: University of California Press, 1973.
Waterbury, J. *The Egypt of Nasser and Sadat*. Princeton, NJ: Princeton University Press, 1983.

3

The Future of Human Rights in the Arab World

Saad Eddin Ibrahim

Some 1,350 years ago, a bedouin client of the Umayyad dynasty stood up in a public meeting in Damascus, pointed at Mu'awiya, the Umayyad Caliph, and proclaimed, "This is the Commander of the Faithful; should he die, this (pointing at Yazid, Mu'awiya's son) is his successor. Should anyone defy them, this (swinging his sword) is the arbiter." Several other clients cheered; Mu'awiya nodded . . . and considered it a unanimous endorsement, or *bay'a*.

Since that day in the first Islamic century, whatever human rights or basic freedoms were enunciated in the Qur'an, followed by the Prophet Muhammad, and adhered to by the first four Guided Caliphs have been abridged time and again. The history of the following centuries shows an endless struggle between true believers in the pure vision of Islam and *realpolitik* usurpers of power by force. To be sure, there have been fair and just rulers in Arab–Muslim history. However, they were the exception; their fairness or justice was due to individual piety rather than to respect of any instituted rules of law or accountability.

Today, despite the transformation which has engulfed Arab society and institutions, most rulers of the Arab world remain guided by the spirit of that proposition proclaimed by the Umayyad client in Damascus 1,350 years ago. Most rulers invest themselves with absolute or near-absolute power. Some of them may coat or soften it by quasi-legal trappings. Some may be more subtle than others. But most of them are equally absolutist in their conception of what they are entitled to. And they hold on to such conceptions until they are removed from power by natural death, killing, or overthrow. Their successors, despite initial claims, soon adopt a similarly absolutist conception and practice of power.

There have been countless attempts in Arab–Muslim history to check absolute power—uprisings, rebellions, and revolutions. Some of these even succeeded briefly in instituting more egalitarian rule. In modern times, several Arab countries practiced or flirted with liberal forms of government shortly before or immediately after securing political independence from Western colonialism. But again, these were exceptions which soon ended.

Absolute power is of course inimical to basic freedoms of individuals and groups. Where power is absolute, human rights as defined by the United Nations' 1948 Universal Declaration of Human Rights are unlikely to be respected.

Most Arab governments have signed the Universal Declaration, and several of them have adopted the 1966 International Covenant on Civil and Political Rights. All of them, furthermore, have voted in favor of the 1984 Anti-Torture Declaration of the United Nations. Arab constitutions, where they exist, include whole sections on basic freedoms and human rights incorporating the content, if not also the letter, of the above international documents. But very few, if any, of these governments observe their spirit.

While no one has illusions regarding Arab governments' strict observance of the human rights of their citizens, no one has expected those rights to be so grossly and widely violated as they have been. The last ten years witnessed an unprecedented scale of atrocities committed by several Arab governments against their own citizens. The annals of Amnesty International (AI), the International Commission of Jurists (ICJ), and the Arab Organization for Human Rights (AOHR), among many others, are full of information, documents, field observations, eye-witness reports, and complaints substantiating these atrocities. There is no need to reiterate the details of such accounts of horror. Suffice it to list some of the general categories of human rights violations. They include—

1. Arbitrary arrest of political suspects and their prolonged detention in the custody of the state security forces without charge or trial. Such detention may last for more than 10 years.
2. Arbitrary arrest and detention of relatives—including women and children—as hostages, pending the arrest or surrender of suspects at large.
3. Summary trials before special courts (e.g., Popular, Military, Revolutionary, State–Security, Values, Islamic). Without offering even basic legal safeguards, these pass severe sentences (including death) against which there is no appeal.
4. Kidnaping and/or killing of known or suspected opposition figures.
5. Torture of detainees to extract confessions.
6. Torture of prisoners of conscience who have not engaged in acts of violence.
7. Mass killing and/or destruction of communities under suspicion of harboring opposition elements. Aerial bombing and artillery barrages may be used against such communities indiscriminately.

In nearly all Arab countries there is an arsenal of laws restricting basic freedoms (such as those of expression, the press, and organization). Only five countries (Egypt, Morocco, Tunisia, Lebanon, and, more recently, Sudan) have some margin allowing the formation of political parties. But even this margin can be used only at the discretion of the government.

The separation of the three branches of government, where it exists, is hardly respected by the executive branch. The legislature is often nothing but a rubber stamp for the executive. The judiciary is often bypassed or circumvented by Special Courts. Even in a country with some tradition of judiciary independence, such as Egypt, the restrictive laws on basic freedoms tie the judiciary's hand. Whenever the government realizes that the existing laws are not sufficient to silence or penalize the opposition, new ones are quickly proposed by the executive and rubber-stamped by the legislature. In the last five days of Egypt's People's Assembly session one year, some 40 new laws were passed with hardly any debate.

Despite the ease with which Arab governments can formulate restrictive bills and pass them through the legislature, making them into laws, these governments still resort to extralegal and illegal means—e.g., harassment, kidnaping, and assassination. In this respect, it matters little what form of political or legal system is formally adopted in a given country. Monarchical Morocco with its largely French legal code and conservative political orientation is not much different from monarchical Saudi Arabia—with an Islamic legal code (*shari'a*). Neither one is much different from republican, secular, "progressive" Syria, Iraq, and Libya. In all these countries, politically suspect individuals have disappeared, been assassinated, or been summarily sentenced to death.

Some heads of Arab states have publicly taken responsibility for such extralegal means of dealing with the opposition. In a televised speech (May 24, 1984), then-president Numayri of Sudan declared that while his newly adopted *shari'a* laws are good for "normal citizens," there are dissidents who do not deserve to be tried according to them. They are to be tried according to the more severe *al-qanun al-battal*. He went on to assert that in the name of Islam and reform he was "entitled to use extralegal means. . . . Islam also allows for emergency . . . we can storm any house . . . search and arrest people anywhere. . . ." Libya's Qadhafi has publicly declared on several occasions that "in the name of the Revolution and the masses . . . enemies of the people will be liquidated wherever they may be in the World. . . ." (May 10, 1980). "If this sacred duty is described as terror . . . then I gladly accept to be the biggest terrorist in the World. . . ." (March 1985).

Egypt's late president Sadat was not so audacious or blatant. He once declared in a televised speech that he would never break the law while dealing with the opposition, but that he would show them that despite democracy, he could still "mince them . . . for democracy has sharp teeth" (September 5, 1981).

Underlying these gross violations of human rights is a crisis of legitimacy. The craving for continuing absolute power in the face of mounting popular opposition makes Arab rulers resort to terror. Sudan's Numayri is a case in point. As he alienated most Sudanese political forces and felt his legitimacy fast eroding, Numayri declared the application of Islamic *shari'a* in September 1983. He thought that this would win him some general support among Sudan's Muslim population, and especially that it would rally the organized Muslim Brothers behind him. For a while this tactic seemed to work. But by April 1984, the misapplication of Islamic *shari'a*, along with a host of other domestic and external failures, made him realize that the threat to his power was growing rather than subsiding. An armed insurrection had broken out in the South, and a series of strikes was paralyzing the country and causing him embarrassment. On April 29, 1984, Numayri declared a state of emergency in the country. The pretext was to face "rampant moral, administrative, and financial corruption." But he did not fail meanwhile to send a bill to Sudan's People's Assembly (June 10, 1984) proposing amendments to the constitution, in his words "to coincide with Islamic *shari'a*." Curiously enough, all the proposed amendments revolved around the presidency. The proposed change in Article 80, for example, read, "The President of the Republic is the Commander of the Faithful and the Shepherd of the Nation. He is the Head of State, has the executive power, and participates in the legislative power. He is to be endorsed according to the *shari'a bay'a*."

Article 84 was amended so as to change the presidential term from six years, making the *bay'a* (endorsement) unbound by any time limit. Another change in the constitution amounted to extending the president's power after his death. For the stipulation (in Article 112) that a new president be elected within 60 days after the death of the Commander of the Faithful, Numayri substituted a provision that he appoint his successor in a "written will which is to be sealed and only read in the People's Assembly upon his death. The Assembly is to ratify the nomination, and grant the nominee the required *bay'a*." The same set of amendments of the Sudanese Constitution provided that the president no longer be accountable. Article 115, which stipulated the principle and procedures for investigating and trying the president, was deleted. The amendments also gave the president the right to appoint the speaker of the People's Assembly instead of his being elected by the Assembly. They made the judiciary "accountable to the President and to God" (Article 187). All the prerogatives of the Supreme Judiciary Council were transfered to the president (Article 191). Finally, the bill (in Article 220) made "the abrogation of the *bay'a* of the Commander of the Faithful . . . a grand treason."

If we have gone to some length with the Sudanese case, it is to demonstrate the link between the quest by Arab rulers for absolute power on one hand and the gross violations of human rights and the use of terror on the other. The Sudanese case graphically shows this link—but it is not atypical. Nearly all rulers in the Arab world have managed, with varying degrees of subtlety, to do the same. They are all heads of state for life. Most of then have near-absolute power. The demarcations between branches of government have been obliterated or greatly blurred. The only processes that remove heads of Arab states from office are death, assassination, and coup d'état. Both ruler and ruled realize this fact. The deep gulf of mistrust between them is filled with mutual fear and actual or potential terror.

Most current Arab rulers have initially predicated their legitimacy on an explicit or implicit covenant with their people. Often this is stated in declarations they make upon assuming power, or in later charters and constitutions. These covenants usually contain a commitment on the part of the rulers to realize such major objectives as rapid development, social justice, Arab unification, liberation of Palestine, cultural renaissance, sound democracy, and the like.

Often, however, it is understood that these objectives may not be all realizable at once, especially in the midst of external threats of "neo-imperialism," "Zionism," or "Communism." Some objectives, therefore, may have to be delayed in favor of others. In the last three decades the candidate for delay has invariably been democracy, and hence basic political freedoms. The majority often acquiesced to this trade-off. Such initial acquiescence seemed in order as new regimes demonstrated effectiveness and delivered on one or more of the other objectives.

The march of sociopolitical and regional events in the past two decades, however, cast growing doubts on the viability of the trade-off formula. Most of the initial successes usually come to an end after a few years, and some of them may even be reversed. Yet the regime gets more entrenched in power, and the delay in instituting "sound democracy" continues. In other words, the trade-off formula becomes meaningless.

Since the mid-1970s, there has been growing popular rejection of a trade-off of basic freedoms and human rights for any other goal—no matter how noble or dear that goal may be. The rejection of the trade-off formula was first made by the highly politicized elements of the Arab population. They were soon followed by organized political parties in the opposition. These included parties and political groups which in the past had not been vocal concerning, or committed to, principles of liberal democracy, such as the Communists and the Muslim Brothers.

The growing demand for basic freedoms and respect for human rights has been reinforced by several structural and situational factors, among which are—

1. The rapid expansion of the new middle class in the past three decades.
2. The growing failure of ruling elites in dealing with domestic and external problems.
3. The sharp rise in the volume and sophistication of state terror.
4. The increased interaction with the outside world by more Arab citizens through large-scale traveling, the mass media, and work abroad.
5. The Arab press in the diaspora, which has, since the Lebanese civil war, displayed a marked margin of freedom of expression.
6. The inter-regime disputes, one manifestation of which is exposing adversary regimes' failures and especially their gross violations of human rights. Each regime engages in harboring and aiding the opposition forces of the countries of its rivals.
7. The limited but significant multi-party experience in Egypt since the late 1970s.

The Israeli invasion of Lebanon and the shameful and inept response of Arab regimes gave the growing opposition to absolute rule a quantum increase. Since 1982, there have been tens of conferences, seminars, and rallies demanding an end to absolutism. Organizations dedicated to the defense of human rights in the Arab world have mushroomed. The most important amongst these is the Arab Organization for Human Rights (AOHR), founded in 1983. Its significance comes not so much from its impact on Arab regimes as from the way it was formed, the quality of its founders, and its reception by the politicized Arab publics. Suffice it to indicate that the AOHR represents what I may call a "new Arab political consciousness" or a "new Arab rationality." Its foundation was a culmination of a process that had been under way for several years. Its founders come from all ideological streams of the Arab world.

The pressures for democratization and for respect and expansion of human rights go hand in hand. The sentiment and voice of each reinforces the other. Together, these developments seem to be the basis of a new, though embryonic, Arab consensus.

I submit that the next decade is going to be one of human rights and democratization in the Arab world. The absolutist regimes will be falling or drastically modified in the years ahead. The geneses of this trend are manifested in the following:

1. Democratic openings in Egypt, Sudan, Tunisia, Morocco, and Jordan. Kuwait continues to consolidate its democratization process. Some of the old liberal parties have been revived (e.g., Egypt's Wafd), and the creation of new ones is under way in several Arab countries.

2. The proliferation of human rights organizations. Currently there are at least five such pan-Arab organizations and more than 100 local organizations in the Arab world. Several branches of these organizations have also been established by Arabs residing in Europe and North America.

3. The revitalization of intermediary and voluntary organizations and professional and trade unions, and the founding of women's associations. While these are not directly involved in the struggle for human rights, many of them have given moral and material support to human rights organizations.

4. New and highly effective intellectual centers which are dedicated to independent free research and dialogue over all major issues of contemporary Arab life. Notable among these are the Centre for Arab Unity Studies (based in Beirut with a branch in Cairo), the Arab Thought Forum (based in Amman), the Thought and Dialogue Forum (based in Morocco), and the Third World Forum (based in Cairo). Many of these have in theory and practice upheld democratic freedoms and human rights. Their publications are distributed in the tens of thousands throughout the Arab world.

5. The growing independence of the judiciary and its active role in interpreting the law in favor of basic human rights (e.g., with regard to torture or to due process). Egypt's courts have, in the last four years, ruled against the government and in favor of the opposition in a number of cases. Several laws were declared unconstitutional and stricken out of the books.

Significantly for the issue at hand, Egyptian courts have sharply condemned the executive branch in cases involving violations of human rights and compelled the government to compensate victims with substantial sums of money (ranging from L.E. 10,000 to L.E. 50,000) in 23 cases in the last three years.

Egypt in 1981 and Sudan in 1985 are previews of things to come. Things in both countries got worse before they got better.

Egypt, always a pacesetter, has recently witnessed steady advances in the field of human rights and democratization. But this could only come after the explosion of 1981 (culminating in the assassination of President Sadat on October 6). Since then, the principles and language of human rights have become integral parts of Egyptian political discourse.

Sudan's experience of the last two years represents another microcosm of things to come in the Arab world. Numayri was overthrown in April 1985 by a popular uprising led by professional associations. Significantly enough, all the first declarations by the new Transitional Regime emphasized a commitment to human rights. It is still too early to know whether this pledge will be kept. But one of the earliest symbolic acts of the popular uprising was the storming of Kubor Prison in Khartoum and the freeing of all prisoners of conscience. Many of the leaders of the uprising happened to be founding members of the Arab Organization for Human Rights (AOHR). Some have become cabinet members in the provisional government. Through these and others, I have no doubt that the commitment to democratization and human rights will be kept.

The cases of Egypt and Sudan represent one possible scenario for several Arab countries in the few years ahead: an absolutist ruler is killed or his regime overthrown as a necessary step for instituting a democratization process. There is another possible scenario: the ruling regime preemptively takes the initiative toward democratization. Morocco, Tunisia, and Jordan are cases in point. After several years of postponement, King Hassan II finally held the overdue Moroccan national election in 1984. Tunisia, a one-party system for nearly 30 years, has recently changed to a multi-party system. Jordan, in 1984, held a parliamentary election, and it has revived its National Assembly, suspended since 1967.

Whether through the first, violent or the second, peaceful scenario, the democratic transformation of the Arab world is already in progress. In this regard, at least, I am optimistic about the next Arab decade.

4

Democracy, Development, and Human Rights: Can Women Achieve Change Without Conflict?

Nadia Hijab

In this paper, I will briefly survey the human rights of women in the Arab world and look at the results of the development process as it affects them. In assessing prospects for future change, it is important to ask if there is sufficient knowledge available to speak with confidence about the present. It is also important to determine whether that knowledge is likely to become available, and whether it will then be used either by those forces seeking change or by those already in power.

In terms of human rights in the Arab world, there is legislation discriminating against women alone. Such legislation violates from one to six of the articles of the United Nations Declaration of Human Rights, depending on the state in question. Some may consider it a luxury to single out laws that discriminate against women, when, on the whole, neither men nor women in the Arab world enjoy basic human rights (about 23 of the Declaration's articles are violated in some way by various Arab governments). However, the laws of the Arab nation-state are becoming increasingly significant in regulating relations among its citizens. And the laws on women apply to all women whatever their political views, whereas others are violated in the case of politically active individuals or groups.

Most constitutions in the Arab world provide, on paper, for full equal rights for men and women with no discrimination, as do most labor laws. But these are undercut by the personal status codes that tackle the most private areas of life—marriage, divorce, custody of the children, and inheritance. I do not propose to argue whether these laws stem from correct application or interpretation of the Qur'an or the Hadith, the main sources of Islamic *shari'a* (Islamic law), or from patriarchal tradition, simply to list briefly the inequalities. Whereas the Declaration of Human Rights specifies in Article 16 that men and women are "entitled to equal rights as to marriage, during marriage, and at its dissolution," Arab women are—to different degrees—discriminated against by the institution of polygamy, by men's unconditional right to divorce and to custody of the children after a certain age, and by unequal inheritance.

Tunisia is the only Arab country to have made polygamy illegal; some others have restricted it. Its practice ranges from 2 percent of marriages and declining to 10 percent in some oil rich states. Tunisia has reformed its personal status codes to give equality in marriage, divorce, and custody, but a woman is still allocated half the inheritance of the man, and the man is still the legal head of the family. Democratic Yemen, the next most progressive Arab state in this respect, particularly as it needs all hands in the development process, has set strict conditions for polygamy. Some Arab states have amended their laws (e.g., Egypt) to allow a woman to request a divorce in case of polygamy, and to make it necessary for a man to inform his first wife of his intention to take a second. In many other Arab countries, amendments now make it more difficult for men to exercise a unilateral right to divorce, and a little easier for women to divorce and to keep the children a few years beyond the usual ages of seven for boys and nine for girls.

There are other laws that discriminate against women. It should be noted that many of these are not unique to the Arab world, but also existed or exist in countries where there are strong religious and patriarchal traditions, as in other Muslim countries and Latin America. These include laws alleviating punishment for "crimes of honor," or laws requiring a male guardian's permission for work or travel. In some Arab countries, the requirement for women to have written permission from their husband to leave the country is no longer applied in practice; in others, she "only" needs written permission to get a passport. I should repeat that the situation is very different from one Arab country to the next; for instance, in some cases a woman's testimony in court is treated as half that of a man; in others there are women judges.

Is change possible in the specific area of the right to equality within the family in the next decade? If one assumes that the present governments or variations thereof will be in power until 1995, then it is safe to answer with a categorical negative. The most that can be hoped for is more of the piecemeal change that has characterized the region since independence. Many reasons have been advanced for the Arab regimes' reluctance to introduce radical change in personal status codes. The most common reason given is that, having taken political and economic decision-making out of the hands of the people, without a mandate to do so, most governments are reluctant to tackle the one sphere where men still have authority left. Thus, while it has been possible to separate between religious tradition and commercial and banking laws, for example, it has proved impossible in the case of personal status laws. So far, attempts at change in family laws have roused such an uproar in defense of culture and tradition—whether those laws could be justified by the Qur'an or not—that the regimes have backed down. Pressure by women for change during this century, as happened most recently in Algeria in 1984 and in Egypt in 1985, has proved only forceful enough to achieve a compromise.

Of course, those in power can be just as attached to culture and tradition as anyone else. The case of Tunisia is interesting in this respect. The radical changes in law were carried out immediately after independence. These were the regime's progressive days, when it pushed the idea of women's equality vigorously. In time, and following internal power struggles, however, the regime lost its progressive vigor. A study carried out in 1967 on attitudes to women's emancipation in 1967 and again in 1973 found that support for women's emancipation had declined. The proportion of men and women believing education to be equally important for girls and boys decreased from 65 percent to 51 percent, while the proportion considering it acceptable for a woman to exercise authority over a man at work declined from 46 percent to 32 percent. President Bourguiba, once a passionate advocate of women's rights, began to feel in the early 1970s that too much reform would loosen society's morals.

Thus, while states like Tunisia used to pursue, and South Yemen still pursues, a vigorous pro-equality policy, there is no guarantee that the momentum, even of progressive regimes, will be maintained until equality is reached. If there is to be change in attitude, it will need to come from other quarters.

But first, it should be asked whether the laws on the books actually reflect the reality in the Arab world. I remarked earlier that the law is becoming more important. Urbanization is placing people within closer access of the law and gives the state closer access to the people. But, does the law reflect real attitudes? And in rural and tribal areas, has state legislation affected people's lives? What application of the *shari'a* exists at the local level and what informal systems exist to regulate social behavior? The Arab world is far from monolithic in its stages of development. As many social scientists have pointed out, much of the information available on Arab society has been produced by non-Arabs armed with definitions and concepts that do not necessarily fit.

Recently, social scientists with an ear more in tune with the culture have questioned whether lack of rights on paper should be confused with lack of respect—respect of women's persons, respect for their ability to carry out a variety of traditional and non-traditional tasks, or indeed respect of the power they enjoy within society. At the simplest level, women traditionally earn a great deal of respect from their role as wives and mothers, with their power growing as they and their children grow older. Moreover, respect accorded to women, and power enjoyed by them, would appear to be greater in tribal communities, peasant communities, and poorer urban classes than in urban middle or upper class settings. It is noted that in the former cases, there is a more active sharing of productive roles. There would also seem to be a system of checks and balances among the extended families and in the community to keep the supposedly unbridled use of patriarchal power in check. Such systems are breaking down with urbanization, with the only new recourse being the incomplete and unequal laws.

Certainly, Arab society has been fragmented by major social upheavals, in part caused by a mode of development chosen by the state without sufficient knowledge or planning. This has resulted in piecemeal industrialization but not self-reliance. There has been aimless modernization, leading to rapid urbanization and labor migration. Individuals in this process are left to fend for themselves, having lost the support of the extended family or the community.

This process has not touched all parts of the Arab world at the same time or at the same rate. It is important to study different areas in order accurately to assess the actual problems faced by men and women. We need to compare the workings of different social systems and their success or failure to provide social justice and stability in order to propose change that is relevant; otherwise, those forces seeking change in the Arab world will find themselves, with the best of intentions, in the same position of Arab governments—of tinkering with society and doing more harm than good.

In this respect, the most positive indicator of change that I can see is the growing awareness of the lack of information on which current theories are based. This is clear at the meetings of Arab social scientists, who are seeking to develop sociological analysis by Arabs about themselves, using relevant theories and developing relevant methodology.

As regards the status of women, 17 Arab women social scientists were brought together at a conference organized by UNESCO in 1982 to study the state of social science research on women in the Arab world. Eight of the papers presented were published by UNESCO,[1] and one can see why the organization has become so unloved by Western nations. Although the authors' backgrounds are not necessarily radical, the book is packed with questions about economic and social fundamentals imported from the West.

In their papers, the Arab women social scientists do not insist that research on women should be exclusively carried out by women. But they are unanimous on the need for research by "women specialists of the region themselves in a manner that reflects the complexities of social reality and the situation of women of different social categories." They further stress the "human rights dimension of research" in that it should "serve to enhance knowledge of women's position and problems faced and should have as one of its principal objectives the improvement of the status of women."

The social scientists each presented a critique of the research done so far in her country. Some pointed out that "much of the research" is "descriptive in nature, with little analysis of how [customs, values, and male attitudes] actually affect women's status." They noted that women do not necessarily share the male view of themselves and that it is necessary to find out how women view themselves and whether this view is changing. The social scientists analyzed the failings of development—the "commercialization of land, heavy investment in cash crops at the expense of subsistence, uneven mechanization of agriculture"—and the resultant rural migration. They questioned prevailing definitions of modernism as opposed to traditionalism, and of women's liberation. They noted the change in economic relations within the family as a result of modernization, and the shift, in women's case, from self-reliance, to dependence on the male, to dependence on the state.

They urged that the specific situations in the Arab world be compared to relevant examples from other parts of the world. In short, they have begun the process necessary to collect and analyze available data, to draw up plans for studies needed in vast uncharted areas, and to develop a general theoretical framework based on actual fact.

Other encouraging signs include the interest being taken in women's studies at various universities and research institutes, for example, the establishment of the Institute for Women's Studies in the Arab World at the Beirut University College in the early 1970s. More conferences are being held, most noteworthy being those organized by Kuwaiti women on Gulf women and development, to which women from the Arab world and abroad are invited. The collection of information on the half of society that has been treated differently one way or the other for centuries is a prerequisite for social change in the right direction.

Meanwhile, the "modern" indicators of improvement in women's status are taken to be education, participation in the work force, and political participation. These are certainly the areas promoted by the Arab state. Perhaps it is hoped that if such matters as personal status laws cannot be tackled head-on, then gradual change can be achieved through education and through "integration of women in the development process."

Certainly education is an area where there has been rapid growth in the attendance rate of both sexes. There is currently little question about women's right to an education, although there are still questions as to the kind and level of education. Illiteracy remains much higher among women than among men, and the school drop-out rate is high for both boys and girls. If there is no constant push on the part of the state and a corresponding opening of opportunities for both sexes to take advantage of their education, even the process of education cannot be taken for granted.

As for labor force participation, the official statistics on this issue are generally too misleading to be valid as they take into account only part of women's agricultural labor and often leave out homemakers and women in the informal sector. According to the—incomplete—statistics, Arab women's participation in the work force is generally thought to be among the lowest of the developing countries.

Of course, in each Arab country some women are active in a variety of professions and at levels quite close to the top. The ease with which they have moved into the formal workforce, when the opportunity or need arises, is an indication that lack of rights on the books in terms of personal status has not necessarily meant a lack of respect for their abilities.

In the political system, women are present in more or less the same proportions as they are in the "developed" countries, where their numbers are also low. A number of Arab governments have appointed a woman minister in their cabinets, where they generally occupy the same portfolios as they do in the West—education, welfare, or culture. Each Arab country also has its women's groups, official and unofficial. The official groups naturally promote government aims and, by and large, focus on integrating women into development.

The question is, what price development? If we look at the economic cake in the Arab world, we will see it has a very thin, rich, upper crust, a rapidly diminishing middle layer of half-baked economic ideas, and a very thick bottom layer of almost inedible burnt-out development. Arab states have lurched from self-sufficiency to major indebtedness, with the Arab countries' overall external debt approaching $100 billion in 1983. It is true that much of this debt is concessionary aid from oil rich Arab brothers to poorer ones, but with the oil windfall rapidly coming to an end, the number of Arab economic basket cases is bound to rise. The service sector is expanding at the expense of productive sectors, imports are rising and cities in the highly populated Arab states are now ringed by belts of poverty. Development in the oil rich states has left the indigenous populations feeling threatened by massive imports of foreign manpower, and unable to run their countries fully themselves.

Surely in this case, the question should not be how rapidly to integrate women into this mess, but how to define development. It is, at any rate, becoming increasingly clear that for women more than men, the promise of education and work, with resulting economic independence within the family, may fade before it has had a chance to become much of a reality. In the North African countries and Egypt unemployment has reached levels that will make it very difficult for women to compete. This comes at a time when the break-up of the extended family and the rise in the cost of living mean that they need paid employment not so much for self-fulfillment, but to survive. In Cairo, some ads for jobs now say bluntly that women need not apply. To cure North Africa's unemployment problems, some Arab brother nations have suggested that they send the women back home. (Even in the "developed" nations, women are still looked on as a reserve pool of labor to be called on in time of war or economic boom and then sent back home.) In the case of Jordan, the government has spent the last decade committed to research and plans to encourage women to enter the workforce to replace the manpower that had drained away to the Gulf. Now the cutback on Gulf projects and employment and the return of Palestinians and Jordanians may reverse the process.

A necessary area of research is the impact of labor migration on the women left behind to manage the families alone. How have they managed, has there been any change in status, and what will happen when the men come home? Another area for research should involve the impact of war on Lebanon and Iraq, where the numbers of men decimated through fighting have meant that women have had both to support their families and to step further into the workforce to replace lost manpower.

With the results of development so dismal in the Arab world, it is hard to see that women's integration in development is an effective way to achieving equality in rights and status. Indeed, some research has shown that urbanization and industrialization have worsened and not improved women's status, through the break-up of family ties, increased dependence on the male, or job insecurity. It is safe to say that if the present government policies continue, there will be little impetus for economic self-reliance and fairness in distributing output. In this case, women can expect to remain for decades even further on the margins of society than their menfolk.

Can women achieve change without conflict by 1995? Of course, social change takes decades and cannot be planned for a ten-year span. What is most likely to happen in the next decade is that women will define the dimensions of change needed and wanted by Arab society, as well as the means to bring it about. That women largely will have to take matters into their own hands on the level of personal status is clear. There is general awareness among educated women that the national liberation movements brought about minimum rights and liberties (for both men and women) and that social liberation movements have not gone far enough. That women will be able to achieve change through women's movements alone—be they official, reformist, or feminist—is less clear. Change in matters specifically related to women, as in personal status codes, cannot be detached from the necessary change in the mode and aims of social and economic development. It will be difficult and probably inadvisable to isolate individual concerns from group concerns.

There are several obstacles that a feminist movement would face and has faced in the Arab world. First, such movements are identified with the West and are seen by Arab men and women, who still suffer from political and economic colonialism and dependence, as just another assault in the form of "cultural imperialism." Second, in an era of rapid change, there is an almost fanatical attachment to "traditional" values. Since women have been responsible for transmitting cultural values from generation to generation, an attempt to change their role will be viewed as an attack on the culture. And, of course, there are patriarchs and businessmen reluctant to give up privileges and to meet the costs of making room for women.

Perhaps the most important factor is that rapidity of change in the Arab world has meant that individualism has not had the time to develop in the way it has in the West. There is still a strong sense of commitment to community life. Women's rights expressed as individual rights will be seen as a threat to the community. Perhaps it is this sense of community that, beneath all the rhetoric, traditionalists seek to preserve; and preserving this may be no bad thing. The challenge will be to bring about individual rights within the community. This will make the difference in years to come between women in conflict with each other and against men, or women and men seeking justice in conflict with state and religious authorities.

For the next decade then, a start has been made by indigenous social scientists in defining the problems; and conferences are being held to share information and tactics, both within the region and abroad. Non-official women's movements are being formed. Women are increasingly active in movements of both the left and of Islamic fundamentalism seeking change—although they hold few positions of power in either as yet. The next step for men and women will be to find the means necessary to bring about political participation and a social and economic development that makes sense. For women specifically, the next step will also be to find the means to achieve change in areas where they are discriminated against. They must find the means to negotiate power-sharing within overall movements seeking change. Only in this way will they ensure that the issue of personal equality is not again left for when the time is right, but happens alongside real national and social liberation.

Notes

1. United Nations Educational, Scientific, and Cultural Organization, *Social Science Research on Women in the Arab World* (Paris: UNESCO and London, Frances Pinter, Ltd., 1984).

PART TWO

The Political Economy of Arab International Relations

5

The Shape of Inter-Arab Politics in 1995

Rashid I. Khalidi

Stagnation and Change

The fate of those who try to predict the future is usually an unenviable one: if not treated as madmen or fools, they are ignored when wrong and resented when their predictions prove correct. It is hard to decide which of these fates is preferable. But if attempting to predict the future has always been a hazardous business, predicting the future in the Arab world presents particular and awesome hazards.

This is partly the case because inter-Arab politics have a peculiar feature which may be shared with other regional subsystems, but which is noticeably acute in the Arab case. While on the one hand events occur with bewildering rapidity in Arab politics, with alliances shifting, instability developing, rulers changing, and new political, economic, and social forces emerging,[1] on the other hand there has been little change in the underlying structure of the Arab subsystem, and indeed in most Arab regimes, for at least the 15 years since 1970.[2]

This paradox, of rapid change combined with stagnation, is perhaps only conjunctural, perhaps only a characteristic of the past 15 years. The Arab system certainly changed fundamentally, repeatedly, and unpredictably during the decades preceding 1970. This is true whether one speaks of the pre-World War I era, the interwar years, or the period after World War II, when most Arab states obtained their formal independence and put an end to the presence of colonial military forces on their territory, and when many underwent socioeconomic upheavals.

But since 1970, with the possible current exception of the government of Sudan, no Arab regime has changed fundamentally: leaders have died, or have been killed or removed, in Algeria, Egypt, Saudi Arabia, Iraq, both Yemens, Kuwait, and now Sudan in the intervening years. But essentially, the regimes in these countries have so far stayed the same, evolving over time, but registering no sharp break from the past. Moreover, as regimes, elites, and social formations in the formerly radical Arab states have apparently become more stable, there has been a certain process of convergence between them and the other Arab states, those formerly labeled conservative.

Even in Lebanon, where there has been a progressive breakdown of the political system since the mid-1970s, civil war and external intervention have almost become routinized: there has been upheaval without real change, or perhaps unchanging and seemingly endless upheaveal. To reverse the title of Elie Salem's 1973 work, over the past eleven years Lebanon has witnessed revolution without modernization,[3] or perhaps neither revolution nor modernization. More important, the Arab subsystem has adjusted with little apparent difficulty to this state of semi-permanent chaos in Lebanon.

Similarly, despite many striking events and burning crises since 1970, many important patterns of inter-Arab politics have remained constant over this decade and a half. With the end of Nasserism, the main axis of the system as it has existed since the mid-1950s—Egypt—disappeared, and systemic polarities shifted in consequence. Certainly one can no longer speak of the Arab world as characterized by a growing radical Arab nationalist and pro-Soviet core of Arab states, opposed by a dwindling number of conservative monarchies and traditional regimes, as one could in the 1960s.

In place of one central focal point in the Arab world, which formerly was Egypt, the past 15 years have seen the emergence of many. Each has become a mini-axis in its own right, but none has succeeded fully in replacing Cairo. Thus, today no actor in the Mashriq can ignore Damascus, none in the Arabian Peninsula can ignore Riyadh, none in the Maghrib can ignore Algiers; but at the same time, Baghdad, Rabat, and Cairo remain important alternative poles of Arab politics.

Since the end of Egyptian preeminence in the Arab world, there has thus been a certain diffusion of power within the Arab subsystem. This has produced a balance of power, or perhaps a balance of impotence, which has remained generally constant for more than a decade, despite periodic shifts in the relative importance of this or that subcenter.

Among the other constants have been certain alliance patterns within the Arab subsystem. Notable among these has been a tacit Damascus–Riyadh axis. This dates back at least to the 1973 war, was cemented by King Faysal in its wake, and since then has been a major, if very underrated, feature of Arab politics. This has not been an exclusive relationship for either partner. Just as Syria has preserved its close ties with Moscow, with which Saudi Arabia does not have diplomatic relations, so has Saudi Arabia maintained strong links with Syria's arch rival Iraq, financing its war effort against Iran, an ally of Syria. Nor has the existence of this axis precluded generally close relations between Syria and Libya. There are other similar consistent patterns throughout much or most of the period.

As far as regional conflict is concerned, after 1973 the Arab–Israeli dispute was largely confined to Lebanese territory, to the relief of all the Arab parties concerned, except of course the Palestinians and the Lebanese themselves. At the same time, and partly as a result of this, the Lebanese conflict has become endemic, and is now apparently impervious to efforts to end it. Two longstanding disputes, those at the western extremity and on the northeastern border of the Arab world, between Algeria and Morocco and between Iraq and Iran, have become semi-permanent conflicts. Other less serious foci of tension exist, but these three have become established as the major ones over the past decade or so.

In terms of external relations, these 15 years have also marked a change from those which preceded them and have seen the development of a clear and relatively stable pattern. In place of what seemed to be an irreversible shift in favor of the U.S.S.R. in the years before 1970, there has occurred since then what appears to be an equally decisive shift in the direction of the United States. On the surface at least, it began in the early 1970s with Sadat, but it was most recently symbolized by the resumption of relations between the United States and Iraq and the visit of Algeria's president to Washington, both pronounced variations from the patterns of the previous two decades.

The End of Stability

Perhaps the key question to ask regarding the shape of inter-Arab politics in 1995 is whether this combination of rapid internal change and both domestic and systemic stagnation will continue. The first thing any analyst worth his Ph.D. will do when faced with a straight question such as this is to dodge it behind a smokescreen of scenarios. The topic is so difficult to deal with that perhaps this would be the wisest course. But notwithstanding the conventional dictates of caution, it is possible to suggest unequivocally that this current pattern will not, indeed cannot, continue for another decade.

The main reason why the shape of inter-Arab politics 10 years hence will not resemble that of the 15 years past is that the emergence of the present regional configuration has depended very largely on the precarious domestic stability and the relative prosperity which have prevailed in most Arab states over this period. It now seems that many of the factors which have contributed to both stability and prosperity are disappearing or have disappeared. The most important of these factors has been the socioeconomic and political impact of the inflow of revenues derived from oil, in both oil-producing and labor-exporting states.

This inflow provided the dynamic socioeconomic force behind the tide of what, for want of a better word, we may label *infitah*, a process which has transformed the appearance of, and at least the top of the social pyramid in, most of the formerly radical Arab states. The way the process worked in oil and gas producers like Iraq and Algeria is easy to trace. But there were similar effects in the many Arab states where remittances from workers abroad, direct subventions from oil producers, and other similar sources of oil wealth produced an analogous transformation. Indeed the Arab labor exporters (Egypt, Syria, Sudan, Tunisia, Jordan, Lebanon, the two Yemens, and the Palestinians, whether in the occupied West Bank and Gaza or the diaspora) were in many ways as profoundly affected by this impact as the oil producers themselves.[4]

The point here is that in the Arab world the age of easy, massive, sometimes excessive, oil wealth is over, at least for the time being. As a result, the social and economic forces which came into being during this period will be critically affected. Not only will oil-producing states have to tighten their belts and make hard choices for the first time in over a decade; in addition, major labor exporters and other Arab states which reaped extensive indirect benefits from oil wealth will suffer serious dislocations.

In consequence, it seems clear that the pattern of superficial stability which has prevailed in the Arab world for the past 15 years will surely change, perhaps radically. The direct effects of such a change on inter-Arab politics are hard to predict, but certain possible outcomes can be suggested.

One is that as labor-exporting countries, such as Tunisia, Egypt, Sudan, the two Yemens, Jordan, Lebanon, and Syria, adjust to the decrease in indirect and direct financial inflows into their economies from the oil producers, the process of convergence between labor exporters and oil producers discernible over the past decade will be reversed. The Arab world may not go back to the 1960s pattern of a clear delineation between haves and have-nots, but there will be new cleavages as a result of these major economic shifts.

Furthermore, many of the links forged between these two groups of countries by migration, remittances, and the like (described aptly in the title of Kerr and Yassin's pathbreaking work as constituting a "new Arab order"[5]) will begin to be broken. Signs of this process can already be seen in the recent expulsion of Tunisians from Libya and the failure of increasing numbers of Palestinians and Lebanese to find work in the Gulf or to have their contracts renewed, combined with the gradual departure of other Arab workers under economic and other pressures.[6]

Parameters of the Future

Accepting that there will be domestic changes resulting from the end of the oil boom and new cleavages in the Arab world as a consequence, how will all this shape the Arab system in the years to come?

It is impossible to answer this question without first setting out at least some of the parameters within which this system is likely to have to function between now and 1995. Specifically, what will be the state of the interaction between the superpowers in the Middle East, and what will be the status of the current conflicts between Arab states and non-Arab ones, such as Israel and Iran?

While no one can affirm with any confidence what will happen over the next ten years regarding either of these conflicts, it can be assumed that there will be a continuation of the rivalry between the superpowers in the Middle East, without either of the two gaining the upper hand or expelling the other. While the Soviet Union seemed on the ascendant in the Arab world during the 1950s and 1960s, the United States gained ground in the following decade and a half. The pendulum may swing back again in the other direction, or equilibrium may obtain for a period, but in any case their rivalry in the region seems bound to continue unabated.

This in turn will probably be a factor in the perpetuation of the current conflicts between Arab states and Israel and Iran. In the past both disputes, and in particular that between the Arabs and Israel, have been exacerbated by superpower rivalry. This was most harmful when it was expressed through attempts by one side to achieve exclusive advantage at the expense of the other through manipulation or exploitation of war and peace in the region. Whether this was done via the arming of one of the conflicting parties, or via "peace plans" which excessively favor one protagonist, the net effect has been the same.

Sadly, it does not seem likely that the United States and U.S.S.R. will allow any consideration, certainly not the achievement of peace in the Middle East, to take precedence over their obsession with one another. Nor does there seem to be any realistic immediate prospect for resolution of the Arab–Israeli or Iran–Iraq conflicts, for this and other reasons.

Occasionally, there appears the glimmer of an oppportunity for a breakthrough in one of these two conflicts, which are now semi-permanent features of the international relations of the Arab world. So far, however, these prospects have proved illusory, due as much to the intractable nature of the conflicts themselves as to the obduracy of the superpowers in pursuit of their narrow aims.

Egypt's Changing Role

If things on the external level are likely to remain largely unchanged, therefore, how can the Arab system be expected to respond to the internal changes we have outlined, and what will inter-Arab politics look like in 1995?

Beyond a number of vague scenarios, all that is possible is to suggest some likely developments in this regard.

The most important will be a fundamental shift in the position of Egypt. This will take place, sooner or later, as a result of two factors. The first is that the enormity of Egypt's socioeconomic and developmental problems is likely to impose a phase of retrenchment, austerity, and investment during the next decade. This will probably once again turn it into a model for other Arab states facing similar problems, as happened during the decade after the 1952 revolution.

The second factor leading to a shift in Egypt's orientation is that it is already suffering from the chafing constraints of its current relationships with the United States and Israel. Growing domestic pressures combined with Egypt's inevitable reemergence as the leader of the Arab world are likely to necessitate at least major modifications in its alignment with the United States and its attitude toward Israel.

There are many ways this could happen. One could be through renewed conflict in and around Lebanon involving Israel, which could well have the same kind of effect in further alienating Egyptian elite opinion from Israel and the current relationship with it as did the 1982 war. Another way this could happen would be through Syrian involvement in a major war with Israel, whether as a result of events in Lebanon or for some other reason. Similarly, Israeli military action against Jordan because of a renewed PLO presence there could severely strain the current network of Egypt's external alignment.

The Egyptian–Israeli peace treaty was never very popular with the Egyptian public. Perceptions of Israeli bad faith over the issue of the Palestinians had a major initial impact. Thereafter, Israel's bombing of the Iraqi nuclear reactor, its annexation of the Golan Heights, and, most important, its invasion of Lebanon, were all serious blows to the spirit and letter of the treaty, from which it still has not recovered. Another such dislocation, whether as a result of the Lebanese situation, a Syrian–Israeli war, or Israeli moves against Jordan, could fatally undermine it.

Another possible cause for a shift in Egypt's current external alignments would be a deterioration of its bilateral relations with the United States, perhaps as a result of trends which are already visible. Resentment at U.S. aid levels and aid disbursement policies relating to Egypt in comparison with treatment of Israel, U.S. inflexibility and bias in favor of Israel as regards the regional peace process, and the political impact of a future economic decline in Egypt could all be factors in such a process. So could unexpected crises in relations such as that in the aftermath of the hijacking of the Italian cruise ship in October 1985.[7]

Such a shift in Egypt's position would inevitably manifest itself in a fundamental revision of the polarities of the Arab system, very likely one initiated by Egypt. Among other things, this would involve an Egyptian–Syrian rapprochement, possibly as a result of the kind of shocks suggested above, possibly as a result of a change of regime or leader in one or both of the two countries, and possibly simply out of a realization that such a move would present both with major new opportunities.

It is unnecessary to stress how great are the obstacles to such a shift. But, just as in the case of the Sino–Soviet split, at least some measure of rapprochement is so clearly in the interest of both parties that given a slight change in the perspective of those concerned, such a move might seem in many ways logical and even inevitable. The various obstacles, incidentally, could be overcome with a little ingenuity, daring, and vision. Just as Sadat flew to Jerusalem and, on a more prosaic level, Mubarak flew recently to Baghdad, leaping over polarizations which at least on the surface looked insuperable, so might it be possible under suitable circumstances for an Egyptian leader to fly to Damascus, or vice versa.

This could perhaps be done in such a way as to attempt to maintain some semblance of peace between Egypt and Israel, possibly by Egypt's describing such a move as part of an attempt to create a broad Arab diplomatic front in order to work for a peaceful, comprehensive resolution of the conflict with Israel. Such an approach would undoubtedly be anathema to both the United States and Israel, but difficult for them to argue with, at least directly. It might also be acceptable to Syria if linked to a clear confidential understanding about the aims and limits of the policy to be followed by such an Arab front.

It may be argued that this is a fantastic scenario, and in some ways indeed it is. But if the internal situation of the Arab states follows the lines suggested above, and if the givens regarding the superpowers and the conflicts with Israel and Iran posited earlier do in fact continue to serve as fixed points in the Arab landscape over the next decade, something has to give and change is inevitable. The factor which would most fundamentally change the shape of the Arab system as it was described at the outset would be a shift in the position of the largest Arab state. For if this system is to overcome the diffusion of power which currently plagues it, Egypt is its only possible central axis.

There is an alternative scenario. This involves the continuation of the status quo, with Egypt remaining relatively isolated in the Arab world. Such an eventuality is unlikely, because the pressures from within Egypt for a change in the Egyptian position seem likely to mount rather than decrease. These are fed by dissatisfaction with some of the options regarding development and Egypt's international alignment chosen during the Sadat period, combined with intense irritation at the continued inflexibility in the U.S. position on a comprehensive peace between Israel and its remaining Arab adversaries and at the immobility of the Israeli position. While other Arab states may modify their orientation, none seems as ripe for a major shift as Egypt; nor does the congruence of domestic and foreign policy considerations dictating such a change seem as great in any other Arab state.

We are left therefore with a picture of an inter-Arab system which can be expected to change dramatically by 1995. There will undoubtedly be changes of rulers, and probably changes of regime. There will be changes in relative wealth of the various countries. But most important, there will be a different pattern of distribution of power within the Arab system, with sooner or later a reemergence of Egypt to play a leading role within it.

This will not mean a move back to the old system of the 1950s or 1960s, for the Arab world has already been transformed so much since then that the system which emerges will be much more complex and nuanced than the earlier one. Certainly transnational ideologies will play a smaller role: Arab nationalism has faded; the current Islamic wave does not appear to have the potential to transcend state boundaries which Arab nationalism had in the 1950s (the seeming imperviousness of Iraqi Shi'a to Iranian appeals to rebel seems strong proof of this); and if the Palestine cause remains important, the Palestinian national movement has lost much of its pan-Arab appeal.

At the same time, interstate boundaries have grown stronger in the Arab world as has *raison d'état* as a force in inter-Arab relations, with the reassertion of the priority of nation-state interests. These trends will most probably not change. Similarly, many regional groupings which have emerged since the 1960s, and many new regional preoccupations, will inevitably continue to exist.

There are other changes of importance. Some states have grown in relative power and importance, and others have decreased. Syria, for example, will always retain some of the increased influence which has accrued to it over the past decade or so. From being an object in inter-Arab politics in the two decades after independence—whence the title of Patrick Seale's book *The Struggle for Syria*[8]—Syria will continue to be a major subject, a key Arab actor. It is unlikely that Saudi Arabia, on the other hand, will ever regain the importance it had in the 1970s, or even the major role it played in the decades before that. In the Maghrib and elsewhere, there are important new realities which will necessarily be reflected in this new pattern.

But it is virtually inevitable that Egypt should resume playing a central role in the Arab world, if only because, as in the early 1950s, such a role is simply waiting for the leader and the regime in Egypt with the confidence and skill to play it.[9] All the contraints and restraints which have been placed on Egypt since then will not suffice to prevent such a development if that confidence and skill are present.

When and how this will happen cannot be predicted, nor can even whether it will lead to a resolution of the problems facing Egypt and the Arabs. The results may well be as somber as those achieved the last time Egypt dominated inter-Arab politics. But it is hard to conceive of such an obvious development not suggesting itself more and more forcefully to people in the Arab world in years ahead as their weighty problems, both internal and external, remain unsolved. Where the initiative will come from, whether starting in Sudan or the Arabian Peninsula, over Lebanon or the Palestine issue, cannot be divined. What seems clear is that major change is on the way, and once it has begun, the directions just outlined seem the most likely ones for that change to take as the Arab system and inter-Arab politics are reshaped in the decade ahead.

Notes

1. One explanation for the instability of the entire Middle Eastern system is provided by L. Carl Brown, *International Politics and the Middle East: Old Rules, Dangerous Game* (Princeton, NJ: Princeton University Press, 1984), pp. 3–18.

2. For more on this phenomenon, see R. Khalidi, "Social Transformation and Political Power in the 'Radical' Arab States" and other chapters in I. William Zartman and Adeed Dawisha, eds., *Nation, State and Integration in the Arab World*, vol. III of *States, Issues and Society* (Syracuse, NY: Syracuse University Press, forthcoming).

3. Elie Salem, *Modernization Without Revolution: Lebanon's Experience* (Bloomington, IN: University of Indiana Press, 1973).

4. For an examination of several aspects of this process, see Malcolm Kerr and El Sayed Yassin, eds., *Rich and Poor States in the Middle East: Egypt and the New Arab Order* (Boulder, CO, and Cairo: Westview Press, American University in Cairo, 1982).

5. *Ibid.* See also, the essays in Ibrahim Ibrahim, ed., *Arab Resources: The Transformation of a Society* (Washington, DC: Georgetown University Center for Contemporary Arab Studies, 1983), most of which deal with this subject.

6. See Judith Miller and John Kifner, "Wave of Arab Migration Ending with Oil Boom," *New York Times*, October 6, 1985, pp. 1, 16, for an assessment of the impact of the end of the extensive migration between Arab countries of the past decade.

7. See Bernard Gwertzman, "A Chill in Egypt Ties: Washington Worries that Mubarak May Move Closer to Other Arab Lands," *New York Times*, October 20, 1985, p. 20, written in the wake of the ship hijacking, for an example of how such an incident might contribute to the impetus for a realignment of Egypt's position.

8. Patrick Seale, *The Struggle for Syria* (London: Oxford University Press, for the Royal Institute of International Affairs, 1965). The subtitle is *A Study in Post-War Arab Politics, 1945-1958*.

9. The reference is to the much-quoted metaphor utilized by Abdel-Nasser in *Egypt's Revolution: The Philosophy of the Revolution* (Washington, DC: Devin Adair, 1955).

6

Unwelcome Guests: The Political Economy of Arab Relations with the Superpowers

Bahgat Korany

Introduction

Analysts and schools of thought have differed on explaining past and present events in the Arab world. Will they agree on accounting for its future? The problems of forecasting in social analysis are only too well-known: the variables are too many and keep changing all the time, thus creating hundreds, if not thousands, of different combinations. Moreover, we do not yet have reliable tools to determine the weighting of the various factors nor to control their movement.

These general problems of social futurology might be further complicated by the topic at hand. For would not the dynamics of relations between the Arab world and the superpowers depend also on what happens within the superpowers, within their blocs, and between them—that is, on no less than the structure and functioning of the whole global system? And would not occasional regional fickleness create what specialists in cybernetics and communication dub "noise" that could make us confuse sensational happenings with long-term structural patterns? It was Sadat who said in 1974 that the Arabs were in the process of becoming the sixth world power, a mere eight years (the equivalent of days in terms of history) before Lebanon's solitary fall on the path of Israel's invading troops. How could we have expected during the "glorious days" of October 1973, when Arab political, military, and economic instruments were so well coordinated, Sadat's separate peace and the general Lebanonization of inter-Arab relations? Those who mistake the tip of the iceberg for the "real thing" might answer: human fickleness knows no bounds, and certainly the Arab world does not have a monopoly on it. Granted. But this complicates, rather than solves, the methodological problems of forecasting. Should we, then, be resigned to accepting forecasting as mere lucrative fortune-telling and an academic pastime?

The way out adopted in this paper is to concentrate on constants or long-term variables that—beyond individual desires and personal actions—shape the evolution of relations and set the limits for personal decisions. In this case, even when surprise actions take place (e.g., Sadat's 1977 Jerusalem visit) we may surmise their degree of success/failure, because we do not lose sight of structural factors, i.e., the parameters.

Consequently, and since forecasting is history extended, this paper sorts out and emphasizes a particular set of structural trends: those of dependency. To deal with the assigned topic, it pursues two lines of the argument:

1. The constant presence of the intrusive global system in the Arab world: historically, at present, and in the future. No structural change would take place at this level before 1995. Certainly some Arab countries could replace the United States by the Soviet Union or vice versa, but this is a change in the dominant partner and not in dependency itself.
2. This dependency is analyzed and measured through five indicators supported by data included in ten tables. Without going into complicated trend extrapolation, it is explained how some facets of this dependency, like debt, might change between now and 1995, but others (e.g., food or arms dependence) change so slowly that no trend reversal is expected at this level.

Consequently, the paper is organized in the following way. The first part deals with the all-important issue of forecasting methodology. The survey of the literature in this area shows its tentativeness and even underdevelopment. If any lesson can be drawn from the existing literature, it is much less from the recipes it gives than from its examples of what *not* to do. The second part analyzes five structural determinants of the Arab world that govern the dynamics of its relations with the superpowers. The data emphasize both economic and cultural dependency, especially on the United States. The third part discusses the more orthodox and widespread view that the relations of the Arab world are dominated not by dependence but by interdependence. This part deals briefly with two aspects of this counterthesis, petropower and Arab investment, to show their relative fragility as bases of power. The conclusion pulls the threads together and raises some issues for discussion.

Inconsistencies and Methodological Difficulties

In the spring of 1983, Egypt's leftist newspaper *Al-Ahali* started publishing part of Heikal's *Autumn of Fury: The Assassination of Sadat*. Heikal was Nasser's alter ego and was Sadat's, too, until 1974, when they parted company over the question of Egypt's relations with the United States after the 1973 October War. Heikal offers a wealth of data, and the publication of his book was bound to initiate a heated debate on Sadat's decade and policies.

Mutual invective apart, some of the exchanges between expert and well-known journalists and intellectuals were so important as to force President Mubarak to intervene. Of special relevance here is the fact that the debate gave us an inkling of the Egyptians' evaluation of both the Sadat and Nasser eras and of the role of their country in the Arab world. But some writings tried to go beyond the immediate context to address themselves to Egypt's future. For instance, in the weekly *Rose Al-Yusef* (June 13, 1983), the seasoned journalist and ex-army officer, Salah Hafez, believed that one of the obstacles to the Arabs' advance was that people were still chained to the past, debating its details and adopting its criteria of evaluation as immutable. Such an approach, he asserted, prevents Arabs from systematically analyzing the present and sorting out basic trends to trace their future evolution. Unfortunately, the discussion of future trends was lost in the heated verbal battle.

This discussion in Egyptian newspapers was crucial not only because of the wide diffusion of Egypt's mass media and the impact of its leadership, Nasser as well as Sadat (obviously in different ways), but also because of the weight of the country and of the urge of its inhabitants for a better future.

A better future? Not only have some Islamic and Christian traditionalists insisted that only God knows and shapes the future, but also some eminent social scientists have ridiculed the "historical prediction business"—"the Year 2000 and all that."[1] Skepticism is bolstered when we consider some worldwide events that were never predicted:[2]

1. The coming of World War I, when the world had looked so peaceful a few years earlier. (It is certainly difficult to predict the "first" of anything!)
2. The coming to power in Russia of what was to become the Communist Party. (Only a year before the Revolution, no lesser authority than Lenin had affirmed that he did not expect to see it in his lifetime.)
3. The rise of Nazi Germany, Japan's attack on Pearl Harbor, the nuclear destruction of Nagasaki and Hiroshima, and the rapid resurgence of Germany and Japan.
4. In the tense atmosphere of the 1950s and the Cold War, who could have predicted that a new world war would not take place within the following ten or twenty years?
5. In that postwar period, who could have predicted that political decolonization would advance so fast, colonial empires would crumble, a United Nations would have more than 150 members, the first man would land on the moon, and the country that sent him would lose the Vietnam War after pouring into it so many thousands of men and millions of dollars, or—much closer to our subject—what would result from the 1967 and 1973 Middle East wars and the oil embargo?

Is the inability to forecast or to err in forecasting a question of "scientific methodology"? In a recent book about the Arab world that will certainly be quoted frequently, the author answers the question about methodology and makes a clear choice. "Social scientists removed from the scene may be able to play with indexes and measurements of power and to determine the ebb and flow in national resources and capabilities, but nations persist in their memories."[3]

And specialists in forecasting do not disagree: after all, it was Harold Nicholson who in his novel *Public Faces* foresaw the atom bomb, while Rutherford, having split the atom, did not think that this great scientific achievement would have practical consequences.[4]

Even in cases of quantifiable trends, margins of error have plagued forecasters. For instance, a Delphi panel grossly underestimated the increase in the world's population. Already at the 4.4 billion mark in 1980, population had surpassed the 4.3 billion of the Delphi forecast long before 1984. Moreover, "many demographers now project a global population of about 7 billion—not 5.1 billion—by the year 2000, and at least 10 to 14 billion—not 8 billion—during the next century."[5]

Does this mean that talking about the future is merely a flight of the imagination or academic fortune-telling? Not exactly, provided we think of the future not as specific events and detailed happenings but rather as patterns of relations and orders of magnitude. In this case the emphasis can be placed on identifiable constants or long-term variables, e.g., the fact of Arab dependency on the superpowers.

This paper's emphasis on the political economy of Arab relations with the superpowers touches on one basic aspect in the sociology of knowledge: whether personalities count or not, and if yes, to what degree. It was, after all, Presidents Sadat and Asad who took the decision to launch the 1973 October War; King Faysal who decreed the oil embargo; and Sadat who went to Jerusalem and ended by signing a separate peace with Israel. And can we imagine Tunisia without Bourguiba? These examples may confirm that "a great man" can occupy a prominent place in history. But can he shape it?

Without discounting altogether the "great man theory" of history, the view adopted here is that real-life factors set the limits for any possible change in the pattern of events. In other words, personal whims, subjective actions, or even the perseverance of "the great man" cannot change the course of history overnight or singlehandedly. An analogy might be drawn in this respect to a restaurant and its menu. If one goes to a Chinese restaurant one cannot normally order and get a pizza; the limits of choice are already set by the menu. Similarly, the margin of maneuverability of any leader of a Third World, i.e., dependent, country is set by the structure, processes, and historical evolution of the global system. The system's structure, processes, and evolution have been shaped by the powers of the day (e.g., think of the Yalta Conference and its impact on present international politics).

Does this mean that leadership in the dependent country has to resign itself to the world system's tyranny and meekly obey global odds? Not necessarily. What is important, however, is that the leadership start from the fact of global dominance, understand its mechanism, and through consistent cumulative behavior aim to influence the rules of the game and the position of the pieces.

Indeed, many of the deficiencies in both political analysis and political behavior stem from failure to grasp this obvious fact: the impact of global parameters. Those local powers that managed to promote their own political objectives did so by standing up to the monopoly of one great power (Great Britain in the past and the United States at present) and bringing in an alternative great power (France in the past and the Soviet Union at present). In this case, exploitation of the differences between the big powers of the day concretized the small state's age-old maxim: divide-that-ye-may-not-be-ruled.[6]

The Continuing Intrusion of the Great Powers

Despite mass media sensational emphasis on "oil power" and "the Arabs are coming," the Arab world has been—in the past and up to the present— highly penetrated by the big powers. The region's strategic importance (in terms both of historical geopolitical significance and of contemporary resource-endowment) has been so emphasized that the point does not need to be labored. Suffice it to say that the United States still imports 49 percent of its total oil needs, Europe 96 percent, and Japan 100 percent, and that the ratio of oil imported from the Gulf to total oil imports is 34 percent, 61 percent, and 72 percent for those three regions respectively.[7] As a result, the Arab world will not be allowed, even if it prefers, to steer its own course. The superpowers will always be too interested in its affairs and will naturally persist in attempting to shape its course. This seems to be a historical fact, independent of who the big powers of the day are. Recent scholarship confirms the continuation of the pattern of balkanization. ". . . For roughly the last two centuries the Middle East has been more consistently and more thoroughly ensnarled in great power politics than any other part of the non-Western world . . . no area has remained so unremittingly caught up in multilateral great power politics."[8]

Penetrated thus by the superpowers, the region's patterns of politics cannot be adequately explained without frequent reference to the influence of the intrusive outside system. The United States, from Truman to Reagan, has tended to interpret many regional political events as "evidence of Communist meddling." Because of the Suez Canal, for instance, "the interests of the entire Free World were at stake in Egypt."[9] Soviet "machinations" were also the determining factor, according to ex-President Lyndon Johnson, in the 1967 Arab–Israeli War and its consequences:

> In an effort to gain influence in the radical Arab states, the Soviet Union shifted in the mid-1950s from its original support of Israel to an attempt to push moderate Arab states toward a more radical course and to provide a

Middle East base for expanding its role in the Mediterranean, in Africa, and in the areas bordering on the Indian Ocean. The Soviets used Arab hostility toward Israel to inflame Arab politics to the boiling point. Country after country had shifted to the Russian view. The expanding Soviet presence in this strategic region threatened our position in Europe. Soviet leaders called publicly for the withdrawal of our Sixth Fleet from the Mediterranean, as well as for the liquidation of NATO. If they gained control of the seas, the oil, and the air space of the vast arc between Morocco and Iran, all that had been done since President Truman's time to achieve stability and balance in the world politics would be endangered.[10]

The reference to the 1967 third link in the chain of Arab–Israeli wars brings in another aspect of the involvement of the intrusive system in inter-Arab affairs: Israel's presence.

Israeli leaders insist on the conception of Israel as the embodiment of the Jewish dream of statehood.[11] As a result, a very complicated set of delicate and original problems, as Nahum Goldmann (former head of the World Zionist Organization and World Jewish Congress) put it, faces Israel in its relations with the Diaspora. In his three-volume classic on Israel's foreign policy, Michael Brecher dealt with this issue in relation to foreign policy analysis:

> The presence of externally based foreign policy interest groups is widespread in an age of "penetrated political systems": no state is totally immune from group pressures stemming from beyond its territorial boundaries. None is comparable to Israel in this respect, however. Israel is a self-conscious Jewish state; indeed that is its raison d'être; and Israel is the only Jewish state, indissolubly linked to world Jewry in the minds of her leaders and of most Jews—and to most non-Jews in the Euro–American world as well.[12]

Among these Diaspora Jews, the six million of North America stand out. Not only are they double the Jewish population of the state of Israel, but they have also provided Israel's basic means of political, financial, and economic support. Without them, Israel would not have achieved international recognition so quickly and surmounted its political, economic, and military challenges so successfully.

The result is that the influence of the global powers has been continuously felt in the daily evolution of the Arab system. From the very beginning, the creation of Israel and the subsequent conflict between Arabs and Israelis was determined by external events such as the 1917 Balfour Declaration giving Britain's promise of a Jewish national home, the Hitler Holocaust and the subsequent Western desire to compensate Jews by helping them to settle in Palestine, and then the decision to partition Palestine.

Even at the level of policy making and implementation, European and American Jews have participated directly in deciding the evolution of the Middle East. In the early years following the establishment of the state of Israel, the World Zionist Organization attempted to secure for its president, Nahum Goldmann, an invitation to attend Israeli cabinet meetings. Israel's prime minister at the time, Ben Gurion, refused. Goldmann returned to this subject in his writings, reviewing the proposals for a joint decision-making organ between Israel and the Jewish Diaspora (e.g., the establishment of a senate, in addition to the Israeli parliament, where the elected representatives of the Diaspora would sit; the creation of a permanent assembly where equal numbers of Israelis and representatives of world Jewry would sit). In the absence of any common decision-making institution, Goldmann found unsatisfactory the existing practice: periodic visits to Israel by leaders of Jewish organizations to discuss with members of the Israeli government the current state of affairs. Thus Israel's extraterritoriality has brought the global system even more concretely into the region's affairs. Possible lines of demarcation between regional interactions and global politics have become even more blurred.

The Primacy of Arab Structural Dependence

The result of this historical pattern of events is a high degree of global dominance in regional Arab politics, translated—from the side of the Arabs—into an equally high degree of dependence that will not be reversed in the next ten years. Five indicators are used to document this dependence and trace its evolution. They are food, trade, arms, debt, and the invasion of "alien" cultural norms.

Food Dependency

In January 1977, the whole of Egypt was caught in upheaval because of the government's decision to withdraw food subsidies.

> By the morning of 20 January, when the military finally restored order, Egypt had been shaken to its very core. For two full days, from Aswan to Alexandria, Egypt witnessed its worst riots in a quarter of a century. It was twenty-five years, almost to the day, since the "Burning of Cairo" riots which were a landmark on the road to overthrow the Faruk monarchy. Some talked of a second burning of Cairo . . . By the official count, which most observers agree was a gross underestimate, 80 deaths occurred, 560 people were wounded and 1,200 were arrested. For two days, political order had broken down completely.[13]

The government had to give in and restore the subsidies. These Egyptian happenings, however, are important not only because of their intensity but also because they reflected the pattern in other Arab countries. Thus 1984 witnessed the intensification of the so-called "bread riots" in two countries of North Africa: Morocco and Tunisia. At the time of writing (1985), Sudan, too, is paralyzed by a general strike and riots, triggered by the withdrawal of subsidies, protesting general government policy.

These examples show how food dependence is basic to the Arab situation and could make Arab governments increasingly vulnerable in their relations with the superpowers, especially the United States (the main provider of wheat). As Table 6.1 shows, the Arab deficit in agricultural products has been, on the whole, rising. In the eight-year period ending in 1983 (the last year for which the FAO data are available) the deficit rose by 304 percent. The Khartoum-based Arab Organization for Agricultural Development (AOAD), an Arab League agency set up in 1970, noted that Arab imports of agricultural commodities such as wheat and sugar soared from $6.6 billion in 1974 to $21.2 billion in 1981. And at this level of dependency, the so-called "rich" Arab states are not spared. "The oil states' food imports grew by an annual average of 27 percent with the growth rate highest in Saudi Arabia at 37 percent. Arab countries now import 10 percent of all food grain on the international market and if present trends continue the figure could easily rise to 50 percent."[14]

Not only increasing Arab demand, but also less world supply could make the Arab food situation worse in the next decade. Suleiman Sid-Ahmed, head of AOAD's production economics department, has insistently rung the warning bell.

> ... the world is getting less and less food on the international market because the countries that used to produce much of the grain such as the U.S., Australia and Canada were not expanding their agricultural production. In fact, the U.S. has taken out of cultivation 80 mn. hectares and has paid its people not to cultivate because it wanted the international prices maintained at a certain level ... Moreover, the U.S.S.R., which was formerly self-sufficient in agricultural commodities, has become a net wheat importer . . . Consequently, if the current trend of production and consumption is sustained until the year 2000, many people would not be able to get enough to get by.[15]

There should not be anything fatalistic about this worsening food situation in the Arab world. Saudi Arabia, for instance, has achieved—though at a high cost—great success in grain cultivation. Its 1980–85 Plan target was to increase wheat production by 56,000 tons, but in 1984 it produced 740,000 tons—a big jump from the 3,000 tons of seven years earlier. Moreover, the region as a whole has a large agricultural potential (e.g., 187 million hectares of arable land, of which only about a third is being used; ample manpower; and a huge market).

But the word "potential" has to be underlined, for most of the 153 projects of the AOAD 1980–85 Plan still remain on paper, with many of them requiring detailed feasibility studies. In addition, little agricultural research is being undertaken in the Arab world to increase productivity; the average yield at present is 1.1 tons per hectare compared with 6.0 tons for developed countries.

There is another obstacle, a political-administrative one, to be overcome, before present food dependence levels can improve: such plans must be separated from inter-Arab politics. Thus, AOAD sources have explained that some of the decisions concerning Arab food security have to be taken at the level of heads of state. Postponements of Arab summits delay the execution of the Plan, and often, as in Fez in 1982, political discussions monopolize summits, leaving no time for so-called nonpolitical issues such as food security.[16]

If the proper political decisions are taken and implemented, the last two obstacles could be overcome. In this case, within the next decade Arab food dependence could be lessened, although not yet reversed.

Trade Dependence

As in many other Third World countries, Arab economies are extroverted and trade constitutes a high percentage of their GNP, as Table 6.2 shows.

One difference between "rich" and "poor" Arab countries is that the former are in fact in a worse situation as far as trade dependence is concerned. For not only is the major part of their national income dependent on their exports in general, but it is dependent on only one commodity: oil. Moreover, their trade dependence is constricted not only by the limited number of commodities exported, but also by concentration on a few partners, i.e., Western countries. The East (or "centrally planned economies" in UN terms) tried to compete, but failed to come even a close second, let alone act as an alternative or even a balancer. Tables 6.3 and 6.4 are very eloquent in this respect.

The tables indicate another important factor: concentration on the West applies equally in the cases of both "moderate" and "radical" Arab countries. Algeria's imports from the West range between 83 percent and 89 percent, while those from the East between 2 percent and 3 percent—that is, a ratio of between 40 and 30 to one. Neither Libya's pattern of trade nor even South Yemen's is radically different.

The reversal of trade dependence on the West is not feasible within the coming ten years, for the political decision has to be taken and implemented before one could set a time for trade dependence reversal. Moreover, nothing guarantees that when a trend of trade diversification is set in place, it will continue until trade dependence reversal is achieved. Egypt's example is a case in point. After huge political investment and some success in trade diversification in the 1960s Egypt rapidly reintegrated with the West and replaced the Soviet Union by the United States in the 1970s. In the 4-year period 1974–78, Egypt's imports (since imports more than exports express a certain choice at this level) from the United States increased by 31 percent.[17]

The objection might be raised that rather than dependence, it is trade interdependence that exists between the Arab world and the United States. In this respect, suffice it to say that between 1983 and 1984 U.S. exports to the *whole Arab world* (as a percentage of total exports) declined from 8 percent to 6 percent (in round figures), and imports from 3.5 percent to 2.9 percent. On the other hand, the average exports of even such radical states as Algeria and Libya to the United States (as percentages of their exports to the whole world) for the 1974–83 period were 37 percent and 24.6 percent, respectively. The asymmetry is too clear to require comment. This asymmetry is even clearer in the case of the next indicator: arms.

Arms Dependence

Whether in the case of food or of trade dependence, the United States and the West generally have occupied the prominent position. In the realm of arms imports and training, however, the Soviet Union is very much present. It is to be remembered that the area up till the 1955 Czech arms deal had been a Western monopoly and that it was precisely the arms issue that brought in the Soviet Union. Moscow, then, came to the Arab world by invitation and not by invasion. The increasing militarization of the Arab–Israeli conflict consolidated Moscow's presence in the area and allowed it to have privileged relations with some influential Arab countries—e.g., Egypt between 1967 and 1972, when around 20,000 Soviet advisors were stationed there.

But if Egypt pioneered in massive imports of Soviet weapons and the signing of friendship and military cooperation treaties with Moscow, this pattern soon passed to other countries, e.g., Syria, Algeria, the two Yemens, Somalia, and Libya. All these countries received East European military advisors and sent their men to be trained in the Eastern bloc countries, as Tables 6.5 and 6.6 show. Thus, for the 5-year period 1976–80, recorded arms sales to 19 Arab countries amounted to just less than $40 billion (or precisely $39.755 billion in current U.S. dollars), of which the Soviet share was 50 percent (or $19.990 billion).[18]

But with the rise of petropowers and the intensification of Soviet–Egyptian estrangement, the biggest contracts were increasingly reserved for Western countries: notably the United States, France, and the United Kingdom, with Italy and West Germany far behind. The Gulf countries are the example that comes readily to mind. The massive inflow of petrodollars not only provided these countries with the means to acquire the latest military gadgets, but also increased their sense of being coveted and vulnerable, and hence pushed them to allocate increasing sums to defense, as Table 6.7 shows.

Thus, between 1972 and 1976 alone, defense expenditure more than doubled in Iraq and rose by 1000 percent in Kuwait and about 1200 percent in Saudi Arabia. In 1980, three of the five biggest contracts signed by Arab countries were for arms.

The beginning of the Iran–Iraq war channelled even more petrodollars toward arms, making arms sales an extremely lucrative business. As *Arabia* put it,[19] delegations arrive and go, heralding the age in which ministers and ambassadors are the new arms sales middlemen. Iraq's defense expenditure in 1982 was $7.7 billion and was geared toward a steep rise in 1983 and 1984. According to London's International Institute of Strategic Studies, the Gulf Cooperation Council (GCC) defense expenditure in 1983 was $28.5 billion, with Saudi Arabia representing 77 percent of the total, or $22 billion.

Given, on the one hand, the level of technological sophistication in the arms imported and, on the other hand, the level of knowhow and military preparedness in, say, the GCC countries, the military build-up is not only an aspect of dependence on the superpowers, but is bound to increase this dependence, especially on the United States. For between 1976 and 1982, U.S. military sales and construction agreements with Saudi Arabia alone amounted to $33.38 billion.[20]

Debt Dependence

Given popular perceptions of the "rich Arab," to talk about a rising external Arab debt might seem to many like a contradiction in terms. But according to a 1984 report by United Gulf Bank (the Bahrain-based offshore bank) Arab countries' total external debt rose from 1982 to 1983 by 10 percent to attain almost $100 billion. This sum amounts to an increase equal to 20 times the 1979 level.[21] The eight biggest debtors together owe about $94 billion, with Iraq, Egypt, Algeria, and Morocco topping the list, followed by Sudan, Tunisia, Syria, Jordan, and North Yemen. Table 6.8 gives details on the evolution of this situation for most of these countries up to 1982.

Compared to food, trade, or arms dependence, the debt problem could easily improve in the short term if seriously tackled, as the projected decline in public debt service shows: from $12 billion in 1983 to about $5 billion in 1991, according to World Bank projections. (See Table 6.9).

However, the debt burden is already crippling the developing economies of such countries as Algeria, Egypt, Morocco, Sudan, and of course Iraq, and these economies will still need some time to recuperate from the debt's adverse effects. Thus the United Gulf Bank estimates Egypt's ratio of debt to exports and invisibles in 1982 at 154 percent and calculates that its international reserves represented just 2.3 months' import cover. As for Algeria, its ratio of debt to exports and invisibles was put at 132 percent for 1982, when it had reserves just above 3 months' import cover. As for Sudan, its bleak state could herald what might befall other Arab countries: the $850 million debt service is almost equal to total earnings from exports, and its debt has been rescheduled several times since 1978.[22] But Sudan is caught in a dilemma. Massive international aid is necessary to save the country from bankruptcy, and foreign agents are thus in a good position to exercise pressure on Khartoum to implement rigorous austerity measures. Yet succumbing to foreign pressure and withdrawing subsidies could topple the government without really solving the problem.

One relatively positive aspect of the debt problem (again, compared to arms, food, or trade dependence) is that a part of the debt is between "poor" and "rich" Arab countries, that is, contained within the family. But with the continuing world oil glut, declining oil revenues, and increasing arms and development expenditures, not as many petrodollars would be available for use as grants or even loans to other Arab countries. Already the United States is increasing its level of aid in the region, and a country like Egypt is absolutely dependent on the more than $2 billion it gets from Washington. If Egypt is a special case because of its separate peace with Israel, consider Algeria, which started to figure on the list of U.S. aid-receivers in 1985 and requested for FY 1986 $100 million in U.S. aid. In this year the U.S. aid level to 14 Arab countries would be approximately $10 billion.[23]

Cultural Dependence

The number of Arab students (i.e., future policy makers) flocking to study in foreign, especially Western, countries is increasing. In the seven years from 1974–75 to 1981–82, the number of students from 21 Arab countries going to study abroad increased from 83,983 to 152,001, as Table 6.10 shows.

Of course the sending of students abroad might be part of an integrated development plan, since these young people represent future knowhow and a basic element of infrastructure. But no one can deny that the majority bring back with them "alien" development models and even "foreign" values. They can thus become value-transmitters and encourage the consumption of foreign products, hence contributing to the dependency syndrome.

But cultural dependency is not only intensified by the sending of students abroad, it can also be consolidated by the importing of, say, foreign films. Thus in 1970, Tunisia, for instance, produced two *long métrage* films, a documentary, and six short films. But it imported 346 *long métrage* films, of which 167 (or more than 48 percent) were from the United States and only seven from India, the world's biggest film producer.

Though less identifiable and quantifiable than economic dependency, cultural dependency can be more basic and harder to eradicate in the short term. It constitutes the basic frame of reference within which different options are evaluated and decisions taken. It can thus be self-perpetuating and self-generating.

Is It Interdependence, not Dependence?

The interdependence counter-thesis is too well-known to be labored. In a nutshell, it propagates the idea that the Arabs not only have leverage on the superpowers but could even hold the West hostage. The main evidence is, of course, the 1973 oil embargo and the long queues in front of petrol stations, as well as the consequences of this embargo in terms of accumulated petrodollars.

But here the French distinction between *structure* and *conjoncture* is very relevant. As G. Homans remarked: "Few words do sociologists use more often than 'structure.' Yet we seldom ask what we mean by the word."[24] It is intended here to indicate the set of fundamental and persistent social phenomena that constitute an interdependent whole. For instance, the pattern of world trade constitutes a *structure* because it is based on a group of international institutions and norms elaborated by the Bretton Woods system (that is, by the big powers of the day). The 1973 oil embargo, on the other hand, is a *conjoncture*, a contextual event that took place in a specific set of circumstances (effect of surprise in an energy-hungry world). It cannot be repeated now in a context of oil glut and abundant reserves in Western countries. This distinction between *structure* and *conjoncture* indicates in fact the limits of power based on primary commodities, in this case oil.

The Limitation of Resource Power

Primary resources—including oil[25]—are subject to fluctuations in global demand, and thus the level of revenue and rate of development of primary producers are a function of what is going on in the economies of developed countries. For instance, between 1979 and 1982, oil demand in the non-Communist world dropped from 52.4 million barrels per day (bpd) to only 45.5 million.[26] Perhaps half of this decline was due to the worldwide recession—U.S. factories, for example, were operating at only 60 percent of capacity—but the developed countries' policy of conservation has turned out to be an even more important factor in the marketplace. Between 1973 and 1980, economic output in the major industrial countries increased by 19 percent, while total energy consumption grew by only 4 percent, and petroleum use actually declined. The problem for OAPEC (Organization of Arab Petroleum Exporting Countries) is that the market loss due to conservation is irreversible. Even lower oil prices will not induce homeowners to rip the insulation out of their attics, or persuade automakers to build gas-guzzling cars, overnight.

Developed countries have also demonstrated the fragility of oil power by entering the market as new producers with oil and gas fields of their own, in Alaska and the North Sea, for example. Because of this increased competition and sagging oil demand, OPEC's sales started to slide in 1982 for the first time in nearly two decades. By February 1983, OPEC's share of the non-Communist world's total oil supply stood at 46 percent, down from 68 percent in 1976. Between 1979 and 1982, world demand dropped by 9.5 million bpd, and OPEC's production fell by more than 12 million bpd, to 17.75 million bpd. Yet according to one estimate, OPEC members need to produce about 21 million bpd to meet the needs of their own economies. Even if the Arab oil producers are not yet in the same economic plight as Nigeria, which had to evict hundreds of thousands of foreign workers almost overnight, the writing is on the wall. Although they appear powerful, oil producers are in fact hostages to the global system and the short-term fluctuations of developed economies.

Even before the 1982–83 world oil glut, oil power could not guarantee the success of the 1975 Paris conference on North–South relations, nor achieve the global change insisted on by Algeria, nor establish the New International Economic Order (NIEO) that the Third World demanded.

The Illusion of Investment

But oil has given birth to petrodollars, a source of both financial power and potential political influence. What about Arab investments then?

The issue of "Arab money" and so-called "Arab takeover" of real estate and financial institutions even in countries like the United States and the United Kingdom has been so repeatedly emphasized that it has become for many a power fact. But a 1985 report from the Brookings Institution sheds some doubt on such a widely-held conception.[27]

It is true that with the rise of petrodollars in countries with limited absorptive capacity in the short term, many of these petrodollars were encouraged to go abroad. For instance, in 1973 Saudi Arabia's net foreign assets totaled $4.2 billion, Kuwait's $3.7 billion, and the United Arab Emirates' (U.A.E.) $0.5 billion. But by 1981, these sums had increased to $163.3 billion, $80.7 billion, and $40.7 billion, respectively. And by 1982, according to U.S. Treasury Department figures, OPEC's identified cumulative investments during 1974–82 amounted to $395 billion (in addition to another $72 billion of cash surplus and less clearly identified investments). Though these sums are impressive cash by Third World standards, it is wealth and not cash—as Adam Smith expressed it almost two centuries ago—that constitutes the might of nations.

For because of widespread antipathy toward OPEC in the United States, coupled with Washington's increasingly close monitoring of foreign investments, Arab investment—as Saudi Finance Minister Abu Al-Khail expressed it—is not large compared with inflows from Japan and Western Europe (or even Latin America); and though relatively large, these funds, in terms of the total U.S. market, are of no great significance.[28]

Moreover, the size of OPEC assets is declining. In 1982, identified overseas investments peaked at $392.5 billion, but one year later they were $9.9 billion less. With the increasing oil glut, declining prices, and rising development and arms expenditure, these investments are getting less and less. In June 1984, Saudi financier Suleiman Olayan, who has a 7.6 percent stake in the First Chicago Corporation, commented that "the flood of Arab capital to Western financial centers has been reduced to a trickle."[29]

Conclusion

Before 1995 the basic asymmetry of relations between the Arab world and the superpowers would not drastically change. Change could take place concerning the position of the different pieces, the evolution of short-term events, and the dialectics between "old" and "new" issues. For instance, within the next ten years Jordan, Israel, and the West Bank will exhaust sources of renewable fresh water if they continue their present pattern of consumption. Consequently, water will loom larger as a strategic factor, and we might increasingly see water-generated conflicts. But this would not change the structural characteristics of the relations of the Arab world with the superpowers. Even a mass revolution or a determined Islamic movement could within the next decade only take steps for disengagement and toward self-reliance, but, as China's case shows, this process is long and not at all irreversible.

Within these parameters, however, some secondary changes and fluctuation in Arab bargaining potential could take place. For instance, with the increasing militarization of the Arab–Israeli conflict, more Arab countries (e.g., Kuwait, Jordan) could be attracted to buy Soviet arms without dropping, however, their relations with the United States. Though Soviet influence might come back partially, it will not be able to replace U.S. and more generally Western presence in the Arab world. Either because of cultural affinity (Arab elites, even the most radical ones, are still consumers of Western literature, fashion, and media) or because the global system is still dominated (in both the norms of its functioning and its institutional mechanism) by the West, the leader of this camp, the United States, will continue its imposing presence—directly or by proxy—until 1995 and even beyond.

Notes

1. Robert A. Nisbet, *Social Change and History: Aspects of the Western Theory of Development* (London, Oxford, and New York: Oxford University Press, 1969), pp. 60–68.
2. Christopher Freeman and Marie Jahoda, *World Futures* (New York: Universe Books, 1979), pp. 2–3.
3. Fouad Ajami, *The Arab Predicament* (Cambridge, U.K.: Cambridge University Press, 1981), p. 104.
4. Freeman and Jahoda, *World Futures*, p. 2.
5. Thomas Jones, *Options for the Future* (New York: Praeger, 1980), p. 57.
6. L. Carl Brown, *International Politics and the Middle East: Old Rules, Dangerous Game* (Princeton, NJ: Princeton University Press, 1984), p. 237.
7. *The Middle East* (April 1984): 13.
8. Brown, *International Politics*, p. 237.
9. Dwight D. Eisenhower, *The White House Years: Mandate for Change 1953–1956* (New York: Signet Books, 1963), p. 150.
10. Lyndon B. Johnson, *The Vantage Point* (New York: Holt, Rinehart & Winston, 1971), p. 288.
11. Bahgat Korany and Ali E. H. Dessouki, et al., *The Foreign Policies of Arab States* (Boulder, CO: Westview Press, 1984), pp. 34–35, and sources cited therein.
12. Michael Brecher, *The Foreign Policy System of Israel* (London and New York: Oxford University Press, 1972), p. 137.
13. Mark N. Cooper, *The Transformation of Egypt* (Baltimore, MD: The Johns Hopkins University Press, 1982), p. 136, and especially Hussein Abdel-Razek, *Egypt on 18th and 19th January (1977): A Political Documentary Study* (Beirut: Dar Al-Kalima, 1981) for a very detailed day-by-day documentation.
14. *The Middle East* (June 1984): 38.
15. *Ibid.*
16. *Ibid.*, p. 39.
17. Korany, et al., *The Foreign Policies of Arab States*.
18. *Middle East and North Africa*, 1984–85, p. 141.
19. *Arabia* (September 1984): 6.
20. Anthony H. Cordesman, *The Gulf and the Search for Strategic Stability* (Boulder, CO: Westview Press, 1984), p. 970.
21. *Middle East Economic Digest* (February 10, 1984): 55.
22. *Middle East Economic Digest* (February 10, 1985): 10.

23. U.S. Agency for International Development, as quoted in the *Middle East Economic Digest* (February 1985): 4.
24. Peter Blau, ed., *Approaches to the Study of Social Structure* (London: Open Books, 1976), p. 53.
25. Bahgat Korany, "Hierarchy Within the South: In Search of a Relevant Theory," in *Third World Affairs Yearbook* (London: Third World Foundation, 1986), pp. 85–101.
26. Korany, et al., *The Foreign Policies of Arab States*, pp. 32–33.
27. Richard P. Mattione, *OPEC's Investments and the International Financial System* (Washington, DC: Brookings Institution, 1985).
28. *Middle East Economic Digest* (February 8, 1985): 28.
29. *Ibid.*

References

Abdel-Razek, Hussein. *Egypt on 18th and 19th January (1977): A Political Documentary Study.* Beirut: Dar Al-Kalima (in Arabic), 1981.
Ajami, Fouad. *The Arab Predicament.* Cambridge, U.K.: Cambridge University Press, 1981.
Blau, Peter, ed. *Approaches to the Study of Social Structure.* London: Open Books, 1976.
Brecher, Michael. *The Foreign Policy System of Israel.* London and New York: Oxford University Press, 1972.
Brown, L. Carl. *International Politics and the Middle East: Old Rules, Dangerous Game.* Princeton, NJ: Princeton University Press, 1984.
Cooper, Mark N. *The Transformation of Egypt.* Baltimore, MD: Johns Hopkins University Press, 1982.
Cordesman, Anthony H. *The Gulf and the Search for Strategic Stability.* Boulder, CO: Westview Press, 1984.
Eisenhower, Dwight D. *The White House Years: Mandate for Change 1953–1956.* New York: Signet Books, 1963.
Freeman, Christopher and Jahoda, Marie. *World Futures.* New York: Universe Books, 1979.
Johnson, Lyndon B. *The Vantage Point.* New York: Holt, Rinehart & Winston, 1971.
Jones, Thomas. *Options for the Future.* New York: Praeger, 1980.
Korany, Bahgat and Dessouki, Ali E. H. et al. *The Foreign Policies of Arab States.* Boulder, CO: Westview Press, 1984.
Korany, Bahgat. "Hierarchy Within the South: In Search of a Relevant Theory," in *Third World Affairs Yearbook.* London: Third World Foundation.
Mattione, Richard P. *OPEC's Investments and the International Financial System.* Washington, DC: Brookings Institution, 1985.

Magazines, Yearbooks, and Other Data Sources

Al-Ahram al-iqtisadi (The Economist) (Cairo, weekly)
Arabia (London, monthly)
Direction of Trade Statistics (International Monetary Fund, Washington, DC, yearly)
FAO International Trade Yearbook (Rome, yearly)
International Financial Statistics (International Monetary Fund, Washington, DC)
Middle East Economic Digest (London, weekly)
Middle East Magazine (London, monthly)

The Middle East and North Africa (London, yearly)
The Military Balance (London, yearly)
UNESCO Trade Yearbook (Paris, yearly)
World Bank Atlas (Washington, DC)
World Debt Tables (World Bank, Washington, DC)

TABLE 6.1
Evolution of Balance of Payments Deficits of Agricultural Products (in thousands of U.S. dollars)

Country	1975	1976	1977	1978	1979	1980	1981	1982	1983
Algeria	-1,275	-911	-1,312	-1,479	-1,689	-2,369	-2,643	-2,765	-2,461
Bahrain	-69	-103	-162	-169	-214	-240	-243	-212	-217
Djibouti	-19	-25	-22	-42	-47	-60	-48	-60	-52
Egypt	-830	-802	-1,139	-1,755	-1,309	-2,123	-3,532	-3,098	-3,408
Iraq	-846	-663	-873	-1,087	-1,544	-2,114	-2,195	-2,221	-2,041
Jordan	-145	-224	-249	-331	-383	-362	-434	-534	-495
Kuwait	-409	-474	-589	-668	-786	-996	-930	-1,045	-1,042
Lebanon	-285	-283	-363	-326	-376	-438	-551	-473	-438
Libya	-701	-546	-792	-856	-974	-1,400	-1,686	-1,392	-1,460
Mauritania	-26	-32	-255	-14	-26	-7	+52	+76	+67
Morocco	-465	-195	-292	-225	-288	-329	-577	-397	-292
Oman	-51	-50	-124	-136	-175	-285	-336	-386	-406
Qatar	-57	-86	-105	-134	-169	-213	-217	-180	-170
Saudi Arabia	-691	-1,223	-1,843	-2,579	-3,526	-4,746	-5,647	-5,893	-5,198
Somalia	+10	+8	-39	+18	+22	-27	-55	+42	+84
Sudan	+203	+405	+457	+291	+380	+149	+122	+174	+380
Syria	-224	-128	-114	-274	-268	-481	-726	-461	-707
Tunisia	-154	-111	-175	-189	-283	-427	-436	-321	-449
U.A.E.	-239	-386	-442	-504	-752	689	-782	-693	-713
North Yemen	-141	-159	-181	-378	-425	-489	-593	-546	-423
South Yemen	-65	-50	-66	-140	-132	-219	-208	-243	-172
Total	-6,479	-6,038	-8,680	-10,977	-12,964	-17,865	-21,665	-20,628	-19,613

Source: Deficit calculated on the basis of data collected from U.N. Food and Agriculture Organization (FAO), International Trade Yearbooks, 1980-83 (Rome: FAO, 1983).

TABLE 6.2
Arab Countries' Exports (as percentage of gross national product)

Country[*]	1974	1976	1978	1980	1981	1982	1983
Algeria	43.8	36.2	28.4	35.8	35.0	26.7	24.6
Djibouti	--	18.8	35.0	27.3	18.3	--	--
Egypt	26.1	25.5	33.0	36.7	30.8	27.2	27.5
Iraq	70.9	52.5	53.1	--	--	--	--
Jordan	41.0	61.2	59.8	69.3	78.8	39.3	34.5
Kuwait	96.7	68.4	60.2	66.9	53.2	34.1	35.5
Libya	80.5	54.8	57.4	76.4	59.7	48.8	47.6
Mauritania	56.5	40.8	32.1	44.2	50.0	33.4	34.2
Morocco	31.3	22.7	21.4	23.5	26.5	20.4	22.5
Oman	97.8	81.4	71.7	79.8	86.6	67.2	50.9
Qatar	78.1	90.5	70.0	83.0	91.0	74.4	60.4
Saudi Arabia	89.6	95.2	61.9	66.1	69.1	67.4	58.4
Somalia	18.0	13.5	12.7	22.8	21.4	11.1	14.2
Sudan	12.6	13.4	11.0	16.0	9.7	8.7	8.1
Syria	27.2	21.9	24.1	18.7	18.0	12.7	11.3
Tunisia	39.3	33.0	31.7	38.6	41.2	36.3	35.2
U.A.E.	69.8	85.4	74.9	76.9	78.9	61.7	71.2
North Yemen	27.2	70.2	66.6	52.0	39.4	6.9	1.3
South Yemen	32.2	51.5	57.6	61.6	43.6	48.2	34.5
Average	49.4	49.3	45.4	47.1	44.8	36.7	33.6

[*]Data for Bahrain and Lebanon were incomplete.

Sources: International Monetary Fund, Direction of Trade Statistics Yearbook (Washington, DC: IMF, 1974-83); International Monetary Fund, International Financial Statistics Yearbook (Washington, DC: IMF, 1974-83); World Bank, World Bank Atlas: Per Capita Product, Population (Washington, DC: World Bank, 1974-83).

TABLE 6.3
Origins of Arab Countries' Imports (as percentage of total imports)

Country	Industrial Market Economies 1975	1980	1983	Developing Economies 1975	1980	1983	Centrally Planned Economies 1975	1980	1983
Algeria	89.3	83.6	83.4	7.3	12.8	14.4	3.4	3.4	2.2
Bahrain	35.2	32.2	39.0	63.6	66.9	60.6	0.2	--	--
Djibouti	57.0	58.8	55.7	42.3	39.5	42.7	--	--	--
Egypt	65.8	72.5	78.8	21.0	17.7	13.9	12.8	5.4	3.5
Iraq	74.5	76.8	57.5	18.9	19.7	40.4	6.5	3.5	2.0
Jordan	52.4	56.4	44.5	31.7	29.2	35.7	2.5	2.7	2.5
Kuwait	77.1	74.1	73.8	18.8	21.3	20.2	2.3	1.2	1.3
Lebanon	71.2	60.2	71.8	23.6	34.2	27.2	5.0	4.9	1.0
Libya	74.1	84.2	79.2	20.6	12.9	16.0	2.8	2.4	2.7
Mauritania	77.2	94.7	55.3	22.1	5.3	17.1	0.7	--	0.8
Morocco	69.9	61.6	60.8	20.5	26.7	29.4	8.6	6.2	8.3
Oman	64.9	63.4	71.2	34.9	34.9	28.7	0.2	0.8	0.1
Qatar	76.9	77.7	78.6	22.5	20.5	17.1	0.3	0.3	--
Saudi Arabia	63.7	79.6	81.7	32.3	15.6	15.4	0.7	1.6	0.3
Somalia	44.4	77.3	68.6	34.2	22.3	30.8	7.4	0.2	0.3
Sudan	59.9	55.1	57.1	28.1	38.1	39.5	4.6	1.8	1.4
Syria	59.2	52.1	44.9	27.5	38.4	44.5	9.2	6.4	8.1
Tunisia	79.5	74.1	79.3	17.4	22.7	17.9	2.9	2.9	2.8
U.A.E.	69.0	70.7	73.9	24.0	26.9	25.8	1.0	0.6	0.3
North Yemen	49.1	53.5	50.6	47.4	43.3	37.6	3.4	1.9	0.7
South Yemen	50.0	29.1	41.4	44.9	69.8	57.0	5.1	1.1	1.3
Average	64.8	66.1	64.1	28.7	29.5	30.1	3.8	2.2	1.9

Source: International Monetary Fund, Direction of Trade Statistics Yearbook, 1982-84.

TABLE 6.4
Destination of Arab Countries' Exports (as percentage of total exports)

Country	Industrial Market Economies 1975	1980	1983	Developing Economies 1975	1980	1983	Centrally Planned Economies 1975	1980	1983
Algeria	88.3	90.3	93.5	7.9	5.4	6.0	3.8	1.8	0.5
Bahrain	51.7	23.0	17.8	43.3	54.6	56.7	--	--	--
Djibouti	6.0	19.6	20.6	93.3	80.4	79.3	--	--	--
Egypt	14.5	59.8	73.3	22.6	31.7	18.0	62.7	7.6	5.1
Iraq	60.1	59.4	34.5	39.5	19.7	65.8	0.2	0.2	0.2
Jordan	8.0	6.5	6.0	62.8	58.5	54.3	5.2	1.4	2.4
Kuwait	62.4	50.3	38.6	33.2	38.6	42.6	--	0.7	0.9
Lebanon	10.2	13.5	12.9	81.5	68.5	71.0	3.1	6.4	2.6
Libya	84.6	89.8	73.7	14.9	9.6	23.4	0.5	0.3	2.4
Mauritania	96.9	94.3	94.0	3.1	5.8	6.0	--	--	--
Morocco	66.3	62.1	64.5	19.5	20.3	27.0	13.6	8.7	5.1
Oman	83.2	77.6	77.3	16.8	15.7	14.6	--	--	--
Qatar	72.1	70.5	67.7	26.8	28.6	29.8	--	--	--
Saudi Arabia	68.3	75.3	58.9	24.2	21.9	37.2	0.1	--	--
Somalia	7.7	15.6	15.5	81.2	84.4	84.4	5.5	--	--
Sudan	51.1	35.3	32.7	43.8	53.4	58.9	3.7	6.4	6.6
Syria	48.7	67.0	36.8	26.7	23.4	45.6	11.4	7.0	16.2
Tunisia	60.1	68.9	81.7	32.8	28.3	16.1	6.1	1.4	1.3
U.A.E.	92.6	81.0	60.6	7.4	18.4	18.2	--	--	--
North Yemen	26.8	28.8	26.0	72.1	66.6	64.1	1.1	3.1	--
South Yemen	85.1	33.6	55.7	12.6	65.8	43.6	0.1	0.1	--
Average	54.5	53.4	49.6	36.5	38.1	41.1	5.6	2.1	2.1

Source: International Monetary Fund, Direction of Trade Statistics Yearbook, 1982-84.

TABLE 6.5
Soviet Bloc Military Technicians in Selected Countries, 1979 (number of persons)

Country	U.S.S.R. and Eastern Europe	Cuba	Total
Algeria	1,015	15	1,030
Libya	1,820	--	1,820
Iraq	1,065	--	1,065
Kuwait	5	--	5
Syria	2,480	--	2,480
North Yemen	130	--	130
South Yemen	1,100	1,000	2,100
Least Developed Countries	15,865	34,315	50,180

Sources: Adapted from the various data sources as indicated in the references.

TABLE 6.6
Middle Eastern Military Personnel Trained in Soviet Bloc Countries, 1955-79 (number of persons)

Country	U.S.S.R.	Eastern Europe	Total
Algeria	2,195	200	2,395
Egypt	5,665	585	6,250
Iraq	3,710	690	4,400
Libya	1,370	285	1,655
Somalia	2,395	160	2,555
Sudan	330	220	350
Syria	4,245	1,210	5,455
North Yemen	1,360	--	1,360
South Yemen	1,075	20	1,095

Sources: Adapted from the various data sources as indicated in the references.

TABLE 6.7
Defense Expenditures of Gulf and Some Other Arab Countries, 1969-81 (in millions of current U.S. dollars)

Country	1969	1970	1971	1972	1973	1974
Gulf						
Bahrain	–	–	–	–	4	7
Iraq	826	822	762	816	1,168	1,510
Kuwait	202	203	185	210	234	568
Oman	–	127	46	77	121	342
Qatar	–	–	–	52	114	104
Saudi Arabia	1,182	1,481	573	792	1,187	2,670
U.A.E.	–	–	–	16	13	20
North Yemen	14	27	36	37	41	59
South Yemen	32	31	39	37	46	53
Total	2,256	2,691	1,641	2,037	2,928	5,333
Others						
Egypt	435	645	811	1,030	1,073	1,524
Jordan	100	78	155	184	182	186
Lebanon	46	48	44	48	54	85
Syria	227	282	235	290	508	497
Subtotal	808	1,053	1,245	1,553	1,817	2,292
Libya	183	302	140	134	193	388
Total	991	1,355	1,385	1,687	2,010	2,680

TABLE 6.7 (continued)

Country	1975	1976	1977	1978	1979	1980	1981[a]
Gulf							
Bahrain	14	28	39	49	57	55	135
Iraq	1,555	1,684	1,891	2,148	2,671	3,790[b]	4,500[b]
Kuwait	731	1,086	1,043	1,076	1,181	1,315	1,300
Oman	698	785	686	768	779	1,179	1,690
Qatar	124	167	230	264	458	555	893
Saudi Arabia	6,519	9,426	9,505	10,751	13,851	16,740	24,400
U.A.E.	32	81	505	791	1,151	1,658	1,700
North Yemen	85	100	130	155	373	325	135[b]
South Yemen	46	61	65	96	104	114	150[b]
Total	9,804	13,418	14,094	16,098	20,625	25,731	34,903
Others							
Egypt	1,929	1,472	1,834	2,044	1,984	1,362	2,100
Jordan	192	337	283	310	382	399	425
Lebanon	86	93	98	—	—	—	232
Syria	1,014	1,055	1,077	1,273	1,577	2,205	2,390[b]
Subtotal	3,221	2,957	3,292	3,627	3,943	3,966	5,147
Libya	243	364	479	729	500	523	630
Total	3,464	3,321	3,771	4,356	4,443	4,489	5,777

[a]Adapted from The Military Balance, 1981-82 and 1982-83 (London: International Institute for Strategic Studies, 1982 and 1983).
[b]Figures highly uncertain; often estimated by author.

Source: Adapted from Anthony H. Cordesman The Gulf and the Search for Strategic Stability (Boulder, CO: Westview Press, 1984), p. 503.

TABLE 6.8
Public Foreign Debt* of Arab Countries (in millions of current U.S. dollars)

Country	1972	1973	1974	1975	1976
Algeria	2,697.4	4,916.4	6,002.1	9,590.8	11,975.9
Djibouti	--	--	--	--	--
Egypt	2,680.0	2,912.9	4,431.3	7,254.1	8,780.9
Iraq	733.0	805.6	728.4	1,356.3	1,448.7
Jordan	238.5	359.3	469.2	501.4	483.9
Lebanon	62.5	98.1	89.7	79.7	73.1
Mauritania	119.6	213.8	373.3	412.6	619.4
Morocco	1,216.3	1,308.9	1,831.2	2,404.9	3,130.9
Oman	32.0	91.7	343.1	571.1	825.9
Somalia	250.7	286.3	413.7	465.1	645.4
Sudan	702.2	971.8	1,483.9	1,960.4	2,526.7
Syria	523.2	707.6	1,280.5	2,221.4	3,129.2
Tunisia	1,083.1	1,268.6	1,478.8	1,729.5	2,277.3
North Yemen	269.0	322.6	380.3	451.9	585.3
South Yemen	149.2	175.5	243.8	292.5	371.0
Total	10,756.7	14,439.1	19,549.3	29,291.7	36,873.6

TABLE 6.8 (continued)

Country	1977	1978	1979	1980	1981	1982
Algeria	14,967.6	20,057.0	23,842.3	23,187.9	21,685.8	--
Djibouti	19.8	21.0	25.4	49.5	71.6	93.2
Egypt	12,607.9	14,310.0	16,129.0	17,810.5	17,334.4	--
Iraq	1,334.2	1,372.0	--	--	--	--
Jordan	1,182.2	1,665.2	1,911.2	2,485.7	2,475.7	2,516.1
Lebanon	190.3	379.3	423.4	425.1	384.8	332.1
Mauritania	684.1	841.6	1,221.5	1,338.0	1,521.0	1,653.0
Morocco	5,093.5	7,403.5	8,519.1	9,155.5	10,677.6	--
Oman	864.2	994.6	759.7	898.5	925.5	1,303.2
Somalia	930.5	1,062.2	959.5	1,143.5	1,316.0	--
Sudan	3,202.4	3,847.2	4,812.3	5,368.1	5,949.1	6,455.9
Syria	3,872.9	4,284.5	4,536.2	4,596.9	4,339.2	4,220.0
Tunisia	3,182.1	3,984.0	4,720.0	4,977.8	4,881.5	--
North Yemen	793.3	1,088.9	1,477.9	1,655.1	2,019.0	2,244.0
South Yemen	435.4	579.9	890.7	1,240.7	1,270.9	--
Total	49,360.4	61,890.9	70,228.2	74,332.8	74,852.1	18,817.5

*Public debt outstanding, including undisbursed.

Source: World Bank, World Debt Tables, External Debt of Developing Countries, 1979-83.

TABLE 6.9
Projected Public Debt Service of Arab Countries, 1986-91* (in millions of current U.S. dollars)

Country	Actual Disbursed Outstanding Debt (end of 1983)	1986	1987	1988	1989	1990	1991
Algeria	12,915.0	3,463.2	2,901.0	2,525.1	1,965.5	1,243.2	784.3
Egypt	15,530.8	1,821.2	1,747.4	1,404.2	1,273.3	1,218.3	1,136.9
Jordan	1,940.1	318.4	332.7	333.7	292.7	257.1	238.7
Lebanon	181.8	20.9	21.7	21.4	20.8	19.4	18.8
Morocco	9,445.3	2,440.2	2,024.3	1,825.8	1,641.1	1,361.8	1,099.6
Oman	1,125.0	333.8	358.0	319.1	218.7	114.1	100.5
Sudan	5,664.5	660.4	527.6	485.9	401.5	297.7	257.3
Syria	2,660.8	471.6	457.9	435.6	403.8	367.7	313.0
Tunisia	3,427.1	597.0	592.5	586.7	550.0	511.3	454.1
North Yemen	1,573.9	168.4	182.0	188.8	190.3	187.2	143.0
South Yemen	1,262.8	117.4	134.5	149.6	146.9	141.6	129.0
Total	55,727.1	10,412.5	9,279.6	8,275.9	7,104.6	5,719.4	4,675.2

*Projections based on data from the early 1980s.

Source: World Bank, World Debt Tables, External Debt of Developing Countries, 1979-83.

TABLE 6.10
Students Abroad from Arab Countries (number of persons)

Country	1974-75	1975-76	1976-77	1978-79	1980-81	1981-82
Algeria	7,968	9,806	12,738	13,342	12,661	12,350
Bahrain	1,427	1,851	1,704	2,054	1,855	1,944
Egypt	7,188	7,924	7,924	7,943	9,150	9,067
Iraq	4,219	4,967	5,551	7,236	7,367	6,507
Jordan	11,601	13,010	13,988	21,310	17,030	15,833
Kuwait	1,548	1,666	2,377	3,893	4,511	3,671
Lebanon	7,321	11,015	11,237	14,276	15,117	13,595
Libya	2,126	2,121	2,652	3,531	3,965	3,516
Mauritania	455	507	558	829	782	929
Morocco	9,344	10,776	13,404	16,285	20,876	20,981
Oman	132	137	265	428	652	729
Qatar	230	310	292	750	950	984
Saudi Arabia	3,835	5,698	7,428	10,113	11,701	9,585
Somalia	511	567	569	775	1,152	1,162
Sudan	2,778	2,986	2,763	8,673	11,008	10,522
Syria	6,069	6,316	6,005	6,726	13,701	13,725
Tunisia	8,460	9,983	11,005	10,739	9,817	9,737
U.A.E.	392	489	595	1,094	1,227	1,006
North Yemen	1,176	1,580	1,445	2,663	3,011	2,445
South Yemen	1,022	804	1,142	1,303	1,145	1,650
Palestine	6,201	7,537	1,960	17,936	15,414	12,953
Total	84,003	100,050	105,602	151,899	163,092	152,891
Number of Foreign Countries Included	50	50	50	45	45	45

Source: UNESCO, Statistical Yearbook, 1977-84.

PART THREE

The Economy: Breakthrough or Breakdown?

7

The Lean Years: The Political Economy of Arab Oil in the Coming Decade

George T. Abed

Introduction

Economic forecasting has always been recognized as an elusive science. Forecasts almost never materialize in the form ordained by their creators, a humbling fact that has caused serious economists to shun this pedantic practice. They have been inclined therefore to leave the field to those who find some satisfaction in the limelight of public attention, while they retire to the more exacting demands of academic inquiry.

But forecasts have a ready market, and the burgeoning demand for learned prognosis has induced a rising supply of willing forecasters. The simple and telling fact that the forecasters' record of performance has been less than overwhelming seems neither to slow the spread of the practice nor to dampen the enthusiasm of the practitioners. The case at hand, that of energy forecasting, is an especially sobering experience. Its quintessential lesson, if lessons are to be learned, is that far from possessing the requisite foresight for unlocking the future, most forecasters have shown themselves to be myopic, subjective, and highly vulnerable to the herd instincts of their own breed.

It is thus that when the price of oil "exploded" in 1974 and OPEC oil revenues began to climb with unprecedented speed, forecasters invariably saw the dawn of a new era when OPEC countries, in control of much of the world's supply of oil, would dictate the course of world energy development and, with their newly acquired wealth, would dominate the world financial system. It is also thus that in the midst of their recent weakness and disunity, the OPEC countries have been deemed to be on the verge of collapse and declared totally powerless to shape the future of the oil, much less the energy, markets of the world. Of course, neither prediction (admittedly oversimplified) has turned out to be entirely correct, a result that gives credence to the seemingly innocent but powerful notion that the truth often lies between two extremes.

It is in this context, and against such background, that one must approach, delicately but with a well-earned sense of humility, the question of the future of oil. It is a difficult and uncertain task, made that much more so when placed in the even more confounding world of the Middle East, and that of the Arab countries in particular.

But forecast we must, and forecast we will, if not entirely without reluctance. In this connection, a brief review of the past decade of oil and development in the Arab countries will serve as a prologue for a careful probe into the future—the next decade and beyond. Quantitative forecasts of certain key variables will be ventured. This proffer is based on the view that it is more useful to offer a quantitative prognosis, even with all of its shortcomings, than to advance only skillfully hedged notions about the "general direction" of future trends. The most likely scenario for the period 1995–2000 will therefore be illustrated with figures. These will be kept to the minimum extent that seems useful for the purpose at hand. Without defending to the last breath one's own figures and forecasts, one can nonetheless draw useful conclusions from them. This can be fruitfully done even in the event that actual developments in the future show less than complete reverence for the commands of the forecaster. It is in this spirit that one must then approach the task of venturing into the next decade of oil and development in the Arab world.

The Boom Years: 1974–81

The sharp increases in oil prices that took place in 1973–74 caused such fundamental changes in the economies of the Arab region that by the time the storm had blown away, the terrain was no longer recognizable. This is not the occasion to expound on the strategic and political ramifications of these financial shocks, but simply to note their magnitudes and the nature of their economic consequences. For these not only irretrievably altered the economic and social structure of the oil-producing countries, but deeply affected the other countries of the region as well—those that produced moderate, but not excessive, amounts of oil, such as Bahrain, Egypt, Oman, and Syria, as well as those that produced none, such as Jordan, the Yemens, and Morocco.

Merely to gauge the size of the economic and financial shocks that occurred late in 1973 and early in 1974, a few illustrative figures would suffice. In the decade ending in 1973, total oil receipts of the seven major Arab oil-exporting countries (Algeria, Iraq, Kuwait, Libya, Qatar, Saudi Arabia, and the United Arab Emirates) rose eightfold, from $1.5 billion in 1963 to $12.4 billion in 1973. Even at this latter level, they remained relatively modest. In the subsequent year alone, such receipts rose by a further $38 billion, and between then and 1980 they quadrupled, to $206 billion. The seven countries' combined total nominal gross domestic product (GDP), which is admittedly distorted by the inclusion of the oil sector, increased by a third in 1974 and by an average annual rate of over 20 percent in the subsequent six years. The gross official foreign assets of the Arab oil-exporting countries rose from about $9 billion at the end of 1973 to about $165 billion in 1982. These countries' share of world trade nearly doubled during the period 1974–82, and the share of their official reserves rose to about 14 percent of total official world reserves. It was such unprecedented changes in the economic and financial indicators that led many observers at the time, especially in the industrial, oil-importing countries, to draw an exaggerated picture of the power of OPEC, especially that of its Arab member states, and to spread the visions of fear of what such a major shift in world economic power could bring about.

The economies of other Arab countries also were swept up by the oil storm, as the nominal GDP of such countries as Jordan, Egypt, and the two Yemens grew by an average annual rate of nearly 20 percent. The average per capita income of these four countries rose from the equivalent of $230 in 1973 to over $700 in 1983.

From the vantage point of the Arab region itself, these changes went beyond the financial dimension. Within a very short period of time, nearly 3.5 million persons crossed their countries' borders into the booming oil-exporting countries, causing enormous flows of remittances to their native lands that, at their peak, amounted to more than $7 billion annually. Several national and regional development assistance institutions were quickly established and began to disburse considerable sums to the poorer Arab countries in the form of official aid. Ambitious plans were formulated for undertaking massive pan-Arab development projects, and inter-Arab trade began to rise, albeit at a much slower rate than one might have expected.

Thus, the boom that followed in the wake of the 1973–74 oil price increases found the Arab world poised at the edge of a new era of rapid transformation and potentially far-reaching social and economic development. The "golden decade" had arrived.

But alas! Even before the decade had come to a close, it began to manifest ominous signs of fatigue and dissipation. The "golden decade" died an early death, as in the period after 1982 the hitherto booming economies began to show negative growth rates. World demand for the supposedly precious black gold began to slump; the price of oil softened, then declined; and the development explosion that had swept up the countries of the region began to dissipate. By 1984 it became obvious that the Arab oil-exporting countries, not accustomed to austerity and decline, were headed for an extended period of adversity and doubt. Budgets had to be slashed, projects cancelled or stretched out, external reserves drawn down to meet current needs. Austerity measures were instituted everywhere. The expatriate workers began to head homeward, and the remittances stabilized, then tended to decline. The volume of inter-Arab trade began to shrink. Development assistance to the poorer countries was cut back, and the mood in the whole Arab region turned from buoyancy and pan-Arab solidarity to caution and provincialism.

To be sure, there were causes other than the slump in the oil market that brought about this sea change in the Arab region of the Middle East. Foremost among these were the Iran–Iraq war and the Arab countries' own excesses, mismanagement, and lack of foresight. This was particularly true of Kuwait, where a "triple whammy" of a sharp decline in oil receipts, the costly impact of the Iran–Iraq war, and the serious repercussions of the collapse of Al-Manakh stock market left the economy in a state of severe depression. An enormous internal private debt led to crippling bankruptcies of a number of important businesses and threatened the survival of many more. Economic growth came to a halt; uncertainties and doubt prevailed in the market. Official immobility and vacillation in the crisis reinforced the loss of confidence and paved the way for massive capital flight out of the once-buoyant economy.

Saudi Arabia, whose economy and development program were far more massive than those of Kuwait, also suffered from the impact of the Gulf war and the decline in oil prices, but the key factor in the sharp drop in its oil revenues (and hence its economic fortunes) was the dramatic decline in its oil output. Saudi Arabia had reveled in its role as a "swing supplier" in OPEC when the market was buoyant, but now that role exacted its price. From a peak of ten million barrels a day (mbd) in 1980 (at the time, over 35 percent of OPEC total production), Saudi Arabia's output had plunged to only about three mbd (or about 20 percent of OPEC's output) in the first half of 1985, as the once star oil producer was stuck with its role of "swing supplier," but this time in a slumping market. Its oil revenue, which had mushroomed from $4.3 billion in 1973 to over $100 billion in 1980, was projected to decline by 60 percent by 1985. As a result, one of the most ambitious and intensive development drives in history had to be reined in as the country experienced its first balance of payments deficit in over a decade. The budget was slashed by nearly 30 percent from its peak levels, and large, capital-intensive industrial projects were either cancelled or stretched out over longer periods.

For Iraq, the impact of its war with Iran was far more devastating. When the war began, Iraq was in the midst of one of the biggest building booms in the history of the developing world. Its oil output was rising, its external reserves ample, and its political leadership confident that it could transform the Iraqi economy, in the short span of one generation, into a major economic force in the region. Less than five years later, Iraq finds itself entrenched in a seemingly endless and costly conflict, drained of external reserves, accumulating a rising level of external debt, and, most telling of all, shifting its once stridently anti-Western political position and drawing closer to the United States.

Other oil-exporting Arab countries appear to have fared no better. Libya, which in less than a decade received more than $125 billion from oil (for about 3 million inhabitants, not an inconsiderable sum) found itself running balance of payments deficits and faced with severe cutbacks in its development program. Even Egypt, which began the "golden decade" as a net agricultural exporter, saw its economy open to exploitation and waste and its dependence on external assistance rising. Its growth potential had been dissipated by an immobilized political leadership, pervasive price and cost distortions, and the pursuit of economic policies geared to foster consumption rather than saving and investment.

In short, the massive resources made available to the Arab countries as a result of the oil boom of the 1970s appeared not to have been used to prepare those countries to deal adequately with the crisis of an oil market slump when it arrived. To be sure, not all was lost, and by any reasonable set of social and economic standards, the Arab countries benefited immensely from the development drive of the 1970s, if at an astronomical cost. In the major oil-exporting countries, per capita (nominal) income rose sixfold between 1973 and 1981, before declining somewhat in the subsequent two years. In the more balanced oil economies (Bahrain, Egypt, Oman, Syria) and in the poorer Arab countries (Jordan, the two Yemens) of the Arab region of the Middle East, per capita income increased fivefold in the decade ended in 1983. Moreover, during this single decade (1973–83), more than $150 billion of investment was undertaken in the infrastructural sectors alone (transport, communication, electric power, etc.), a task that would have taken decades to accomplish in more normal circumstances. This is in addition to what may be estimated to have been nearly twice this amount spent on directly productive activities (industry, agriculture) and on essential services (such as health, education, and government).

This is not the place to argue whether these enormous expenditures were undertaken efficiently, nor to judge whether a considerable proportion of them were even necessary; the large number of loss-making projects and the even much larger number of men of influence who were enriched through the widespread greed and corruption are a clear testimony to the inefficiency and waste that accompanied this explosive drive for development in the region. Nonetheless, some facts are indisputable. The illiteracy rate in the Arab countries dropped dramatically—from 70 percent to 40 percent—during the decade. Electricity and the means of communication, as well as such basic services as transportation, education, and health care, reached areas of the Arab countries that would not otherwise have been touched by modernization for decades. College enrollment in the Arab countries rose threefold. The numbers of physicians and of hospital beds per capita more than doubled. Infant mortality rates plunged, and life expectancy rose dramatically. Thus, although some of the impact of oil income on the Arab region in the 1970s had been dissipated by the early 1980s, a considerable part of this impact had nonetheless been internalized into the new Arab reality. It is this part which, in the final analysis, will constitute the new material basis from which the coming decade will need to be examined.

The Transition Years: 1984–95

If the past decade began as one of material abundance and ended as one of missed opportunities, what does the next decade portend? The starting point this time is a more sobering reality, and one is therefore tempted, given the myopic view to which forecasters are prone, to predict a future that is unrelievably bleak. Indeed, as indicated in the preface, most observers of the oil scene, especially in the West, appear to have made up their collective mind that OPEC is dead, or nearly so, and that the oil-exporting countries of the Middle East are therefore doomed to their present condition—fighting for market shares in an ever-shrinking oil market, losing oil revenues, and drawing down their external (financial) reserves to meet current requirements. OPEC, it is now widely surmised, will either wither into irrelevance or, if given enough time, collapse altogether.

It is my humble opinion that such a view is unduly gloomy, for reasons that will become clear in a moment. One aspect of this assertion is worth pursuing a little further, however. An important point that one needs to emphasize is that OPEC is not synonymous with the Arab oil-exporting countries. Indeed, the incongruity between OPEC and the Arab oil-exporting countries, moderately important at present, will become even more crucial in the coming decade. For OPEC as a whole may in fact manifest signs of weakness in the coming 10 to 15 years as some of its members contribute a declining share of total oil output, but these will not be the Arab countries of the Middle East. Indeed, if anything, the Arab oil producers possessing considerable oil reserves—Iraq, Kuwait, Saudi Arabia, and the United Arab Emirates—are bound to become *more*, not less, important to world oil supply, even as the remaining members of OPEC (except Iran) gradually lose their influence in the world oil market. But this may be taking us ahead of our story. Let us step back a little.

In order to highlight the role the Arab oil-exporting countries might play in the evolving oil market, it is necessary that the outlines of this market be sketched out first.

The demand for oil is positively associated with the level of economic activity and negatively with its price. As the average world economic growth rates (for both industrial and developing countries) have been lower since the early 1970s than in the two preceding decades, it was only natural that, other things remaining the same, the demand for oil should not rise so fast. But other things did not remain the same. The price of oil rose steeply throughout the 1970s, restraining the growth in demand and inducing additional supplies (mostly from non-OPEC sources) onto the world market. Shifts to non-oil sources of energy were made almost everywhere, and the demand for OPEC oil slumped. Thus, whereas OPEC supplied approximately 44 percent of total world oil consumption in 1979, its share declined to 26 percent by early 1985.

For the coming decade, we may assume that growth rates in the industrial countries will remain moderate, in the range of 2.25 to 2.75 percent per annum, while the corresponding rates for the developing countries will be somewhat higher. As for the price of oil, we may assume no change in the *nominal* price through 1990 and no change in the *real* price (i.e., the price adjusted for the average rate of inflation) from then through 1995. This assumption does not rule out fluctuations from year to year such as a possible substantial drop in price in the immediate period ahead; it is only a statement about average trends during the period.

These and other factors are expected to continue to bring about changes in the structure of demand for energy, with substitution of non-oil sources for oil and with energy conservation measures proceeding, albeit at a somewhat slower pace than in the past decade. The oil consumption/GDP elasticity (the ratio of percentage change in oil consumption to percentage change in real GDP), which had been in excess of unity for more than two decades before 1975 and which declined thereafter, may continue to drop, but not so fast as most recently. It may be expected to remain in the range of 0.4 to 0.71. Price elasticity of demand (the ratio of a percentage change in demand to a percentage change in price), on the other hand, is expected to be somewhat higher (in absolute terms) than has been historically the case—in the range of -0.3 to -0.4.[1]

OPEC's own consumption of oil, which has been rising faster than that of any other group of countries and is now estimated at about 3.6 mbd, is projected to continue to increase, if somewhat more moderately, to a range of 6.0 mbd to 6.5 mbd by 1995. Of this volume, the Arab oil producers will probably account for about half of the total by then.

Non-OPEC supply, which rose sharply from the mid-1970s through the early 1980s, is expected to continue to rise through 1990 but is projected to peak around that time and start declining thereafter, so that by 1995, non-OPEC sources of supply (excluding the socialist bloc) may be in the range of 26 mbd to 27 mbd, or somewhat below current levels.

These assumptions are consistent with a gentle rise in world demand for oil over the coming 10 to 15 years—perhaps only marginal or even nonexistent at first, then somewhat stronger in the late 1980s and early-to-middle 1990s. Indeed, this seems to be the consensus of most forecasts, although, understandably, divergencies among them tend to widen as the projection horizon recedes into the more distant future. It should be noted that total world oil consumption, including that of the centrally planned economies (CPEs), which had risen to a peak of 64.4 mbd in 1979, has declined since then (even as the world economy continued to grow), although most observers now believe it may have reached a trough and may begin to rise again soon, with some relief for the OPEC countries.[2]

On the basis of these considerations, one may summarize as follows (Table 7.1) the world oil market in the period "around 1995." (One need not be unduly precise about the exact period, as margins of error in all such forecasts are sufficiently large that the projected developments could occur a year or two earlier or, as I am inclined to think, a year or two later, say between 1995 and 1997.)

Thus, according to a reasonable set of assumptions, it is quite likely that the major Arab oil-exporting countries will be producing, by 1995 or shortly thereafter, a volume of oil near the peak level of 1979 (when it was 21.1 mbd).

TABLE 7.1
Projection of World Oil Market, 1995

Sources of supply and demand	Millions of barrels per day
World demand (excluding centrally planned economies [CPEs])	51.0-53.0
Less: non-OPEC, non-CPE supply	-26.0-27.0
Less: CPE net exports and natural gas liquids (NGL)	-1.5-2.0
Equals: supply required from OPEC	22.0-25.5
Plus: demand within OPEC	+6.0-6.5
Equals: OPEC production	28.0-32.0
Of which: Arab share	20.0-22.0
(of which exports)	17.0-19.0
Of which: Saudi Arabia's share	8.5-10.5
(of which exports)	7.0-8.5

As to oil revenues, these will depend on the evolution of the combination of export volume and export prices. As the price of oil is assumed to remain stable in nominal terms through 1990, and as export volumes are projected to rise only marginally until then, oil receipts of the Arab oil-exporting countries are likely to remain depressed during this period, although they may rise somewhat toward the end of the decade, from the present level of about 45 percent of the peak (1980) of $206 billion to about 50 percent. Beyond 1990, given the assumption of some movement in the nominal price, oil receipts of the Arab oil producers can be expected to rise more noticeably, first gently and then perhaps more rapidly as the world oil market begins to firm up. Depending on a number of other important factors (e.g., the levels of world stocks at the time, the direction and strength of expectations about possible price movements, possible disruption of supplies), the price of oil could rise rather rapidly just before or around 1995.[3] It is conceivable therefore that the Arab oil producers' export receipts could begin to rise again around 1990 and, if the above scenario materializes more or less as outlined, could grow so as to exceed the previous peak level in nominal terms by about the mid-1990s.

Before proceeding to discuss the implications of this result, we must make some observations on the key assumptions used in generating this scenario. In the first place, the assumption on oil supplies from the non-OPEC sources is crucial to the whole scenario. It derives from the fact that the search for new oil supplies outside OPEC began to run into visibly diminishing returns by the early 1980s. Ait-Laoussine and Parra, for example, have calculated that in the decade 1963-73, world production of oil (excluding CPEs) rose by 25.5 mbd, the increase having come mainly from the Middle East. This additional supply was brought onto the world market at a total capital cost of $76.2 billion, or about $3,000 per additional b/d. In contrast, in the period 1973–82, net new additions to world oil supply from non-OPEC sources amounted to 5.8 mbd (gross additions of 7.1 mbd and a reduction in supplies originating in the United States and Canada of 1.3 mbd). This incremental amount was produced at a capital cost of $420 billion, or about $60,000 per additional b/d. This is a staggering amount in comparison with the negligible cost of producing an additional b/d from existing OPEC sources. It is simply uneconomical, a point evidently well taken by the oil companies, which have slowed their exploration activity considerably since 1985. Furthermore, virtually all of the gross additions to supply made during this latter period originated from three key non-OPEC areas—Mexico, the North Slope, and the North Sea. All three areas have either peaked or are likely to do so in the coming few years. Given these considerations, it is quite unlikely that any substantial sources of oil will come on stream in the coming decade, especially if oil prices remained soft for a few more years.[4]

Other assumptions are less crucial for the scenario and, in any event, the margin of error implicit in them is rather limited. The centrally planned economies will at best barely keep up with their own demand and, more likely, will supply declining volumes to the world market in the coming years. As to OPEC's own demand for oil, the assumed rate of increase of about 6 percent annually is conservative, given the 7.5 percent annual rate of increase experienced in the period 1979–84 and the somewhat higher rate recorded for the 1974–84 decade as a whole.

As regards OPEC's production potential, it is worth noting that although OPEC's maximum installed capacity is currently estimated at a little over 41 mbd,[5] its maximum sustainable capacity is only a little under 35 mbd. Moreover, the production capacity of several members of OPEC is expected to decline during the coming decade. These include Algeria, Indonesia, Libya, Ecuador, Gabon, Qatar, and possibly Venezuela and Nigeria. The total reduction in capacity in OPEC may be in the range of 2 to 3 mbd by the mid-1990s, leaving a maximum total sustainable capacity of about 32 mbd, of which Iran and Iraq will account for nearly 9 mbd—if by then the Gulf war has ended or the belligerents have found ways around currently imposed obstacles to increased exports.[6] If, on the other hand, Iran and Iraq do not or cannot supply this volume (the two countries' combined output is currently running at about 3.5 mbd) the pressure on the remaining members of OPEC, especially Kuwait, Saudi Arabia, and the U.A.E., would be enormous. Hence the plausibility of the conclusion that the world oil market will begin to firm up during the early 1990s, placing pressure on the price of oil and inducing a rise in the Arab oil-exporting countries' export receipts.

It is of course conceivable that at least some of these assumptions may not turn out to be valid and that other developments, not directly incorporated into the analysis, may intervene so as to invalidate the projections. Political developments could indeed upset the basis of the forecast, and, in the context of the Middle East, one has come to expect the unexpected. Moreover, some of the underlying economic assumptions may be incorrect. For example, growth rates in the oil-importing countries may turn out to be at variance with what was assumed, or the oil/GDP coefficient may in fact be lower than expected. Energy conservation efforts may remain vigorous and the drive for the substitution of non-oil sources of energy may continue at a more rapid pace than is assumed. Non-OPEC supplies may also materialize in larger volumes than is anticipated. Indeed, any combination of these factors may reduce world demand for oil and postpone or eliminate the time when the high-capacity members of OPEC will become dominant again.

My own view is that with some largely inconsequential detours along the way, the basic trends in the world oil market over the coming 10 to 15 years are clear. The difficulties that have afflicted the oil market and have adversely affected the OPEC countries, and especially the main Arab oil exporters, since 1982 are likely to persist for a few more years, perhaps until the end of this decade, although indications are that the severity of the OPEC crisis will gradually subside. At around the end of the decade, world oil demand will rise, slowly at first and then more visibly. After 1990, non-OPEC sources are not likely to add significant new supplies to the market;[7] thus OPEC will be left to gradually restore its "swing supplier" role in a tightening world market and thereby reestablish at least some of its former power in this market. Moreover, OPEC's own production capacity can be expected to become increasingly concentrated in the five major Middle East producers—Iran, Iraq, Kuwait, Saudi Arabia, and the U.A.E. Of course, if the war between Iran and Iraq drags on and these two countries' production remains constrained by the exigencies of their conflict, the pressure on the three remaining Gulf producers will be even greater. Beyond the year 2000, it becomes extremely hazardous to make any predictions, as the new, and critically important, factor of the technology of energy production and use could introduce an entirely novel set of considerations and therefore invalidate any predictions that might seem reasonable at this distance.

The Lean Years:
Preparing for a Second Chance?

The conclusion is that the Arab oil-exporting countries will continue to confront the challenges of reduced levels of oil revenues for several years. The 1982–92 decade is therefore likely to shape up as a period of painful adjustment to a different reality than was characteristic in the heady period of the oil boom. In many fundamental respects, this decade (1982–92) is closer to being "normal" than the eight years which preceded it. More important, the Arab oil-producing states now have the opportunity to undertake the much-needed and long-overdue adjustments in outlook and policies that will better prepare them for extracting greater benefits for the development of the Arab region when and if a second opportunity for substantially higher oil revenues materializes in the mid-1990s.

From this standpoint, the important question is not what the Arab countries will do in 1995 and beyond, but what they will do in the intervening period to improve their indigenous capacity to deal with the improved resource availability more effectively and to exploit the new opportunities for genuine and sustained economic development of the Arab region as a whole. More specifically, can the Arab countries, both the major oil exporters and others, internalize the lessons learned from the first oil boom and from the experience of the current period of "relative austerity" so as to extract maximum pan-Arab benefits from the new opportunity that may arise in the mid-1990s? Although the answers to this and related questions depend to a large extent on external factors, it is ultimately what the Arab countries themselves do that will determine the final outcome.

Let me highlight two sets of considerations that will bear directly on the course of economic development in the region in the coming decade. The first set relates to fundamental questions of political economy and development strategy, while the other set comprises considerations of a more technical nature, bearing on specific economic and financial policies that may be pursued by the Arab countries in the years ahead.

One basic consideration relates to our own view of economic development—its nature, its processes, and its objectives. Reviewing the process of economic transformation that swept the Arab region during the turbulent 1970s, one is struck by the peculiar view of development that appeared to prevail at the time, both among policy makers and, with minor but significant exceptions, among academics and practitioners. This view assumed that economic development was something new, an economic and financial superstructure that could simply be imported and superimposed on existing social and economic systems. It was in affirmation of this view that the Arab countries, both the "rich" oil exporters and the "poor" remittance-receiving oil importers, embarked on such a dizzying import binge. The flood of imports, grossly subsidized by artificially elevated exchange rates, virtually wiped out traditional or potential import substitutes. Investment was associated with shiny, and massive, turn-key projects, which, because calculations of their benefit and costs were made in terms of artificially distorted costs and prices, have turned out to be uneconomical as soon as economic and financial conditions returned to a semblance of normality. The pervasive effects of oil revenues so severely distorted relative values throughout the economy that traditional industries withered and died. Again, what damage the oil revenues did to the oil-exporting economies was mirrored in the harm done by remittances and foreign aid to the economies of the poorer, labor-exporting countries.

To be sure, the increase in the oil revenues did confront the oil-producing countries with difficult choices regarding development strategy, but the lack of discipline to resist the temptations of higher spending was rooted in the inherent weakness of the political systems of the Arab states. These systems not only sailed rudderless into the storm that engulfed them, but also lacked the internal controls to exploit the prevailing forces for the benefit of a well-defined set of strategic objectives. What is needed, therefore, in order that greater use be made of the second opportunity (if and when it does come) is that we Arabs begin to view the development process in a new light. We must approach it as an internal process of discovery of our own resources and endowments, of clear definition of our own objectives and long-term goals, and only after that has been accomplished must we begin to call on external resources (and oil revenues in this case are viewed functionally as external resources, similar to remittances or foreign aid) to intensify, facilitate, and accelerate the process of social transformation in the desired direction. As an illustration of this point, had such a view of development prevailed in the middle and late 1970s, the Arab oil producers would not have produced so much oil as they did nor would they have undertaken all the derivative activities that emanated from the momentous decision in favor of high production. A more balanced sort of development would have been achieved, and many of the regrettable consequences of the development course taken would have been avoided. It is quite likely, in this connection, that a careful study of the process of economic development in such countries as Japan in the late nineteenth century and China and India in the more recent past would reveal that the benefits of interaction with the more industrial societies were internalized so effectively only after a certain degree of introspection and self-preparation had been achieved.

A second fundamental point that needs to be considered in preparing for the "second opportunity" is the inseparability of politics and economics in designing appropriate development strategies. Much of the reason why Arab development strategies have in part failed has been the prevailing illusion that economic and financial development can be accelerated in the absence of clear movement toward political modernization. Thus the absence of fully developed political institutions deprived broad sectors of the population of participation in (as distinct from benefit from) the development process and preempted the emergence of the minimal norms of public discourse and accountability essential to the prevention of waste and corruption. The absence of minimal guarantees of basic civil rights and individual freedoms led to a steady and substantial brain drain from the region. Major development decisions taken by autocratic regimes in a political environment filled with fear, indifference, corruption, or some combination thereof have resulted in the initiation of disastrously bad programs and projects. Furthermore, as long as these conditions prevail (and they still do in most, if not all, of the Arab countries), there is no likelihood that the "second opportunity" will be more productively exploited than the first one.

A third issue, related in many ways to the one just raised, bears on the question of the duties and responsibilities of the public sector in the development process. The absence of democratically based political systems has permitted the state apparatus in several of the Arab countries to use the newly available resources (from oil) to augment their own power to such an extent that, with or without the need to resort to directly destructive measures, they have left little room for the independent development of alternative centers of economic power in society. This has not only enhanced the oppressive capacity of the state but prevented the emergence and growth of a private sector or popularly based cooperative movements capable of sufficiently absorbing new technology and of providing the necessary flexibility and resilience in times of crises. I do not wish to convey the mistaken impression that I would be in favor of a system of "unbridled capitalism" in the Arab countries. What is needed, however, is an appropriate delineation of roles for a public sector truly accountable to the public and a private sector operating under limits and guidelines developed within a sound political process.

The fourth issue that must be addressed is that of Arab integration. Despite a plethora of pronouncements and a multitude of pan-Arab institutions spawned by the oil boom, little has been achieved in genuinely integrating the Arab economies. (The modest exception may be the Gulf Cooperation Council, but this organization is regionally truncated by design and does not therefore advance the cause of Arab unity as it is commonly understood.) As indicated earlier, the oil-induced economic boom led to a vastly larger volume of bilateral economic exchange between the Arab oil-exporting countries and the industrial West than among the Arab countries themselves. Although manpower movements and the offsetting flows of remittances increased dramatically during the 1974–82 period, very little lasting impact was left when the tide began to turn the other way. It is simply an exercise in self-delusion to pretend that individual Arab oil-producing countries can achieve self-sustained economic development either in isolation or in small exclusive "rich man's clubs." At the same time, one need not take the argument too far and propose immediate and complete merger among all the Arab countries. One may say, however, that the ability of the Arab countries to exploit any economic opportunity that may arise out of favorable external conditions in the mid-1990s will depend in no small measure on the progress those countries will have achieved by then in breaking down barriers to the movement of manpower, capital, and goods; in facilitating the construction of the massive pan-Arab transportation and communication infrastructure so essential to the integration of the Arab economies; and in harmonizing investment, fiscal, monetary, and external sector policies within a broader regional framework.

The fifth and final issue centers on the economic relations between the Arab countries and the rest of the world. Briefly stated, the problem is that one would have expected the Arab countries' enhanced financial resources to lead to a commensurately greater leverage of the Arab countries on the industrial West, especially in relation to issues that may be considered of overriding pan-Arab importance. One finds instead that the enhanced financial and economic links with the West have produced a fragile relationship of interdependence at best, and one of greater and unhealthy dependence at worst. Even on issues that may be considered technical and narrow in scope, such as Saudi Arabia's current drive to gain unhampered access to European markets for its petrochemical products, the past ten years of massive economic exchange, which benefited the European countries so immeasurably, seem to count for very little when it is the Arab country which is in need. For the coming period, it is essential therefore that the Arab countries, both the oil exporters and the others, redefine the nature of their relationship primarily with the industrial West, but also with the Eastern Bloc countries and the Third World, so as to be in a better position to exploit their combined bargaining power to a pan-Arab, national advantage.

These are some of the key issues that urgently need to be addressed and resolved if the Arab countries are to benefit from the transitory conditions that exist now and that are likely to prevail until the early to mid-1990s. For only with successful resolution of these issues can the Arab countries approach the "second opportunity" that may materialize a decade hence and exploit it to achieve sustained economic and social development.

The other set of considerations touches on such technical issues as the choice of an appropriate development strategy, the development of built-in incentives to investment and disincentives to consumption, the appropriate mix of fiscal and monetary policies to achieve acceptable growth with financial stability, and the choice of exchange rate policies and other instruments of external management to achieve specified developmental and financial objectives. Space limitations prevent detailed description of these issues, which in any event are familiar and require no amplification in this context. The Arab countries, if they were to undertake the more fundamental political reforms discussed earlier, would lack neither the indigenous talent nor the expertise from abroad to advise them on the appropriate choice of economic and financial policies.

Conclusion

Projections and forecasts are inherently hazardous to make. In the case of energy and in the context of future developments in the Middle East, they may be foolish even to attempt.

Nonetheless, available indications are that during the coming decade the Arab oil-producing region may gradually approach a constellation of favorable conditions in the world energy market that will permit oil revenues to rise considerably, thus creating a second "window of opportunity" for improved access to resources for development. The ability of the Arab world to exploit this opportunity for broad national developmental goals will depend critically on its success or failure in resolving certain fundamental issues related to the nature of the Arab society, the choice of political systems, a redefinition of relations with the rest of the world, and issues related to Arab integration. If the Arabs fail, the second opportunity may be squandered even more wastefully than the first. If, on the other hand, they succeed, they will have a better than even chance to set their economies on a course of genuine, self-sustaining economic and social development. The Arab world will then have the capacity to approach the twenty-first century as a dynamic, cohesive, and increasingly productive society. A new opportunity to achieve much higher oil revenues will greatly facilitate this task. In any event, the Arab countries' success in resolving these fundamental issues in the transitional decade ahead will undoubtedly enhance their chances of accomplishing the task, even if the second opportunity fails to materialize.

Notes

1. These coefficients are useful only for medium- and long-range forecasts, as they have been known to take on perversely negative values in some of the recent years.

2. Data on world demand for OPEC oil (during 1984 and 1985) are clouded with imprecision because, given the prevailing uncertainty with regard to price, considerable drawdown of stocks has taken place, offsetting possible increases in OPEC oil output. Such drawdowns cannot of course continue for long.

3. One can easily envisage the dynamics of the developing situation in the early to mid-1990s; the pent-up desire of at least some OPEC producers who see a tightening oil market on the horizon may then be reflected in strong demands for substantial price adjustments.

4. The slowdown in exploration and production augmentation activities is not uniform in all regions outside OPEC, as such activities are affected by a complex set of factors, including price expectations and tax treatment of expenditures. The general trend, however, especially since 1982, has been downward.

5. Including an assumed capacity for Iran of 5.5 mbd and for Iraq of 3.5 mbd.

6. It should be noted that the maximum capacity allowable, i.e., in conformity with OPEC members' own self-imposed restrictions on maximum output, may be significantly smaller still, perhaps by 2 to 3 mbd.

7. This is not to deny that relatively small suppliers such as Egypt, Brazil, Colombia, India, and some West African countries may continue to raise their output, nor to ignore the possibility that possible new suppliers, e.g., North Yemen, may provide some additional output. But the net impact of all such developments on the world oil market will nonetheless be small.

Selected Bibliography

Abed, George, T. "Arab Oil-Exporters in the World Economy." *American-Arab Affairs* no. 3 (Winter 1982–83): 26–40.

Abed, George T. "Arab Financial Resources: An Analysis and Critique of Current Deployment Strategy," in *Arab Resources: The Transformation of a Society*, edited by Ibrahim Ibrahim. Washington, DC: Center for Contemporary Arab Studies and and London: Croom-Helm, 1983.

Ait-Laoussine, Nordine and Parra, Francisco R. "The Development of Oil Supplies During the Crisis of the 1970s and Some Questions for the Future." *OPEC Review* 9, no. 1 (Spring 1985): 29–62.

Al-Janabi, Adnan. "Estimating Energy Demand in OPEC Countries." *Energy Economics* (April 1979): 87–92.

Attiga, Ali A. "Energy and Development in the Arab World: Present Situation and Future Prospects." *OPEC Review* (Summer 1984): 127–49.

Arab Fund for Social and Economic Development (in cooperation with other Arab regional organizations). *The Arab Economic Report, 1984*. Kuwait: Arab Fund for Social and Economic Development, 1985 (in Arabic).

Brookes, L.G. "More on the Output Elasticity of Energy Consumption." *Journal of Industrial Economics* no. 1 (November 1972): 83–92.

Deagle, Edwin A. Jr. *The Future of the International Oil Market*. New York: Group of Thirty, 1983.

Deagle, Edwin A. Jr. and Mossavar-Rahmani, Bijan. "Oil Demand and Energy Markets: An Interpretation of Forecasts for the 1980s." *OPEC Review* no. 2 (Summer 1982): 140–60.

Gately, Dermot. "OPEC: Retrospective and Prospects 1973–1990." *European Economic Review* no. 21 (1983): 313–31.

Gately, Dermot. "A Ten-Year Retrospective: OPEC and the World Oil Market." *Journal of Economic Literature* 22 (September 1984): 1100–114.

Ibrahim, Ibrahim. "Energy Forecasting and Energy Data in the Arab Countries." *OPEC Review* 9, no. 2 (Summer 1985): 125–40.

Kouris, George. "Oil Trends and Prices in the Next Decade." *Energy Policy* (September 1984): 321–28.

Mohnfeld, Jochen H. "European and World Energy Perspectives: The 1980s and 1990s." *Intereconomics* (July/August 1982): 159–66.

Odell, Peter R. and Rosing, Kenneth E. "The Future of Oil: A Re-Evaluation." *OPEC Review* (Summer 1984): 203–28.

OPEC Energy Studies Department. "Domestic Energy in OPEC Member Countries." *OPEC Review* (Spring 1984): 111–25.

OPEC Papers. "Future Demand for Refined Products in OPEC Member Countries and Possible Export Outlets." *OPEC Papers* 1, no. 3 (December 1980).

Stevens, Paul. "The Future of World Oil Prices: The End of an Era?" *Overseas Development Institute Review* no. 2 (1982): 1–19.

Styrikovich, M. A. "An Approach to Evaluating the World's Medium-Term and Long-Term Oil Demands." *OPEC Review* (Spring 1983): 14–31.

Totta, Lisa and Johnson, Todd. *OPEC Domestic Oil Demand: Future Scenarios of Product Consumption*, Program Report PR-82-2. Hawaii: East–West Resource Systems Institute, October 1982.

Totta, Lisa. "OPEC Domestic Oil Demand: Product Forecasts for 1985 and 1990." *OPEC Review* (Summer 1983): 190–211.

World Bank. *Petroleum: Price Prospects for Major Primary Commodities* 4 (September 1984): 38–68.

Zilberfarb, Ben-Zion and Adams, F. Gerard. "The Energy-GDP Relationship in Developing Countries." *Energy Economics* (October 1981): 244–48.

8

Arab Agriculture in 1995: Apocalypse or Muddling Through?

Alan Richards

Introduction

One of the most serious problems facing the Middle East and North Africa is the region's growing inability to feed itself. The rising imbalance between consumption and domestic production constituted the Achilles heel of the oil boom of the 1970s. Despite slackening oil prices and (for many) declining export revenues, this "food gap" has continued to grow. Rapidly escalating effective demand and sluggish domestic supply response have made the Middle East and North Africa the least food self-sufficient region in the world.

What are the implications of this situtaion for the political economies of the region during the next ten years? Will this situation improve or deteriorate? Can such a "food gap" be sustained? What public and private responses to this gap are likely? These are some of the questions which should be asked in assessing the implications of the food security and agricultural development situation in the area over the next ten years.

There are two principal approaches to discussing the future: forecasting and scenario construction. Forecasters usually construct a formal model of an economic process and then obtain estimates for past rates of growth of critical variables by making assumptions on some crucial parameters. These are then projected, usually linearly, into the future. Uncertainty is commonly handled by varying one or several parameters to obtain "high" and "low" projections.

While such forecasts are often useful exercises, they necessarily exclude the more qualitative, explicitly political variables from their analysis. The assumption of linearity also is questionable; however, identifying the length and periodicity of cycles is typically quite difficult, especially in less developed countries (LDCs), for which sufficiently long data sets are often unavailable and in which rapid structural change is taking place, altering many underlying parameters.

An alternative approach is "scenario construction." One variant, increasingly used by business planners, is to identify the "principal structural features," that is, the variables which are assumed to be quite stable, and then to discuss the "principal uncertainties." The first step is really very similar to forecasting, and such scenario builders commonly draw freely on available forecasts. But the focus is on the uncertainties, and especially on how the policy responses to one problem may exacerbate others. Such an approach has the defect of considerable subjectivity; however, it has the merit of explicitly including qualitative aspects of the problem and of openly recognizing the extent of our ignorance. It is really an exercise in identifying problems rather than in offering solutions to them.

This paper will adopt the second approach to the question of what Arab agriculture might look like in 1995. Rather than construct yet another forecast of the demand–supply balance of foodstuffs in the region, I will draw freely on several useful existing forecasts and devote most of my attention to such qualitative issues as the causes and consequences of policy responses to the "food gap."

Some Forecasts of the Food Gap in 1995

At least three major forecasts of the demand–domestic supply imbalance in the region are available.[1] Despite differences of detail, the "bottom line" is the same for each: the food gap is large and will continue to grow for the rest of the century. The International Food Policy Research Institute (IFPRI) finds the deficit in food staples rising at about 1.5 metric tons per year, with a predicted deficit of cereals of roughly 30 million tons by the year 2000. The UN Food and Agriculture Organization (FAO) estimate is quite similar. The Arab Organization for Agricultural Development (AOAD) estimate, the most optimistic, still projects a gap of nearly 25 million tons at the turn of the century. Other estimates run even higher: the U.S. Department of Agriculture (USDA), for example, finds that total imports of wheat and flour, rice, and feed grains for all Arab countries were already close to 28 million metric tons in 1981![2] All agree that demand will continue to grow rapidly, while supply response faces both natural and social constraints. Policy innovations to relax these constraints are likely, but their success is in doubt. Even if they should be successful, the transformation of Arab agriculture under the twin spurs of the food gap and state policies may add to the various social problems and political pressures on governments. The rest of this paper is devoted to cataloging the uncertainties surrounding each of these aspects of the food gap.

Uncertainties on the Demand Side

Let us first look at the uncertainties on the demand side. There are three determinants of demand growth: population growth, per capita income growth, and the income elasticity of demand.[3] Population growth is often stressed to the exclusion of all other factors, especially in the popular press. However, even for cereals, much, and in some cases most, of the growth in demand has been due to expansion of per capita incomes. Of course, rapid population growth made a substantial contribution to increased demand for food (Table 8.1). All countries' population growth rates exceed 2 percent per year, and many are considerably higher. Indeed, the region of the Middle East and North Africa as a whole has the highest rate of population increase of any region in the world except sub-Saharan Africa. Further, in comparison with a sample of 68 LDCs, the World Bank finds fertility in the region generally higher than would be expected, given income levels.[4] The low levels of female literacy surely contribute to this pattern, as do poor health conditions, especially in the rural areas.[5] It is true that there have been some declines in fertility recently reported for Egypt and Tunisia; however, declines in mortality have swamped this effect, leaving the rate of population growth essentially unchanged.

While further increases in female literacy, in health, and in labor force participation might reduce population growth, there are two obstacles to such changes having a noticeable effect on food demand in 1995. Although most Arab countries have made progress in improving health conditions, some have reduced their spending on health and education recently as a result of the economic austerity enforced by declining export revenues.[6] Further, relatively few countries have programs to make contraceptives readily available to those who want them. And finally, such changes typically take some time to have much impact; even under the best of conditions (which are not very probable), we would expect relatively little effect of altered population policies on the demographic situation in 1995.

Even if the population growth rate were to fall, demand for food would continue to increase; consumption per capita of most foodstuffs has been growing during the past decade due to the very rapid growth of incomes. For five countries, incomes grew faster than 5 percent per year, a rate that will double incomes in 15 years. Further, since the numbers used in Table 8.1 are for GDP, which excludes remittances, the estimates for countries such as the Yemen Arab Republic (Y.A.R.) are underestimated. There can be no doubt that per capita incomes advanced swiftly in the region during the past decade, although in some of the larger countries, e.g., Morocco and Sudan, growth has been much more disappointing.

Of course, the infusion of revenues from the oil price revolution of the 1970s was the "engine of growth" for the entire region. Since such rapid changes seem unlikely in the near future, continued growth for oil-exporters will depend on pay-offs from existing and planned investments. Most projections assume continued relatively rapid growth of incomes in the oil-producing countries.[7] Continued increases in income for labor-exporters (e.g., Egypt, Y.A.R., Jordan) depend on the pattern of growth of demand in the oil-exporting countries. The principal forecast of such demand predicts a shift in its composition from unskilled labor toward more skilled labor, which could imply a reduction in remittance flows.[8] However, the very

TABLE 8.1
Selected Agricultural Indicators, Middle East and North Africa, 1970-82

	Population growth rate 1970-82 (as annual percentage)	Growth rate of per capita gross domestic product 1970-82 (as annual percentage)	Index of food production per capita 1980-82 (1969-71 = 100)	Growth rate of agricultural output 1970-82 (as annual percentage)	Growth rate of value-added in agriculture 1970-82 (as annual percentage)	Growth rate of cereal imports 1974-82 (as annual percentage)
Algeria	3.1	3.5	75	3.9	3.1	9.3
Egypt	2.5	5.9	85	3.0	3.1	6.8[a]
Iran	3.1	N/A	111	N/A	N/A	5.3
Iraq	3.5	N/A	87	N/A	N/A	2.3
Jordan	2.5	6.8	70	0.2	3.0	17.0
Kuwait	6.3	-4.2	N/A	5.5	N/A	18.4
Libya	4.1	-1.7	127	10.5	9.4	4.1
Morocco	2.6	2.4	84	0.1	0.5	9.6
North Yemen	3.0	5.5	93	3.6	5.0	15.8[a]
Oman	4.3	1.5	95	N/A	N/A	17.0
Saudi Arabia	4.8	5.0	N/A	5.6	5.2	30.1
South Yemen	2.2	N/A	92	N/A	N/A	7.4
Sudan	3.2	3.1	87	4.1	3.7	19.8
Syria	3.5	5.3	168	10.0[b]	9.1[b]	2.9
Tunisia	2.3	4.7	128	3.6	4.4	14.1
Turkey	2.3	2.8	115	3.2	3.3	-10.6
U.A.E.	15.5	N/A	N/A	N/A	N/A	9.5

[a]If food aid is included, the rate is 8.2 percent per annum.
[b]Figures are for 1970-80.

Source: World Bank, World Development Report, 1984 (Washington, DC: World Bank, 1985).

large demand for reconstruction labor in Iraq once the war ends may swamp such an effect.

Continued strong growth of income for both labor- and oil-exporting countries, then, seems a reasonable assumption. But the patterns of the demand for labor and of remittances, in turn a function of the pattern of growth of oil exporters and of the outcome of the Iran–Iraq war, remain major uncertainties.

It is much more difficult to be sanguine about some other countries, especially Tunisia, Morocco, and Sudan. Much depends on internal developments and responses to the current economic and political crises and on the revival and growth and decline in protectionism in the European Economic Community (EEC). The latter is especially important for the Maghrib countries. We will deal with these cases in somewhat more detail below.

Despite these uncertainties, scenarios which include continued growth of incomes in the region seem quite reasonable. The impact of such income growth upon food demand depends, of course, on the specific foodstuff. If we use an income elasticity of 0.7 and 0.9 for foods as a whole for middle- and low-income countries, respectively, we find that for many countries it is the growth of incomes, not population growth, which is the principal source of demand growth.[9] And by far the largest impetus to the increased demand for such "luxury" products as meat, fruit, and vegetables, which have higher income elasticities, comes from the expansion of incomes due to the oil boom. Indeed, the derived demand for imported feedgrains for livestock is the fastest-growing component of the food gap in the region. Finally, in some countries urban consumer tastes have shifted away from local grains toward bread wheat.[10] Such taste shifts are very unlikely to be reversed; indeed, continued increases in incomes make it very likely that they will continue into the next century.

It seems that even if population growth decelerates markedly (and even if the food subsidies which receive so much attention are withdrawn), the demand for food in the region will continue to increase rapidly. Only if oil prices, government revenue, and economic growth in the region were to collapse would the rate of growth of demand decelerate markedly. Although not impossible, such a collapse seems quite unlikely. And such a grim conjuncture would still leave a large gap between current consumption and domestic production, since food consumption is highly inelastic downward: governments are likely to cut everything else except national defense before they reduce the nation's food supply. We may conclude that any reduction in the "food gap" coming from the demand side is unlikely.

An Overview of Supply Response

Let us now turn to the supply side. First of all, it should be noted that by international standards, Middle Eastern agricultural output has grown relatively respectably. According to the World Bank, the average annual rates of growth of agricultural output during the decade 1970–80 for low-income, middle-income, and industrialized market economies were some 2.3 percent, 3.0 percent, and 1.8 percent, respectively.[11] As a glance at Table 8.1 shows, many Middle Eastern countries have performed better than this. However, when we turn to a regional comparison, a somewhat different picture emerges. From 1961 to 1967, food production in the Middle East and North Africa (MENA) grew 2.5 percent per year, less rapidly than Latin America (3.22 percent) or Asia (2.78 percent), but more so than sub-Saharan Africa (1.6 percent).[12] It is important to note that MENA countries' agricultural sectors have lagged primarily in relation to their own rates of growth of demand; the problem is *not* one of stagnation or retrogression, as is often the case in sub-Saharan Africa.[13]

It is also important to note that increasing yields accounted for some 55 percent of this growth in food output, while extension of the cultivated area explained the remaining 45 percent. Output per unit of land increased at roughly 1.4 percent per year, a rate roughly equal to that of Latin America and well above that of sub-Saharan Africa, but far below that of Asia (2.1 percent).[14] Apart from Sudan and perhaps some areas of Iraq, little potentially cultivable but uncultivated land remains in the region. Consequently, the rate of expansion of the cultivated area during the past generation (1.1 percent) will almost certainly decline. Therefore, further growth of output in the region can come only from increasing land productivity: the region is shifting from "extensive" to "intensive" growth. Indeed, Khaldi argues that this shift occurred during the 1970s, when 88 percent of the growth of domestic cereal supply in the Middle East and North Africa was due to increases in yields.[15]

Continued advance along these lines will be both difficult and expensive. The process will deeply involve the state and will both require and stimulate considerable rural social change. State policies and the responses of private agents to these policies and to the opportunities provided by the food gap itself comprise a central set of uncertainties on the supply side. Both public and private responses encounter a series of natural and social constraints. Much depends on the extent to which these constraints can be relaxed.

Constraints to Accelerating Supply Response

The supply response of Arab agriculture is constrained by both ecology and history. The natural difficulties are rather straightforward. Since roughly 80 percent of the agricultural area is rain-fed, inadequate and undependable water supplies limit domestic supply response. The main source of food insecurity, both globally and in the MENA region, is fluctuation in domestic production, not price instability. Many countries face a high probability that production will fall at least 5 percent below trend in any one year. Planners must find supplementary foreign exchange to buy "unusual" (i.e., at least 5 percent above trend) amounts of food four years out of ten.

The problems posed by the natural environment are underscored by the devastating impact of the recent droughts in the Maghrib and in Sudan.

The situation in Sudan is especially troubling, given its size and its potential regional role as a producer of sugar and feed surpluses. Climatologists agree that the African monsoon shows cyclical patterns; they also agree that we are currently in a "dry phase" of the cycle. Although the length of the cycle is in dispute, most believe that the current relatively dry phase is likely to persist for at least the next 30 years.[16] The consequences for the entire Nile Valley of such an eventuality constitute one of the major uncertainties and sources of concern about the future of domestic food supplies in the region. There is an unknown potential for real disaster here.

The social constraints also are severe. We may divide such constraints into three groups, each the inheritance of a particular historical period. These are, roughly speaking, the constraints of urban bias and bimodalism (the *ancien régime*), the effects of import-substituting industrialization policies (the era of nationalism and populism), and the affliction of the "Dutch disease" (the period of the oil boom).

Urban bias has deep roots in the region. With a few exceptions, regimes have always been based in the cities and have neglected, abused, or simply ignored the rural areas. Whether measured by rural–urban income gaps, by differences in education and health facilities, or even by food subsidies, urban bias is a central fact of most Arab countries' political economy.[17] Only the Syrian regime's social origins and political base lie in the countryside. It may not be accidental that Syria's agricultural performance has been among the best in the region.

Land tenure systems continue to restrain the growth of agricultural output in the region. There is by now a large body of literature which criticizes the impact of a "bimodal" distribution of farms on both the equity and the efficiency of the farm sector. The combination of a large number of small farmers exploiting large, modern farms with the large majority of the peasants eking out a subsistence on dwarf holdings either retards the growth of land yields or, at a minimum, biases the direction of agricultural growth against the interests of the rural majority.[18] The absence of linkages between industry and agriculture and the distortions in factor and input markets are usually cited as among the most significant unfortunate results of such a land tenure system. At the same time, excessive fragmentation of farms also impedes agricultural development.

The gross inequalities evident in Table 8.2 are the fruits of the ancien régime in the region, that is, the period of colonial rule or influence and its immediate aftermath. The process could be characterized as the "premature spread of private property rights in land."[19] European colonists or modernizing indigenous regimes imposed private property rights in Egypt, Iraq, Algeria, Iran, and Syria. Urban-based landlords, whether wealthy merchants as in Syria or court favorites as in Egypt, accumulated large tracts of land due to their connections to state power. Just as in Latin America, the region consequently developed gross inequalities in the distribution of land ownership. This process was especially marked in the Maghrib, with its history of settler colonialism. In Morocco, some 75 percent of farmers hold less

TABLE 8.2
Gini Coefficients of Farm Size

Country	Gini Coefficient	
Brazil	.831	(1960)[3]
Chile	.933	(1960)[3]
Colombia	.868	(1960)[3]
Egypt	.601	(1961)[2]
	.460	(1974)[2]
	.550	(1979)[2]
India	.585	(1960)[3]
Iran	.624	(1960)[3]
Kenya	.822	(1960)[3]
Republic of Korea	.195	(1960)[3]
Mexico	.747	(1960)[3]
Morocco	.640	(1960)[3]
	.588	(1981)[4]
Pakistan	.631	(1960)[3]
Peru	.935	(1960)[3]
Senegal	.399	(1960)[3]
Syria	.461	(1970)[1]
Taiwan	.401	(1960)[3]
Tunisia	.645	(1961)[3]
Turkey	.629	(1960)[3]

Sources:
1. Calculated from data in Raymond Hinnesbusch, <u>Party and Peasant in Syria</u> (Cairo: American University in Cairo Press, 1980).
2. Egyptian Ministry of Agriculture, unpublished data (1961, 1975, 1979).
3. World Bank data in R. Albert Berry and William Cline, <u>Agrarian Structure and Productivity in Developing Countries</u> (Baltimore, MD: Johns Hopkins University Press, 1979), pp. 36-39.
4. Irrigated sector, in Saad Eddin Ibrahim, <u>Population and Urbanization in Morocco</u> (Cairo: American University in Cairo Press, 1980).

than 5 hectares each and account for some 25 percent of the cultivated area.[20]

Land reforms undertaken during the past generation modified, but failed to transform, this picture. Although land reforms succeeded in breaking up the largest estates and in eliminating much of the political power of their former owners, many peasants either received no land at all (e.g., in Egypt only 12 percent of the peasantry received land) or received parcels too small for subsistence (in Iran, 75 percent of peasants received such dwarf parcels). The landless class remained large; in 1970 about one third of the rural population in the region was landless.[21] Throughout the area, the upper strata of the peasantry benefited most from land reform.

The administration of land reforms often created additional obstacles. Confiscating land proved easier than redistributing it. Especially in Iraq, delays in redistribution, failures to provide credit and other complementary inputs, and the lack of trained rural cadres undermined agricultural production. Too often, governments removed large landowners, who often had also supplied credit and seed, without replacing them with anything else. More successful reforms, like those in Egypt, instituted "cooperative" societies to supply inputs and tax outputs of farmers. Better-off farmers usually dominated such cooperatives.

The resulting rural class structure has been characterized as a "kulak–bureaucrat" system, although some have argued that the former are far more potent than the latter. The rural societies of the region are not entirely polarized, however. There are several intermediate strata whose members are often linked to their richer neighbors through various social and economic ties.[22]

It seems quite unlikely that the land tenure situation in most Arab countries will change in the near future. Land reforms of the past era were aimed at foreigners or at holders of very large estates which could be characterized as "semi-feudal" without excessive violence to reality. By now, however, most large private farms in the region are capitalist farms; it seems unlikely that they will divided.[23] Indeed, the tendency is clearly in the opposite direction, toward increasing government support of relatively well-off private farmers. Governments hope to solve some of the problems of cooperatives by increasing reliance on private farming, as recent moves in Iraq and Algeria show. The two main uncertainties here are the extent to which governments will actually support these farmers with reliable input supply and output marketing and the extent to which such policies will imply neglect of the large majority of small farmers.

The regimes which instituted land reforms also embarked on ambitious programs of import-substituting industrialization. Such policies, still operative in many countries in the region, constitute the second set of social constraints to agricultural growth. For example, Egypt, which had no alternative source of investable surplus, used the cooperative system to shift the terms of trade against agriculture, ostensibly to increase the rate of investment.[24] The bias against the agricultural sector which resulted from such "macro price" policy has been extensively documented.[25] Such policies go a long way toward explaining the failure of Sudanese agriculture to fulfill its hoped-for regional role as a "breadbasket" ("feedbag" or "sugar bowl" would be more apt).[26] In addition, the stress on industrialization led to allocation to agriculture of a very low share of total public investment.

It should be noted here that *some* source of investable funds is, after all, necessary. Only if some alternative source is available can a country which wishes to accelerate its growth rate avoid a net outflow of resources from the agricultural sector.[27] Many regimes did acquire such an alternative source of foreign exchange during the 1970s—oil revenue (or remittances, in turn dependent on oil money). However, it is well known that the inflow of oil wealth was a "very mixed blessing"[28] for oil exporters' agricultural sectors. Although there are somewhat different versions of the "Dutch disease" argument, all focus on the shift in the terms of trade against tradables (including, of course, agriculture) and in favor of nontradables (services and construction) as the real exchange rate appreciates.[29] This may occur either because the rates of inflation in the oil states exceed those of their principal trading partners, the Organization for Economic Cooperation and Development (OECD) nations, or because of differential supply elasticities.[30] The shift in these relative prices leads to an outflow of resources from tradables into non-tradables; consequently, agricultural (and industrial) growth suffer.

It appears, however, that the impact of the "Dutch disease" has been overrated. According to the World Bank, middle-income, oil-importing countries' agricultural sectors grew at 2.8 percent during this period, while middle-income, oil-exporting countries' agricultures grew at 3 percent and high-income oil exporters' agricultures grew at 5.6 percent. At the national level, a glance at Table 8.1 shows that some oil-exporters' agricultures have performed quite well. They seem to have survived the "Dutch disease," largely because the state intervened directly to offset the shift in the terms of trade against agriculture. This was done both by launching investment projects and by either subsidizing agricultural inputs directly (e.g., in Saudi Arabia) or by shifting agricultural price policies which had formerly taxed agriculture heavily (e.g., in Egypt).[31]

We may conclude that although the problems of urban bias and bimodalism are likely to persist, unfavorable price policies and terms of trade shifts may recede in importance as constraints on supply growth. Such developments, however, presuppose alternative, nonagricultural sources of revenue. And here, of course, there are numerous, serious uncertainties. Further, it is most unlikely that even with the best possible luck with each of these constraints, Arab agricultures could have succeeded in reversing the trend toward an increased reliance on food imports. Let us now turn to uncertainties surrounding such imports.

State Responses

Food Imports

The imbalance of supply and demand in the 1970s led to an extremely rapid growth of imports (Table 8.1). This food import boom had several components. First, as mentioned earlier, domestic production was (and is) highly unstable due to erratic rainfall. Second, the barter terms of trade moved sharply in favor of oil-exporting food importers. In 1970 a barrel of oil would buy roughly a bushel of wheat, but by 1980, the same barrel would purchase six bushels. Although oil prices have fallen since 1980, wheat prices also have, and the relative price ratio still stands at roughly six to one. Third, most MENA countries had ample supplies of foreign exchange; the balance of payments did not constrain food imports during the 1970s.

Increased reliance on food imports was also politically attractive for governments in the short run. First, they really had no choice if consumption were to rise. Second, food imports afford a government a high degree of political control over strategic urban food supplies. It is much easier to collect and administer food which arrives at one or a few ports than to collect grain from the hundreds, perhaps thousands, of local markets in the countryside. Since most governments subsidize urban food consumption, and since urban food supply is a national security issue, governments were and are reluctant to rely on private grain traders to supply cities with food. In the 1970s, then, the forces favoring increased imports were overwhelming.

Since the demand for imports is likely to remain very strong for at least the next decade, we should ask what uncertainties surround such reliance on imported food. We may divide these uncertainties into the economic and the political. On the economic side, the real issues are the continued ability to finance food imports and the opportunity costs of the foreign exchange so used. Reliance on food imports exposes a country to substantial risks should foreign exchange availability decline, as the cases of Tunisia and Morocco illustrate. In addition, investment is usually reduced as a result of the use of imports to stabilize food consumption.[32]

The potential risks may be listed as follows. First, the price of cereals could rise suddenly. Although there is no doubt that the long-run trend of cereal prices is downward, there have been occasional (usually brief) periods of sharp upward movements in prices (e.g., 1972–74, 1950–52). Such a development could occur either because of a large-scale weather disaster in North America,[33] or because of a sudden increase in purchases by industrial countries (e.g., especially the U.S.S.R.) in a context of relatively limited grain stocks. A repeat of the experience of 1972 would be very costly for many Middle Eastern countries.

Although North American livestock herds continue to represent substantial "excess capacity" in grain, it should be noted that the current wave of difficulties and contractions of American agricultural land area due to very high interest rates and resulting farm foreclosures may set the stage for a relatively inelastic short-run supply of U.S. grain. Should a sudden increase in demand coincide with the trough of the U.S. agricultural production cycle, price developments similar to 1972 could recur. But since such events are conjunctural, they are very difficult to predict.

Perhaps more serious are developments on the foreign exchange side of the ledger. Of course, a major decline in the price of oil could reverse the favorable trend in the barter terms of trade. The overvaluation of the U.S. dollar has not affected petroleum exporters' food import bill because both oil prices and wheat prices are denominated in dollars. The really difficult cases are, again, countries like Sudan, Morocco, and Tunisia: non-oil-exporting countries, which experienced dramatic declines in foreign exchange revenue at the same time as their food demand mounted steadily and domestic food supply growth was constrained by both bad weather and bad policies. The problem was exacerbated for Morocco and Tunisia by the increase in the price of the dollar relative to the French franc, to which those Maghrib countries' currencies are tied.

The principal future uncertainties in such cases are the following:

- Will there be a dramatic reversal of the prices of these countries' principal commodity exports?[34] This depends mainly on the prospects for a revival in OECD growth.
- Will tariff barriers to textiles and fruits and vegetables in the EEC fall? This seems quite unlikely with the accession of the Iberian countries to full membership in the EEC.
- Will there be a revival of opportunities for emigration to the EEC? Again, this is possible, but unlikely.
- Can these countries find alternative markets and perhaps also promote labor-intensive manufactured exports? Perhaps, but the world economy can accommodate only so many Koreas and Taiwans.

In addition to problems of sluggish growth in the OECD countries, these Arab countries' internal problems and policies create further barriers to such expansion. And regionally, important competition may be expected from Turkey, which is determinedly pursuing an "export-led growth" strategy and which has certain advantages, such as its relatively skilled industrial workforce. Unless there is a dramatic revival of growth in the world economy, it is difficult to be sanguine about these Arab countries' ability to finance growing imports over the longer run through exports.

How long can these countries continue to finance large food imports and to run large balance of payments deficits? In the 1970s they borrowed fairly heavily (although not nearly so heavily as the Latin American debtors like Brazil and Mexico).[35] Obviously, sources of such private loans are unavailable now. Instead, however, it can be argued that countries like Morocco and Egypt can continue to finance food imports by collecting "strategic rent." Neither the United States nor the conservative states of the Gulf want to see a change of regime in countries like Morocco, Tunisia, and Egypt. They have (so far) been willing to provide grants and aid to cover food imports and to shore up the very weak balance of payments position of these countries. How long such countries can and will be willing to underwrite balance of payments deficits and growing food imports is thus an additional fundamental uncertainty surrounding the continued viability of the food gap for some countries.

Receiving such "strategic rents" has its price in reduced maneuverability of the recipient in regional politics. Indeed, the levels of food dependency shown in Table 8.3 prompted widespread alarm in the region in their own right, leading to fears of the U.S. "food weapon." The risk of a politically motivated food embargo became almost an obsession with many government planners.

For most countries in the region, it seems fair to say that this fear was excessive during the 1970s; the effectiveness of the "food weapon" has

Arab Agriculture in 1995

TABLE 8.3
Food Self-Sufficiency Ratios for Selected Foods and Countries, 1970 and 1981

Country	Cereals 1970	Cereals 1981	Vegetable Oil 1970	Vegetable Oil 1981	Meat 1970	Meat 1981	Sugar 1970	Sugar 1981
Algeria	73	40	26	11	97	87	--	--
Egypt	81	49	56	32	94	75	100	52
Iran	98	66	33	11	90	66	100	38
Iraq	91	47	15	4	98	44	--	--
Libya	25	20	42	28	60	30	--	--
Morocco	94	60	51	16	100	100	36	55
Saudi Arabia	22	7*	--	--	38	27	--	--
Syria	73	84	100	90	100	75	17	24
Tunisia	61	54	100	99	98	84	10	--

*Saudi Arabia was by 1984 self-sufficient in wheat.

Source: U.S. Department of Agriculture.

probably been overrated. First, the U.S. agricultural lobby constitutes a powerful domestic force against restricting grain exports to attain political goals. Second, the weapon is ineffective because of the fungibility of grain and the multinational scope of the grain trade. Number 2 Hard Red Wheat is Number 2 Hard Red Wheat, whether it comes from North America or Argentina. There is evidence that just as the multinational oil companies restructured their global oil flows to evade the Arab embargo of that commodity to the United States and the Netherlands in 1973, so did the grain multinationals evade the U.S. wheat embargo of the Soviet Union after the invasion of Afghanistan. Finally, many countries in the region have diversified their sources of food. As Table 8.4 shows, relatively few countries depend heavily on the United States (the only potential embargoer).

Nevertheless, heavy reliance on food imports undeniably carries political risks. Two Arab countries purchase at least 20 percent of their total food supply from the United States: Egypt (25 percent) and Morocco (20 percent). Furthermore, for highly strategic *wheat* supplies the percentage is even higher in some cases: Egypt gets nearly 50 percent of all its wheat and wheat flour from the United States. Clearly, a cut-off of U.S. wheat to Egypt would be catastrophic; the small size of the country relative to the world market implies that the U.S. farm lobby would be less opposed to a politically motivated boycott there than to a similar action against the much larger Soviet Union. Second, giving food aid is commonly thought to be a more effective political instrument for the supplier than is withholding.[36] The United States has extended food aid as part of "policy packages," in which the recipient makes concessions to U.S. strategic interests; for example, the Camp David Accords could be interpreted in this light.

TABLE 8.4
Proportion of Total Agricultural Imports Coming from the United States, 1983

Country	Imports (As percentage of total agricultural imports)
Algeria	8.1
Bahrain	4.8
Egypt	25.0
Iran	<1.0
Iraq	11.8
Israel	34.0
Jordan	14.4
Kuwait	4.4
Lebanon	9.2
Libya	4.0
Morocco	20.3
North Yemen	9.1
Oman	2.6
Qatar	3.1
Saudi Arabia	7.0
South Yemen	<1.0
Syria	3.0
Tunisia	16.8
Turkey	15.2
United Arab Emirates	4.5

Source: U.S. Department of Agriculture

The potential for future leverage of the United States over Arab food importers thus constitutes an additional set of uncertainties. The "food weapon" is the stronger, the tighter the market for foodgrains. A conjuncture of increased food prices with a political situation pitting some set of Arab regimes against U.S. policy could make this weapon more potent in the future than it was during the 1970s. My own guess is that such a conjuncture is relatively unlikely, but it is certainly one of the most dangerous possibilities for Arab states.

Investment Policies

Whatever the risks of relying on imports, few countries anywhere are willing to rely exclusively on comparative advantage and market forces in their food systems. Not surprisingly, therefore, state reactions to the imbalance of domestic supply of and demand for food have included changes in investment and technological policies and changes in price policies. Although such policy shifts have contributed to domestic supply growth, all too often

TABLE 8.5
Share of Agriculture in Public Investment, According to Development Plans, 1975-80

Country	Share (as percentage)
South Yemen	35.0
Syria	23.9
Iraq	23.6
Sudan	22.6
Libya	17.6
Morocco	16.3
North Yemen	14.2
Tunisia	11.9
Algeria	11.0
Jordan	5.2
Egypt	3.5
Saudi Arabia	0.9

Source: Yusif A. Sayigh, The Arab Economy: Past Performance and Future Prospects (New York: Oxford University Press, 1982), p. 116.

they have also either ignored the mass of rural producers or have been made at the expense of the long-term viability of agricultural production. As during the period of land reform, state action, by favoring some and disfavoring others, contributes to peasant differentiation and class formation. The consequences of such social changes, occurring in response to policies adopted to reduce the food gap, create additional uncertainties for assessing the future state of agriculture and rural society in the region during the next ten years.

As is so common in the LDCs, agricultural investment has suffered from relative neglect in MENA (Table 8.5).[37] It is likely that agriculture will require large sums in the future, since the need to expand irrigation will probably raise the incremental capital-to-output ratio. Some governments have recognized this problem during the past five years. For example, Saudi Arabia has made a major effort to expand domestic food production; agricultural project loans in 1982 exceeded $1.18 billion. Algeria has recently reoriented its investment priorities toward its woefully lagging agricultural sector. But many countries have done relatively little.

The principal future uncertainties here are whether more governments will recognize the need to accelerate agricultural investment (reasonably likely, given the growing food gap) and how the particular pattern of investments will shape rural society and long-run agro-ecological viability. Existing investment projects are commonly marred by a bias in favor of those farmers who are already relatively well-off. Such favoritism has both political and administrative roots and is reinforced by the "food security" fear. The governments' main concern is to increase production. Whether in their investments in irrigation, in input subsidies, and/or in the promotion of specialty crops and livestock, governments believe that a "wager on the strong" is the way to close the food gap. Even if such responses accelerate the growth of production, the Middle East and North Africa may run the risk of replicating the Latin American experience: rapid agricultural output growth coupled with expanding rural poverty. This may be an expected consequence of the underlying distribution of property and power in both regions. The political and social consequences of such developments bear careful monitoring.

Consider the experience of irrigation expansion. Given the link between irrigation and increased yields, governments understandably push irrigation as the solution to the food gap. Two kinds of inequalities have been exacerbated by such policies, within irrigated areas and between irrigated and non-irrigated areas. MENA experience with respect to the irrigated areas themselves has often resembled that of northern Mexico from 1940 to 1960: when irrigation is introduced or expanded in an already highly dualistic agrarian system, the existing inequalities in the irrigated areas are reinforced.[38]

The concentration on irrigation has too often implied neglect of the rain-fed areas, where usually some 80 percent of the rural population live. The lack of knowledge of how to raise productivity and incomes under such conditions contributes to this neglect. It is by now widely realized that a "farming systems" approach is essential to designing successful small-farmer projects in dry areas. But such an approach requires slow, patient accumulation of considerable socioeconomic data. Recommendations may run against powerful rural social groups' interests (e.g., if small farmers have more and better livestock, their family members may insist on higher wages for work on nearby large farms). Government engineers can rightly argue that they *know* how to build a dam, and although the evidence in favor of small-farmer, farm systems projects accumulates, the engineers' case typically persuades the planning ministry. Professional training and inclination thus reinforce political biases in shaping investment programs.

The long-run ecological and sociopolitical consequences of the relative neglect of the rain-fed sector constitute an additional uncertainty. The demand for livestock products is growing extremely rapidly; the very large majority of such products is produced by small farmers under rain-fed conditions. Government promotion of feed-lot operations (so far the main response to soaring livestock product demand) may neglect an important, long-run resource. The relative lack of adequate small-farmer projects also contributes to the rural exodus (with its attendant social and political strains) and to the ecological destruction (especially deforestation) which is undermining irrigation systems in both Tunisia and Morocco. Implementing recommendations to increase the supply of fodder crops like sorghum and barley, which are usually grown under rain-fed conditions, will require greater use of the farm systems approach.[39] Although the numbers of people involved as well as the need to maintain existing irrigation systems and to increase domestic fodder supplies suggest increasing the emphasis given to raising the productivity of small farmers in rain-fed areas, so far little has been done.

Ecological dilemmas and uncertainties are not limited to the rain-fed areas. Some of the attempts to expand production via irrigation have also had unfortunate ecological consequences. Too often in recent experience, output now has been "purchased" at the expense of output in the future.[40] Of course, this phenomenon is hardly limited to MENA or indeed to the LDCs. But the problem is acute. Salinity plagues much of Egyptian and Syrian land because adequate drainage was not provided when irrigation was expanded. Despite ten years of effort and substantial funding from the World Bank, a majority of Egyptian land still suffers from some degree of salinity. Libyan and Saudi Arabian agricultural expansion has been criticized as "water-mining" agriculture. In some areas of the Gafara coastal plain in Libya, the water table has fallen at a rate of five meters per year; many hydraulic scientists believe that the coastal resources are now at serious risk due to excessively rapid expansion of well irrigation.[41] Consideration of such factors highlights some additional uncertainties surrounding agricultural performance during the next ten years. Many Middle East agro-ecologies are rather fragile; they will be abused at the peril of future productivity.

Price Policies

Additional uncertainties surround governments' pricing policies. Some believe that government output pricing policies are *the* cause of the food gap. The argument holds that if only governments could "get the prices right," specifically, permit cereal prices to rise to international levels, the food gap would shrink dramatically. Although current pricing policies do indeed introduce significant distortions into many agricultural sectors in the region, correcting such biases will provide no panacea for agrarian problems. It remains to be demonstrated that *agricultural output as a whole* is elastic with respect to price: most of the relatively scarce studies of aggregate agricultural supply response to shifts in the terms of trade find elasticities of around 0.2 or 0.3. Individual crops are indeed highly responsive, but the case for sectoral output is much less persuasive.[42]

But the reallocation of crops is a serious problem in its own right. In Tunisia, where nominal protection coefficients for cereals are less than 1.0, but those for livestock products, fruits, and vegetables are above 1.0, it is not surprising to find sluggish growth of cereal output. Similarly, Egypt now devotes nearly 25 percent of its extremely scarce land to growing fodder for animals. Saudi Arabia pays farmers at least six times the international price for wheat; not surprisingly, they now have a wheat surplus. But at the same time, the barley area has declined and therefore animal feed imports have soared.

These policies may simply accelerate a trend which we might expect anyway. After all, as incomes rise and demand shifts increasingly to high-value crops, farmers might be expected to shift into "semi-tradables" like fresh fruit, vegetables, and livestock products, whose prices are likely to rise faster than cereal prices under free-trade conditions.[43] An uncertainty here, then, would be whether governments will permit such developments, or whether they will try to promote cereal production through subsidies.

Oil revenues have played a critical role here. At the same time as the food gap grew, taxing agriculture via price policies became less essential for providing funds for accumulation or for providing adequate food supplies for the cities. Consequently, governments that worried about food security modified their policies. This is clear in Egypt, Saudi Arabia, Jordan, and Syria. In all of these countries the farmers' tax burden has declined; in the last three, farmers now receive prices above international levels. Yet so far, both Jordan and Syria remain heavily dependent on food imports. Price policy reforms could ameliorate the food gap in cereals, but such changes are no panacea for the food gap facing Arab states.

Conclusion

The future of Arab agriculture is murky. It is probably safe to assume that for the foreseeable future demand will continue to outrun domestic supply in most countries. Very large food imports will be necessary if standards of consumption are to continue to rise. This situation is probably not an unduly heavy burden to oil-exporting countries, unless, of course, the international price of oil collapses. Labor-exporting countries face a more uncertain situation, given the historic instability of remittances. Adjusting to a reduction in remittances would be difficult, especially for countries like the Yemen Arab Republic, with very limited alternative export potential. Finally, the non-oil Arab countries of Africa face the most severe problems of financing future food imports. These countries have recently faced dramatically unfavorable conjunctures of bad weather; policies disfavoring agriculture; adverse movements in their terms of trade; and sluggishly growing, increasingly protectionist export markets. Their situation is already quite serious, and could easily become worse.

Apocalypse is always possible. The areas of "potential disaster" include collapse of the international price of oil, continued or still-worsening drought in Africa, continued slow growth in the world economy and increasing protectionism, and persistence of government policies which impede agricultural growth. No one knows the probabilities attached to any of these outcomes; I would guess that bad weather and poor growth in the world economy may be somewhat more likely than an oil price collapse. Policy reforms are already underway in many countries; their sustainability, however, is crucially dependent on alternative, non-agricultural sources of public revenues. If the Arab oil exporters continue to enjoy substantial revenues, they may be able to continue to underwrite the food imports for their poorer relations. Unless they wish to see regime changes, they will have little choice but to do so.

Despite such dire possibilities, great disasters are mercifully the exception in economic life. "Muddling through" seems much the most likely outcome. Despite the growing food gap, Arab governments are likely to find some way to finance imports. At the same time, they may have little choice but to redirect investments and energies toward the agricultural sectors of their economies. Given the current pattern of the distribution of assets, successful promotion of agricultural output growth is likely to accelerate social differentiation within the rural population. Such social change will probably have important political and economic consequences, but they are almost impossible to predict. Experience in the region and elsewhere indicates that such processes are highly heterogeneous, characterized by many reversals, unexpected contradictions, and unforeseen results. Few predicted the tumultuous events of the decade of the oil price revolution. It is unlikely that in pondering the future of agriculture we will do any better.

Notes

1. Those of the Arab Organization for Agricultural Development (AOAD), the Food and Agricultural Organization of the UN (FAO), and the International Food Policy Research Institute (IFPRI): Ahmad Goueli, *Future of the Food Economy in the Arab Countries* (Khartoum: AOAD, 1979) (in Arabic); FAO, *Agriculture: Toward 2000* (Rome: FAO, 1981); Nabil Khaldi, *Evolving Food Gaps in the Middle East/North Africa: Prospects and Policy Implications* (Washington, DC: IFPRI, December 1984).

2. See "Middle East and North Africa: Outlook and Situation Report," (Washington, DC: USDA, Economic Research Service, RS-84-3, April 1984).

3. The formula is $D = N + Ye$, where $D =$ the growth of demand; $N =$ population growth rate; $Y =$ rate of growth of per capita incomes; and $e =$ the income elasticity of demand. Cf. John Mellor and Bruce F. Johnston, "The World Food Equation: Interrelations Among Development, Employment, and Food Consumption," *Journal of Economic Literature* 22 (June 1984): 531–74.

4. World Bank, *World Development Report, 1984* (Washington, DC: World Bank, 1985).

5. Female illiteracy is above 50 percent in many countries. See, among many others, M. Riad el-Ghonemy, *Economic Growth, Income Distribution, and Rural Poverty in the Near East* (Rome: FAO, September 1984), and World Bank, *World Development Report, 1984*.

6. See el-Ghonemy, *Economic Growth, Income Distribution, and Rural Poverty*. Few Arab countries have been among the top performers among LDCs in increasing longevity or in reducing illiteracy. See the comparative analysis of 100 LDCs in Amartya Sen, "Public Action and the Quality of Life in Developing Countries," *Oxford Bulletin of Economics and Statistics* 43, no. 4 (November 1981): 287–319. Only Tunisia and Jordan ranked among the top one third of LDCs by his measurement of improvement.

7. For example, Khaldi assumes income growth of 5.4 percent per year.

8. More skilled workers more often have their families with them, reducing the incentive to remit. See Ismail Serageldin, et al., *Manpower and International Labor Migration in the Middle East and North Africa* (Washington, DC: World Bank, 1981).

9. John W. Mellor, "Food Prospects for the Developing Countries," *American Economic Review* 73, no. 2 (May 1983). Khaldi argues that population growth is the main source of demand growth for "non-oil, non-labor exporting" countries, while income growth is more important for oil exporters and for labor exporters.

10. For example, Yemenis and Sudanese shifted away from sorghum and millet, North Africans away from *couscous* made from durum wheat, and rural Egyptians away from maize flour; all replaced these local foodstuffs with wheat flour and bread.

11. World Bank, *World Development Report, 1983* (Washington, DC: World Bank, 1984).

12. John Mellor, "Food Prospects for the Developing Countries."

13. Aggregate data conceal wide differences among countries and among crops. Using FAO data, we find that the output of "luxury" foods such as fruits, vegetables, poultry, and livestock products has usually increased more rapidly than wheat, the staple cereal of the region. Note also that for several countries, food production per capita has declined while *agricultural* production has increased; these countries have pursued a "food last" strategy. This underscores the important question of long-run comparative advantage and paying for food imports; it is quite sensible for Egypt to concentrate on cotton production for export, rather than on trying to grow its own food (clearly impossible in any case). The risks inherent in such a strategy are considered below.

14. J. Mellor, "Food Prospects for the Developing Countries."

15. Khaldi, *Evolving Food Gaps in the Middle East/North Africa*, p. 27.

16. Personal communication, Prof. Michael Watts, Geography Department, University of California, Berkeley. See, e.g., A. Biswaf, ed., *Climatic Constraints and Human Activities* (Chicago, IL: Chicago University Press, 1981).

17. See the evidence marshaled in el-Ghonemy, *Economic Growth, Income Distribution, and Rural Poverty*.

18. Bruce Johnston and Peter Kilby, *Agriculture and Structural Transformation: Economic Strategies for Late-Developing Countries* (London and New York: Oxford University Press, 1975); Alain de Janvry, *The Agrarian Question and Reformism in Latin America* (Baltimore, MD and London: The Johns Hopkins University Press, 1981).

19. That is, the diffusion of individualistic tenure forms before the ratio of population to cultivated area had created conditions favorable to such institutional change.

20. World Bank, *Morocco: Economic and Social Development Report* (Washington, DC: World Bank, 1981).

21. World Bank, *Land Reform: A Sector Policy Paper* (Washington, DC: World Bank, 1975). Landlessness is by now less prevalent, largely as the result of migration patterns stimulated by the oil boom.

22. See, e.g., Richard Adams, *Growth Without Development in Rural Egypt: A Local-Level Study of Institutional and Social Change* (Ph.D. dissertation, University of California, Berkeley, 1981).

23. Cf. argument of David Lehmann, "After Chayanov and Lenin: New Paths of Agrarian Capitalism," *Journal of Development Economics* 11 (1982): 133–61.

24. Whether the actual result was an increase in investment is debatable. See, e.g., Bent Hansen and Karim Nashashibi, *Foreign Trade Regimes and Economic Development: Egypt* (New York: Columbia University Press, 1975).

25. On the concept of macroprices (i.e., wages, interest rates, foreign exchange rates, and the rural-urban terms of trade), see C. Peter Timmer, *et al.*, *The Choice*

of *Technology in Developing Countries: Some Cautionary Tales* (Cambridge, MA: Center for International Affairs, Harvard University, 1975). On the Egyptian case, see my review article, "Ten Years of *Infitah*: Class, Rent, and Policy Stasis in Egypt," *Journal of Development Studies* 20, no. 4 (July 1984), and the literature cited therein.

26. See, e.g., Shakar N. Acharya, "Incentives for Resource Allocation: A Case Study of Sudan," World Bank Staff Working Paper No. 367 (December 1979).

27. Turkey, whose agricultural performance has been among the best in the Middle Eastern region in the past generation, illustrates this point. There, abundant non-agricultural sources of funds (U.S. aid in the 1950s and workers' remittances in the 1960s) and peasant political leverage joined to create a favorable policy environment for the only agricultural sector of the region to generate net grain exports.

28. The phrase is that of Jahangir Amouzegar, "Oil Wealth: A Very Mixed Blessing," *Foreign Affairs*, 60 (April 1982): 814–35. A fuller analysis is available in his *Oil Exporters' Economic Development in an Interdependent World* (IMF Occasional Paper 18, April 1983).

29. See, among others, Sweder van Wijnbergen, "The Dutch Disease: A Disease After All?" *Economic Journal* 94 (March 1984): 41–55; indeed, some authors (e.g., Gelb) define the real exchange rate as the relative price of tradables to nontradables. Alan Gelb, "Capital Importing Oil Exporters: Adjustment Issues and Policy Choices," World Bank Staff Working Paper No. 475 (August 1981).

30. Tradables are supplied perfectly elastically to a "small country," while the elasticity of supply of nontradables such as construction is much smaller.

31. This is consistent with the argument of Robert Bates, *Markets and States in Tropical Africa* (Berkeley and Los Angeles: University of California Press, 1981); see also van Wijnbergen, "The Dutch Disease." The question whether such growth rates are ecologically sustainable will be taken up below.

32. See, e.g., Grant M. Scobie, *Food Subsidies in Egypt: Their Impact on Foreign Exchange and Trade*, Research Report No. 40 (Washington, DC: IFPRI, August 1983).

33. This is relatively unlikely because the North American wheat belt runs North–South while most climatic problems occur within a fairly narrow band of latitude. See Philip M. Raup, "Some Domestic Consequences of the Expanded Role of the United States in Meeting World Food Needs," in Kenneth C. Nobe and Rajan K. Sampath, eds., *Issues in Third World Development* (Boulder, CO and London: Westview Press, 1983).

34. Sudan, for example, lost approximately 1.5 percent of total 1970 GDP due to a decline in its terms of trade during the past decade. World Bank, *Toward Sustained Development: A Joint Program of Action for Sub-Saharan Africa* (Washington, DC: World Bank, August 1984).

35. Morocco's debt was roughly $12 billion and Sudan's about $8 billion in 1984. Although this seems small compared to Brazil's more than $90 billion, Morocco's debt/GDP ratio was nearly 80 percent before rescheduling, while Brazil's ratio was about 33 percent.

36. Mitchel B. Wallerstein, *Food for War—Food for Peace: United States Food Aid in a Global Context* (Cambridge, MA: MIT Press, 1980) and Robert M. Hathaway, "Food Power," *Foreign Service Journal* (December 1983): 24–29.

37. Raj Krishna, "Some Aspects of Agricultural Growth, Price Policy, and Equity in Developing Countries," *Food Research Institute Studies*, 28, no. 3 (1982) has argued that agriculture should get at least 20 percent of public investment.

38. See, e.g., Cynthia Hewitt de Alcantara, *Modernizing Mexican Agriculture: Socio-economic Implications of Technological Change, 1940-1970* (Geneva: United Nations Research Institute for Social Development Report No. 76.5, 1976).

39. See the recommendation in Khaldi, *Evolving Food Gaps in the Middle East/ North Africa*. At the International Center for Agricultural Research on Dry Areas (ICARDA), for example, it has been found that Syrian farmers in the drier zones will not harvest higher-yielding varieties of barley unless they are also assured of an adequate supply of roughage for their sheep. This helped to account for the difficulties in diffusing a yield-increasing technology. Thomas L. Nordblom, "Livestock–Crop Interactions: The Decision to Harvest or to Graze Mature Grain Crops," Discussion Paper No. 10 (Aleppo, Syria: ICARDA, May 1983).

40. For countries such as Egypt, this problem has a history of nearly 100 years. See my *Egypt's Agricultural Development, 1800–1980* (Boulder, CO and London: Westview Press, 1982).

41. J.A. Allan, *Libya: The Experience of Oil* (London and Boulder, CO: Croom Helm and Westview Press, 1981).

42. See Raj Krishna for the general argument; for a specific, detailed study, see Joachim von Braun and Hartwig de Haen, *The Effects of Food Price and Subsidy Policies on Egyptian Agriculture*, Research Report No. 42 (Washington, DC: IFPRI, November 1983). They show that permitting all prices to move to international levels would likely lead to a *reduction* in Egyptian wheat production, given the strong "comparative disadvantage" which Egypt faced in that crop.

43. This may be conceived as part of the "Dutch Disease" phenomenon, in which the agricultural sector itself is disaggregated by "degree of tradability."

9

The Prospects of Technological Growth in Arab Societies: An Analysis of the Potential for Progress Toward Technological Autonomy in the Arab World, 1985–95

Michael J. Simpson

For a developing country seeking to attain an advanced level of technology, there are four key requirements. The first is a social force—a class or elite—capable of identifying realistic technological goals and organizing the human and material resources of the country to achieve them. The second is the attainment of a critical mass of scientists and technically skilled manpower to generate and sustain the level of technology desired. Third, the country must possess, or have easy access to, sufficient resources, in the form of raw materials or capital, to ensure that technological progress is not prevented by the absence of raw materials or capital inputs alone. A final prerequisite is the existence of a market for the products of advanced technology.

Among countries that have attained an advanced level of technology to date, the driving social force has not been identical in each case. The basic paths have been those taken by capitalist and socialist countries, although there have been differences among countries within each of the two categories. In the capitalist countries, the entrepreneurial and corporate class has played the major role, with varying kinds and amounts of support from the state. On the whole, the importance of the state role has differed according to the historical period and the ranking of the country in the world system of states: the usual tendency has been for the state to be more active in the twentieth century than earlier, and more active in countries catching up with economic leaders than in those at the forefront. In socialist countries, on the other hand, the elimination of private entrepreneurialism has made the development of technology entirely the province of the state and, consequently, oriented toward state objectives (national infrastructure, heavy industry, military requirements, and the provision of basic necessities for the population).

Despite the difference in the driving force between the two systems, an analysis of their development suggests that some common commitments and forms of organization have been adopted by the elites or classes that have been responsible for technological progress in each case. These include:

1. *Strong commitments* of material resources to the development of technology. These arise from a perceived interest by the elite or class in this kind of development. In the private sector of capitalist countries, this has basically been an interest in high revenues and profits, and in establishing, maintaining, or improving the market position of companies. Among state elites, the perceived interests tend to be crucial state objectives, which may range from survival to the attainment of greater regional or international stature.

2. *Effective coordination* with the groups in society which possess scientific and technological knowledge, in cases where these groups are not already part of the dominant class or elite. Societies in which there are strong social barriers between economic and political elites, on one hand, and groups skilled in science and technology, on the other, or in which scientific activity is stifled or unsupported by political elites with little knowledge of what it entails are less likely to achieve favorable results.

Without the presence of an organizing social force, the existence of skilled manpower, resources, and an adequate level of demand does not in and of itself guarantee rapid technological development. Historically, it has not been uncommon for countries to possess rich natural resources which are unexploited or are exported abroad to be processed for industrial purposes. A population may also have large amounts of material capital that are not used for technological purposes at all. In relatively poor countries, there may be reserves of skilled manpower which are not used for technological development, but migrate elsewhere as part of the brain drain. In most Third World countries, there exists a demand for industrial products which is met through a dependence upon imported industrial goods from the West and not by local efforts.

The Missing Combination

For advanced technological development to take place, it is important that there exist a combination of all four factors—the social force, manpower, resources, and demand. The principal difficulty facing the Arab world arises from the general absence of this *combination* of prerequisites.

We can address the problems of Arab technological development on either of two levels: the pan-Arab level, which deals with the Arab world as a whole, or the level of the individual state. In each case, there are major obstacles to technological development. If we consider the Arab world as a whole, it is well-endowed with capital and at least some important resources. Recent educational developments, moreover, have given it a pool of educated and skilled manpower that is now substantial. It is also an important world market for the commodities produced by industrialized countries. Because of the lack of political or economic unity, however, no social force exists that is capable of organizing these resources toward common technological goals.

If, on the other hand, the Arab world is examined at the level of the individual Arab state, not one combines all the factors mentioned. Egypt, which has the most advanced pool of manpower and the most developed (although imperfect) system of promotion of science and technology, is lacking in resources. Elsewhere, even when lack of resources is not the fundamental problem, there is a lack of a critical mass of scientific and technological manpower and of effective commitments and organization by economic or political elites.

In Arab countries where the economy is based strongly on private enterprise, there is only a weak industrializing entrepreneurial class, and a problem exists of inadequate commitment of private investment to economic sectors in which indigenous technological development can take place. A principal reason for this lies in the structure of opportunities for profit that has been created by the role of the Arab countries in the world economic system, and particularly by the greatly increased inflow of oil revenues, following the rapid price rises of the 1970s. The result has been major opportunities for profits in construction, finance, real estate, services, and import trade. The latter is particularly important in the Arab world, where the value of imports and exports as a proportion of GDP is higher than that of any other region in the world.[1]

Dependence on imported technology is at present built into the economic structure of Arab countries, and the import of manufactured commodities is often so profitable in countries with private enterprise that serious problems confront attempts to escape dependency. By the early 1980s, about $100 billion worth of industrial goods were imported annually into the Arab world. For business groups with capital to invest that are considering ways of meeting this demand, the question is likely to be whether more profit is to be obtained from attempting to import foreign technological products into the Arab world or from the development of a local industry competing with these products. Although there has been an increase in local Arab industrial investment, a number of considerations have weighed heavily in favor of the course of seeking profits from the import of industrial goods or other business ventures. Industrial products, especially where the technology needed to create them is relatively sophisticated, require long-term investments. They also lack the quick return of trade deals and some alternative means of investment, such as real estate. If they are import substitutes, they are often competing with the established products of strong and stable manufacturing companies, and the proposed local enterprise may fail because of this international competition. Moreover, in an area of the world where fears of political instability are strong among investors, an investment in plant and machinery that may easily be expropriated by a radical government in the future is an unattractive proposition. Indeed, it has been common to export to the West profits from current financial, trade, and real estate deals as a safeguard against future governmental policies.

Arab business groups with a strong stake in continued imports have proliferated, because of the share of the approximately $100 billion worth of imports that accrues to them in profits as agents for foreign companies.[2] In the day-to-day business of promoting these products to local consumers and government departments, they constitute a source of regular pressure on governments and consumers to purchase products derived from foreign technology. There is no equivalent strong source of pressure promoting products based on the development of local technology. The result is an economic system structured in such a way that foreign technology is strongly promoted and, with few exceptions, local technology is not.

Even in countries with a freely operating private sector, a major role in the promotion of technology devolves upon the state because of the weakness of the private sector in this field. In those countries where the private sector is restricted in any case for political reasons, the state is already responsible for organizing technological development. In neither type of country, however, have state elites been able to create an organizational system for the promotion of science and technology that is likely to lead to major breakthroughs or rapid progress toward technological autonomy. One important reason seems to be the weakness of the links between political elites and scientific communities. A second reason may be that technological development is not regarded by state elites as central to their attempts to build up regional influence, which currently depend heavily upon factors such as military strength, the ability to disburse foreign aid (for countries with oil wealth), or the promotion of political beliefs which appeal to significant constituencies throughout the Arab world.

A key indicator of a state's efforts in the field of science and technology is its commitment to research and experimental development. The latest available statistics show these commitments to be generally weak in the Arab world. Table 9.1 shows, in fact, that as a proportion of GNP, the commitment of the Arab world in 1980 was lower than that of any world region. The absolute total spent by the Arab world is less than a third that of Latin America. Some Arab countries, such as Egypt and Iraq, had somewhat higher proportional commitments than the average in the late 1970s—about 0.9 percent of GNP for Egypt and 0.7 percent for Iraq.[3] Despite this, the absolute totals spent in each case represent only a modest investment in research.

Because of the great difficulty faced by developing countries in closing the gap between them and developed countries with large technological establishments and great resources to invest in further development, the assigning of a top priority to scientific and technological development is needed for a successful effort. In countries where the state is officially committed to active sponsorship of science and technology, one indicator of such a commitment is the designation of responsibilities at the cabinet

TABLE 9.1
Commitments to Scientific and Technological Research and Experimental Development in Different World Regions, 1970-80

Region or Type of Country	Expenditure (in millions of dollars) 1970	1975	1980	Expenditure (as percentage of GNP) 1970	1975	1980	Research and Development Scientists and Engineers (per million persons) 1970	1975	1980
World total	$62,101	$113,815	$207,801	2.04	1.87	1.78	790	803	847
Developed countries	60,677	109,330	195,377	2.36	2.25	2.24	2,290	2,696	2,954
Developing countries	1,424	4,485	12,424	0.30	0.36	0.43	81	101	125
Arab states	115	334	1,027	0.31	0.23	0.27	123	165	207
Africa (excluding Arab states)	105	300	698	0.33	0.35	0.36	29	43	52
Asia (excluding Arab states)	4,540	12,304	30,661	1.02	1.08	1.18	225	270	284
Europe	15,739	36,455	70,649	1.70	1.78	1.79	1,253	1,552	1,743
Latin America	498	1,686	3,745	0.30	0.44	0.49	136	181	253
North America	27,620	38,382	66,646	2.59	2.26	2.23	2,521	2,369	2,677
U.S.S.R.	12,987	23,194	32,421	4.04	4.79	4.67	3,882	4,809	5,172

Source: UNESCO, Statistical Yearbook, 1984 (Paris: UNESCO, 1984), pp. V-27, V-28.

level for the promotion of science and technology. In one case, that of India, for example, there were four ministries by the late 1970s that were exclusively or overwhelmingly devoted to scientific and technological development.[4] In contrast, by the end of 1982, only four Arab countries (Algeria, Egypt, Iraq, and Tunisia) had ministries of technology. In all four cases this ministry was still combined with the Ministry of Higher Education, rather than being a separate body.

A further problem arises in the organizational system of Arab states for the advancement of science and technology. State-organized technology requires the establishment of coordinating bodies responsible for overseeing and guiding research in different areas of science and establishing links with the various clients for technology (e.g., in industry or in agriculture) to ensure the practical applicability of the research. The objective is to establish an effective "research triangle" linking governments, universities, and enterprises. The Arab world is generally deficient in such bodies. Only Egypt has policy making or coordinating bodies for most of the relevant fields of scientific research that have been in existence for ten years or more. Despite the fact that the Egyptian system of organization of science and technology is comparatively advanced for the region, a number of defects in it have been pointed out by a recent study which compares the Egyptian organization of science and technology with those of a number of other developing countries, including some, such as South Korea, Brazil, and India, which have made important technological advances. The study finds major problems in Egypt to be lack of finance, weak communications and coordination between industry and the scientific community, and lack of a clear direction and effective control by the official science-policy making bodies.[5] Such problems are also likely to be acute in other Arab countries, which all have systems for the promotion of science and technology that are less developed than that of Egypt.

In a recent analysis, a leading Arab expert on science and technology, A.B. Zahlan, has underlined some of the problems that are general in the relationship between state elites and the scientific community.

> During the past three decades, enormous personal effort has been deployed by fairly large numbers of Arab scientists. Many have willingly given up their professional occupations to work on applied problems, to administer national research centres or to staff SPMBs [Science-Policy Making Bodies]. It is my observation that it has been the rule, rather than the exception, to find competent scientists and mathematicians who are willing and capable to apply themselves to practical problems. One would be ill-advised to seek the causes of the present situation in the professional chauvinism of scientists or in their lack of concern for their societies . . .
>
> A political leadership that is deeply committed to a scientific culture could provide an alternative basis for sound development planning . . .
>
> The absence of an established scientific tradition in the Arab world, the dependence of decision makers on a small number of technical advisors, the ease with which individuals arrogate to themselves paramount roles, the insecurity of power and the ease with which ill-qualified individuals can

progress to the top of a party machinery, the forced politicisation of professionals and thus their reduction to serving as rubber stamps, and the ease with which intellectuals, scholars and independent opinions can be terrorised into silence, have virtually paralysed the so-called STS—science and technology system—laboriously constructed on paper. . . .[6]

In the 1970s, almost all Arab countries launched or developed bodies for science-policy making or for the coordination of various kinds of scientific research. The problems described by Zahlan are not, however, resolved simply by the establishment of institutions, but require considerable changes in the relationships of state elites to scientific communities. These would include a greater receptiveness by states to proposals by groups of highly-skilled scientists with a realistic sense of the practical applications of existing or possible research work, respect and support for the operational autonomy of the scientific community, and sponsorship through state initiatives or incentives of closer links between the scientific community and industrial and agricultural clients for its research. Without such commitments, it is unrealistic to expect major state-sponsored technological progess.

The Next Decade: Three Scenarios

What, then, are the prospects for Arab science and technology in the next decade? An objective declared by states and receiving overwhelming support from public opinion is progress toward technological autonomy, which we shall treat here as a situation in which the Arab world has the indigenous capacity to satisfy most of its material needs. In this situation, it would be able to manufacture a significant portion of the industrial and agricultural products which it consumes or uses and to construct a substantial number of machines with which to produce them; to process its important raw materials without great foreign assistance; and, in the health sphere, to spread modern health technology through the population and to research, prevent, treat, and eradicate local diseases through the efforts of Arab personnel.

The first and most optimistic scenario would see breakthroughs in achieving technological targets that have long been an objective of some Arab countries: large-scale production of steel; major advances in the manufacture of industrial motors and machinery, chemicals, and a wide variety of light industrial products; substantial substitution of local crops and produce for imported agricultural products; and a major reduction through local efforts of some of the diseases and health hazards that are endemic to Middle Eastern countries.

A second scenario envisages some progress without major breakthroughs. Overall industrial production would improve, with the development of the petrochemical, steel, cement, fertilizer, and textile industries and the establishment of a moderate capacity in other products, not to an extent that would put the Arab countries firmly on the industrial map of the world. Some improvement in agricultural production would take place, and, in the field of public health, some inroads into disease rates would be made, but without a dramatic alteration in the existing situation. Great dependency on Western industrial products would remain.

The third scenario is the stark one of general stagnation, and even regression in some areas: failure to increase industrial production, or reduction in output of a number of industries because they are uneconomical to run; lack of improvement or falling off in agricultural output; and an inability of existing health systems to keep up with the health problems of a rapidly growing population. Dependence on more advanced foreign countries for industrial products would be almost total. In this scenario, the Arab world would appear to have the inescapable destiny of being no more than a supplier of minerals and raw materials for an international economic system that might not always need them.

My argument will be that the second scenario—that of some progress—is the most plausible to envisage for most of the Arab world in the next ten years. One basic reason for this is the effect of the rapid development of skilled manpower as a result of the very strong investment in human capital that has been made by almost all Arab countries in the last two decades. A second reason, despite the weakness of Arab entrepreneurialism in technology-related areas, is the a relatively high existing level of capital for investment in the Arab world, where there exist both oil revenues and a trickle-down movement of oil money to countries that are not oil-rich—a movement that can be expected to continue even in the event of a moderate decline in oil prices. Because of these factors, the most pessimistic scenario is not likely to materialize in the majority of Arab countries. On the other hand, the above discussion of the weakness of both state organization of technology and private entrepreneurial commitments to it suggests that there is no basis at present for the most optimistic scenario postulating major breakthroughs by 1995.

The Development of Manpower

One of the most important factors reducing the chances that the most pessimistic scenario will materialize is the rapid development of scientific and technological manpower in the Arab world. This has occurred at all levels: that of scientists capable of advanced research; that of university-trained practitioners of science working in applied fields (engineers, physicians, etc.); and that of technicians with lower levels of formal training, but with relevant applied skills, such as those obtained at vocational schools.

An important question arising from these developments is the extent to which they reflect not merely an increase in the number of pure and applied scientists, but the growth of scientific communities, with their own autonomous bodies, formal or informal systems of ranking the achievements of members, and a strong sense of a shared professional identity and commitment to the promotion of scientific culture in their countries. Unfortunately, these important groups have received much less attention than they merit, so that this kind of development cannot at present be addressed. Assessments of progress are dependent on a survey of available quantitative data, from which the broad outlines of educational changes can be derived.

At the highest level, that of scientists engaged in research and experimental development, the number more than doubled in the Arab world from 1970 to 1980, rising from about 15,000 to almost 34,000.[7] In most individual Arab countries, however, the number remains small, despite the increase.[8] Closely associated with this increase has been a growth in the number and scale of scientific research establishments specializing in subfields of science and technology relevant to a particular country (e.g., in that country's major agricultural crops or its most prominent local diseases). Although available information on these establishments is difficult to compare between countries because of different systems of classification of institutes engaging in research, Egypt has the highest number, and Iraq seems to have the second highest. In Egypt there are probably more than 70 enterprises and government agencies and institutions performing research and development activities.[9] The scope of research conducted includes the industrial, agricultural, medical, and other fields.

There has been a steady growth in other indicators of research productivity, such as local periodicals devoted to scientific or technological subjects, and articles from the Arab world published in professional journals indexed in international scientific bibliographies. In a period of about eight years (approximately 1972 to 1980), the number of periodicals rose by about 25 percent in seven countries that provide data to UNESCO (Algeria, Egypt, Jordan, Kuwait, Saudi Arabia, Sudan, and Tunisia).[10] During the 1970s, the number of articles from the Arab world indexed in international scientific bibliographies doubled.[11] However, the totals for individual countries are still low, and in almost all Arab countries, the range of research seems to cover only a minority of scientific subfields.[12]

A further problem is the small amount of postgraduate science education in the Arab world. This is particularly important because it is at the postgraduate level that research skills are developed. Indeed, some of the costs of the rapid expansion of scientific education at the bachelor's level have been developments that inhibit the preparation of students to conduct research, such as poor teacher–student ratios, which prevent individual attention from faculty to students, and laboratory and library facilities that cannot meet the demands being made of them. Recent statistics allow an assessment to be made of the extent of post-B.Sc. education in a number of Arab countries: Algeria, Egypt, Jordan, Kuwait, Lebanon, Qatar, Saudi Arabia, Sudan, Tunisia, and the Yemen Arab Republic. Of these, only Egypt appears to have a strong and extensive commitment to this kind of scientific education, with more than 10 percent of its students at the post-B.Sc. level.[13]

Table 9.2 illustrates the development of scientific and technological education in the Arab world at another level, focusing upon students obtaining university degrees in scientific subjects. It is clear that this number increased dramatically over the ten-year period until about 1981, rising from an annual

TABLE 9.2
Students Graduating in Scientific Subjects at the University and Equivalent Levels Within the Arab World, c. 1981 and 1971

	Number of Students	As Percentage of All Graduating Students	Number per 100,000 Population	Number of Students Graduating in Science and Technology Ten Years Earlier	10-Year Increase (ratio of later to earlier figure)
Algeria (1981)	3,545	45.4	18	649	5.5
Egypt (1981)	31,028	36.7	72	14,382	2.2
Iraq (1978-79, average)	9,600	45.2	74	2,915	3.3
Jordan (1982)	2,150	17.4	62	282	7.6
Kuwait (1982)	493	29.8	32	69	7.1
Lebanon (1981)	865	9.3	30	716	1.2
Libya (1978)	510	22.6	19	121	4.2
Morocco (1979)	636	14.1	3	176 (est.)	3.6
Saudi Arabia (1980)	1,350	16.5	16	125	10.8
Sudan (1981)	1,466	31.6	9	540	2.7
Syria (1981)	8,168	56.5	88	2,113	3.9
Tunisia (1982)	2,015	40.8	30	269	7.5
U.A.E. (1982)	80	13.4	10	0	--
North Yemen (1980)	17	4.5	1	0	--
South Yemen (1981)	151	20.3	7	0	--
All Arab world (1981 estimate)	64,000	33.5	40	24,000	2.7
Comparisons:					
Brazil (1980)	57,091	24.4	46	21,993	2.6
India (1978)	223,097	20.4	35	113,209	1.9
South Korea (1981)	53,387	44.2	140	20,520	2.6

Source: Computed from the statistics on education at the third level in UNESCO Statistical Yearbooks, 1970-75 and 1980-84.

The fields included in the table are natural sciences, mathematics, computer science, engineering, medical sciences, and agriculture. Due to some difference in reporting by governments, the statistics indicate approximate rather than absolute levels of attainment. The Lebanese statistics may be unreliable as a result of the war.

total of about 24,000 to about 64,000. Combining projections based on these trends with estimates made by Zahlan,[14] it can be estimated that there are currently about one million B.Sc.'s in the Arab world, and that this number should double by 1995.

Although one area of traditional weakness in the Arab world has been vocational training, there have also been important advances in this field in recent years. Between 1970 and 1981 (a period for which statistics are available for 16 Arab countries), the total number of students undertaking vocational training rose from about 350,000 to 1,030,000 in the Arab world as a whole. While more than two-thirds of these students are in Egypt, countries such as Iraq, Syria, and Tunisia also have made significant progress, with fourfold or greater increases during this 11-year period.

Changes are thus taking place in the Arab world that result in major increases in the pool of skilled scientific and technical manpower. At the pan-Arab level, the totals are impressive, although it should be borne in mind that the existing drive toward scientific and technological development is more realistically analyzed at the level of individual states. Scientific and technological development requires not only that a relatively high proportion of the population be trained in the required fields, but, if the development is to be extensive rather than consist of achievements in isolated fields, it requires a high critical mass of skilled manpower, which can be difficult for small states to achieve. If we examine the latest UNESCO Statistical Yearbook (that for 1984), for example, we find that among developing countries which have attained technological breakthroughs, there are especially high absolute numbers of scientifically and technically skilled persons: for India in 1977, 2,328,200; for China in 1980, 5,296,000; for South Korea in 1981, 2,025,639; and for Brazil in 1980, 6,870,828.[15] While these statistics are to be handled with particular caution because of different reporting procedures, Egypt appears to be the Arab country closest to this kind of total, though well behind it. The latest statistics on this kind of manpower in other Arab countries date mostly from the early 1970s, but they fall far short of the levels that were registered at that time by the developing countries referred to above. Indeed, apart from Egypt, no Arab country had the same level as the 80,000 total of scientific and technical personnel of Hong Kong in 1971.

While these statistics indicate that technologically ambitious development aims in the Arab world during its period of grand nationalistic aspirations two decades ago were unrealistic because of the small supply of skilled manpower, Table 9.2 suggests that the situation is changing. The increased scientific educational attainments offer the chance for at least moderate technological progress.

An obstacle to even more dramatic progress is the brain drain taking place from a number of Arab countries. Some Arab countries with high science educational attainments (see Table 9.2) also have standards of living that are well below those of the West and oil-rich countries. Although the brain drain problem was once mainly one of migration to the West of scientists with qualifications that were highly competitive internationally, the export of talented manpower from poorer to richer Arab countries now greatly exceeds the migration of skilled labor to the West. There is clearly a substantial number of cases where well-trained scientists leave productive scientific and technological occupations entirely for general managerial, administrative, sales, or service occupations in oil-rich countries, simply because even modest jobs in the latter fields offer much higher pay than university, secondary school, or government positions in the home countries.

Resources

Resources are the third key factor determining the chances of advanced technological development. Two kinds of resources are relevant to our consideration. First, there are natural resources that are marketable under current economic conditions or can be processed into marketable commodities. The nature of these resources will often strongly influence the kind of industrial technology a country acquires since a natural first step in industrialization is to process raw materials that are close at hand. The second kind of resource is capital that can be invested in projects that expand the technological capacities of the country.

Oil is by far the most important natural resource in the Arab world. The large reserves of oil are, nevertheless, concentrated in a few Arab states. While this provides them with major development opportunities, it leaves countries without oil with major problems of financing investments in technology. One example of a country under severe constraints of this nature is Egypt, where a large pool of skilled manpower has been built up and an organizational system has been created for the promotion of science and technology, but where attempts to utilize this manpower in major scientific and technological projects have often been frustrated by the lack of resources. A second, even poorer example is Sudan, which has great agricultural potential but is lacking in the resources to develop the communications and transportation systems necessary to exploit these resources.

While the oil-rich Arab countries have sufficient capital to invest in a variety of industrial projects, their basic thrust has been toward the development of oil-related industries. The results will be impressive in the coming decade, when they will manufacture a number of petrochemical products (e.g., ethylene glycol, low-density polyethylene, and methanol) in substantial quantities. The plants that have been constructed in the Arab world to manufacture these products incorporate state-of-the-art technology. The petrochemicals produced in the Arab world can be expected to have a major impact on the international market. Indeed the prospect of competition from plants in the Arab world has already caused considerable concern among, and moves toward protectionist measures by, European petrochemical industries. The technology required is, however, extremely sophisticated, and products from the Arab world will compete with those of countries that are highly economically developed, so that to maintain competitiveness, the Arab petrochemical industries will need to continue to rely on the most advanced technology in the field. Technological autonomy in this field is not a short- or medium-range prospect, although there will be a significant growth in Arab manpower capable of operating and maintaining petrochemical plants.

A number of oil-rich countries envisage important developments in other major industrial fields (steel, pharmaceuticals, motor vehicles), but it is generally too early to predict the outcome of these ventures.

In terms of capital, a number of countries that are not oil-rich have resources which, although slender, permit moderate progress in the coming decade. Some (e.g., Syria, Jordan, and Lebanon) have benefited from substantial remittances from their nationals who are working in oil-rich states, or from direct aid from those states. Even with a decline in oil prices, these revenues are likely to play a significant role in their economy in the coming decade.[16] In terms of natural resources, some countries that are not oil-rich (e.g., Morocco, Tunisia, and Jordan) have important phosphate reserves which are not only a source of capital through export, but can be used as an input in local fertilizer industries. Growth in a number of other industries also has taken place in the non-oil-producing countries in the last decade. In the latest period for which industrial statistics are generally available (1970 to 1982),[17] there were important increases in the production of steel in Egypt and of cement in Jordan, Morocco, Syria, and Tunisia. Further progress is likely in these fields and possibly in chemicals, textiles, and other light industries. Local scientists, technicians, and managers are likely to acquire knowledge and experience that represent an advance in Arab capacities, although dependence on foreign machinery and precision instruments will continue in the next decade.

As might be expected, the level of capital resources affects the chances not only of developing technology that can be used for modern industrial and agricultural purposes, but also of spreading medical technology. Although statistics are imperfect, those provided by recent editions of the United Nations *Demographic Yearbook* suggest that during the 1970s an increase in life expectancy of two to three years was not atypical for most Arab countries without major oil reserves and one of six to seven years was typical for those with major reserves. The least promising developments were for three of the poorest Arab countries, where the available statistics suggest that there may even have been a decline of life expectancy. In Sudan, life expectancy was estimated at 47.3 years for men and 49.9 for women in the 1970–75 period, compared to 43.9 for men and 46.4 for women over the 1975–80 period. The estimate was 43.7 for men and 45.9 for women in both Yemens combined in 1970–75; but over the next five years it was 40.4 for men and 42.2 for women in North Yemen and 43.0 for men and 45.1 for women in South Yemen.[18]

Demand for Products
Based on Advanced Technology

A final prerequisite for technological development is the existence of a market for the products for which the new technology is to be used. In the Arab world at present, lack of markets does not appear to be a major obstacle to development. About $100 billion is spent per year on imported industrial products, and there are clearly major opportunities for import substitution in many fields.

The Arab demand for advanced technological products is disproportionately concentrated in oil-producing countries. For Arab countries without oil but with industrial aspirations, this is a regional market. There is a disadvantage in this kind of market, as compared with a local market falling within state borders, since the latter can be protected for emerging local industries by special tariffs, whereas the regional Arab market is not so protected for the industries of the Arab world as a whole. Industrial products in the Arab world also face the usual problems of new products attempting to break into existing markets dominated by well-established enterprises. The recent entry into these markets of goods from other developing countries, such as South Korea and Brazil, indicates, however, that these problems are soluble once there has been a solution to the basic problem of the efficient production of goods requiring new technologies.

Conclusion

In summary, the outlook for most Arab countries seems to be one of some technological progress in the coming decade. The growth of human capital and the resources available in a number of countries suggest that stagnation will not be the general rule. The principal obstacle to even greater progress is that no single Arab country combines the key requirements of a strong industrial entrepreneurial class or state elite committed to technological development, the necessary level of scientific and technological manpower, and the resources necessary for this development.

If the Arab world is analyzed as a whole, rather than at the level of individual states, the existing manpower and resources are impressive. It can be tempting to imagine the effects of a situation in which the scientific communities of the different Arab countries worked with adequate funding on projects in those fields in which they had the greatest research experience and capabilities according to a coordinated plan. The lack of any effective unifying economic or political framework, however, has been decisive in preventing this kind of use of Arab material and human resources.

Notes

1. Estimated from the tables for different countries in the World Bank publication *World Tables, 1980* (Washington, DC: World Bank, 1984).

2. The case of a country, which, like Algeria, prohibits its nationals from acting as agents for foreign companies is rare in the Arab world. Some countries, such as Saudi Arabia, in fact require that foreign companies doing business in the country employ local businessmen as their agents.

3. United Nations Education, Scientific, and Cultural Organization (UNESCO), *National Science and Technology Policies in the Arab States*, Science Policy Studies and Documents, No. 38 (Paris: UNESCO, 1976) and *Science and Technology in the Development of the Arab States*, Science Policy Studies and Documents, No. 41 (Paris: UNESCO, 1977).

4. Jack N. Behrman, *Industry Ties with Science and Technology Policies in Developing Countries* (Cambridge, MA: Oelgeschlager, Gunn and Hain, 1980), pp. 50–51.

5. *Ibid.*, pp. 17, 23, 25.

6. A. B. Zahlan, *Science and Science Policy in the Arab World* (New York: St. Martin's, 1980), pp. 176, 182.

7. UNESCO, *Statistical Yearbook, 1984* (Paris: UNESCO, 1984), Table 5.0.

8. In Jordan, Kuwait, and Lebanon, for example, which provide statistics on scientists active in research and development in the late 1970s, the total was less than 1,000 in each case (*ibid.*, Table 5.2).

9. This is a projection on the basis of data in UNESCO, *National Science and Technology Policies in the Arab World*, p. 73.

10. UNESCO, *Statistical Yearbook, 1984*, Table 7.22, and UNESCO, *Statistical Yearbook, 1974* (Paris: UNESCO, 1974), Table 12.3.

11. This estimate was derived from the Institute for Scientific Information, *Who Is Publishing in Science, Annual Publication, 1974 to 1978* (Philadelphia, PA: 1978), and from Zahlan, *Science and Science Policy in the Arab World*, p. 30.

12. For an assessment of the situation in the mid-1970s, see J. Davidson Frame and Aileen Sprague, "Indicators of Scientific and Technological Efforts in the Middle East and North Africa," unpublished report prepared for the Office of Science and Technology, U.S. Agency for International Development, by Computer Horizons (1978).

13. UNESCO, *Statistical Yearbook, 1984*, Table 3.13.

14. Zahlan, *Science and Science Policy in the Arab World*.

15. UNESCO, *Statistical Yearbook, 1984*, Table 5.1.

16. In Egypt, too, revenues from oil-rich countries have been a major source of income mitigating the overall poverty of the country.

17. In United Nations, *Statistical Yearbook, 1982*.

18. All information in this paragraph is from the United Nations *Demographic Yearbook, 1983*, Table 4, and *1977*, Table 4. All statistics are estimates by a United Nations commission. While the statistics should be treated with some caution, they suggest serious obstacles to the spread of medical technology in the Yemens and Sudan during this period.

Bibliography

Behrman, Jack N. *Industry Ties with Science and Technology Policies in Developing Countries*. Cambridge, MA: Oelgeschlager, Gunn and Hain, 1980.

Durbin, Paul, editor. *A Guide to the Culture of Science, Technology and Medicine*. Riverside, NY: Free Press, 1980.

Frame, J. Davidson and Aileen Sprague. "Indicators of Scientific and Technological Efforts in the Middle East and North Africa." Unpublished report prepared for the Office of Science and Technology. U.S. Agency for International Development, Computer Horizons, 1978.

Gaston, Jerry. "Sociology of Science and Technology," in Paul Durbin, ed. *A Guide to the Culture of Science, Technology and Medicine*. Riverside, NY: Free Press, 1980.

Institute for Scientific Information. *Who Is Publishing In Science, Annual Publication, 1974 to 1978*. Philadelphia, PA: The Institute, 1978.

Jones, Graham. *The Role of Science and Technology in Developing Countries*. London: Oxford University Press, 1971.

Kazimi, M. S. and J. I. Makhoul, eds. *Perspectives on Technological Development in the Arab World*, Monograph No. 8. Belmont, MA: Association of Arab–American University Graduates, 1977.

Layton, Edwin. "Conditions of Technological Development," in Ina Spiegel–Roesing and Derek J. de S. Price, eds. *Science, Technology and Society*. Beverly Hills, CA: Sage, 1977.

Merton, Robert K. *The Sociology of Science*. Chicago, IL and London: University of Chicago Press, 1973.

Moore, Clement H. *Images of Development: Egyptian Engineers in Search of Industry*. Cambridge, MA: MIT Press, 1980.

Morgan, Robert P. et al. *Science and Technology for Development*. New York: Pergamon, 1979.

Nader, Claire and Zahlan, A. B., eds. *Science and Technology in Developing Countries*. Cambridge: Cambridge University Press, 1969.

Nagi, Saad and Corwin, Ronald, eds. *The Social Contexts of Research*. New York: Wiley, 1972.

Skorow, G. E., ed. *Science, Technology and Economic Growth in DevelopingCountries*. Oxford: Pergamon, 1978.

Spiegel–Roesing, Ina and Derek J. de S. Price, eds. *Science, Technology and Society*. Beverly Hills, CA: Sage, 1977.

United Nations. *Demographic Yearbook, 1977*. New York: United Nations, 1977.

United Nations. *Demographic Yearbook, 1983*. New York: United Nations, 1983.

United Nations. *Statistical Yearbook*. New York: United Nations, annual.

United Nations Educational, Scientific, and Cultural Organization (UNESCO). Science Policy Studies and Documents, No. 3. *National Science Policies in Countries of South and Southeast Asia*. Paris: UNESCO, 1965.

UNESCO. Science Policy Studies and Documents, No. 13. *Bilateral Institutional Links in Science and Technology*. Paris: UNESCO, 1969.

UNESCO. Science Policy Studies and Documents, No. 18. *The Role of Science and Technology in Economic Development*. Paris: UNESCO, 1970.

UNESCO. Science Policy Studies and Documents, No. 38. *National Science and Technology Policies in the Arab States*. Paris: UNESCO, 1976.

UNESCO. Science Policy Studies and Documents, No. 41. *Science and Technology in the Development of the Arab States*. Paris: UNESCO, 1977.

UNESCO. *Statistical Yearbook, 1974*. Paris: UNESCO, 1974.

UNESCO. *Statistical Yearbook, 1984*. Paris: UNESCO, 1984.

World Bank. *World Tables: 1980*. Washington, DC: World Bank, 1984.

Zahlan, A. B. *Science and Science Policy in the Arab World*. New York: St. Martin's, 1980.

Zahlan, A. B. "The Science and Technology Gap in the Arab–Israeli Conflict," *Journal of Palestine Studies* 1, no. 3 (Spring 1972): 17–36.

Zahlan, A. B. ed. *Technology Transfer and Change in the Arab World*. Oxford: Pergamon, 1978.

PART FOUR

Cultural Change, Creativity, and Authenticity

10

Challenges to Arab Cultural Authenticity

Issa J. Boullata

In current discussions of Arab intellectuals on cultural change in the Arab world, the fear is sometimes expressed that too much change will eventually alter Arab identity. Advice is therefore offered that Arabs should restrain the process of change in order to preserve their cultural authenticity and keep their specificity as a people with a distinct national heritage.

While I grant that the culture of any society ought to have its own checks and balances, and that it ought to develop its own principles of inclusion and exclusion in the dynamics of change, I believe that too protective an attitude in this regard is not only unwarranted in the contemporary Arab world, but also inimical to the very cultural authenticity that is being adduced to justify it. In my view, this excessively protective attitude is indeed a camouflage for attempts to reduce the pace of change or even keep the Arab world in the grip of traditionalism and hence under the hegemony of the present power systems at the national and the international levels.

It is true that, in the last few decades, there has been a tremendous move toward modernization in the Arab world, greater in certain regions than in others. But to say that the Arab world has become modern in its sociopolitical and economic structures; its thought; its sciences and arts; its values, attitudes, and behavior; and the lives of its individuals is a gross overstatement. There is still ample room for further change before the Arabs can begin to be a modern people who are effective in the world community. They may therefore continue to change with little or no fear for their cultural authenticity. In fact, they can and should change in order to become truer to themselves.

At this point one may ask: And what is Arab cultural authenticity, anyway? Is it a quality that is a permanent attribute of the Arabs? Are the Arabs endowed with a quintessential characteristic that distinguishes them from all other peoples? Is their culture so different from everybody else's in the world that it is to be differently treated in modern times?

Let me quickly admit of the difficulty of these questions which have recently engaged the attention of Arab intellectuals, especially since the 1967 Arab defeat that has been for many of them an imperative to rethink, an opportunity that has evoked a vast and continuing literature in self-analysis, including a significant amount of self-criticism. In the limited space of a paper, one can hardly do justice to all that literature except to say that there is in it a general agreement on the existence of an Arab cultural authenticity but hardly on its nature. As a consequence, there is disagreement regarding the degree of cultural change that Arabs can initiate and yet continue to be true to their cultural authenticity.

The problem, as I see it, arises from the notion that Arab culture is considered a monolithic entity, permanent and static in its nature, given once and for all, then handed down from generation to generation. To be culturally authentic, an Arab must—according to this view—preserve this monolith and faithfully hand it down intact to posterity. This formulation obviously oversimplifies the problem, but the fact remains that we have here an unhistorical and, indeed, an incorrect view of culture. For the culture of any human group is its collective experience in time. As the group moves in time from generation to generation, it continually meets with new needs that challenge it. The response of the group shapes its experience of reality, which, in turn, adds to its culture. The group learns to acquire new cultural elements and discard others, so that its culture continues to develop in the service of group survival and enhancement. Culture is thus continually changing and accommodating the group's institutions, beliefs, and values to its ever-rising needs, both material and otherwise. Certain cultures may be more open to change than others. But there is no culture that does not change unless it is a dead culture—i.e., an archeologically reconstructed culture of an extinct group. Furthermore, the unity of a living culture contains diversity. Certain cultures may allow a larger latitude of diversity within them than others, but there is hardly any culture that exhibits total and solid uniformity.

In the current discourse on Arab culture (*thaqafa*) and Arab cultural authenticity (*asala*) in the Arab world, there is serious discussion of the Arab heritage (*turath*). In articles, books, and specially-convened conferences and symposia, contemporary Arab thinkers have presented insights on what they consider to be the Arab cultural heritage of the past and what they believe ought to be its function in the present and the future. This discourse is a significant aspect of contemporary Arab thinking in general, but it is especially significant with regard to the concept of Arab authenticity. Although it deals with the Arab past, in fact it reveals the concerns of the contemporary Arab mind about one of its most important intellectual problems in the struggle to achieve a place for the Arabs in the modern world amid conflicting international forces and ideologies, and in difficult conditions of dependency, national development, and social change.

Contemporary Arab thinkers view their cultural heritage in a variety of ways. This variety is a function of the variety of ideological stances of the thinkers. Thought does not exist in a vacuum. It is a reflection of objective reality. By reflection, I do not mean a mechanical, mirror-like image formed in the consciousness by an object outside it. I rather mean the product of a dialectical relation between the object and human consciousness. This relation has to be dialectical because human consciousness is not a *tabula rasa*, but rather a complex result of inherited individual characteristics and societal environmental influences. The heritage, likewise, is not a simple object to be perceived, but a complex cultural entity formed in the past as a result of a multitude of societal and psychological forces and still living and effective in the present. The relationship between the heritage and thought is, therefore, one of constantly changing perception, since every generation views the past from a different perspective, which is its own and strongly governed by its needs. Furthermore, though individuals differ from one another in their perceptions of the heritage, there are discernible affinities of perception among individuals belonging to one class. Hence, difference in one generation reflects not only individual idiosyncrasy but also class distinctions which are in reality ideological distinctions.

With regard to present-day Arab culture, we must first recognize its long and variegated history, during which it has been continually evolving and developing. Depending on when they deem it to have begun, contemporary Arab intellectuals have variously assessed its dominant features. But if there is anything almost consensual about Arab culture, it is that it underwent a revolutionary change with the advent of Islam in the seventh century and that it has nevertheless continued to retain and develop cultural elements from periods before and since then, during which it was in contact with peoples of other cultures—such as the Babylonians, the Assyrians, the Aramaeans, the Phoenicians, the Hebrews, the Canaanites, the Pharaonic Egyptians, and the Berbers, as well as the Greeks, the Romans, the Visigoths, the Franks, the Chinese, the Indians, the Persians, the Turks, and modern Western nations—and with religious traditions like Judaism, Christianity, Hinduism, Buddhism, and Zoroastrianism. The culture of Arabia revolutionized by Islam and enriched by elements from the cultures of other peoples is today the heritage of what has come to be called the Arab world, inhabited by over 185 million Arabic-speaking people.

One of the greatest impacts on Arab culture in its recent history has been a function of its contact with modern Western culture. This contact has been going on now for over a century and a half, in varying degrees of depth and intensity, at different times and in different regions of the Arab world. Like any other culture, Western culture is not a static monolith, and the Arabs have been exposed to various trends in it. The modern cultural encounter with the West is perceived by the Arabs to be more forceful and pervasive than others in their past, not only because the West is more powerful, but also because they view it from the position of their contemporary weakness following several centuries of virtual stagnation and surbordination.

Arab culture has adopted many elements from modern Western culture, notably in the realm of material civilization but also in societal organization and in ideas. Yet there has been increasing resistance to this process. As the countries of the Arab world moved toward political independence after Western colonial rule receded, the demand for the preservation of the national cultural heritage and of cultural authenticity intensified. Tradition loomed to many Arabs as a rock of sure durability, safety, and strength to which they could cling amid the insecurity and instability of change. Only in tradition could many of them find their identity and their cultural authenticity. The 1967 Arab defeat, after decades of modernization, confirmed their belief in tradition.

But there are other Arabs who think otherwise. In this paper, I will attempt to present three contemporary trends of Arab thought: (1) that of the traditionalists, (2) that of the liberals, and (3) that of the radicals. Admittedly, this categorization is not adequate because, in fact, intellectuals cannot be tightly compartmentalized and intellectual life is very complex. But it will do for the present purpose of giving an idea of the main trends.

Among the traditionalists, I place writers and thinkers like Sayyid Qutb and other intellectuals of the Society of Muslim Brothers and its recent offshoots, as well as most persons in the Islamic religious establishment. The traditionalists believe in the necessity of restoring an Islamic society based on what they perceive to be values and institutions derived from the Qur'an and the teachings of Prophet Muhammad. For them, the Arab heritage is basically the Islamic heritage, because they view the Islamic elements of Arab culture as the principal, if not the only, ones that must predominate. They advocate the elimination from Arab society of external cultural influences, particularly Western ones, and they call for a return to the pristine essence of Islam as they perceive it to have been in the early centuries, particularly during the Prophet's lifetime. The heritage for them has been given once and for all. Modern life, according to them, must conform to this heritage. They do not negate science and technology, but consider them to be modern products of the earlier efforts of Muslims during the heyday of Islamic civilization, and they teach that those products must be re-acquired. They want the economic system and, in fact, the totality of life to conform to the rules and ideals of the Islamic heritage, which they consider to be as sufficient for human well-being in modern times as they were in old times.

Those Arab intellectuals who support this view write extensively to defend it. Although they do not all necessarily agree with each other, they help to increase the atavistic tendencies among large sections of the populace and to foster the idea that the Arab past offered ideal paradigms in one bygone period or another but especially the early period of Islamic history. The visions of the past that underlie these paradigms are mostly romanticized, but this does not make them less appealing, as they are considered to be at the roots of Arab culture, where genuine cultural authenticity resided and gave the Arabs their historic power and greatness. Recreating this past and its institutions in contemporary Arab society has become a value worth living and dying for. In this perspective, Arab culture is increasingly considered self-sufficient, and it is confident of its authenticity.

This traditionalist view of Arab culture and the heritage is static. It does not take into consideration the historical factors that went into the formation of the cultural heritage in the first place. If it concedes change, it does not relate it to the continuous influence of historical factors in society, but rather to the perversion of human willfulness and to evil external factors with nefarious anti-Islamic intentions of undermining the heritage. The traditionalists sincerely believe they have the truth, and they present that position as such to their contemporaries. They believe that any other conception of the heritage is wrong and doomed to eventual failure.

Among the liberals, I place writers and thinkers like Qustantin Zurayq, Zaki Najib Mahmud, and Muhammad al-Nuwayhi; nationalists like Sati' al-Husri; and educationalists like 'Abd Allah 'Abd al-Da'im. These liberals consider certain elements in the Arab heritage to be viable in modern times if only they are reinterpreted and understood better and developed in the light of modern Arab needs and the experience of modern nations. Their major thrust is toward renewal rather than radical change. They want to reform, not transform, Arab society. Though they want to discard many traditional values and institutions of the Arab heritage, they continue to believe in some others, which they like to reinterpret and supplement with new elements that, according to them, will make Arabs function better in modern times. Some of them may endorse a socialist economy, but most would only want some improvement in the present economic system in the Arab world to ensure a reasonable distribution of wealth. Many among them look with favor on the introduction of Western cultural elements, including concepts of freedom and democracy, parliamentary life and party systems, equality of men and women, secularization of the political and legal systems, equality of all citizens before the law, emphasis on individual rights, and reliance on science and technology. Some among them, like Muhammad al-Nuwayhi, reinterpret a selection of Islamic cultural elements so that they may function in a way that suits the modern age.

Some other liberals view Western culture as *the* universal culture of the modern world *par excellence*. They do not all necessarily agree with each other, but most are as romanticizing as the traditionalists. Their vision of an idealized Western culture is as fatuous as the simplistic way they think it can be transplanted without much consideration for the quality of receptivity in the Arab soil. Yet they write extensively to defend their view and manage to win over small segments of the Arab population, mostly among those exposed to Western systems of education.

Although this liberal view of Arab culture and the Arab heritage is not quite static, it all but ignores the fact that the heritage is a communal product of the social conditions of its times. Liberals regard thought as if it were an independent individual factor, and they credit it with the ability to change social conditions. They also place high value on the innovative individual and they credit him with the ability to initiate change by himself or as a member of an elite. They suggest that if persons are properly prepared to accept change, society as a whole will eventually be made to change by democratic will. Thus they ignore the basic economic structure of society which is the material background of the heritage that gives it its content. They advocate the selection of what seems best to them from both Arab culture and Western culture. By ingenious mental acrobatics, they sometimes interpret elements of the foreign culture in terms of the indigenous one to make them acceptable to the Arab public, but they often borrow Western cultural elements, especially in technology and societal organization, without much ado and place them next to selected Arab ones with little concern for integration. Because of its practicality and the possibility of fast implementation, the resulting cultural hybrid is attractive to many Arabs, particularly to most Arab governments bent on speedy modernization. But questions of cultural authenticity keep cropping up among the populace, and opposition occasionally interrupts the process.

Among the radical writers and thinkers, one may mention on the one hand intellectuals like Adonis ('Ali Ahmad Sa'id), 'Abd Allah al-'Arwi, Anwar 'Abd al-Malik, who have leftist tendencies mixed with a liberal tinge, and on the other hand Marxist intellectuals like Tayyib Tizini, Husayn Muruwwa, Mahmud Amin al-'Alim, and Samir Amin, whose vision of history is inspired by dialectical materialism. The radical thinkers recognize the Arab heritage as a historical reality whose life has continued into the present. To understand it, they advocate a historicist approach, and the more leftist among them take a hard look at its socioeconomic and political setting, epitomized in the relations of production, which they consider to be the matrix within which the heritage developed and of which it is the product. They consider the religious content of the Arab heritage as an expression, in part, of the socioeconomic and political conditions of Arab history.

The Marxists posit class struggle as the mover of history. Change, for them, is the outcome of class struggle. As the mode of production develops in response to local and world markets, class relations change and thought also. The prevalent ideology, they believe, is always that of the dominant class which controls the mode of production. At present, they see that the Arab bourgeoisie is dominant and that its interests are aligned with those of capitalist imperialism in the world, on which it is dependent. This bourgeois ideology is threatened by the rising power of the Arab lower classes, which have a necessarily different ideology.

For the Marxists, the Arab heritage has two aspects, one cognitive, the other utilitarian. The cognitive aspect is connected with the scholarly study of the heritage in order to bring out its true nature as the historical product of the socioeconomic and political interests of the dominant class in the Arab Islamic society of the past. The utilitarian aspect is connected with understanding this nature of the heritage as a continuing reality in the present and the necessity to transcend it by bringing about new thought, based in theory on Marxism and rooted in practice in the Arab working class and its experience, the aim being the eventual elimination of the Arab bourgeoisie and the establishment of scientific socialism. They sincerely believe they correctly interpret the Arab heritage by bringing out this truth about its nature. They maintain that in all scientific study truth is not made truth by being utilitarian but rather, on the contrary, it is made utilitarian by being true.

Despite this lofty idea and other sound principles, including a belief in some independence of thought from social reality, the approach of the Arab Marxists suffers from too rigid an application of theory to the facts of Arab history and to the conditions of contemporary Arab society. There is in it a facile transposition of analytical categories applicable perhaps to classical, medieval, and modern European society, but little, if at all, to Arab–Islamic society, whose past institutions of land and capital ownership, forms of slavery and labor relations, class systems, and political-legal structures were totally different from, and whose contemporary conditions are not quite parallel to, those that prompted Marx's analysis. The attempt by Arab Marxists to elaborate on Marx's and Engels' concept of "the Asian mode of production" has not produced insights of any profundity with which to correct or wholly replace other views on the subject, and the facts of Arab–Islamic history relating to political economy still need years of scholarly work before they are all unearthed so that a new history may be written in their light.

The further application by Arab Marxists of Leninist, Stalinist, or Maoist theorization only reveals dogmatic or derivative stands, shedding little additional light on Arab culture and the Arab cultural heritage. Anwar 'Abd al-Malik's new theorization on the social dialectics of Third World countries and the interaction between the Orient and the West is too specious to be acceptable even to the Arab Marxists themselves, bold though his attempt may be. In general, the Arab radicals have not been able to attract many followers besides a sector of intellectuals and workers. Their efforts, however, have occasioned a debate among themselves and with other Arab ideologues which may bring about deeper research and a better understanding of Arab culture and Arab history.

From the foregoing, one may observe that although the Arab cultural heritage is one, views of it are several, depending on the ideology of the perceiver. It is essentially their ideological commitment that dictates the way Arab intellectuals view their cultural heritage in the light of present conditions locally and internationally. It is also their ideological commitment that is decisive in identifying what the cultural heritage is and how it is to function in present and future Arab society. Hence, what Arab authenticity is and should be is an ideological question. Each ideological group sincerely believes it has the truth regarding Arab authenticity and tries energetically to present it as such to its contemporaries. This variety of visions is reflected in much of the indecision prevailing today in the Arab world with regard to policies and the general orientation of development and social change.

Claims have begun to arise that there is a cultural crisis in the Arab world. By counterclaim, some say that it is the crisis of Arab intellectuals, others that it is rather the crisis of Arab regimes. The Kuwait symposium of April 1974 evasively called it "The Crisis of Civilizational Development in the Arab Homeland," and Kuwait University and its alumni association assembled some of the best-known Arab intellectuals to discuss the matter. Since then, symposia, books, and articles on the subject have multiplied, and they continue to do so. The Cairo symposium of September 1984, convened by the Centre for Arab Unity Studies (of Beirut), did not use the term "crisis" in its conference theme, "The Heritage and the Challenges of the Modern Age in the Arab Homeland: Authenticity and Modernity." But the unfortunate placement of "authenticity" in opposition to "modernity" in its thematic consideration is the result of a misconception which is shared by many people in the Arab world and thus is in itself evidence of the crisis. Authenticity does not necessarily have to be a quality that locks people up in the past or in a limited understanding of Arab culture and the Arab heritage as products of an ideologically-selected, specific period of the past. For Arab culture and the Arab heritage are alive today, and they remain the basis of Arab authenticity.

There is no doubt, therefore, that there is a cultural crisis in the Arab world and that the situation is in flux. This is further complicated by the state of dependency in which the Arab world finds itself, by the clash of superpower interests in the area, Zionist and Israeli schemes to keep the Arab world under control, and the Arab regimes' glaring ineptitude and often unwitting bungling of internal and external affairs to the detriment of the Arab masses and their real interests.

The question now is: What are the cultural prospects of the Arab world for the coming decade?

A decade is too short a period for perceptible change to occur in the life of a people like the Arabs, whose culture has a long history. Yet, judging by what has been done so far and by what ought to have been done, I venture to say that the crisis will not be resolved by 1995, but that its dimensions will become clearer. The Islamic resurgence will continue to spread among the Arabs because, more than any other ideology, Islam can readily capture the imagination of the expanding lower middle class and lumpen urban proletariat, and can give them a sense of orientation and meaning in the flux of the new social order emerging in several Arab countries. Arab governments will continue to use Islamic symbols and to introduce desultory legislation with some Islamic flavor to meet the demands of resurgent Islamic masses. This may continue to keep such Arab governments in power for a certain period.

Sooner or later, the Arab masses will realize that this governmental patchwork will neither produce real progress nor bring about a return to the power and the glory of the past. More deeply, they will realize it does not embody the cultural authenticity they like to have. As they were earlier disillusioned with Arab nationalism and its drive in the 1950s and 1960s toward Arab national unity, they will also be disillusioned with the Islamic resurgence and its attempt in the 1980s and 1990s to recapture an idealized past. They will be disillusioned not because Arab nationalism and the Islamic resurgence have no elements that can succeed, but because neither has been realistically grounded in the present-day conditions of the Arabs, neither has been genuinely acquainted with the actual contemporary conditions of the modern world at large, and both have only a vague and romantic view of the historical Arab culture and the historical Islamic heritage.

These are very important factors of past failure which should be seriously understood before a reverse trend can be established. Arab national unity and Islamic reconstruction cannot be achieved by wishful thinking and emotional romanticizing. The socioeconomic and political forces that have militated against them should be faced and treated. The demographic realities of the various sectors of the Arab world should be taken into account, including differences in mode of production, degree of urbanization, level of education, and extent of political consciousness, as well as the problems of a variety of minority religions and sects and of ethnic groups. All centrifugal and hostile tendencies should be understood objectively, and the methods of dealing with them should be scientifically and democratically conceived and implemented with the full participation of all. This process will take a long time, but it will at least avoid future frustrations.

Similarly, Arab-Islamic thinking will have to come to grips with the actual realities of the modern world: it will have to genuinely understand and begin to apply the principles of modern science, not merely acquire and consume its finished technological products; it will have to really comprehend the necessity and the mechanics of modern societal organization, not merely copy its institutional structures; it will have to learn the real nature of modernity, including its positive and negative features. In the light of this understanding as seen through the prism of Arab culture, it will have to rethink the values of Arab-Islamic life in order to modernize them and help society to institutionalize them. Emotional religious resurgence and the concomitant political and social turmoil will have to be recognized as fruitless, and rational Islamic reconstruction in modernizing society as potentially fruitful.

Arab culture and the Islamic heritage will have to be subjected to historical scrutiny and critical study. Otherwise, what is desired alone will be highlighted, seen in rosy colors, and considered to be real. Selectivity will not reveal the truth. A comprehensive acceptance and study of the whole past with all its detailed facts, welcome and unwelcome, will alone reveal the authenticity of the Arab self that should survive to the present.

By the turn of the twenty-first century, the Arab masses will realize—as some Arab intellectuals have only recently begun to realize—that Arab culture and the Islamic heritage will inevitably have to be taken into serious consideration in any modernization process, yet both have to be adapted to the needs of the present and the future. The Arab-Islamic cultural heritage will remain a necessary basis upon which to build Arab modernity and preserve Arab cultural authenticity, but elements of it will have to be discarded or reinterpreted.

Hard choices will have to be made. Arabs must face the fact that they cannot continue to play Dr. Jekyll and Mr. Hyde. They cannot be modern and traditional at the same time. Some inoperative elements of their culture will have to be discarded irrevocably, however dear those elements may be and however painful that action may be. Some other elements of the Arab–Islamic cultural heritage will have to be changed boldly, just as many others will survive because they will continue to be relevant and useful. But the Arabs will have to stamp modernity with their own Arab identity. They must not adopt Western modernity wholesale, because that will only lead to alienation and continued inner tensions. And since to recreate the Arab–Islamic tradition *in toto* is impossible, and the attempt to do so is not only unrealistic, but deleterious to their contemporary growth (as experience has already shown), they must create their own Arab modernity. This is the challenge they must accept.

Creating Arab modernity that retains cultural authenticity requires vision, imagination, and courage as well as a leadership which is well-informed of the niceties of Arab–Islamic culture, the complexities of modern Western culture, and the present and future needs of Arab society. Arab intellectuals are challenged to take the leading role in responsibly orienting public opinion, so that they may influence the direction of change in societal reorganization and government action and may foster the climate that will promote the development of new attitudes, new values, and new patterns of behavior and eventually the establishment of viable new institutions to sustain them.

There will be heated debate. There should be unqualified freedom. Nothing short of this will resolve the continuing cultural crisis of the Arab world and bring about the birth of the New Arab Man and Woman. This debate should be carried across the whole Arab world and should use all possible channels, including ALECSO (the Arab League Educational, Cultural, and Scientific Organization) and the Centre for Arab Unity Studies. It should reach the home of every Arab family through television, radio, or the written word in a single-minded and concerted effort at spreading awareness of the problems and needs of the Arabs. It should aim at reaching the younger generations in their schools, colleges, and universities, and the workers in the fields and the factories. It should reach men. It should reach women. It should be a national debate. Input should be encouraged from all. Participation should be assured for all.

Different ideologies should democratically accept one another's existence and should allow interaction. There will continue to be conflictive differences and contending viewpoints which should have free play. These are not merely stubborn and vindictive attitudes, but reflections of real division in Arab society. But there will also be a possibility for reconciling some contentions as the Arab masses begin to realize their power in deciding the outcome of the discourse.

The outcome cannot be easily predicted. But I suspect there will eventually emerge a synthesis that will fuse living elements of the Arab–Islamic tradition and relevant elements of modern culture and thus create an organically integrated Arab modernity. The sociopolitical and economic conditions of the Arab masses will affect the nature of this cultural synthesis, but these conditions in turn will be dialectically affected by the synthesis as the process of change moves on.

It is likely that the emerging modernity of the twenty-first century in the Arab world will have rationalism as one of its formative and animating principles, but it will in my estimation be tempered by a humanist qualification. It will endorse and acquire science and technology, but will admit of human limitation. What is indubitable is that it will culturally be an Arab modernity, an authentic Arab way of life in modern times, not a Western one. Just as the Japanese have created a Japanese modernity, totally their own, successfully contributing to the well-being of the modern world, so will the Arabs at long last create their own modernity, which will make them again an effective community in the family of nations and full participants in the world's well-being and civilization. This modernity of theirs will be more authentically Arab than their present-day irresolute society. To be sure, the Arab world will have new problems to solve as well as some remaining old ones. But on the whole, it will be an Arab world on the move toward progress and better living, an Arab world looking forward to new and open horizons.

Arab cultural authenticity will have been redeemed and justified.

Selected Readings

On sociocultural change in the Arab world in general: Daniel Lerner, *The Passing of Traditional Society* (Glencoe, IL: Free Press, 1958); Abdulla M. Lutfiyya and Charles W. Churchill, eds., *Readings in Arab Middle Eastern Societies and Cultures* (The Hague–Paris: Mouton, 1970); Jacques Berque, *Cultural Expression in Arab Society Today*, trans. Robert W. Stookey (Austin, TX: University of Texas Press, 1978); Talal Asad and Roger Owen, eds., *Sociology of "Developing Societies": The Middle East* (New York: Monthly Review Press, 1983).

On the impact of the June 1967 war on the Arab psyche and culture: Sadiq Jalal al-'Azm, *Al-Naqd al-dhati ba'd al-hazima* (Beirut: Dar al-Tali'a, 1968); Nadim al-Bitar, *Min al-naksa ila al-thawra* (Beirut: Dar al-Tali'a, 1968); Qustantin Zurayq, *Ma'na al-nakba mujaddadan* (Beirut: Dar al-'Ilm li-al-Malayin, 1967); Lewis R. Scudder, Jr., "Arab Intellectuals and the Implications of the Defeat of 1967," unpublished M.A. thesis (American University of Beirut, 1971); Al-Sayyid Yasin, *Al-Shakhsiyya al-'Arabiyya bayna surat al-dhat wa-mafhum al-akhar* (Beirut: Dar al-Tanwir, 1983).

For studies on the Arab-Islamic heritage and the Arab struggle for modernity: Adonis ('Ali Ahmad Sa'id), *Al-Thabit wa-al-mutahawwil*, 3 vols. (Beirut: Dar al-'Awda, 1974–78); Bulus Khuri, *Al-Turath wa-al-hadatha* (Beirut: Ma'had al-Inma' al-'Arabi, 1983); Hasan Hanafi, *Al-Turath wa-al-tajdid* (Beirut: Dar al-Tanwir, 1981); Tayyib Tizini, *Min al-turath ila al-thawra* (Beirut: Dar Ibn Khaldun, 1978); Victor Sahhab, *Darurat al-turath* (Beirut: Dar al-'Ilm li-al-Malayin, 1984); Ghali Shukri, *Al-Turath wa-al-thawra* (Beirut: Dar al-Tali'a, 1973); Al-Sayyid Yasin, ed., *Al-Turath wa-tahaddiyat al-'asr fi al-watan al-'Arabi (Al-Asala wa-al-mu'asara)* (Beirut: Markaz Dirasat al-Wahda al-'Arabiyya, 1985).

For studies on Islam in the process of change: Hasan Sa'b, *Al-Islam tujah tahaddiyat al-hayah al-'asriyya* (Beirut: Dar al-Adab, 1965); Hisham Ju'ayyit, *Al-Shakhsiyya al-'Arabiyya al-Islamiyya wa-al-masir al-'Arabi*, trans. al-Munji al-Sayyadi (Beirut: Dar al-Tali'a, 1984); Yvonne Yazbeck Haddad, *Contemporary Islam and the Challenge of History* (Albany, NY: State University of New York Press, 1982); Ali E. Hillal Dessouki, ed., *Islamic Resurgence in the Arab World* (New York: Praeger, 1982); Michael Gilsenan, *Recognizing Islam: Religion and Society in the Modern Arab World* (New York: Pantheon, 1983); John Obert Voll, *Islam: Continuity and Change in the Modern World* (Boulder, CO: Westview Press, 1982); John L. Esposito, ed., *Islam and Development: Religion and Sociopolitical Change* (Syracuse, NY: Syracuse University Press, 1980); R. Hrair Dekmejian, *Islam in Revolution: Fundamentalism in the Arab World* (Syracuse, NY: Syracuse University Press, 1985).

On the Arab cultural and intellectual crisis: Abdallah Laroui, *The Crisis of the Arab Intellectual: Traditionalism or Historicism?*, trans. Diarmid Cammell (Berkeley, CA: University of California Press, 1976); Shakir Mustafa, ed., *Azmat al-tatawwur al-hadari fi al-watan al-'Arabi: Waqa'i' nadwat al-Kuwayt, April 7-11, 1974* (Kuwait: Jam'iyyat al-Khirrijin/Jami'at al-Kuwayt, 1975); 'Amil Mahdi, *Azmat al-hadara al-'Arabiyya am azmat al-burjuwaziyyat al-'Arabiyya?* (Beirut: Dar al-Farabi, 1974).

For critiques of Arab thought: Sadiq Jalal al-'Azm, *Naqd al-fikr al-dini*, 2nd ed. (Beirut: Dar al-Tali'a, 1970); Zaki Najib Mahmud, *Mujtama' jadid aw al-karitha* (Beirut-Cairo: Dar al-Shuruq, 1978); Muhammad 'Abid al-Jabiri, *Al-Khitab al-'Arabi al-mu'asir: Dirasa tahliliyya naqdiyya* (Beirut/Casablanca: Dar al-Tali'a/al-Markaz al-Thaqafi al-'Arabi, 1982); Louis 'Awad, *Thaqafatuna fi muftaraq al-turuq* (Beirut: Dar al-Adab, 1974); 'Abbas al-Jarrari, *Al-Thaqafa fi ma'rakat al-taghyir* (Casablanca: Dar al-Nashr al-Maghribiyya, 1972).

On the modernization of Arab thought and culture: Hasan Sa'b, *Tahdith al-'aql al-'Arabi*, 2nd ed. (Beirut: Dar al-'Ilm li-al-Malayin, 1972); Zaki Najib Mahmud, *Thaqafatuna fi muwajahat al-'asr* (Beirut-Cairo: Dar al-Shuruq, 1976); Idem, *Tajadid al-fikr al-'Arabi*, 4th ed. (Beirut-Cairo: Dar al-Shuruq, 1978); Adonis ('Ali Ahmad Sa'id), *Fatiha li-nihayat al-qarn: Bayanat min ajl thaqafa 'Arabiyya jadida* (Beirut: Dar al-'Awda, 1980); Muhammad al-Nuwayhi, *Nahwa thawra fi al-fikr al-dini* (Beirut: Dar al-Adab, 1983); 'Abd Allah 'Abd al-Da'im, *Fi Sabil thaqafa 'Arabiyya dhatiyya: Al-Thaqafa al-'Arabiyya wa-al-turath* (Beirut: Dar al-Adab, 1983); Anwar 'Abd al-Malik, *Rih al-sharq* (Beirut: Dar al-Mustaqbal al-'Arabi, 1983).

For accounts of various ideologies in the Arab world: Leonard Binder, *The Ideological Revolution in the Middle East* (New York: John Wiley & Sons, 1964); Fouad Ajami, *The Arab Predicament: Arab Political Thought and Practice* (Cambridge: Cambridge University Press, 1981); Sami Hanna and George Gardner, *Arab Socialism: A Documentary Survey* (Leiden: E.J. Brill, 1969); Tareq Y. Ismael, *The Arab Left* (Syracuse, NY: Syracuse University Press, 1976); Maxime Rodinson, *Marxism and the Muslim World*, trans. Jean Matthews (New York-London: Monthly Review Press, 1981); Ilyas Murqus, *Tarikh al-ahzab al-shuyu'iyya fi al-watan al-'Arabi* (Beirut: Dar al-Tali'a, 1964); *Al-Qawmiyya al-'Arabiyya fi al-fikr wa-al-mumarasa*, proceedings of a symposium organized and published by Markaz Dirasat al-Wahda al-'Arabiyya, Beirut, 1980; Ma'n Ziyada, ed., *Buhuth fi al-fikr al-qawmi al-'Arabi* (Beirut: Ma'had al-Inma' al-'Arabi, 1983); Bassam Tibi, *Arab Nationalism: A Critical Inquiry*, eds. and trans. Marion-Farouk Sluglett and Peter Sluglett (New York: Macmillan Press, 1981); Richard P. Mitchell, *The Society of the Muslim Brothers* (London: Oxford University Press, 1969); G. H. Jansen, *Militant Islam* (New York: Harper and Row, 1979); Ali E. Hillal Dessouki, ed., *Islamic Resurgence in the Arab World* (New York: Praeger, 1982); John L. Esposito, ed., *Voices of Resurgent Islam* (New York-Oxford: Oxford University Press, 1983); R. Hrair Dekmejian, *Islam in Revolution: Fundamentalism in the Arab World* (Syracuse, NY: Syracuse University Press, 1985).

For views on the Arab future: Qustantin Zurayq, *Nahnu wa-al-mustaqbal* (Beirut: Dar al-'Ilm li-al-Malayin, 1977); Edward Said and Fuad Suleiman, eds., *The Arabs*

Today: Alternatives for Tomorrow (Columbus, OH: Forum Associates Inc., 1973); Michael C. Hudson, ed., *The Arab Future: Critical Issues* (Washington, D.C.: Georgetown University, Center for Contemporary Arab Studies, 1979).

On modernization in Japan (for comparative purposes): Robert E. Ward and Dankwart A. Rustow, eds., *Political Modernization in Japan and Turkey* (Princeton, NJ: Princeton University Press, 1964); Donald Shively, ed., *Tradition and Modernization in Japanese Culture* (Princeton, NJ: Princeton University Press, 1971); Yasumasa Kuroda, "Al-Tahdith wa-al-ightirab fi al-Yaban," in Al-Sayyid Yasin, *et al.*, *Al-Turath wa tahaddiyyat al-'asr fi al-watan al-'Arabi (Al-Asala wa-al-mu'asara)*, Proceedings of the Cairo Symposium of September 24–27, 1984 (Beirut: Markaz Dirasat al-Wahda al-'Arabiyya, 1985), pp. 223–41.

11

Cultural Creation in a Fragmented Society

Kamal Abu-Deeb

The purpose of this paper is to situate cultural creation in the wider context formed by the social, political, and economic reality of the Arab world over the past 15 years and to project the lines of development which emerge out of such an act onto the next decade. I shall argue that the characteristics of Arabic writing, particularly on the level of its structure, have been determined by an intensifying process of fragmentation in the various spheres of life. I shall argue further that this process of fragmentation will continue in an even more acute form over the next ten years, hence writing itself increasingly will display these properties associated with fragmentation. Although cultural creation might develop a more active response of resistance to fragmentation and consequently move into completely or almost completely new areas of human existence, creating in the process new structures and acquiring new structural properties, it seems to me that such a possibility will not materialize in the space of ten years—a decade is too short a time for such major changes in art and literature. In the course of its formulation, this study will consider a number of forces and factors which it conceives of as having generated and/or contributed to the process of fragmentation. It will also discuss the role of some reemerging traditional forces in Arab society which have materialized both as products of fragmentation and as causes of its further spreading and domination.

Finally, this paper will suggest that a new order of being in the Arab world may not take form unless the fragmentation reaches into even deeper levels and affects existing social and political institutions, particularly the structure of the state, authority, and ideology.

Situating Cultural Creation

Cultural creation over the last 15 years will have to be situated within the larger social, political, and economic structure, if we are to achieve a better understanding of its properties and orientation. It has to be situated in the context of successive Arab failures and the increasing hegemony of the colonialist and imperialist forces, including Israel; in the context of the internal divisions and conflicts along political, religious, sectarian, and social (class) lines, and especially the conflicts between the advocates of modernity and modernization and those of traditionalism—between a futurist vision and a past-oriented vision; and in the context of a regression toward the latter and a gradual ebbing of the former.

Recent cultural creation must be situated within the structure of the increasing violence exercised by authority, particularly as embodied in the demonic growth of the power of the state and the diminishing power of "civil society." It should be situated also within the context of the emergence of a truly consumer society—the growth in some parts of what we can call one-dimensional man, and the growth in other parts of a society with no middle class—only the very rich and the very poor.

Cultural creation should be situated further in the context of a fundamental split between reality and thought. The reality is that of the intensification of the drive toward Westernization, to put it simply, whereas in thought (which is divided) we witness a strong current of awareness of the dangers of Westernization and, more recently, another current of much louder voices advocating the "return" to "national" tradition and "national" identity. In other words, we must place cultural activity within the space of two opposing forces: the shock of modernity (or the shock of *other* as an external entity), and the shock of tradition (or the shock of *other* as a distant self). So far Arab intellectuals, outside the traditional sphere, have been fighting to *internalize the other*, to absorb the other into the organic structure of the culture. Now, they are trying to externalize the self, to turn the tradition into a force capable of shaping the present and to prove that it is more relevant to our problems than the external other.

Finally, and more importantly, perhaps, cultural creation should be situated within the context of the domination of cultural life by preconceived models which fluctuate between Islam on the one hand and the West on the other. All major currents of thought in the Arab world have suffered from this defect: that they were borrowing models little related to the reality of the Arab world—Western models or ancient Islamic models—and the latter are no less surreal, if you like, than the former.

Once we have situated cultural creation in these contexts, the important questions become: how do all these conflicts end in the future? What direction do these processes take? It seems to me that the next decade will witness a greater degree of fragmentation and the dissolution of entities, and more fundamental splits within the culture. I shall argue later, perhaps surprising some of you, that this process is a necessary condition for the emergence of a different Arab world, in a more positive sense.

Fragmentation

I shall characterize the last decade in the Arab world as "the decade of fragmentation." For the previous half century at least, Arab political and cultural life had been motivated by a collective project, a collective vision, dream, yearnings, and aspirations. Cultural creation derived its vitality, importance, and relevance from its immersion in this collective project, this *consensus*. At times vague or emotional, it was a *consensus* nevertheless. It represented a process of growth, an organic totality within which a great number of details, tendencies, and currents of thought were assimilated and (at least partly) integrated.

Cultural creation in all its forms, from poetry to sculpture, embodied this wholeness; it developed a sense of totality of its own, a fullness of presence, an organic or indeed structural balance of which it had never been capable before. In poetry, emphasis on unity, freedom of formation which allowed the production of a work governed by its own inner laws and needs, became the fundamental condition for artistic creation. In the novel, a hero—an individual—enjoying a high degree of well-formedness, fullness, power of action, self-esteem, and significance in the social context in which he moved became an artistic reality never before achieved in Arabic writing. Such fullness existed in a time-context which was itself perceived as possessing this organic nature; time appeared to be a meaningful historical time, i.e., a process of purposeful and meaningful change, evolution, progress. This was the epoch in which fiction embodying this organic process was possible to produce, in which very often time, character, and narrative did not begin and end within the limits of one novel, but extended, in an evolving process, through trilogies or narrative sequences which embodied a sense of continuity throughout the whole work of a given artist.

In this epoch, we witnessed the prominence on the cultural stage of writers, dramatists, poets, and painters who possessed a total vision of reality, man, society, cultural change, form, the artistic process, as well as language itself. In poetry, figures like Adonis, al-Bayyati, Hawi, al-Sayyab, 'Abd al-Sabur, Hijazi (and in other fields of cultural activity, figures of similar stature) achieved prominence. This was also the epoch which made possible Gamal Abdel-Nasser's embodiment on the political and social levels of the collective project, dream, or "consensus."

Up to 1973–75, then, a consensus motivated Arab life, a consensus even on frustrations, failures, sufferings; the 1967 defeat was a tragedy on all levels, except on this particular one: it still embodied a collective "event," a collective collapse, collective disillusionment; cultural creation embodied powerfully the collective nature of the tragedy in lamentations, elegies, satires, self-torturing criticism, characters, and voices. Poetry was totally dominated by this elegiac tone. So were other forms of cultural creation.

The End of Consensus

Then came the fragmentation; who can now see in the events taking place in Lebanon a collective vision, tragedy, or fate? Some voices applaud and glorify; other voices lament. Some saw (and still see) in the victory of the resistance movement against Israel (limited though it might be) a new

Arab dawn (we have had so many of them in the past, but to little avail); others saw it as a menace to their own identity and have been fighting it. Similarly, who can see in literary production in Lebanon over the past decade a collective vision, voice, or lamentation? Who can see anything but the "babel of voices, bombs, and missiles" that I personally wrote about in 1971–72? I have jumped suddenly to the present moment, because what it embodies is the mark of the entire period. This is why I have called the past decade "the decade of fragmentation." The fragmentation continues and, in my assessment, will continue to make the coming decade an even more nightmarish one.

The Deconstruction of the Center

The fragmentation I have been discussing is best embodied, on the political, social, and cultural levels, within a single entity, Lebanon (where, significantly, a large body of modern cultural creation was instituted and produced). But such fragmentation has also taken shape on a much higher level, transcending the space of the individual state. I shall call this manifestation of fragmentation "the deconstruction of place" or, more accurately, "the deconstruction of the center."

I am not using "deconstruction" in a metaphorical fashion, but in a literal, *physical* sense. The center, Beirut for instance, was physically destroyed, Arab writers and intellectuals dispersed all over the world, the Palestinian liberation movement was physically deconstructed and scattered. It is this physical, material weight of deconstruction that I wish to emphasize here. It is this physical deconstruction which needs—and rather desperately—to be overcome if the Arab world and Arabic culture are to have any future at all.

The deconstruction of place, or the center, has had, and will continue to have, far deeper and more fundamental effects on Arab society and Arabic culture than almost any other single factor, specifically after 1973. The center, with its relatively long history of liberalism, secularism, nationalism (both regional and pan-Arab), socialism, and closeness to the West and Western culture in particular, was dealt a heavy blow and began to crack up. A new center began to emerge out of the peripheries which had been almost totally the opposite of the center—traditional, religious, royalist (Shaykhist and Amirist), antagonistic to nationalism and socialism. The new center was also traditionally the least affected by the close contact between the Arabs and the West over the last 100 years. Suddenly, it came to control much of the new wealth and economic resources, new technology (imported, of course), and ability to accelerate the purely material aspect of development, the technical aspect. It began to exert its political influence throughout the Arab world on every major issue. For the past 25 years at least, such issues had been dealt with in the old center from the perspective of modernization, socialism (liberalism if you like), orientation toward the West, nationalism. Now these same issues were being approached from a fundamentally different perspective. This is exactly what I mean by deconstruction of the center.

But the new center was culturally *lean*, to put it kindly. Its cultural outlook and cultural perspectives were different, narrower, far more provincial and conservative than those which dominated the old center. This deconstruction of the center has been largely responsible for the present state of cultural and political fragmentation in the Arab world.

The future of cultural creation depends in great part on two factors: first, the outcome of this process of deconstruction of the center on the level of the relative positions of power that the old and new centers are going to occupy vis-à-vis each other and vis-à-vis the West; and second, the internal developments—economic, political, social, and cultural—that take place within the new center. But it must be emphasized that all these relations take place in the context of the struggle with Israel (militarily, politically, peacefully, or by any other means). And they will be determined by, just as much as they will determine, the shape of the struggle and its outcome.

There are signs that the old center is beginning, and will continue, to react to the new center and attempt to reassert itself after a decade of heavy blows, frustration, and skepticism which sometimes reached the point of a total loss of faith. There are signs that the two-fronted struggle for the rejuvenation of the Arab world—I mean the struggle against traditionalism and against colonialism, imperialism, and Israeli domination and occupation—will continue, having learned a great deal from its previous failures. The next decade is decisive precisely on this level: the fate of the nationalist, socialist, liberal, leftist, secular currents of thought and forms of cultural creation, and their ability to reformulate a collective vision, to embody a new consensus.

I do not personally believe that the traditional forces have the power or coherence to formulate this new collective vision. I do not believe that they have the relevance to the modern world which enables them to formulate such consensus. And it is precisely on who manages to formulate such a collective vision and embody such a new consensus that the future of Arab society depends. The present state of fragmentation will not be finally overcome unless such a collective vision is formulated. And cultural creation itself, over the next ten years at least, will be given its shape by what happens on this level.

The Domination of the State

One dominant, and tragic, feature of social life over the past 30 years in the Arab world as a whole has been the cancerous growth of the power of the state in all areas of human existence. This is true of the most anti-socialist regimes just as it is true of the most ardently socialist (in name at least) regimes. In the Arab world the struggle between socialism and capitalism manifests itself in many forms, but certainly not in this particular one: the degree of intervention of the state in social, political, economic, and cultural life. I have just used an odd word to apply to the position of the state in Arab life, namely "intervention." I am being a bit absurd; for the real position of the state in Arab life cannot be described in terms of intervention. Look for the most complete and violent forms of control, dominance, hegemony, usurpation, coercion, etc., and you might come near enough to finding a proper term.

In fact, if "intervention" is to be used at all, it should apply in a reverse fashion: Arab life, Arab society, can be said to represent—at times—a mild form of intervention in the life of the state. I say "at times" and "mild" because Arab society is on the whole cancelled out as a reality of political significance in the reckonings of all Arab regimes. It is a sort of metaphysical entity which can be actualized only on occasions such as a 99.99 yes-vote "election," or at moments when it becomes necessary to demonstrate the loving loyalty of the people to their eternal rulers—often for the benefit of visiting foreign heads of state—in the form of public marches, or great gatherings to celebrate the numerous "historic" days in the life of a ruler, from his birthday, to the occasion of his ascension to the throne (and I am not here referring to kings in particular, for Arab presidents have their own thrones as well—why shouldn't they?) to the occasion of the "historic" battles he led against plotters or traitors or, occasionally, imaginary external threats to the very existence of the nation, to his present moment on the summit of the world and the throne. I exclude his "death" because Arab rulers often do not "die" although they are sometimes "killed." And this of course changes everything. The new "eternal" ruler assumes the position of the old was-eternal-but-is-no-longer-so one, and the wheels of time start rolling afresh to write a great new history for the nation which usually begins by wiping out the presence, traces, and finally, the memory of the old regime. Exceptions here are, however, known to exist, particularly where a son inherits from his father or a brother succeeds his brother. But these cases have not been many in my own lifetime.

The cancerous growth of the state has been accompanied—and not accidentally so, nor as an act of nature (or, in the Arab context, God)—by the increasingly diminishing power of everybody and everything else, especially what some Arab thinkers and leaders enjoy calling "The People." The word is still known in modern Arabic usage, but only in limited contexts. Its disappearance in the immediate future will not be a surprise; nor will it be against the grain of our history, in which the word was never known as such. In Gramsci's term, "civil society" is disappearing, and we are left with the state versus individuals—millions of them, but no society. Sometimes certain groupings are put together for definite purposes: they are called "parliaments," or "people's councils," or "consultative councils," or "*shura* councils," or whatever. But they have little to do with any of the normal functions which institutions in a civil society usually perform. They are rubber stamps in the hands of various regimes, "progressive" and "regressive," revolutionary and reactionary alike (one exception might prove to be Kuwait).

The power of the state on the political and economic levels has been reflected throughout the Arab world in a corresponding power within the cultural sphere. Ministries of culture have been set up, incorporating publishing organizations, drama groups, national theaters, museums, national galleries, and in some countries, distribution companies and even the cultivation of a reading public, all of which give a state an unprecedented degree of power to control cultural activity on the levels of both production and consumption.

Even more significant, perhaps, is the incredible growth of state-owned journals and cultural periodicals. Journals have been the most influential means of dissemination of ideas, ideologies, and cultural currents. They have replaced the book as the means of influence. The major literary (and political) movements over the last 30 years have all been connected with major journals such as *Shi'r Mawaqif, Al-Adab,* and *Fusul*. The seriousness of the new situation is that the state now controls the major journals (the few exceptions include *Mawaqif; Al-Thaqafa al-jadida*—closed down in 1984 by the Moroccan regime; and *Al-Mahd; Kalimat*). The spread of this control outside the Arab world is an even more frightening phenomenon. Various regimes have set up their own journals, magazines, newspapers, and now even their publishing houses in capitals not only in Cyprus, but as far away as the United States.

In this atmosphere, which might appear positive in that the state is apparently contributing to the advancement of knowledge, the real tragedy is the total loss of freedom and possibility of critical thinking or expression. A few free platforms remain (e.g., *Mawaqif*), but these are blocked by various Arab regimes for one reason or another. When one adds to this the absolute control of mass media (radio, television, and most of the press) throughout the Arab world, the picture of the demonic power of the state becomes clearer and more depressing. The future can only be more suffocating, as Arab regimes have begun to control space through their purchase of the so-called "Arabsat."

Westernization and Backlash

The last 30 years have witnessed the most violent critique of Arab culture, society, and history ever made. The defeat in the June war of 1967 generated a new wave of self-criticism, satirization, and lamentation which left no sacred gods, hidden or manifest. From the religious to the profane, everything was torn apart; political authority, institutions, as well as the basic forms of social organization, especially the family, came under severe scrutiny and criticism. The cultural traditions, the "Arab" mentality, the language and history, were all seen as decadent, crumbling, empty, dead. The most dominant image in this period has been that of the wasteland.

The process was exhausting; but no alternatives were discovered; no new possibilities, institutions, or horizons were found. The decadence continued unabated. Next came the oil explosion, whose most direct and damaging effect has been the emergence of a consumer society and the total fragmentation of the class structure. The process by which this came about was one of unprecedented openness to the technological achievements of the West. The process was dramatic, huge, so fast and immediate that it generated a violent backlash which took the form of clinging to national identity and the Arab tradition.

In this sense, the traditional wave in the Arab world now can be seen largely as a product of the violent process of modernization brought about by the oil explosion. A traditional society experiencing the pains and pleasures of a slow process of change and responding to it positively was suddenly exposed to tempests of change which appeared to threaten not so much to "change" its ways and modes of life, but to blow it up, to uproot it completely. The process was further complicated by two factors: the legendary wealth suddenly enjoyed by a large number of individuals (almost forming a new class) acting mostly as agents for Western exporting firms (or as agents, or partners, for powerful figures in most Arab regimes) and the increasing dominance by the West and Israel of the political process in the Arab world. Sadat's peace with Israel threw the Arab world more deeply into frustration, desperation, and fragmentation, furthering the deconstruction of the center I described above.

The situation looked absurd: tremendous power, financial and economic, was coupled with total impotence, political and military. A revolution was needed, but none was possible; for the oppression had been so total that no chances of any sort were left for rebellion. Indeed, even the notorious process of change familiar in the Arab world, namely, the coup d'état, has ceased to happen.

The violent oppression (in an atmosphere of total frustration) could only be met by a similar degree of violence, which in turn could only come from the one ideology that had for long been absent from the political sphere and had as a result not been so totally battered as other forces, on the one hand, and not been associated with Arab defeats, on the other. Furthermore, it is the ideology which is identifiably "specific" or "authentic," capable of defining itself oppositionally, especially in relation to the West and Israel. This ideology can only be Islamic "thought."

Romanticization of the Tradition

In an earlier section of this paper, I described the struggle of the modern against the dominant culture as a struggle between a future-oriented and a past-oriented vision of man, society, and culture. The most positive achievements in the Arab world today, particularly on the cultural level, owe their existence to this modernist outlook. Yet, for reasons that sociologists and social psychologists are better qualified to determine than I am, but at some of which I have already hinted, the struggle of the modern has elicited reactions from the dominant, traditional culture which have taken the form of a violent rejection of the West—for long associated, indeed identified, with modernity—and a clinging to "specificity," national character, tradition, and "authenticity." All these epithets are variants of a much simpler term: *the past*—the golden age (which nobody has defined clearly so far).

Earlier, I described this reaction as the "shock of the tradition," opposing it directly to what Adonis, for instance, has called "the shock of modernity" (*sadmat al-hadatha*). One must distinguish here between the forces of traditional culture—still deeply immersed in itself as a past-in-the-present form of existence—which have over the last decade begun to fight back with a remarkable degree of vigor, and the neo-traditional forces (rather, groups or individuals who had belonged to the modernist movements) which comprise Arab intellectuals who have suddenly discovered that they have intellectual achievements, methodologies, etc., which make it more than relevant to the modern world. Such individuals suffer deeply from "the shock of the tradition," and one of the most immediate consequences of their shock is the new phenomenon of romanticization of traditional culture, a romanticization which has produced a complete loss of historical perspective and, indeed, of balance.

I do not want to exaggerate the importance of the reaction of traditional forces today, and I believe that such exaggeration has been the hallmark of a lot of reporting in the media and writing even in serious journals by serious thinkers. Furthermore, I believe that creating such an aura around this reaction and blowing up its significance is precisely what the powers-that-be have wanted to achieve and have indeed achieved. A lot of Arab writers have fallen prey to this ploy and begun to play the disastrous game. In my own assessment, this is an ordinary occurrence in an Arab world torn by so many conflicting ideologies and currents of thought. It is no more than yet another trend coming to some prominence in a cycle of rising and falling ideologies. It is, as I said earlier, a passing phenomenon.

All societies are familiar with the phenomenon of traditional reactions appearing at times as if they were dominant forces in cultural and social life. The West has experienced a "spiritual" sort of reaction over the last three decades; but it has not changed much. Arab society is no different, except in one sense: the traditional base is stronger. But it is not sufficiently strong to cause an Islamic revolution over the next decade.

The force with which the Islamic reaction has expressed itself is proportionate to the force of the shock of "modernization" after 1973. The suddenness, pace, and volume of the opening up of Arab markets and Arab life to the overwhelming flood of imported projects, people, ideas, and technological devices have caused a genuine cracking up of social structures, especially within a certain class: the small bourgeoisie which had been on the rise and suddenly found itself incapable of absorbing the new flood. Only the established, traditional commercial class could reap the huge benefits, together with two other groups: those in power because of their royal or presidential origins, and those who have come to possess and exercise power through their army careers.

The Emergence of Islamic Movements

Earlier on, I argued that the emergence of religious (Islamic) movements is directly related to two factors: the oppression by Arab regimes of all political opposition and the violence and extent of the process of modernization over the past 15 years. I should here mention specifically the changes affecting the position of women in Arab society. In my own view much of the religious reaction is motivated by fears of a sexual revolution, fear for honor, and fear of the radical effect women's liberation will have on the position of men enjoyed for 1,400 years. You need only teach at an Arab university to discover this "revelation."

There is, however, a third dimension related directly to the process of fragmentation to which I have devoted so much time. For, in such a state of fragmentation—the collapse of the progressive collective vision and project and the disappearance of the future as a possibility for fulfillment—only the past appears to remain meaningful, coherent, solid, and easily accessible. When the present offers nothing and the future appears aborted, only the past, with its *real* achievements, becomes capable of offering the security of promise and the promise of security as well as the promise of achievement in the present by emulating its modes of feeling, thinking, and operating. And the past in Arab consciousness exists only in one form: as a *religious* experience and modes of political, social, and cultural organization.

This fact in itself testifies to the failure of the efforts made by modern Arab writers, thinkers, and artists alike to reinterpret Arabic history in terms other than those of the dominant traditional culture. Perhaps only the reinterpretation of the Ottoman period of colonization of the Arab world has met with success, i.e., has influenced modern Arabic thought and social life in changing the view of this colonization as a legitimate continuation of the caliphate. But even here, we witness now a reaction led and directed by the Islamic movements which are constantly spreading the view that Ottoman rule was the legitimate rule of Islam and that the movement for independence was a Western-led attack on Islam, contributed to by the anti-Islamic nationalist forces.

This view of the past as a refuge, an ideal, a motivating power, a project for the creation of a better future has not yet had any real impact on the level of cultural creation. But the coming decade will almost certainly witness a definite growth in this direction. Already the number of Islamic publications—books, journals, newspapers—is on the increase.

On the Uses of the Tradition

It was Frantz Fanon, I think, who first described the intricate process by which a colonized society asserts its cultural identity in response to a colonizing society. I shall use the outlines of his model, without taking all its details as part of my argument.

What seems to me most significant in Fanon's description is the way in which a colonized society responds first by trying to assimilate the cultural forms of a colonizing society. The ability to assimilate such forms becomes a criterion of the ability of the colonized society to survive the period of colonization. The process implies both a recognition of the superiority of the cultural forms of the colonizing power and an identification of this superiority with the position of power occupied by the colonizing society. The colonized, in this condition, responds to the challenge of the colonizing power by trying to acquire its own language (and by "language" I mean the entire semiotic system developed within the colonizing society, especially those aspects of the system which relate to cultural phenomena). By acquiring such a semiotic system and the ability to use it effectively (i.e., as creatively, expressively, and powerfully as the colonizing power), the colonized develops a new sense of power, of capability, of equality with the colonizer. If it can use those forms most intimately related to the "secrets" of power of the colonizing society and most intimately expressive of its inner world and inner vision, then a colonized society proves both to itself and to the colonizing power that it can stand on an equal footing with it and claim to belong to its own universe.

Once the culture has established its ability to compete with the colonizing power, it acquires the self-confidence to allow its own cultural forms to come into play. Such forms, however, being part of the traditional system which had been in the first place associated with the inability of the culture to maintain its strength and independence, will now tend to lose their original significance. They will be used afresh as a new semiotic system whose main function is not to denote traditional concepts or meanings or modes of thinking and existence but, to a large extent, to assert national identity as an opposing identity, i.e., in the face of the colonizing identity. This largely *assertive* function of the new semiotic code comes as a second phase in the struggle between the colonized and the colonizer. It generates a process of conscious search for "authentic" forms of expression—dance, singing, folklore generally, literary forms—especially those most intimately rooted in the culture, forms which might have been dead, or left unused for a long period of time.

These forms will now be imbued with different meanings and be endowed with a definite symbolic function in the context of the ongoing struggle. When Emile Habibi writes in Israel, in a situation where the *identity* of the Palestinians as Arabs is threatened, he uses forms which are deeply rooted in the traditions of Arabic writing, going back to al-Jahiz in the eighth and ninth centuries. The "content," so to speak, embodied in these forms is totally different; it has nothing to do with the world view expressed by al-Jahiz, or by Islamic society (or Arab society) in the eighth and ninth centuries.

Nor do the issues over which the struggle is taking place have much to do with the issues originally expressed by these ancient forms. When the form itself becomes a weapon, it becomes a statement of identity. Thus Mahmoud Darwish shouts "Write down, I am an Arab," using the symbols of Arabism which sound naïve and irrelevant on the level of reality in the struggle between the Palestinians and the Israelis, and he does that in the form which is the most intimate to the culture: poetry. Equally, when Jamal al-Ghitani uses traditional forms of narration in his *Al-Zaini Barakat* or his *Tajalliyat*, he is using form as part of a total semiotic system, whose function is largely that assertive function I pointed out earlier.

I am not saying, and I will make this more explicit later, that the world view of the culture dies away, or that its content dies away. I am making a vital distinction between the use of a semiotic system of cultural forms to imbue it with a new content, and the actual continuation of traditional forms still possessing their original content. In other words, I am making a distinction between two currents which exist in the culture. The first is the still traditional current of thought, i.e., traditional ideology and world view; the second is the new ideological structure, new world view, using the semiotic system of cultural forms which belongs to national culture in opposition to the hegemony of invading cultural forms.

This distinction can be expressed in terms of the inside and outside. The insiders carry on with their traditional life and modes of conception and expression, offering resistance of a specific nature to the dominating power. Their resistance is the less significant and less powerful. The outsiders are those who have first attempted to break out of the boundaries of traditional culture, and who have assimilated the cultural forms of the dominating power. They turn inward now with this new sense of achievement and self-confidence to revitalize traditional cultural forms and give them new significance. Their resistance is the more expressive, more powerful.

The insider culture remains imprisoned within its own traditional world view and weaknesses. The outsider culture is the one which possesses vigor, power, and a new sense of itself. It works to achieve four things: first, to assert national identity and, second, to counter the dominance of the outside power. Third, and very importantly, it works to assert its creativity, to demonstrate its ability to create, and to add to the very rich stock built up by the dominating culture. Its creativity is best achieved and expressed on this level, for it brings in new forms, new abilities, and a new language (for a good example of this, see how Roland Barthes views the work done on the semiotics of popular culture by 'Abd al-Kabir al-Khatibi). Four, it works to reinterpret the tradition from a new "revolutionary" perspective or, at least, a perspective of change.

In Arabic culture the first current remained dominant for a long period of time, and it has been the one least capable of resisting outside domination. It is precisely the second current, which broke out of the limits of traditional culture, assimilated Western experience, then turned inward with this new power that I have been describing, which has been responsible for most of the achievements and the cultural contribution the Arabs are making, and which will be, over the next decade (and for much longer than that), the current capable of furthering such a contribution.

The Islamic and the Tradition

What I have been saying will immediately raise the question: How about Islamic "fundamentalism"? How about the movements which call for return to the golden past? How about those "reactionary"—in the literal sense of the word—currents of thought within Arabic culture now? In this regard, it seems to me that what we might call "the internal resources of the artist" in the Arab world will become increasingly based in national culture, by which I do not mean Islam. Undoubtedly, Islam formed the context within which Arab society has existed, but as far as cultural creation is concerned, I do not think we can identify a single period of cultural vitality as an Islamic period or as a period in which a religious view of the world formed the main source of inspiration for the artist. The main exception to this statement is not so much a period as a current within the culture, namely the *sufi* tradition. Outside this, Arabic literature and other cultural forms of expression have constantly been dominated by secular world views, by what Edward Said likes to call "worldliness."

In literary criticism, for instance, the main currents of thought were never formed as an expression of a view of literature as an instrument of propagating faith or embodying a religious attitude to the world. In fact, the striking characteristic of all Arabic criticism (with very minor exceptions) is that it insisted on the autonomy of literary texts, on the separation of religion from literature. It is also striking that the only literary current in prose and poetry alike which was dominated by a spiritual or religious world view, namely, sufism, was totally ignored by literary critics.

The major figures in Arabic writing are those poets who were nonreligious or anti-religious, from Abu Nuwas to Al-Ma'arri. The only exception to this statement might be—and only might be—what we now call Islamic art, which was non-representational, and in its non-representationality is said to have derived its sources of inspiration or its artistic language from a religious world view. I am not personally confident that arabesque was to the people practicing it an expression of a religious world view. I am not confident that it is even now in the forms in which we see it, in mosques, on brass trays, on furniture, in the markets of Damascus, produced by Muslims and non-Muslims alike, an expression of a religious spirit. In fact, I see arabesque as precisely the outcome of the artists' having to work within the constraints, restrictions, and taboos imposed by Islam, rather than being inspired by it. Not one account by those who practiced arabesque suggests that this was its essence.

On the other hand, the nonrepresentational aspect of Arabic art has been highly exaggerated. We now know that representations existed in the early Umayyad period. And, more important, we also know that wine scenes, sexual scenes, hunting scenes, and worldly scenes, rather than any religious experience, formed the basis of much Arabic art in both architecture and illuminated manuscripts, with the very natural exception of Qur'anic manuscripts. When a modern artist uses arabesque or Arabic calligraphy he is, therefore, not necessarily expressing a religious or spiritual sentiment or vision of the world. Some artists undoubtedly do this, but the majority are still using arabesque and Arabic calligraphy in a totally separate context and mainly because of their function as assertions of identity. The folkloric themes of Iraqi, Moroccan, or Syrian art emphasize not an Islamic world view, but a sense of national identity in "Arabic" culture. This is no less true of the calligraphy of the Palestinian artist Kamal Boullata, although in his work we do find an almost mystical way of seeing things which I personally attribute more to personal experience than to a collective surge in the culture of Islamic themes or religious experience (it might be of significance to mention here that Boullata, like many other artists working with calligraphy, is not Muslim).

Ultimately, the main current in the culture will in my view develop in this direction, the direction of extracting from the semiotic system of traditional culture those elements most intimately national, i.e., most deeply and explicitly in opposition to Western forms, emptying them of their traditional significance, ideology, and world view, and endowing them with a modernist sensibility. This has been happening in drama, in poetry, in the novel, in literary criticism, in art, and to a lesser extent in music. Indeed, this began to happen at a point in time when national identity as such was threatened, but not the religious dimension of the culture. The process, that is, began long before this recent emergence of Islamic "political parties." The dramatist, Sa'dallah Wannus, for instance, was trying to explore the possibilities of popular traditional forms (the storyteller in particular) before anybody in the Arab world or in the West—where it mostly happened—was talking about "Islamic revival." Adonis was using such symbols as al-Husayn, al-Hallaj, and 'Umar bin al-Khattab when the question of Islamic identity was not at all in evidence. So was Emile Habibi, who, in fact, argues constantly for deeprootedness in the traditions of Arabic writing and in the language itself as an ideological (Marxist) and artistic issue rather than as a religious (i.e., Islamic) one (he is not a Muslim). He sees the use of tradition as a device, an artistic means of getting the message through to the "masses" who fail to understand when Western symbols are used.

A further point needs to be made, and made with special emphasis. The use of symbols of national culture and forms of expression which originated in that culture did not acquire any real significance so long as it was practiced within the world of traditional culture. It acquired significance only when it began to be practiced by the "modernist"—to use a single adjective—writers. And in this new context, its frame of reference was not Islam or, more specifically, Sunni Islam, i.e., the official culture, but what I have often called counterculture or marginal culture. From Arwa bint al-Ward in pre-Islamic poetry to al-Ma'arri in "Islamic" poetry, the chain of symbols developed—developed in the texts produced not by the religious establishment but by figures who belong to the culture of the outsider.

This fact is important in two ways. First, the nature of the symbolic figures themselves is significant: they all belong to the counterculture—sufis, Shi'a, rejectionists, revolutionaries, outsiders, wine poets, poets of sexuality and homosexuality, anti-religious and anti-tribal poets, socialists, nationalists. Second, one must note the nature of the poets who evoke these symbols—and who belong to the same current of thought: nationalists, rejectionists, non-religious and anti-religious types, poets of sexuality (not so much homosexuality), modernists, non-traditionalists, socialists, revolutionaries, i.e., outsiders. The body of literature read in the Arab world today and considered to be representative of cultural creation and cultural activity is produced by such figures and dominated by such symbols.

It may be very significant to point out here that even figures who were religious personalities (who included figures like al-Husayn, al-Hallaj, and Christ, but rarely Muhammad) have been stripped of their religious character.

Even religious vocabulary, when used in modern poetry or narrative, is stripped of its religious connotations. In modern poetry, a strong tone of what I have called *ibtihal* emanates, but its "religious" vocabulary and its spirit are totally secular, nationalist, and revolutionary. *Salat*, for example, no longer means prayer as part of a religious code of practices, and the title of a Kuwaiti book, *Prayer in a Deserted Temple*, no longer has much to do with Islam. Hence, phrases like "I pray to your eyes," which is meaningless and even indicative of religious infidelity, are extremely common in modern secular poetry.

All this use of religious symbolism, religious language, and mythology has played a significant role on one important level. At the time when the struggle of the modern had a definite secular, nationalist, socialist, liberal, and Marxist content totally devoid of religious connotations, religious symbolism in myth emerged and prevailed. That was back in the 1960s. Paradoxically, perhaps, such religious symbolism has almost completely faded out now, precisely at the point when a strong, truly religious current of thought begins to make itself felt.

This stripping away of religious substance is a phenomenon of real importance; if we read it correctly, we will see that it contributes to sustaining the argument I have been making. I do not personally see that much is going to change in this regard during the next ten years.

The Half-Formed and the Disintegrated

In the epoch of totality and fullness I described earlier, many writers, artists, and thinkers came to embody this wholeness and integration in their work. Thus we had a generation, in the precise sense of the word, in the works of whose members internal links and associations were far more powerful than internal contradiction, as they all derived their inspiration from the collectivity of vision, the collectivity of the project or dream, or what I have called "consensus." The generation immediately following has never managed to make itself as powerfully felt in modern Arabic writing. It is, in a sense, just half-felt, which is extremely significant in the present context. The members of this generation, or rather the group of individuals producing in these years, began earlier, in the period of wholeness and integration, and they began to make themselves felt as a new generation. But suddenly, in the middle of their life and work, they were struck by history—they were cut down to size, if you like, and they crumbled. They were subjected to and subjugated by the process of disintegration. The work they produced after that possessed the quality which the entire culture, the entire society possessed: absence of internal links and relationships, of a collective vision, of a consensus. They have remained since hanging in the air, half-formed, half-deformed, half-integrated, half-disintegrated. Many readers will know the names—in poetry, for instance, they include such individuals as Sa'di Yusuf, M. 'Afifi Matar, Amal Dunqul, and their contemporaries in Iraq, Syria, Lebanon, and Egypt.

The new generation or new large group of individuals producing on the cultural scene after this half-formed, half-disintegrated group, began and continues to function in the context of disintegration. They do not even have the bliss of half-formedness, nor do they form a generation in any artistic or cultural sense. They are as scattered and fragmented as people are in any other area, social, political, or economic.

In neither of these two successive waves of groups do we see an artist with a total vision of reality, of humanity, of the past and present and future, of the Arab world and Arabic culture. Nowhere do we see meaningful structures, structures imbued with totality and wholeness. On the contrary, we see total fragmentation. The works of the prominent Egyptians, from A.H. Qasim to Yusuf al-Qa'id, offer a good example of this. In Syria, in the work of Hani al-Rahib, we see another. In poetry the examples are many and it will be almost pointless to quote names.

Here we do not see a great figure or individual artist. It is as if the age of heroic acts or individuals who were well formed, totally integrated, has gone. We see some extremely good individual pieces of writing, individual poems, individual short stories, novels, plays, paintings, but we do not see a "body of literature," a body of cultural creation. This is the hallmark of Arabic cultural production today, and, as I suggested earlier, this will continue to be the hallmark of Arabic cultural production at least for the next decade.

And what I am saying now applies, and will apply, on two different levels. I have so far described it on the level of the creator, but it is also true on the level of the created artistic object itself. In other words, the absence of the individual heroic act; of well-formedness; and of totality, wholeness, and the integrated self are as evident in the creator, the poet, the novelist, the dramatist, the thinker, and the painter, as they are in the character in and the total structure of the novel, or the character in a play or in a short story, or the "voice" in a poem, or the composition of a painting. For, on this level also, we see the disintegration of character, the absence of center, of wholeness, of totality, of integrated structures.

Fragmentation in Literature

I have already mentioned certain names and works in the context of the fragmentation I have been describing. I would like to concentrate now on the structure of the poem and take as an example Adonis's recent major poem, *Isma'il*. My intention here is not to present a study of this complex work, but to refer simply to the fact that it represents a very different work from many of Adonis's poems written in the epoch of totality, wholeness, and organic fullness.

Isma'il, even physically, looks fragmented. It is divided up into sections, and in each section the poet breaks the narrative in two different ways. Internally, closed boxes suddenly occupy the center of the text, standing unrelated, or little related, to the development of the individual section as a whole. Externally, the poet adds footnotes, which, however, differ from normal footnotes in that each derives from and continues the line in the text to which it is related, but continues it not as organic narrative, not as a genuine continuation of syntax or imagery, but in the form of a commentary on that particular line, which at times adds a new dimension to it and at other times changes its course and nature. This constant breaking up of the text internally and externally is an embodiment of the process of fragmentation of structure that I have been discussing.

If I may refer to my personal work, as far back as 1970 I wrote a poem called "Opposition" (published in *Mawaqif* in 1972) which was received with a great sense of shock by a number of major poets who had reached their maturity in that epoch I called the epoch of fullness, organic growth, and integration. The poem was very long, some forty odd pages, all divided up, broken, disconnected, disembodied. Parts of it consisted of maps, musical scores, photocopies of poems by other poets, photocopies of stories of oppression and horror coming from the classical tradition, a painting by Picasso, and white pages or pages occupied by fading small dots. The text consisted of a large series of oppositions and contradictions, all tearing apart the body of the poem and the nation, which was symbolically called the "Babel of Voices." That may have been the first major work of disintegration and fragmentation not only to embody this period, but also to anticipate it.

As in poetry, in the novel and in drama we witness the same process of fragmentation and disintegration. In his novel *Alf layla wa laylatan*, Hani al-Rahib produces a long text consisting not of a sequential narrative embodying time as an organic process of growth from A to B to C to D and so forth to Z, i.e., not diachronically, but as a whole series of layers in the text which exist synchronically and depict the world of a huge number of characters and phenomena and events and contradictions, with a conception of time as static, non-organic.

The novel, like the poem, was met by violent attacks. But in its structure, or rather lack of structure, it embodied the same process or state of disintegration and fragmentation that many other works were to embody a little later on.

Reification

One major aspect of this state of fragmentation I have been trying to describe relates directly to another important property of both contemporary reality and cultural creation in the Arab world—reification. This is a phenomenon of such major importance that it deserves a more detailed discussion than is practical here. I shall therefore offer the mere outlines of the way in which it has been manifested.

We owe to Lucien Goldmann our understanding of the mechanism by which reification as a psychic and mental state of man in capitalist society is embodied in the structure of the novel. It was Goldmann who analyzed the French new novel and demonstrated, convincingly I think, that the obsession with objects and the way objects occupy the center of the stage in the novel is an embodiment of "the human condition," to use Malraux's phrase, in that stage of the development of capitalist society which Marx had predicted and to which he had assigned the term "reification." In this stage, according to Goldmann, "the intellectual and effective life of men is progressively reduced and severely diminished. A type of man arises whose psychic structure is essentially passive, who is estranged from all responsible decisions, and who is oriented essentially toward consumption (which of course also includes the ensemble of leisure and cultural consumption)."—*Cultural Creation*, p. 85.

It is probably ironic to see similar structures in the novel emerging in an "underdeveloped" society, decades away from the capitalist stage of development. However, it is not for the sake of irony that I am referring to Goldmann's study here, but because the coincidence helps to raise fundamental questions concerning culture, literature, creativity, and authenticity.

The obsession with objects and the implicit state of reification it represents is fast becoming a common characteristic in modern Arabic fiction. Ibrahim Aslan's novel *Malik al-Hazin* (*The Heron*) is a perfect example of this. I shall only quote a passage from this novel and leave it with you to contemplate in the light of the discussion I have presented:

> The walls of the room were crowded with tightly arranged books on shelves suspended by braided ropes. There were two paintings as well, one on each side of the window. One was a print of the Mona Lisa. It was spread on the wall and fastened with a small metal pin at the top. The other was on the right side along the edge of the couch on which he was sitting. It was drawn with black ink on yellowish white paper, and had been put in a wide frame without glass. The frame's golden paint had faded and it now had the color of old pounded copper. The etching showed a man on an old mule. He had a thick coat on his back and carried a stick-like spear. There was a follower on an ambivalent short donkey bearing two saddlebags. The follower had his eyes raised silently to look at his mounted knight. The background was a group of lines completed with Picasso's signature and the date. Also in the background, in the distance, between the donkey's and the mule's legs, were a few small windmills like children's toys. The sun was suspended like a crooked incomplete ring sending out its rays in short and long lines.
>
> There was also an old hunting rifle in the room and an assortment of empty wine bottles, glasses, pencils, a metal helmet full of medicine boxes and matchboxes, a desk, a heavy mirror in a carved frame, and a short chest with a turntable on top and two pairs of shoes underneath.
>
> Behind the door, his clothes were suspended on a small brass hanger.

A close analysis will reveal that the characters, situations, and concepts depicted by the Arab novelist in the new structure (which he might have learned from the West) originate in conditions similar in nature, although different in roots, to those experienced by the individual in a reified society. The human individual in Arab society is negated by authority and oppression—mostly of a political nature; psychic life is essentially passive, and the person is estranged from responsible decisions and oriented to consumption because of the crushing effects of authority. The Western individual is negated by authority and exploitation, mostly on the economic level. But as al-Mutanabbi said, "Various are the causes, but death is one."

In Western society the context of the individual's loss of importance is that of organizational capitalism and the emergence of totality (embodied in the process of a conscious self-regulating mechanism). The Arab individual has lost whatever importance may have existed through the self-regulating exertion of authority on all levels and the crippling pressures of the value-system as a total structure, in its political, social, cultural, linguistic, and moral dimensions. The emergence of consumer society over the last decade has aggravated the situation and crystallized—prematurely, perhaps—the conditions of reification.

The structure capable of embodying the second experience is capable of embodying the first. Cultural "invasion" here is a very enriching act; it represents no threat to authenticity. (An authentic expression would probably have taken the form of a *maqama* or an anecdote [*khabar*], both embodying different attitudes, psychic lives, and characters; both would have been less capable of performing this new function of structure.)

Is not this state of disintegration and reification which produces an individual "whose psychic structure is essentially passive, who is estranged from all responsible decisions," precisely the state of mind of the millions throughout the Arab world who listened and looked passively and then went about their daily affairs as Israel was destroying the Lebanese and Palestinians across Lebanon and in Sabra and Shatila? In the epoch of fullness, as I will simply call it now, these millions would have at least exploded on the streets of Arab cities in huge, emotionally violent demonstrations. But those were very different times.

The Possibilities of Fragmentation

Let me now end where I started—with fragmentation—and offer my last testimony, not by way of summing up, but by way of restating a half-formed, half-deformed vision of the shape of things to come.

Arab society is threatened over the next decade by the possibility of total fragmentation. The most obvious type of fragmentation is that caused by sectarian divisions, on the one hand, and ethnic diversity, on the other. Purely ideological fragmentation is already prevalent and will reach new dimensions. Moreover, we will also witness an intensification of class struggle, within each Arab state first and on the inter-Arab level second. In some countries the social structure will reach a point where an equilibrium taking the form of a "one-dimensional person" or "one-dimensional society" will prevail. Class struggle will be muted by the benefits that the working classes derive from an affluent society. In other countries, the middle class will almost vanish as society is divided into the very rich and the very poor. In still others, a more classic pattern will emerge or survive: a small rich class, a bourgeoisie, and the poor masses of the people.

In the midst of all this, the power of the state will reach its zenith in some parts and begin to crumble in others. Cultural creation will embody such states of being and attempt to transcend them at the same time.

The idea of, and the possibilities for, a collective project, an Arab dream, will be diminished even further than they are now—and they are already at a very low point.

The Arab Synthesis

From the process of total fragmentation and disintegration which I have been depicting, the possibility of a new, more solid project might emerge. Whatever emerges will, in my assessment, be more deeply rooted in the realities of the Arab world. In this sense, it will be more authentic. Preconceived, totalitarian models will probably fade out, including both Marxism and Islam. If the last hundred years have been characterized by the precedence of such models over reality, the next 25 to 50 years are more likely to be characterized by an exploration of reality, of social structures, economic conditions, and cultural forms which will help to formulate a new, specifically Arab, way of seeing things; an Arab mode of existence, of social and political organization; an Arab synthesis.

Such a synthesis will assimilate fundamental principles of the ideologies current in Arabic culture today, but none of these is likely to survive *in toto* as a dominant ideology. Aspects of traditional culture (including Islam) will undoubtedly be incorporated into this new system of belief and organization. But Islam as a total order of social and political life, as a preconceived model existing in the "golden" past, will not dominate Arab life.

This is only a prediction. But predictions can sometimes be recognized as intuitively valid.

Cultural Creation:
Fragmentation and the New Model

To close now, I would like to contemplate the possibilities that can be opened up for cultural creation by the state of affairs I have been depicting and predicting.

Arabic culture has been dominated for centuries by ideology and authority. This domination turned cultural creation into an instrument for both ideology and authority or an instrument for one fighting against the other. In ancient times, ideology and authority derived from a religious world view and, to some extent, from a religious organization of society. Over the past 40 years or so, the nature of both ideology and authority have changed, but their relationship to cultural creation has not, except in a marginal way: from the consensus of Islam there has been a shift to the consensus of nationalism, socialism, "revolution," and from the authority of the politico-religious figures, we have moved to the authority of the single party or to the personification of God in the military ruler or in the shaykh or the amir or king. In all cases, however, cultural creation remained to a large extent dominated by ideology and authority. There has not been a single period when a state of free search dominated the culture: a search for alternatives, for freedom of creation—of personal interaction with the world and interpretation of reality, of offering individual answers to the deeper questions facing humanity, both within society and, in a sense (maybe not very accurately) outside society, e.g., questions of a metaphysical nature.

Now, for the first time in centuries, we are beginning to see a situation, to live in a social environment, in which both authority and ideology are to some extent being challenged. It is to intensify this challenge, to bring about a fragmentation, not of social forces this time, but of authority and ideology, that Arabic writing and cultural creation in general seem to aspire. For the first time we see a type of literature governed not by collective vision, by ideology or authority, but by an almost free search. We witness the highest degree of experimentation ever known in the culture. We witness a genuine sense of adventure in exploring reality and the mediums of expression in drama, poetry, fiction, painting, sculpture, and even music. We begin to see a genuine state of *multiplicity* as opposed to the one-dimensional vision, and one-dimensional form, generated in the past by the dominance of ideology and authority. It is this state of flux and free search which underlies the feeling of angst gripping people in the Arab world today. It is this condition which makes people declare that we live in a state of crisis: crisis in creativity, crisis in poetry, crisis in thought, crisis in criticism.

I suggest that we do not live in a state of crisis. We live in a state in which consensus as such has been fragmented and a new spirit is struggling to emerge. This is powerfully reflected in a new type of writing in, for instance, Egypt, which for the first time enters the state of free search and experimentation. We see it in the new writing which I can call the post-Lebanese civil war writing, and, more significantly perhaps, we see it even in the context of the Palestinian struggle, specifically in the recent poetry of Mahmoud Darwish. The process is far from completed, but we are approaching the point where ideology and authority might collapse as sources for, and dominant forces in, cultural creation. With this will collapse also the dominance of preconceived models, whether of Western or of ancient Islamic origin. I am fully aware as I say this that other intellectuals and analysts talk about an Islamic revival. But, as I made clear earlier, I personally discount this phenomenon as mainly a chain of reactions against a dislocating, violent process of clash with the West, its technology, material advancement, and hegemony, which a traditional society has not been able to accommodate or cope with.

We are approaching a point, and the next decade will be decisive in this, where the fragmentation, having now occurred on the level of civil society, political parties, various social groupings, and various cultural entities, will begin to reach to the very basis of authority and ideology and to affect the basis of the power of the state. All this has been, and will be to a far greater degree, to the advantage of cultural creation, in the sense that it is likely to make it richer, more varied, more humanistic; even in its involvement in the social and political struggles, it will cease to be purely ideological and develop a more humanist language.

Individual experience, within this new context, is likely to become of far greater importance than it has ever been. Humanity's yearnings, frustrations, hopes, desires, questions, and answers will be more powerfully and richly explored in all forms of cultural creation, which will have liberated themselves to a large degree from the dominance of both ideology and authority. The changes crystallizing over the last ten years suggest that this prediction may be correct.

Another dimension of this breakdown of ideology, authority, and preconceived models is of extreme importance. What appears as a crisis in creativity in the Arab world today stems partly from the fact that certain forces now reject the West as a model to be emulated, just as much as others reject traditional Islamic culture as such a model. This is a crucial impulse in the culture today: for once, the Arab world may meet the challenge of modern civilization without a preconceived model. And without a model it will recognize that its choices are limited: either it perishes or it develops its creative powers, its ability to explore and create and, ultimately, to develop its own model. This will generate new forces and a new drive in the culture. And it is this more than anything else that will shape the future of things to come.

Naturally, authority and ideology will strive to maintain their historic hold on cultural production, and we will see vigorous attempts to subjugate cultural creation both by the state and by the traditional, basically religious, movements which have now emerged under the banner of an Islamic "revival." But I am personally confident that in the long run, the outcome of this struggle will not be a victory for these forces.

PART FIVE

Social Transformations

12

Future Arab Economic-Demographic Potential: Whither Policy?

Ismail A. Sirageldin

Introduction

Changes in stable socio-demographic systems have occurred (except in cases of environmental accident) when major new production technologies are widely adopted and socially institutionalized. In most instances, this process of change is associated with increasing specialization and thus with the opening up of local markets and their integration into the wider regional and international system of trade and exchange. It must be emphasized that major technological changes are but one facet, albeit central, in the development of our ever-evolving technological civilization. But as major new production technologies take hold, a new system of human settlements and social relations evolves that is in harmony with the new wave of emerging techniques.

During these periods of structural change, mortality and reproductive behavior tend to adjust toward new levels that are compatible with the new sets of production relations and their associated social formations. This movement from one equilibrium level of vital rates to another is called in the population literature a "demographic transition." Indeed, the current "demographic transition"[1] is the consequence of the world's dramatic experience with technological change, dubbed the Industrial Revolution. This socio-demographic transition, which had its origin in the seventeenth century and accelerated during the second part of this century, has influenced all the parameters of human and nonhuman life, including the vital rates, and has apparently set the world society on an irrevocable path of "technicalization."[2]

Demographic transitions, accordingly, cannot be defined independently of their socioeconomic context and, more fundamentally, the prevailing production technology. It is possible for the demographic parameters of a system to change as a result of changes in social relations without associated significant changes in the technological parameters. But such changes are necessarily limited by that system's production potential, which, in the final analysis, should be able to provide the necessary biological support for the growth of population.

Contemporary discussions of demographic change that theorize about or prescribe ways and means of influencing fertility or migration behavior without first considering the structural causes that ignite that change are doomed to failure. It does not follow, however, that knowledge about structural causes alone is sufficient for the correct diagnosis of and prescription for development problems. Once set in motion, demographic change has its own momentum, which interacts with the socioeconomic parameters of society. Understanding both the determinants and the consequences of demographic change is essential.

Accordingly, discussions regarding economic development or the choice of appropriate developmental styles that do not integrate population dynamics in the sense just outlined are deficient. Indeed it is the main thesis of this paper that such deficiency characterizes analysis of socioeconomic development, especially of the Arab world. As will become evident, while a localized analysis of demographic change is not necessarily complete, an integrated "world view" of socioeconomic development that does not treat the dynamics of demographic change as endogenous is internally inconsistent. Our focus, however, is diagnostic rather than prescriptive.

In the second section we examine demographic trends in the Arab region through the end of the present century and evaluate their momentum. Our focus will be on the vital rates. The important phenomenon of intra-regional migration will be examined later in the paper. In the third section we review various development paradigms to examine the role of population dynamics in their specified structures. Our next step is to assess the applicability of these various paradigms to the economic demographic potential of the Arab world; this will be the topic for the fourth section. In the last section we discuss briefly some policy implications, including those of international migration.

Demographic Transition in the Arab World: A Predetermined Destiny?

In 1960, crude birth rates in the Arab world were more than 40 per 1,000 for all countries without exception and were closer to 50 for most of them. Crude death rates, on the other hand, were more than 17 per 1,000 for all except two countries (Table 12.1). In 1982, fertility continued in general to maintain its high levels, with a few countries attaining somewhat lower levels. Mortality, however, declined dramatically, reflecting a combination of improved health status and young age structure, thus creating a dramatic increase in the natural rate of population growth. Figure 12.1 shows the situation between 1960 and 1980 and the expected trends through the year 2000.

TABLE 12.1
Demographic Change in Arab Countries, 1960-2000 (rates per 1000)

Country	1960 BR	1960 DR	1970 BR	1970 DR	1980 BR	1980 DR	1990 BR	1990 DR	2000 BR	2000 DR	NRR = 1
Sudan	47	25	47	22	47	18	44	16	41	12	2035
South Yemen	50	29	49	24	48	20	48	17	44	14	2040
North Yemen	50	29	49	27	49	23	48	20	45	16	2040
Egypt	44	20	40	17	40	13	33	10	27	8	2015
Morocco	50	21	48	17	45	13	41	11	33	8	2025
Tunisia	47	19	40	14	35	11	32	8	25	7	2015
Lebanon	43	14	36	11	30	9	28	8	24	7	2005
Syria	47	18	47	14	47	8	43	6	34	4	2020
Jordan	47	20	48	16	46	10	47	7	42	5	2020
Algeria	51	20	49	16	46	13	45	11	40	8	2025
Iraq	49	20	48	16	46	12	43	9	36	7	2025
Oman	51	28	50	22	48	17	42	13	35	10	2020
Libya	49	19	49	16	47	12	44	10	41	8	2025
Saudi Arabia	49	23	48	18	45	13	43	11	40	8	2030
Kuwait	44	10	48	6	40	4	32	3	25	3	2010
U.A.E.	46	19	36	11	29	6	26	4	25	5	2015

BR = Birthrate
DR = Deathrate

Sources: Data for 1960: World Bank, World Development Report, 1984 (Washington, DC: World Bank, 1984). Data for 1970 and 1980: World Bank, World Population Projections, 1984 (Washington, DC: World Bank, 1984) and U.N. publications.

It is evident that with the exception of Egypt and Lebanon, whose rates of growth are expected to be just below 2 percent, the rate of population growth in the Arab countries will be more than 2 percent per year and in most countries will exceed 3 percent by the year 2000. The potential for high rates of population growth will persist into the twenty-first century. In other words, the completion of the demographic transition in its narrow sense will not materialize in the Arab world until well into the twenty-first century.

What are the socioeconomic implications of this demographic picture, and how do they affect the developmental potential or limit the viability of the available policy options? In attempting to answer this fundamental question, we may follow either of two possible paths. The first is to project and examine a battery of consequence indicators in order to illustrate what the Arab society has to deal with during the next few decades. For example, the aggregate size of the Arab population is estimated to be between 190 and 200 million in 1985. Making some plausible assumptions regarding the paths of fertility, mortality, and net migration, we can expect that between

188

Crude Birth Rate

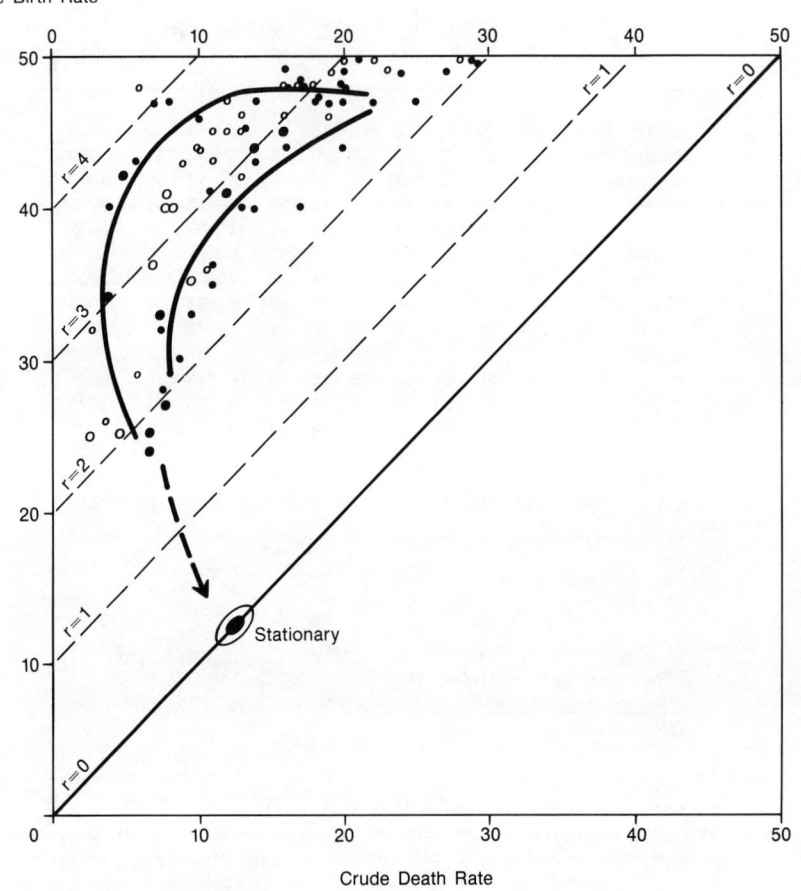

Key:

○ *Capital exporting countries, 1960-1990*
● *Labor exporting countries (Arab), 1960-1990*
o *Capital exporting countries, 2000*
● *Labor exporting countries (Arab), 2000*
  r = *rate of natural increase*

FIGURE 12.1 Demographic Transition(s) in the Arab World, 1960-2000. *Source:* Data for 1960: World Bank, World Development Report, 1984 (Washington, DC: World Bank, 1984). Data for 1970 and 1980: World Bank, *World Population Projections, 1984* (Washington, DC: World Bank, 1984) and United Nations publications.

140 and 150 million births will take place between 1985 and the end of this century, and about 40 to 45 million deaths will occur during the same period. Assuming a net out-migration of about 5 to 10 million, we would expect the total size of the Arab population to reach between 275 and 305 million people by the year 2000. We can safely assume that about half the 40 to 45 million deaths will be among infants and that the income and wealth distributions of these 40 to 45 million deaths will be very skewed (e.g., the Gini coefficient will exceed 0.6).

In more programmatic domains, demographers, economists, and sociologists may quibble about the assumptions underlying this projection, when attempting to estimate, for planning purposes, the number of additional jobs that need creation. Similarly, the implication of population growth for the social investments necessary for education, health, housing, and other basic needs and their incorporation in a macro economic framework opens up a very substantial role for a skilled technocratic cadre of economists, sociologists, and demographers. It also provides a lively—but a serious—numbers game. This is the approach that is most widely used in dealing with population implications. It does not, however, probe into the fundamental forces that brought the demographic picture to its present status.

The second approach, which is the one we will adopt, is to investigate the determinants of the system parameters and relate them to consequences. More specifically, we will investigate how endogenous the demographic factors are in the current phase of Arab socioeconomic development. But the policy conclusions derived from such an examination can be interpreted only in the context of developmental paradigms. For that purpose we need to understand how population is treated within the various development perspectives. It is not our aim to provide a comprehensive assessment of the current debate on development paradigms. That task is too large and fundamental to fall within the scope of the present study. Our own understanding of the role of population dynamics in the various developmental paradigms will be presented in order to relate the demographic situation just outlined to the developmental context of the Arab world.

Population in Development Paradigms

It seems that the pace and diversity of national and international events and the associated structural changes that took place in the world during the past two decades have had the effect of discrediting a number of comfortable generalizations that had been nurtured and cherished across a diverse spectrum of development paradigms. These events include the changing role of China, in both its internal and international policies; the changing fortunes of the Organization of Petroleum Exporting Countries (OPEC); the emergence, from within the ranks of the less-developed countries, of a set of Newly Industrialized Countries that may be labeled semi-imperialistic; the apparent decline of some previously industrial nations; the rise in Latin America of a new brand of military-bureaucratic regime in close alliance with international capital; and disappointment with the progress of the North–South negotiations. These events have disillusioned social scientists concerned with development studies. For those whose perceptions of the world are based on instant analysis, the 1970s and 1980s must have surely projected a state of confusion. Regardless of one's ideological leanings, it was increasingly difficult to identify international friends or enemies or to predict even short-term trends during that period.[3] As a result, development economics as a subdiscipline was put to task.[4]

It is apparent that the current status of development economics is rather fluid. We need not be dogmatic in taking stances before making a careful survey of the grounds. In what follows we present a brief review of various development paradigms, starting with the classical model. Our interest is to illustrate how population is treated in these models. We must, however, be aware that our rejection of a given paradigm, if based on moral grounds, may result not from the unsoundness of its analytic structure, but rather from its unsound application. The same knife can save or take a life, depending on whether it is used by a surgeon or a criminal.

From Malthus to Marx

Malthusian theory (as a system of analysis and not of exploitation) was born a long time before the birth of Malthus. Two major Malthusian assumptions—that the average productivity of labor declines with an increase in population size, and that a fixed resource base and a fixed technology imply the idea of an optimal population size, defined in the context of a desirable average level of welfare (or subsistence)—were elucidated by Confucius and his followers in China almost two millennia before Malthus' time.[5] It is hard to perceive Confucius as Malthusian.

Malthus was a classical economist. According to the classical (as well as the neo-classical) thesis, in a perfectly competitive economy and in the absence of externalities, market forces operating through the price mechanism assure an optimal allocation of resources, statically and dynamically. This paradigm has been open to three major lines of criticism: first, that it is unjust and exploitative; second, that it is unstable, prone to crises, and doomed to collapse; and third, that its quintessential mechanism of market forces operating through the price system fails to work because of a distorted signaling mechanism, an inadequate response of labor and other factors of production to price signals, or the lack of mobility of such factors.[6]

A critical examination of the classical system is that of Marx, who considered the exploitative nature of the capitalistic system to be inherent in the working rules of the system. As put eloquently by Joan Robinson— "Exploitation is the great engine for accumulation and what is nowadays called economic growth. The capitalists extract surplus value, not to enjoy luxury, but to accumulate the means of increasing employment so as to extract more surplus."[7]

Indeed, it is a tightrope game. If capital accumulates faster than the labor force grows (in the extreme case, the reserve of labor is exhausted), real wage rates rise and profit per worker falls, slowing down accumulation relative to the growth of labor. A new cycle begins when relative increase of the labor force tends to reduce real wages and accordingly to increase surplus and accumulation. It is evident from this analysis that "In a class society (whether feudal or capitalist) a growth of numbers is advantageous to the owners of property. It provides them with more people to exploit, as tenants, servants, slaves or workers."[8]

In essence, Malthus considered the functional distribution of income as datum in his system and blamed poverty and unemployment on the reproductive behavior of the working classes. It is the growing subsistence consumption needs of this group that outpace output growth, thus reducing profit and accumulation. The responsibility for misery lies squarely on the shoulders of the proletariat and not in the characteristics of the social structure of the capitalistic system and its production relations.

It is evident, therefore, that population plays an important—albeit differing—role in the functioning of both the classical and the Marxist systems.

In the Malthusian framework (ignoring its reactionary interpretation) population is treated as endogenous in the sense that its rate of growth is a positive function of real wages. But the conceptual framework that underlies the relationship is never articulated; it appears to be mainly based on passion as a biological force. It is of interest, however, that the recent revival of the classical theory of profit ignored even this weak link and treated population as completely outside the system.[9] In Von Neumann's world, the employment of labor grows automatically as the flow of output of wage goods increases. To assume such a state of affairs is to imply either that population is always growing at just the right rate or that there is an indefinite reserve of potential labor living on nuts in the jungle, always ready to take employment when the standard real wage is offered.

The neo-classical (neo-Malthusian) school developed the Malthusian analytic frame one step further. However, it narrowed the focus of the inquiry to the individual as the decision unit of analysis and isolated individual decisions from the long-term dynamics of economic growth and social class formations. It has attempted to show, through the calculus of maximizing behavior based on individual self-interest, that fertility behavior is responsive to changes in the relative costs and benefits associated with different reproductive strategies. The paradigm has been criticized on various grounds.[10] The debate has, however, advanced knowledge about the complexity of the reproductive structure and its time dimension. But in the analysis, the focus is on individual action. It is assumed that the worker can improve his situation without appeal to class solidarity—a questionable proposition.

Evidently there is a need for clearer conceptual guidelines. Does the new "world system" perspective on development and underdevelopment provide these?

A World-System Perspective

Development studies tend to regard underdevelopment as a social "problem," a syndrome which Third World countries suffer from, called "underdevelopment" or "lack of modernity." The less-developed countries should take the industrial nations for their model of a healthy body and follow their path in terms either of specific processes or of historical stages. But the disease is diagnosed as self-inflicted and localized inside the patient's body. Research and policy analysis guided by this diagnosis concentrate on problems internal to Third World countries. Linkage mechanisms between the developing and the developed nations are outside the paradigm and are not examined. The world system perspective, on the other hand, considers development and underdevelopment as parts of an integral totality. It must be emphasized that the world system paradigm is not a uniform entity. There are differences of opinion with regard to conceptualization and empirical methods.

At present there has been a return to the original conceptualization of Lenin and Luxemburg.[11] This is being accomplished through the elucidation by Arghiri Emmanuel and Samir Amin of a world system based on the principle of unequal exchange.[12]

In general, the world system paradigm views the world economy as one of a dual dialectic: the dialectic between production and circulation internal to each sector of the system, and the dialectic between center and periphery.[13]

Unequal exchange implies that surplus value, after different capital investment or differential productivity are allowed for, flows from peripheral production to the core because of different levels of remuneration to labor. Amin estimated that in 1966 the value of this hidden transfer was about U.S. $22 billion, almost twice the amount of "aid" and private capital that the periphery received.[14]

Indeed, according to this paradigm, the continuing existence of a labor surplus in the periphery is a necessary condition for depressing wage rates and, accordingly, perpetuating the system of unequal exchange. Amin elaborates on the dynamic nature of accumulation on a worldwide scale: ". . . the system tends to *reproduce unceasingly* the reserve army which it needs to ensure the profitability of capital. This fundamental law of accumulation . . . inherent in the capitalist mode of production, operates in our time on a worldwide scale and no longer on that of each of the central regions . . . [and . . . has] now reached the state of establishing a *worldwide labour market*."[15] (emphasis added)

But what is the mechanism through which this "unceasing reproduction" of the labor surplus or "reserve army," which is essential for this fundamental law of accumulation, takes place? The determinants of this implied demographic behavior are not articulated in the system's analytical framework. For example, it is not evident why the reproduction of the peripheral labor force should, as a behavioral response, be automatic.

Recent empirical demographic evidence (e.g., the *World Fertility Survey* findings) seem not to support these hypothesized general laws of reproductive response. There has been a long-term trend of fertility decline across the various social classes in the industrial countries. This decline has been led by the educated and the professionals (core), while the cyclical behavior of fertility cuts across all social groups. In the less-developed countries, experience suggests that reproductive behavior is a very complex phenomenon. Generalization should be guarded, and its context specific.[16]

Toward an Arab Population–Development Paradigm

We conclude this section by examining whether an "Arab population–development paradigm" exists that differs from those reviewed above. This is a difficult question. There has been a large and growing literature on Arab development styles by Arab economists and social scientists, but no dominant development philosophy that may be labeled "Arab" has emerged. At the cost of underrepresentation (and probably oversimplification), we will focus on four recent contributions. The first, by Galal Amin, is an attempt at classification and evaluation of the various development paradigms reflecting the planning experience in the Arab world. The second is a collection of articles on Arab development from the Centre for Arab Unity Studies (CAUS). It includes contributions on the subject published in the periodical *Arab Future* in 1983–84 and reviewed by Abdel-Khalik. The third is an interview with Samir Amin on independent development in the Third World. The last is two recent contributions by Ramzi Zaki and Nader Fergani on population problems, with emphasis on Arab development.

Galal Amin[17] argues that the development experience in the Arab world has been a result of the dynamic interaction of three schools of thought: laical liberalism, laical Marxism, and traditionalism. Traditionals regained purpose after the collapse of the Nasserist experience by blaming that collapse on the system's failure to acknowledge religion as the foundation for inspiring development strategies. The side effects of the "open policy" and the Iranian Islamic revolution reinforced the traditional stance, defining the development problem as a lack of purpose. In their view societal problems have solutions in Islamic principles and not in imported ideologies.

Laical liberals also gained ground after Nasser and Sadat. This school considers the real problem of underdevelopment to be a lack of scientific development and the application of scientific methods and techniques not only in production and organization, but also in governing and in personal relations. They view independent development as unrealistic in a highly interdependent world. They adhere to the principles of the market, competition, and a small government. To a large extent, laical liberalism may be labeled neo-classical.

Laical Marxists, according to Galal Amin's typology, are equally enthusiastic about the power of science and technology but see the international system of dependency and unequal exchange as the major obstacles to development. They also differ from the laical liberals in stressing the need for restructuring society as a prerequisite to ensuring long-term equity, even at the cost of a slower pace of development.

The liberals and the Marxists do not present new paradigms. It is curious that the traditional paradigm was not represented in that important collection of articles from CAUS, *Arab Development: Present, Possible, and the Future*.[18] In the discussions of the six theoretical contributions, no attempt is made to provide the conceptual basis for a unified population and development policy.

In a stimulating interview, Samir Amin examines development in the Arab world from the viewpoint of his familiar worldwide unequal exchange system.[19] The solution he offers is to focus on the agricultural sector, fully utilize the potential labor force, increase demand through more equity (wage equalization), and subordinate industry to agricultural development, i.e., produce what is required to enhance agricultural productivity. The general outline is reminiscent of the original Chinese model. Details, especially as to how this development vision relates to the particular nature of population dynamics and labor mobility in the region, are left out at this stage.

Zaki makes an ambitious attempt to provide such a vision.[20] His book provides a well-researched historical perspective on population in economic thought. Most of it, however, is an attack on the neo-Malthusian framework, repeating and reinforcing well-known reservations. The analysis falls far short of integrating population dynamics with development in a systematic framework. The same reservations apply to Fergani's discussion of population and development in the Arab world.[21] One of the possible sources of confusion is mixing short- with long-term changes in population, and accordingly, their determinants and consequences.[22]

To summarize, population plays an important role in the various development paradigms reviewed in this section. Its growth is important for capital accumulation in the capitalist system. In the Marxist system, its differing growth in different social classes provides the bases for exploitation as well as for the ultimate demise of the capitalist system and for paving the way for socialism. The paradigm of unequal exchange expands this last proposition to a worldwide scale. However, the determinants and consequences of population dynamics are not critically examined in either case. The neo-classical analysis attempts to develop a behavioral theory of reproduction, but, being individualistic in scope, it divorces itself from the very context of development as a social issue.

However, regardless of whether we examine the classical, Marxist, or unequal exchange system, an important conclusion emerges. Changes in the structure of population and its growth are assumed to have causal linkage to the dynamics of production, accumulation, and distribution. There is a delicate balance between the reproduction of population and that of capital. The system of distribution of the social product determines the stability of the system. Population change does not act in a vacuum, but is an integral part of the socioeconomic system.

This is an essential point to keep in mind when we examine, in the following section, the applicability of the various paradigms to the Arab situation.

Development Paradigms: How Applicable to the Arab Case?

The current phase of population and economic change in the Arab world is unique in terms of the magnitude of change in its parameters, but it is not unexpected. The general demographic-economic characteristics of the system are rather simple. The story is familiar. Our purpose is not to document events and trends, but rather to evaluate them in the context of the applicability of the various development paradigms in explaining and predicting their patterns.

The general outline of the demographic picture has been presented earlier. The Arab population is one of the fastest growing in the world and, because of its young age structure, has a long-term built-in growth momentum. Arab demography follows the familiar transitions of the less-developed countries that experienced colonial domination. Our contention is that this transition is part and parcel of the technological development of capitalism and the international exchange system it implies. At the turn of the century, investment in public health measures started slowly and was limited to ensuring the adequate reproduction of the work force involved in the production of the export primary goods needed to fuel the engine of the industrial revolution (e.g., cotton in Egypt and Sudan) and in the civil and police administration required for ensuring the efficient flow of these goods and the safety of the colonial presence. Countries or areas outside this international exchange system did not have this limited social benefit. A global conscience demanding an international health policy had not yet been born.

As "direct" colonialism declined, interest in economic development among the newly independent countries became a primary focus on both the national and international levels. In many countries, "average" health status improved. Among the Arab countries, the decline in mortality became more dramatic after World War II and accelerated, especially in the oil-exporting countries, after the oil boom. Fertility, on the other hand, has not shown any significant departure from its high level up to the present.[23] Accordingly, the rate of population growth accelerated.

This demographic picture raises a pivotal question: is the accelerated reproduction of the potential labor force in the Arab world warranted by the pace and structure of capital accumulation and by the structure of the production relation in the region? Our answer is negative. We even assert that within the present sociopolitical context, the long-term demographic trends implied by the current structure and parameters of the population could have dire consequences for the countries of the region as a whole, whether labor/capital importers or exporters. We have reached this conclusion in the face of what appears to be clear contradictory evidence, for example:

- A huge inflow of expatriate non-Arab labor.
- Apparent underpopulation, illustrated by such crude measures as density.

- A large financial capital outflow that finds no adequate internal outlet.

Our main argument depends on a modified classical Marxist dictum: capital has no feelings. It only reproduces what it needs for its own reproduction and accumulation. When it operates on a worldwide scale, it disposes more freely of redundancy. As the world society becomes more "technicalized," where "technique" controls "technology," the criterion of efficiency takes supreme status and disposing of redundancy becomes more cruel.[24]

Let us elaborate. First we will outline the current Arab–international system of production and exchange from the perspective of a worldwide system paradigm, then we will evaluate the system. Figure 12.2 provides

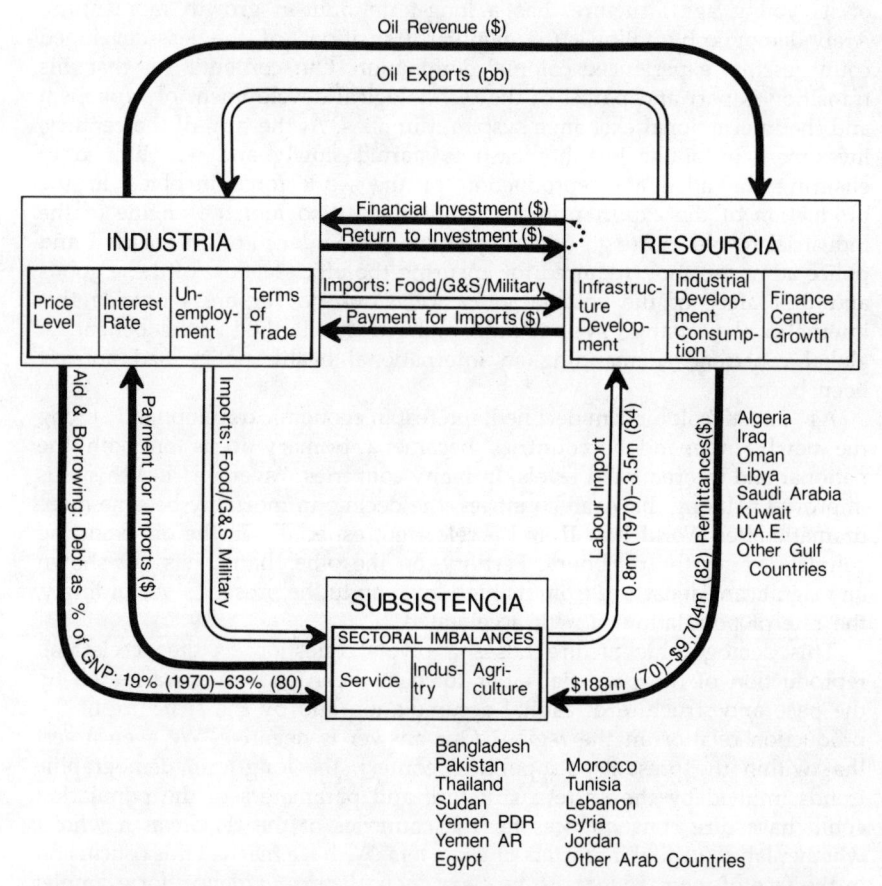

FIGURE 12.2 Socio-Demographic Transitions: A New International Revenue System (NIRS).

Source: Data in figure based on Table 12.2. Figure previously published in Ismail Sirageldin, "Potential for Economic-Demographic Development: Whither Theory?" *Pakistan Development Review* vol. XXV, no. 1, 1986.

a schematic presentation of the operation of the system. As mentioned earlier, the story is a familiar one, which needs no detailed elaboration or documentation. For simplicity, only the Arab and industrial countries are identified in the schematic presentation. The Arab countries are divided into two main groups: Resourcia and Subsistancia.[25] The group of industrial nations (the core) is labeled Industria. There are three direct pairs of relations: Resourcia–Industria, Subsistancia–Resourcia, and Subsistancia–Industria. Each relation has its own past history, present short-term dynamics, and future long-term paths. The first two relations will be examined in turn, first from the perspective of each group in isolation, then from that of an integrated Arab nation within a worldwide system. Discussion of the third relation will be incorporated in the concluding remarks.

Resourcia–Industria

The past experience of this relation is wide-ranging. Its roots lie in the Ottoman Empire and the colonization of the French in Algeria, the Italians in Libya, and the British in Iraq and Arabia. The colonial past is important in understanding the present pattern of development. But the present is largely dominated and shaped by oil. Here is the story of Resourcia's changing fortunes during ten years. Resourcia exports oil to Industria. Oil revenue exceeds Resourcia's initial capacity to invest, and Resourcia embarks on a spectacular program for building physical and human infrastructures. Excess revenue is ploughed back to Industria.

Resourcia has limited manpower relative to the pace of its investment expenditure, and opens its doors to expatriate labor. With the exception of Iraq, Resourcia does not opt for naturalization as a way of reducing the "transitional" shortage of its national labor supply, but adopts a strong pronatalist policy. For social and political reasons, Resourcia transfers part of its new wealth through producer and consumer subsidies to its nationals, and with an open-door policy for admitting expatriates from all nationalities, new high levels of per capita consumption in general and conspicuous consumption in particular take hold in a very short period. Resourcia also commits itself to an expensive arms purchase program and to financing local wars and uprisings.

Resourcia's initial expenditure plans are based on optimistic expectations of trends in oil demand and prices. Prices and volumes of Resourcia's imports increase relative to the value of oil exports realized, which are short of expectations. Being committed to OPEC production, ambitious development plans, and social welfare expenditures, Resourcia runs a sizable deficit. Resourcia has to evaluate its stance on investment criteria, subsidies and welfare, and expatriate labor.

What does the future hold for Resourcia? The future results from the interaction among the forces of accumulated experience, exogenous factors (whether international or incidental), and the conscious effort within Resourcia to shape its future. Let us consider these issues within the context of the various paradigms.

For many futurists, oil is the main actor. As Mabro and Sayegh illustrate, there is now a change from a sellers' to a buyers' market.[26] According to many scholars, oil was for a time beneficial, not only in igniting economic activities in Resourcia but also as a weapon in the hands of the South for the North–South negotiations.[27] This last view was also advocated by Samir Amin, a champion of the unequal exchange paradigm.[28] Ironically, the weapon seems to have another edge, which integrates Resourcia into the international market and international system, cementing its "dependency."

The relevance of the sellers' and the buyers' market-types to the analysis of long-run dynamics, especially in the context of Resourcia development, is not, however, evident to us. The oil market has always been a buyers' market. Demand for oil stems from the technological needs of Industria. Capital needs oil for its own reproduction. This is the long-run view of the sociodemographic transition that has taken place since the beginning of the Industrial Revolution. The events of the 1970s are short-term repercussions from specific events. The 1980s return to the long-term course. There are important insights that arise from this last view:

- Oil production is a highly capital-intensive activity. The idea of a "reserve army" of labor or the "reproduction" of capital through labor or mutual, though "unequal," benefit between core and periphery becomes irrelevant in elucidating the Industria–Resourcia relation.

- The dramatic increase in revenue supports the institution of small, otherwise non-viable states within Resourcia.

- High oil prices will be maintained until Industria adjusts to the diffusion of new technologies. In 1975, Henry Kissinger was quoted as presenting, in Europe, a plan for "an investment programme of one thousand billion dollars for the development of new sources of energy . . . Dr. Kissinger has also been very particularly adamant—that the price of petroleum had to rise and remain high in order to make it profitable to develop these alternative sources of energy."[29] In 1979, there was another price hike. In 1980 the Iran–Iraq war started. One of its outcomes was the reduction of oil supplies. In that respect, M.A. Adelman indicates that "Another cartel resource is the instability and violence of some members . . . The Iran–Iraq war has been a piece of great good luck; the next fighting may be due more to good management."[30]

- Human resource development is a long-run commitment. The fast pace of building the necessary infrastructures implied in the socioeconomic plans and the large inflow of expatriate labor required for that phase of economic activities have generated confusing signals between short-term and long-term needs. The "Dutch Disease" that is being blamed for the decline of non-oil traded goods from the manufacturing sector in new oil-exporting industrial countries, such as the Netherlands and England, might be responsible for creating serious imbalances in the human resource section in the Arab world. In that context, it may be labeled the "Human Resource Disease." There is a dire need for a full analysis of the relationships between policies that provide subsidies to producers, to education, and to housing as well as the importation of labor on the one hand, and the attainment of desired social objectives on the other.[31]

- In the midst of the expenditure euphoria generated by the expanding oil revenue, a fundamental truth seems to have been forgotten: the dramatic expansion of the native population could not have been supported without the oil revenue. Without that revenue, growth of the native population is excessive. The vital question to be addressed is "Do current efforts provide the base for viable employment for the existing and growing labor supply?" As matters stand, the demand for expatriate labor is a consumption demand; it will become a production demand if the answer to the above question is in the affirmative.

- Finally, the long-term negative impact of the emerging pattern of consumption behavior needs no emphasis. The intergenerational implication of this behavior is yet to be assessed. What will be the public and private adjustment mechanism to a decline in oil revenue, and at what cost, are questions that need inclusion on the current agenda of research on future Arab development.

These last two points have serious implications for the development case of Subsistancia.

Subsistancia–Resourcia

The literature on the development experience of the Subsistancia group is substantial.[32] Our focus is limited to a few issues in recent Subsistancia–Resourcia interaction. For many analysts, interregional labor migration is the main focus. The emphasis has been on the role of remittances, on the social and political impact of Arab vs. that of non-Arab expatriate labor in the receiving countries, on the sectoral imbalances created in Subsistancia as a result of selective immigration, and on civil rights issues. As Figure 12.2 indicates, the migration flow (and its remittance counterflow) has been substantial. This is evident in Table 12.2, in the rise of unrequited transfers to Egypt from abroad from $29 million in 1970 to $2,074 million in 1982, or, expressed as a percentage of merchandise exports, from 63.9 percent in 1973 to 72.5 per cent in 1980.[33] For Syria, official unrequited transfers went up from $7 million in 1970 to $140 million in 1982, or from 53.5 percent of merchandise exports in 1974 to 72.0 percent in 1980. Other Subsistancia countries show a similar increase in unrequited transfers.

We argued above that the occurrence of the migration flow has been an outcome of the specific resource base characteristic of Resourcia and the demand for oil generated in Industria. The demand for labor in Subsistancia is derived from Industria as demand for oil and only conditioned by the

TABLE 12.2
Economic Indicators, Selected Arab Countries, 1970-82 (with percentages)

Country	VA Agriculture (in millions of dollars) 1970	%	1982	%	Cereal Imports (in thousands of tons) 1974	%	1982	%	Food Aid (in thousands of tons) 1974/75	%	1981/82	%	Per Capita Income (in dollars) 1982
Sudan	1,367	19	2,127	23	125	2	611	5	50	5	185	7	440
South Yemen	–	–	–	–	149	2	271	3	38	4	25	0.9	470
North Yemen	221	3	401	4	158	3	560	4	0	0	13	0.5	500
Egypt	2,683	38	3,878	42	3,877	60	6,703	53	610	66	1,952	69	690
Morocco	1,725	24	1,836	20	891	14	1,913	15	75	8	465	16.4	870
Tunisia	480	7	816	9	307	5	946	8	1	0.1	96	3.4	1,390
Lebanon	*	–	*	–	354	6	529	4	21	2	11	0.4	(1,500)
Syria	595	8	*	–	339	5	426	3	47	5	8	0.3	1,680
Jordan	92	1	132	2	171	3	668	5	63	7	73	3	1,690
Algeria	952	36	1,375	57	1,816	45	3,831	28	54	98	5	100	2,350
Iraq	1,172	45	*	–	870	21	2,510	18	1	2	*	–	(6,000)
Oman	*	–	*	–	52	1	217	2	–	–	–	–	6,090
Libya	126	5	388	16	612	15	849	6	–	–	–	–	8,510
Saudi Arabia	331	13	616	26	482	12	5,584	41	–	–	–	–	16,000
Kuwait	20	1	30	1	101	3	439	3	–	–	–	–	19,870
U.A.E.	*	–	*	–	132	3	282	2	–	–	–	–	23,770

TABLE 12.2 (continued)

Country	Average Growth (percentage) 1960-82	Current Account (in millions of dollars) 1970	Current Account (in millions of dollars) 1982	Merchandise Balance (in millions of dollars) 1982	Remittances (in millions of dollars) 1970	Remittances (in millions of dollars) 1982	Import Reserves (months) 1982	External Public Debt (as percentage of (GNP)) 1970	External Public Debt (as percentage of (GNP)) 1982
Sudan	(0.4)	(42)	(248)	(768)	—	131	0.2	16	48
South Yemen	6.4	(4)	(221)	(613)	60	411	3.4	—	80
North Yemen	5.1	—	(610)	(1,943)	—	1,118	2.9	—	36
Egypt	3.6	(148)	(2,216)	(5,958)	29	2,074	1.9	24	53
Morocco	2.6	(124)	(1,876)	(2,256)	63	849	1.1	18	61
Tunisia	4.7	(53)	(657)	(1,334)	29	372	2.1	38	42
Lebanon	—	—	—	(2,644)	—	—	*	4	*
Syria	4.0	(69)	(493)	(1,989)	7	140	1.5	13	15
Jordan	6.9	(20)	(336)	(2,488)	—	1,084	3.8	23	43
Algeria	3.2	(125)	85	1,596	211	447	4.6	19	32
Iraq	—	105	—	(9,972)	—	—	—	9	—
Oman	7.4	—	358	1,739	—	43	4.8	—	12
Libya	4.1	645	(2,977)	977	—	—	6.9	—	—
Saudi Arabia	7.5	71	45,125	38,469	—	—	5.9	—	—
Kuwait	(0.1)	—	5,786	8,519	—	—	7.5	—	—
U.A.E.	(0.7)	—	—	7,464	—	—	—	—	—

*Data not available

Source: World Bank, World Development Report, 1984 (Washington, DC: World Bank, 1985).

pattern of development expenditure in Resourcia. It has two main effects. The first is to diffuse any concern for a serious long-term population-development policy that could deal squarely with the imbalances between reproduction and the accumulation of capital and labor. The fact that the reproduction and "accumulation" of population in Subsistancia have been ignited and accelerated by forces external to the pace of social change, and the fact that they need to be dealt with by simultaneously adjusting the two sides of the equation as well as the social framework to accommodate these necessary changes, have been brushed aside. Short-term events provide apparent relief. There is a similarity here between, on the one hand, the rejection by Marxist thinkers of the neo-Malthusian population solution on the premise that it may provide a diversion from the long-run march to the ultimate solution and, on the other, rejection of the consequences of the pattern of emigration on the development potential of Subsistancia.

The second main effect of emigration from Subsistancia has to do with sectoral imbalances. Again, the story is known, although empirical evidence is not always conclusive. The dramatic increase in remittances has created an equally dramatic increase in the demand for goods and services in Subsistancia. For example, food imports increased substantially in all countries of Subsistancia between 1974 and 1982, as illustrated in Table 12.2. Some countries, like Egypt, Sudan, Morocco, and Jordan, received substantial food aid as well. However, food production did not keep pace with the exogenous and sudden increase in demand. The issue has been examined extensively in the literature. It is arguable that another reason for sectoral imbalance has to do with the dynamic interaction of emigration and agricultural production on the micro level.[34]

As a consequence, the merchandise balance was negative for all countries in Subsistancia and exceeded the value of remittances by a wide margin. Subsistancia fell into the international debtors' circle. External public debt as a percent of GNP increased from an average of 19 percent in 1970 to 47 percent in 1982.

Indeed, there are positive elements to emigration, and the argument can continue almost indefinitely as to its net socioeconomic benefit.[35] But that is precisely the point being made in this paper. Concentrating on the temporary nature of emigration and almost treating it as a permanent phenomenon—as is illustrated by proposals to maximize the returns from migration by establishing training programs for an efficient trade in labor export—results in ignoring its long-term basic nature. Consideration of that long-term nature is, however, the only proper perspective for countries in the midst of their socio-demographic transition.

Conclusion

This paper discusses issues of concept and application. On the conceptual level, the main thesis may be summarized on the basis of the following proposition (mentioned earlier):

Changes in the structure of population and its growth have causal linkage to the dynamics of production, accumulation, and distribution. There is a delicate balance between the reproduction of population and that of capital. The system of distribution of the social product determines the stability of the social system.

In the Western as well as the Eastern experience, the balance between the demographic forces and capital accumulation was maintained within tolerable bounds. When relatively large diversions (but never so large as in the present experience of the developing countries) occurred, outlets were found in the colonization of new land. Changes in fertility and mortality were negative functions of the process of industrialization. They were endogenous to the system. Indeed, if they were not, the system must have found a different solution and accordingly had a different outcome. This simple truth seems to be forgotten when the various paradigms are applied.

A decline in fertility independent of, and in the absence of, a self-sustained process of capital accumulation in the context of an integrated framework of social development cannot be considered a necessary or a sufficient condition for development. The same is true of mortality. It does not follow, however, that managing fertility is not a priority in any development strategy. It is precisely the exogenous nature of the large mortality decline that makes it imperative to reduce fertility. In practical terms, no development policy can succeed unless both mortality and fertility are endogenized. In the concluding chapter of one of the most thorough analyses of the Egyptian economy during the Sadat era, Adel Hossain raises the question of how it was possible completely to uproot the foundation of Nasser's social revolution in such a short time.[36] The question was left less than half answered. Is it possible that in the presence of a huge demographic imbalance, cosmetic policies of distributing the social product, e.g., through increased public employment or consumer subsidies, were not sufficient to provide true system stability?

On the application side, the current socioeconomic status of the Arab world can be better understood within the long-term perspectives of the worldwide demographic-industrial transition, a transition that has two known effects. The first is the latent but dramatic increase in rates of population growth in the less-developed countries—the Arab world being no exception. This sudden and unbalanced (only mortality declined) demographic change does not necessarily produce those positive outcomes predicted by the classical, Marxist, or post-Marxist paradigms. Logically, the same paradigms could equally indicate an unnecessary cost if trends are left unchecked.

The second effect is the role of the Arab world as a provider of the resource necessary to fuel the demographic-industrial transition. Since the decline of the English textile industry, an industry that relied on labor-intensive cotton cultivation, the demographic component of the transition has lost its relevance. Oil is now the main actor in the equation. It is a highly capital-intensive industry located in areas limited by national boundaries and lacking in other resources. From this perspective, conventional paradigms fail to give guidance. Economic and demographic trends in Resourcia indicate severe imbalances.

This overall picture can be viewed as overly pessimistic. But there are positive notes. The Arab nation cannot continue to live beyond its means, expanding and changing the pattern of its consumption far faster than its real production capabilities. The present national boundaries are preventing the whole nation from achieving its full potential. Within these limited boundaries, potential growth is limited at best and continuous dependency is inevitable. Even if more efficient economic policies are pursued, as long as they are pursued in isolation, this will be the case. The momentum of population growth, if capital accumulation is not adequate to generate a real and balanced demand within a cohesive socio-cultural framework, will bring about the nation's demise. We feel that this will be the future if the Arab world continues to be divided—and political unions are not sufficient to end disunity.

Finally, we conclude with a vision that we hope crosses national, ideological, and even species boundaries in this ever-shrinking world that hosts us. It is evident that we are witnessing the birth of a new scientific revolution: the post-industrial information society. A new core will be established.[37] But, more important, the information revolution will certainly bring with it new rules governing the accumulation–reproduction game, thus setting the stage for a new socio-demographic transition. The relevance of current paradigms has to be critically examined continuously.

As we adjust to the present difficult situation, we must also keep an eye on the future. Basic research in genetic engineering in the functioning of the brain and in artificial intelligence are trespassing on each others' domains, producing exciting and unexpected results. It is possible, and evidence is accumulating, that fundamental changes may occur that will influence all facets of human organizations, including the biological and social foundations of reproduction as we know them now. As we mentioned earlier, we cannot judge the utility of the end result of this relentless "march of technique," since technique has no social welfare objective.

There is a written rule in at least one leading scientific research institute that forbids its members to sleep during working hours. But how could we advance without dreams, even if they are nightmares?

Notes

1. As is well known, the current demographic transition, associated with the Industrial Revolution, has not been the only one, nor will it be the last. For a review and discussion, see Ismail Sirageldin, *Population Policies and Development in the 80's* (Pakistan: Pakistan Institute of Development Economics, 1984).

2. "Technicalization" and "techniques" are used according to Ellul's definitions in *The Technological Society* (New York: Vintage, 1964), which differ from "technology." In this sense, "technique" refers to ". . . any complex of standardized means for attaining a predetermined result" (p. vi), while to "technicalize" is to "compel the

qualitative to become quantitative . . . [and] force every stage of human activity and man himself to submit to its mathematical calculation" (p. xvi).

3. Alejandro Portes and John Walton, *Labor, Class and the International System* (New York: Academic Press, 1981), p. 1.

4. The response by development economists has been varied. See, for example, Joan Robinson, *Economic Philosophy* (Chicago, IL: Aldine, 1962); A.O. Hirschman, *Essays in Trespassing* (Cambridge, U.K.: Cambridge University Press, 1981); Dudley Seers, "Birth, Life and Death of Development Economics," in *Development and Change* (London: Sage, 1979); the special issue "Economic Development and the Development of Economics" of *World Development* (1983); Jagdish N. Bhagwati and John Gerard Ruggie, eds., *Power, Passions and Purpose: Prospects for North–South Negotiations* (Cambridge, MA: MIT Press, 1984) and its review by Hans W. Singer, "Further Thoughts on North–South Negotiations: A Review of Bhagwati and Ruggie," *World Development* 13, no. 2 (February 1985): 255–60; Shigeto Tsuru, ed., *Human Resources, Employment and Development, I: The Issues* (London: Macmillan, 1983) and Samir Amin, "Introduction," in Samir Amin, ed., *Human Resources, Employment and Development, V* (London: Macmillan, 1984); Thomas E. Weiskopf, "Economic Development and the Development of Economics: Some Observations from the Left," *World Development* 11, no. 10 (1983): 895–99; Portes and Walton, *Labor, Class and the International System* (which includes, aside from a penetrating analysis, an extensive bibliography); S.N.H. Naqvi, "Development Economists in Emperor's Clothes?" *Pakistan Development Review* 23, nos. 2 & 3 (Summer–Autumn 1984) on defense of the "discipline" of development economics; and H. W. Arndt, "The Origins of Structuralism," *World Development* 13, no. 2 (1985): 151–59, among others.

5. E. A. Hammel, *The China Lectures*, Program in Population Research Working Paper No. 10 (Berkeley, CA: University of California, 1983).

6. See, for example, the discussion of Arndt, "The Origins of Structuralism."

7. Joan Robinson, *Aspects of Development and Underdevelopment* (Cambridge, U.K.: Cambridge University Press, 1979), p. 27.

8. *Ibid.*, p. 8.

9. Von Neumann, "A Model of General Economic Equilibrium," *Review of Economic Studies* 13, no. 30 (1945–46).

10. Ismail Sirageldin and United Nations Secretariat, "Demographic Transition and Socio-Economic Development," *Demographic Transition and Socio-Economic Development*, United Nations Department of International Economic and Social Affairs, Population Studies, No. 65 (New York: United Nations, 1979); and Ismail Sirageldin, *Population Policies in the 80's*.

11. V.I. Lenin, *Imperialism, the Highest Stage of Capitalism* (New York: International Publishers, 1939); Rosa Luxemburg, *The Accumulation of Capital* (London: Routledge and Kegan Paul, 1959).

12. Samir Amin, *Unequal Development: An Essay on the Social Formations of Peripheral Capitalism* (New York: Monthly Review, 1976) and Arghiri Emmanuel, *Unequal Exchange, A Study of the Imperialism of Trade* (New York: Monthly Review Press, 1972). For a brief survey of the issues, see Portes and Walton, *Labor, Class and the International System*, especially the first and last chapters. A detailed review should include Bukharin, *Economics of the Transformation Period* (New York: Bergman Press, 1929 and 1971); V.I. Lenin, *Economic Theory of the Leisure Class* (CT: Greenwood Press, 1927); Evgeny Preobrazhensky, *The New Economics* (Oxford: Clarendon Press, 1965); Rosa Luxemburg, *The Accumulation of Capital* (London: Routledge & Kegan Paul, 1959); Paul Prebisch, *The Economic Development of Latin America and Its Principal Problems* (New York: United Nations, 1950), *The Economic Development of Latin*

America in the Post War Period (New York: United Nations, 1964), and *idem*, "The Latin American Periphery in the Global System of Capitalism," in Shigetu Tsuru, ed., *Human Resources, Employment, and Development*, pp. 3–19; Andre Gunder Frank, *Capitalism and Underdevelopment in Latin America* (New York: Monthly Review Press, 1967); J.A. Hobson, *Imperialism* (Ann Arbor, MI: University of Michigan, 1971); Immanuel Maurice Wallerstein, *The Capitalist World Economy: Essays* (New York: Cambridge University Press, 1979); and Samir Amin, *Unequal Development* and *idem*, *Human Resources, Employment, and Development*. For a critique, see R. Brenner, "The Origins of Capitalist Development: A Critique of Neo-Smithian Marxism," *New Left Review* 104 (1977): 21–25; Philip O'Brien, "A Critique of Latin American Theories of Dependency," in Ivar Oxaal et al., eds., *Beyond the Sociology of Development: Economy and Society in Latin America and Africa* (London: Routledge and Kegan Paul, 1975); Ernest Laclau, "Feudalism and Capitalism in Latin America," *New Left Review* 67 (May–June 1971); Robert L. Bach, "The Reproduction of Triviality: Critical Notes on Recent Attempts to Test the Dynamics of World Capitalism," mimeographed (Binghamton, NY: Department of Sociology, State University of New York, 1978); Aidan Foster-Carter, "From Rostow to Gunder Frank: Conflicting Paradigms in the Analysis of Underdevelopment," *World Development* 4, no. 3 (March 1976): 167–80; and Gary Gereffi, "A Critical Evaluation of Quantitative Cross-National Studies of Dependency," paper presented at the panel on Dependency Theory, Toronto, March 1979. Quoted in Portes and Walton, *Labor, Class and the International System*.

13. Alain De Janvry and Carlos Garramon, "Laws of Motion of Capital in the Center–Periphery Structure," *Review of Radical Political Economies* 9 (Summer 1977): 29–38; Portes and Walton, *Labor, Class and the International System*, p. 68.

14. Samir Amin, *Unequal Development*, p. 144.

15. Samir Amin, *Human Resources, Employment and Development*, p. xiii.

16. Ismail Sirageldin and UN Secretariat, "Demographic Transition and Socio-Economic Development"; Ismail Sirageldin and John F. Kantner, "Equity, Social Mobility and Fertility Control Policies," *Research in Human Capital and Development*, 1 (Greenwich, CT: JAI Press, 1979).

17. Galal A. Amin, "Heritage of Arab Development," *Al-Mustaqbal al-'Arabi*, no. 72 (1985): 4–22 (In Arabic).

18. Centre for Arab Unity Studies, *Arab Development: Present, Possible, and the Future* (Beirut: CAUS, 1984) (in Arabic). The volume includes a penetrating review by Adel Hossain and contributions by N. Fergani, Y. Sayegh, A. Al-Kawari, M. Masoud, M.A. Saeed, N. Ramses, and I.S. Abdullah, among others.

19. Samir Amin, "Independent Development and the Third World," in Arabic, *Al-Mustaqbal al-'Arabi*, no. 59 (January 1984): 114–24.

20. Ramzi Zaki, *The Population Problem: The New Malthusian Myth*, in Arabic (Kuwait: 'Alam al-Ma'rifa, 1984).

21. Nader Fergani, "Population and Development in the Arab World," in Arabic, *Al-Mustaqbal al-'Arabi*, no. 67 (1984): 73–91. Fergani adopts the view that the impact of population on development can be assessed only within a socioeconomic and historical context. He also asserts that theoretical frameworks that link population and development are not applicable to the Third World situation (pp. 78–79). However, he takes a strong policy stance.

22. Ismail Sirageldin, *Population Policies and Development in the 80's*.

23. World Fertility Survey, *World Fertility Survey: Major Findings and Implications* (London: Alden, 1984).

24. For definitions of the terms "techniques" and "technology," see note 2 above. Although it is not evident in which direction the technological society is leading us,

i.e., Panglossian or catastrophic, it is certain that techniques are imposing more standardization on all facets of human affairs—and the process is cumulative.

25. *Resourcia* includes the major oil-exporting, financial-capital-surplus countries (Algeria, Iraq, Qatar, Libya, Saudi Arabia, Kuwait, the U.A.E., Bahrain, and Oman). *Subsistancia* includes the rest of the Arab countries—the labor-surplus, capital-deficit ones. This classification follows that of the Arab Monetary Fund's *Unified Arab Economic Report*, 1984 (Kuwait: Arab Monetary Fund, 1984) (In Arabic). We put groups one and two from the *Report* together under *Resourcia* and added to them Bahrain and Oman. Although the classification of the *Report* is more detailed and refined, to use it would complicate the discussion without affecting its general conclusion.

26. Robert Mabro, "Economic Consequences of Future Decline in Oil Prices," *Al-Mustaqbal al-'Arabi*, no. 78 (1985): 54–70; Yusuf Sayegh, "Current Oil Crises and Arab Economic Future," *Al-Mustaqbal al-'Arabi*, no. 59 (January 1984): 15–29.

27. Bhagwati and Ruggie, eds., *Power, Passions, and Purposes* and Singer, "Further Thoughts on North–South Negotiations," p. 255.

28. Amin, ed., *Human Resources*.

29. Andre Gunder Frank, "Economic Crises, Third World and 1984," *World Development* 4, nos. 10/11 (1976): 854.

30. M.A. Adelman, "An Unstable World Oil Market," *Energy Journal* 6, no. 1 (1985): 20.

31. For example, housing subsidies may discourage labor mobility. Import of labor with critical skills may depress relative wages and reduce incentives for training and occupational mobility for the national labor force. Also educational incentives that do not discriminate between short- and long-term skill requirements create misleading signals for individuals making occupational choices and create a division between private and social objectives, especially when public sector employment is perceived as a major source of national employment. For an analysis of the case of Saudi Arabia, see Ismail Sirageldin, N. Sherbiny, and M.I. Serageldin, *Saudis in Transition: The Challenges of a Changing Labor Market* (London: Oxford University, 1984).

32. For a recent global assessment, see the Arab Planning Institute, *Socio-Economic Development in the Arab Countries* (Kuwait: Arab Planning Institute, 1982) (In Arabic) and also Centre for Arab Unity Studies, *Arab Development*. The recent proliferation of literature, conferences, and symposia on international migration to the Gulf countries (*Resourcia*) has been exponential.

33. International Monetary Fund, *Supplement on Output Statistics* (Washington, DC: International Monetary Fund, 1984).

34. Ismail Sirageldin, "Some Issues in Middle Eastern International Migration," *Pakistan Development Review* 22, no. 4 (Winter 1984).

35. For a recent assessment of the Egyptian case, see Adel Hossain, *The Egyptian Economy: From Independence to Dependency, 1974–79* (Cairo: Dar al-Mustaqbal al-'Arabi, 1982), vol. 2, pp. 560–625.

36. *Ibid.*, p. 641–42.

37. Leon F. Bouvier, *Planet Earth 1984–2034: A Demographic Vision* (Washington, DC: Population Reference Bureau, 1984).

13

Arab Women: 1995

Leila Ahmed

All clothing, of course, not only the veil, is in some way symbolic as well as to some degree functional: it may well be, though, that the veil is both the world's most visually powerful and its most symbolic garment. Far more than the robed, sexually neutered Islamic dress for the body, it is the veil, the facial covering, which historically has most particularly been charged with powerful and often quite different significations. It has had, for instance, quite different significance for the Islamic world and for the Western—for which its meaning has been perhaps equally portentous. Commonly, also, it has had different and apparently more powerful connotations for those encountering it (generally men) than for the women who actually wear it. Confronted by the veil in place of the human face (that one part of our anatomy that is quintessentially the focus of human interchange), people experience it as blankness, refusal, absence, and even as promise, imbuing that emptiness with their own meanings. To some extent, no doubt, its connotations for Middle Eastern women coincide with those it has for Middle Eastern men. For women, however, it is in addition a material presence, and as such may be experienced by them as physical encumbrance, as protective garb, and even, as I will suggest, as means of empowerment.

Before discussing these connotations, I would like to register that for myself, in preparing this paper I experienced the veil not physically but mentally as a haunting, insistent presence: I found it impossible, that is, to even attempt to broach the topic I was invited to discuss, "Arab Women: 1995," without the thought of the veil's reemergence constantly obtruding itself as the necessary and only starting point and even as central to any discussion of the entire subject. I attempted in fact to resist taking this approach, because in giving the veil centrality I might be taken to be conflating Islamic and Arab identity, and I would not like even by implication to be seen to be doing this. I can think of few obligations more essential than our obligation to reiterate that neither today nor at any time in history have the Middle East's societies and civilizations been exclusively Islamic, and that on the contrary, if anything is authentically and intrinsically part of our heritage, it is the very fact of its ethnic and religious plurality, preserved through millennia—a heritage which should be among our own most cherished and guarded legacies to the future.

Repudiating that connotation, therefore, I return to the veil. At its most obvious level, its reemergence today is merely a visually somewhat dramatic signal that Middle Eastern societies are plunged into turmoil over the issue that has created turmoil in other world societies also, including the United States: the question of women. No one who has witnessed the U.S. presidential debates, watched the rise of religious fundamentalism in this country, or seen the fierce contentions about the nature of the family and the passions and open violence generated by the abortion issue can have much doubt that turmoil over what is known as "the question of women" is, in reality, turmoil not merely over the roles of men also, but actually over all social and human issues that "the question of women" in the end entails, from how people should dress to what might be the nature and significance of human life.

Just as in the United States, the ideological turmoil into which the Middle East is plunged was preceded and at least partially precipitated by enormous economic and social changes that had already occurred in women's and men's roles and lives in those societies. Women's increasing participation in the workforce, their access to education, their entry into the professions are, for example, today increasingly facts of Middle Eastern life, as are the displacement of the nuclear by the extended family and even the emergence and increasing prevalence of the female-headed household as a result of extensive male migration from the poorer Arab countries, such as Egypt and Jordan, to the oil states.

Neither the problems, then, nor the attempted resolutions are less complex than those in process in the United States. If anything, indeed, both are more complex, in that they are refracted by the West's economic, political, and cultural domination. Two of the veil's major connotations in its reappearance today, for example, highlight that double vision, doubled awareness which Middle Eastern peoples are compelled perpetually to exercise in thinking out their future. One connotation, the affirmation of a belief in a particular culture with a particular notion as to the proper relations between women and men, is clearly inward-looking, and the other, the rejection of Western civilization in its moral and social (though not technological) arrangements is as clearly outward-looking.

Why the veil should have come today to signify rejection of the West is a question that is worth briefly pondering, for as a statement the veil's resumption turns out to have a historical density similar and parallel to the statement "Black Is Beautiful." From their first encounter with it, the veil has stood, for Europeans, for the oriental oppression of women, which in turn came to denote oriental backwardness generally. Why Westerners so construed the veil is not clear. After all, in itself, it is an innocuous enough garment which—unlike corsets or high heels, for example—causes no physical damage.[1] Similarly, given the history, until this century, of

European laws and mores respecting women, one might be at a loss to account for European men's solicitous concern over the fact that *oriental* men oppressed women, unless one read it as having chiefly the function of presenting Western man as, by contrast, humane, rational, unoppressive.[2] In any case, by the time of European colonial expansion, such ideas, which had their origins in the Middle Ages, were fully established in Western culture, and, by the end of the nineteenth century, as the Middle East was increasingly drawn into the West's economic and political orbit and as its elites absorbed Western culture, those ideas—of the veil as the symbol of female oppression, and of female oppression as both cause and epitome of its oriental backwardness—became the ideas of the elites also. And so this century opened with the formal casting off of the veil, explicitly equated by Middle Eastern leaders—Atatürk, Qasim Amin, and others—with the oriental backwardness of their societies, which also, they asserted, must be cast off as those societies marched forward along the road then known as "progress" and today called "Westernization."

The resumption of the veil symbolically repudiates the culture's—or, more precisely, the elite's—acceptance and internalization of the values that the West for its own reasons had applied to the culture and society and repudiates also the earlier naïvely enthusiastic admiration for the West. This is precisely what many young women who have now adopted the veil express. "Once we thought that Western society had all the answers for successful, fruitful living," one woman said in an interview. "If we followed the lead of the West we would have progress. Now we see that this isn't true; they [the West] are sick societies; even their material prosperity is breaking down. America is full of crime and promiscuity. Russia is worse. Who wants to be like that?" How extensively and comprehensively the veil connotes a rejection of the West and a resumption of an intrinsic, once-repudiated identity is suggested by the following analysis by Afaf Lutfi al-Sayyid Marsot. Writing of the appearance of Islamic dress in Egypt, she states:

> It was a sign of opposition to the government and its policies . . . the one-sided treaty with Israel, the excessive westernization with consumerism as its manifestation . . . [the dress] indicating that the wearer espoused the code of ethics and morality of Islam, and set aside the moral "decadence" of the West. It was equally a statement eschewing Western ideology, although not Western technology, and stressing that legitimacy lay within a religious framework and not within any "ism" imported from outside.[3]

The veil, then, emerges as first of all an important counter in an intercultural discourse, a counter whose first value—as symbol of the oppression of women—was set, ironically, not by Middle Eastern women who experienced it, nor even by Middle Eastern men, but by European men. It is noteworthy, for example, that we have no records, so far as I know, prior to Western cultural domination, of women protesting against wearing the veil. (This is not to say that we have no record of women's protest: only that the veil specifically does not appear in itself to have been the object of protest.)

Like its casting-off some 60 years ago, then, the veil's resumption today is, in this framework, preeminently a statement about whether Middle Eastern societies do or do not accept Western values and Western views of themselves; it is thus paramountly, in this context, a statement of self-affirmation, and affirmation of the values of the indigenous culture as against the geopolitically dominant ones of the West. It is also, nevertheless, inevitably a statement about women—although indeed one does distinctly get the sense from the rhetoric of advocates both of its abolition early in the century and of its resumption today that women perhaps are of rather secondary importance, and that it is "progress" on the one hand and "cultural authenticity" on the other that its most vociferous male advocates were and are really concerned about. However this may be, while its casting-off 60 years ago seemingly could only augur well for women (and indeed it did, in that it indicated the direction those societies would take with respect, for example, to the education of women), its resumption today, with its connotations of adherence to a legal and religious system which unambiguously subordinates and discriminates against women, seems, on the face of it at least, unmistakably ominous.

The declarations on this subject of women who have taken the veil (not to mention those of its male advocates) indicate that its implicit burden of female subordination and restriction to the domestic sphere is indeed, at least verbally, an acknowledged and accepted part of its meaning. The leading Islamic activist Zeinab al-Ghazali, for example, has stated that "Islam . . . does not prevent women from working, entering politics, etc.," so long as these do not "interfere with her first duty as mother . . . [for] a woman's first, holy, and most important mission . . . is to be mother and wife." Younger women's words echo this: "Yes," she would work, Ilham, a medical student, informed an interviewer, provided her husband approved and it did not conflict with her duties as wife and mother. And "No," another young woman declared, she did not believe women had the right to choose their husbands, although they might express an opinion. "We women," she declared, "do not have the experience that men have, and my father can judge another man better than I could."[4]

However, if we examine the function that the veil *actually* serves in women's lives, it becomes apparent that we would be wrong to see the phenomenon of reveiling (and by this I mean, broadly, adopting Islamic dress) as necessarily a negative one for women. Ilham, for example, the medical student already mentioned, was interviewed by Saad Eddin Ibrahim, who describes the circumstances of her veiling as follows. Hailing from a provincial town in Egypt, she earned grades good enough to gain her entrance to Cairo University, which she then chose to attend rather than the university in her home town because of its superior reputation. She found Cairo, however, bewilderingly different from her home town: her classmates and roommates had more money and better clothes than she and seemed to know about dating, drinking, and sex. Unable to compete in money and clothes and uncomfortable with their city mores, she felt isolated and disoriented until she met a veiled chemistry student. In similar circumstances, this young woman had resolved her difficulties by adopting Islamic dress, which, helping her identify herself as adhering to conservative mores, also solved her difficulties over the lack of glamorous clothing. Ilham also then adopted Islamic dress (a decision at first opposed by her family as regressive) with the same happy result.

The one option that neither Ilham nor her family appear to have considered was precisely that which old-style orthodox Islam would have imposed as the only option: that is, of her abandoning her studies in the city and returning to live under the protection of the male members of the family, who technically alone are capable—and indeed have the responsibility—of protecting female honor. Islamic dress here functioned in practice therefore to invest Ilham herself with the responsibility for her own honor and allow her to continue to pursue, on her own terms, her self-appointed goals. Research among other young women suggests that Ilham's case is typical rather than exceptional, and that the adoption of Islamic dress often does function to extend female autonomy. As Safia Mohsen has pointed out, in the context of the rapid social, economic, educational, and professional changes that have occurred, and when, on the other hand, traditional views of women have not kept pace with those changes, the veil provides a viable strategy by which women negotiate the tensions between old views and new roles. Thus Islamic dress, for instance, divesting women's presence of sexual connotations, enables them to share work-space—offices, classrooms—with men without becoming sexually suspect. "Before I wore the veil," she cites one interviewee as declaring, "I always worried what people might think when they saw me speak to a man in a cafeteria or in class. I even wondered what the man himself thought. . . . [Now] I don't worry any more. Nobody is going to accuse me of immorality or think we are exchanging love-vows. . . . I do not hesitate as I did before to study with . . . men . . . or even walk with them to the train."[5]

The most startling case of Islamic dress as means of female empowerment is that afforded by Zeinab al-Ghazali herself, the Islamic leader cited earlier to the effect that woman's principal and sacred duty is that of wife and mother. In an interview she explains that she separated from her first husband because "I found that my marriage took up all of my time and kept me from my mission, and my husband did not agree with my work. I had made a condition that if we had any major disagreements we would separate and that the Islamic cause was essential." On marrying her second husband she obtained a written (i.e., legally binding) agreement that he would not come between her and her cause (read "career"), which took precedence over all else, including family life, and that he would on the contrary "help her and be her assistant." She stipulated also that she would freely meet with men whenever she wished and describes how in fact men came to their home at all hours to confer with her (as leader of the Muslim Women's Association), her husband showing them in and retiring himself to bed.[6]

In her case, then, the active assumption of Islam in practice abolished or reversed all restrictions, releasing her even from the primacy of her duty as wife and mother and enabling her to freely interact with men, including two husbands, on her own terms. Al-Ghazali started out life working for Huda al-Sha'rawi in the Egyptian Feminist Union, from which she resigned, aged 18, to found her own Muslim Women's Association, because she believed that that "foreign importation," a women's movement, had become necessary only because Islam had fallen into backwardness, and therefore that a regenerated Islam would make the movement redundant. The daughter of an Azhar-educated cotton merchant who was also a preacher, she belonged to that middle class which articulately opposed the Westernizing trends of the upper classes, and her father apparently actively raised her as Islam's future answer to Huda al-Sha'rawi's imported feminism. "He would say to me," she recalls, "'Huda Sha'rawi does this, Malak Hifni Nassef does that, but among the Companions of the Prophet . . . there was a woman named Nusayba'. . . . He would tell me how she struggled in the path of Islam, and then he would ask me, 'Whom do you choose? Do you choose Huda Sha'rawi or will you become Nusayba, daughter of Ka'b al-Mazini?'"[7]

These examples of the functions which the adoption of Islamic dress actually serves for women today emphasize the enormous tensions and contradictions inhering in "the return of the veil." While, on the one hand, its return has all the appearance of endorsing patriarchal values (and regardless of whether the veil is or is not intrinsically more or less patriarchal than corsets or high heels, and of how deftly its meaning has been manipulated by Western powers, it is nonetheless today an emblem of patriarchal Islam), the examples cited compel us to recognize that on a practical level Islamic dress often serves actually to enhance women's autonomy. That is, despite the rhetoric of subservience with which the women adopting it may surround their action, in practical terms the goal they pursue and often actually achieve by its means is most commonly the extension of their personal autonomy. It is at once apt and ironic that it is most particularly in the life of al-Ghazali, that avid advocate of patriarchal Islam, that the disparity between explicit rhetoric and actual function is at its most glaring.

In a sense, therefore, the movement could be represented not as a reversal but instead as a continuation, now in vernacular idiom (in place of the Western idiom used by the old upper classes) of that feminism launched in the Arab world earlier this century, by such figures as Bahithat al-Badayia and al-Sha'rawi; a pursuit by women of autonomy through an idiom not easily recognized as feminist because we are used to the idea of feminism as Western and easily recognize it only expressed in Western idiom. However, unlike these earlier feminists, the women today adopting the emblems of patriarchal Islam—either in some sort of pursuit of women's rights within "an Islamic framework" (as al-Ghazali's words cited above in part seem to suggest) or, at the other end of the spectrum, simply as the pragmatic route to their particular goals—cannot be regarded in any substantive or long-term sense as advancing women's cause. For though the emblems of patriarchal Islam—the veil, Islamic dress—might fortuitously at certain moments in history prove to be pragmatically serviceable and provisionally empowering for women, nevertheless that version of Islam (of which they are today inescapably the emblem) is unequivocally committed to the subordination of women, and it cannot be invoked to facilely and temporarily serve women except at the cost of intellectual evasion and obfuscation entailing perilous consequences. As we saw in Iran, women may indeed invoke Islam as an affirmation of self-definition—only to be then coopted and crushed by a state that construes Islam not merely as patriarchal but even as misogynist; and throughout history that is how states have construed it.

Further, an element important to bear in mind with respect to the reveiling movement is the coerciveness of the environment in which the choice of whether to veil or not has to be made today. That is, as the very examples cited illustrate, the adoption of the veil may significantly alleviate the arduous economic and human exigencies of daily living, as well as enhance the respect with which one is treated in public spaces and perhaps also guarantee one an important measure of personal safety. It is obviously easier for those of us currently based in societies where such a choice is not exacted of us to discern and analyze the perilous ambiguities of adopting the veil. Certainly we are in no position to condemn women resorting to it, but it is our obligation nevertheless to point out those perils. In a discussion of these ambiguities with Nawal Sa'dawi, she pointed out that the veil may indeed be enhancing women's autonomy and giving them a measure of protection—but at a cost. "If I carry a gun," she declared, "also I will be protecting myself. Wearing the veil is like having to carry a gun." And indeed, it should not be necessary for women—any more than for men—to have to either wear a veil or carry a gun to protect themselves or guarantee that their fellow citizens respect their dignity.

Despite the perils just noted, this is a moment with perhaps unprecedented potential for positive and radical change in the areas of both gender and class structures in Middle Eastern societies. Enormous changes for women have taken place between the casting off and the resumption of the veil. I will here focus on only one which, outwardly undramatic, is perhaps the most momentous. That is the new conjunction that has appeared in this age, a conjunction in practice rigidly prohibited for most of our history—the conjunction between women and knowledge. The figures on women's access to education over this period alone almost tell the story, shifting from scarcely any in school in the Arab world at the start of the century to 6.3 million girls in primary education, some 2 million in secondary school, and 237,000 at university level in 1975 (and the numbers are considerably higher today). This has changed a whole range of women's relations, firstly to the creation of knowledge; for from the moment of their access to education—and to the language and literature of "high" Arab culture from which they had hitherto been debarred—women have soared to the heights of literary and intellectual excellence. Nazik al Mala'ika,

Amina al-Sa'id, Muna Sa'udi, Etel Adnan, Salma al-Jayyusi, Hanan Mikha'il, Fadwa Tuqan, Fawziyya Abu Khalid, Saniyya Salih, Layla Ba'labakki, Fadela M'Rabet, Ghada Sam'an, Raymonda Tawil, May Sayegh, Fatima Mernissi, Nawal al-Sa'dawi—to name only a few.

Each has written of the full range of subjects preoccupying her male colleagues—and they have also written of something quite new in the literature. They have written of the experience of being female, of being female in the Arab culture. Nazik al-Mala'ika, for example, in a poem called "Washing Off Disgrace" decries the savagery and hypocrisy of the murder of females for "honor":

> She's gone
> Washing off disgrace!
> Tomorrow
> wiping his dagger before his pals
> the butcher bellows
> "Disgrace?
> A mere stain on the forehead
> now washed."
> At the tavern
> turning to the barman he yells,
> "More wine
> And send that lazy beauty of a nymphet
> you got, the one with the mouth of myrrh."
> . . .
> Women of the neighbourhood
> women of the village
> we knead dough with our tears . . .

Fadela M'Rabet, writing of the Algerian establishment's declaration that they intended to be modern while preserving their traditions regarding women, declared: "In 1965 I saw a child of 12 already married and a mother: sickly herself, she carried her child with difficulty. . . ." *That* is tradition, and it is tradition that a husband beat his wife "for some little thing or for nothing . . . An Algerian peasant working in the fields saw his two nephews leaving his house. Convinced that his wife has made a fool of him, he runs in and cuts her up about the head and nose. . . ." This man, explains the lawyer, "avenged his honour according to custom . . . Each country has its customs. He could kill her. He did not do it. That is in his favor . . . Honour is very much respected in Islamic countries." Tradition, she continues, is "not to learn anything . . . to be married very young and condemned [continuously] to reproduce, not to have any social life, not to take part in the conduct of public affairs—these are some of our traditions, solid traditions." And finally Nawal al-Sa'dawi, who probably more than any other writer has graphically mapped the territory of the Arab female experience, describes how from the very moment she is born the female infant experiences aggression. People, writes al-Sa'dawi, "do not welcome her coming into the world . . . this . . . [her birth may] even [leads] to the punishment of the mother with insults or blows or even divorce."[8]

And—so as not to represent only the extremes—one final example from middle class life (reflecting a scenario perhaps familiar to Western readers): "He thinks a husband is a god in his own home," says one woman describing her life. "Everything he says has to be taken as the truth without discussion. What he thinks is right is right and what he thinks is wrong should be wrong for everyone else in the family . . . From an objective point of view we certainly cannot afford my not working. But the way he sees it is that if I stay at home and quit my job, I would be able to economize . . . by doing all the work myself and saving the maid's expense . . . He says my mother lived on ten pounds a month, why can't you live on sixty? . . . He resents the time I spend working for my Ph.D. If he comes back to the house and finds me working on my research, it's the end of the world."[9]

As this new geography of female experience, of human experience, is being illuminated, as women are passionately and grievingly exposing the inhuman and inhumane treatment that underlies such mystifications as "tradition" and "honor," and as they document, as Virginia Woolf did in her day and American women are doing today with respect to their societies, how searingly different a thing it is to be female and Arab from being male and Arab, another revolution in knowledge, and in that new conjunction women-and-knowledge, is also in process.[10] Scholars and historians, for example Elaine Pagels in her study the *Gnostic Gospels* and Fazlur Rahman in his works, are ranging through texts and histories exposing the androcentrism, the erasure and exclusion of women, and the misogyny that have gone into creating the traditions and texts of both Islam and Christianity that are in place today.

Also, reworking Middle Eastern history and analyzing the structures of modern society are scholars such as Talal Asad, Saad Eddin Ibrahim, Afaf Lutfi al-Sayyid Marsot, Suad Joseph, Judith Tucker, Hisham Sharabi, Halim Barakat, and many others, who are changing our understanding of the roles of women in our economy and history and revealing the damage to all of society and not only to women of the female's subordination to the male. In the West, studies of Western women in history and society already crowd the shelves and have transformed our understanding of the past—men's as well as women's. With respect to the Middle East, Christian and Islamic, that work has only just begun; and today women are graduating by the hundreds of thousands and perhaps already by the millions capable of studying, evaluating, and redefining traditions, laws, culture, scriptures, and capable therefore of transforming the entire system of knowledge that informs, controls, and governs those societies—and so of transforming the possibilities of the future.

I take therefore an optimistic view of that future—not because of any faith in the governments of those nations, but because, rather, of a faith in the resilience and creativity of the people who, both men and women, for the first time in history have, a majority of them, access to education, and therefore the potential for political and social consciousness and with it the will to work for a just society. It is not a naïve optimism, and it is an optimism for the long- rather than the short-term. By 1995 for example, perhaps the struggle will have only just begun. Resistance to that struggle I do not doubt will be fierce; but the ground already gained, being that of knowledge, is a momentous gain and one that cannot easily be again erased. To control knowledge, to control who creates, interprets, and disseminates it, to allow access to it only to males and only those among them who could be inducted into the governing and lawmaking classes—that has been the real source of power—and it is that hegemony so essential to the perpetuation of the old social order and its moral—or immoral—vision that has now been broken.

The struggle for justice for women is intrinsically and inseparably a struggle for justice for men, for there can be no such thing as justice for women only, no more than for men only. This is not the place to develop in any sustained way the necessary connection between the struggle against women's oppression and that against other oppressions, and I will only point to it here by quoting the words of two women who wrote succinctly and eloquently on the matter.

The first is the historian Joan Kelly, detailing what should be today's feminist agenda. "It is a program," she wrote, "that penetrates both to the core of self and to the heart, or heartless center of the male domain, for it will require a restructuring of all social institutions . . . restructur[ing] how we come to know self and others in our birthing, growing up, loving, and working [and it] must reach the institutions that fatefully bear upon sexuality, family, and community. Schools and all socializing agencies will have to be rid of sex and sexual bias. Work and welfare will have to be transformed, placed in the humane context of the basic right of all to live, work, and love in dignity." Kelly was writing of American society, but it is an agenda that I think would suit the Middle East, too, pretty well.

The second quotation is from the 19th-century Black activist Anna Cooper, writing on the very question of what justice for women might mean. "We take our stand," she declared, "on the solidarity of humanity, the oneness of life, and the unnaturalness and injustice of all special favoritism, whether of sex, race, country, or condition . . . not till race, color, sex, and condition are seen as accidents and not the substance of life . . . not till then is woman's cause won—" and that cause, she continues, is not only women's cause, but "the cause of every man and every woman who has ever writhed silently under a mighty wrong."[11]

To sum up, then: the dilemma confronting thinking Arab women and men today through the issue of Islamic dress for women is in reality, for all its apparent novelty, a dilemma that has haunted Arab society this century, now in a slightly new guise. Throughout the century, the dilemma has been at its most acute concerning the question of women. Because, throughout, the debate on that issue within those societies has seemed to be, fundamentally, about whether Arab society should adopt Western values and attitudes and, in imitation of the West, grant women education, entry into the professional workforce, etc. (women, of course, had always been part of the working class workforce), or whether Arab society should, on the other hand, remain true to the "Islamic" heritage; continue to deny these opportunities to women; and continue to insist, as "Islam" required, that women's only proper role is subservient and domestic. Earlier this century, Arab intellectuals and politicians, arguing for the importance to society as a whole of women's education and advancement, maintained that far from being un-Islamic, this, indeed, was in full accord with the true spirit of Islam.[12] This, too, however, seemed in the final analysis to be merely an adroit ploy whose function was to disguise Western-inspired goals in acceptable Islamic dress. Today, no less, the issue is being fought as if it were fundamentally about competing cultural visions, as the very fact that the veil has become the emblem of the debate itself attests. That is, the issue is being debated as if the idea that women might be fully human, fully autonomous individuals responsible for their own actions and as entitled as men to obtain an education, to practice a profession, and to be treated with full justice before the law were merely a "Western" idea. At the same time, the "intrinsically" Islamic position is presented as one in which essentially (the disguising rhetoric once stripped away) women, even if fully human, are yet not fully responsible and are to be subservient to men who have responsibility for them and authority over them. In this view, Islam classifies women's rights to education, a profession, etc., not as inherent rights but as privileges which their male guardian—in the fullness of his wisdom—may see fit to grant or not grant them. Furthermore, everyone (this is the implication), including women, had been contentedly living within this God-given arrangement and any questioning of it had been quite unheard of—until the interference of Western colonialism.

This mystification of the issue of women through posing it as if it were a matter essentially of different cultural visions (which has been highly serviceable to the mullahs, clerics, and others exercising enormous influence in Islamic societies) is as absurd as the suggestion, also common among this group, that there are no classes in Islam and no class conflict, only a God-given order—occasionally challenged, to be sure, by heretics and other godless individuals, whom the guardians of Islam swiftly and successfully eliminate.

On the contrary, however, as recent trends in historical research make ever clearer, movements such as that of the Karammita, for instance, ruthlessly eradicated by orthodox Islam and surviving in their historical works merely as "heresies," were important and widespread, and concerned with issues that we would today term class issues (as indeed early Sufism, for all its mystical leanings, also appears to have been). Both movements, furthermore, (as I have elsewhere argued) on explicit and implicit levels radically contested orthodox views on women as well as on class.

In the Islamic world as elsewhere, in other words, the versions of history perpetuated as authoritative do not bear the privileged "impartial" relation to reality to which they lay claim but, rather, present a version representing the interests and vision of the male governing classes. Similarly, the versions of Islam and what constitutes "true" Islam that have held sway for so many centuries are essentially the versions that it suited this class to perpetuate. They controlled cultural, historical, and ideological production and other mental production such as the development of the law, just as they controlled economic production. And again (as the Karammita and the early Sufi movements, to mention only the clearest instances, suggest) in the Islamic world as elsewhere, the oppressed resisted and resented oppression. Just as elsewhere, in the Islamic world also, evidently the desire for justice in society, whether in the area of gender or of class, has been persistent and endemic.

These, which should after all be evident truths (of course the oppressed in the Arab world as elsewhere resent oppression on whatever grounds it occurs, biological or economic, and of course females as well as males passionately desired justice) are not self-evident only because so much ingenuity has been expended to conceal them. It is important to insist on their factuality, in part, because the notion that the desire for justice for women is merely a Western idea has proved so serviceable in the hands of those who, ignorantly or willfully, seek to persuade Arab women (and well-intentioned men) that the choice before them is a choice between adopting alien Western ideas and betraying their culture on the one hand, and accepting women's inferiority and inability to be responsible for themselves as an intrinsic and immutable part of their "authentic" cultural heritage on the other. Whereas, as suggested above, the fact is not that Middle Eastern women did not desire justice as strongly as their sisters elsewhere, including those in the West, but only that the forces controlling the making and writing of the area's history hitherto have been particularly ruthless and successful at suppressing resistance and at deleting it from the pages of history. More importantly, however, it is necessary that ideological distortion be recognized for what it is, and that the class and gender interests which shape and inform the "authoritative" and "impartial" versions of history and of Islam that are in place today also be clearly recognized for what they are; that we may form an accurate sense of the forces to be contended with, and dismantled, in the quest for an equitable society.

Notes

1. At least one early European woman, Lady Mary Wortley Montague, seems to have suspected this fact; see E. Wharncliffe, ed., *The Letters of Lady Mary Wortley Montague* (London: 1887), vol. 1, p. 247.

2. That strategy, by and large, appears to have been quite effective in that European women apparently completely accepted the view that they were very fortunate to be European and not Muslims (or "Turks"). "When some of them [men] will not let us say our souls are our own," protests a 17th-century female author, "we then must ask their pardons if we are not yet so completely passive as to bear all without so much as a murmur. We complain that here is a plain and an open design to

render us mere slaves, perfect Turkish wives, without properties, or sense, or souls. . . ." And from that period to the present, the notion of the Muslim wife as a slave by comparison with whom the Western woman is fortunate is an accepted "truth" within the works of Western female as well as male writers—in the works of Simone de Beauvoir, for example, in our own day. Lady Mary Wortley Montague (referred to above) constitutes a significant exception in her refutation of the notion that Turkish women were more oppressed than European women; significantly, she was the only one who based her remarks on her observations in Turkey rather than on the texts and observations of Western men.

3. John Alden Williams, "A Return to the Veil in Egypt," *Middle East Review* (Spring 1979): 54; Afaf Lutfi al-Sayyid Marsot, "Religion or Opposition? Urban Protest Movements in Egypt," *International Journal of Middle East Studies* 16 (1984): 550.

4. Valerie J. Hoffman, trans., "An Islamic Activist: Zaynab al-Ghazali," in Elizabeth Warnock Fernea, ed., *Women and the Family in the Middle East* (Austin, TX: University of Texas, 1985), p. 236; Saad Eddin Ibrahim, *The New Arab Social Order* (Boulder, CO: Westview, 1982), p. 19; Safia K. Mohsen, "New Images, Old Reflections: Working Middle Class Women in Egypt," in Fernea, *Women and the Family in the Middle East*, p. 70.

5. Mohsen, "New Images, Old Reflections," p. 69.

6. Hoffman, "An Islamic Activist: Zaynab al-Ghazali," p. 237.

7. *Ibid.*, pp. 237–38.

8. Nazik al Mala'ika, "Washing Off Disgrace," in Kamal Boullata, ed. and trans., *Women of the Fertile Crescent* (Washington, DC: Three Continents Press, 1981), pp. 20–21; Fadela M'Rabet, "Future Directions?" in Elizabeth Warnock Fernea, ed., *Middle Eastern Muslim Women Speak* (Austin, TX: University of Texas, 1977), p. 324; Nawal al-Sa'dawi, *The Hidden Face of Eve* (London: Zed Press, 1981), p. 6.

9. Mohsen, "New Images, Old Reflections," p. 66.

10. Virginia Woolf, citing the English Lord Chief Justice's words on patriotism to the effect that "England is the home of Liberty," and that the "Englishman's home is his castle," and that patriotism therefore is the Englishman's fight in defense of these, asks: What, then, of the Englishwoman? "What does 'patriotism' mean to her? Has she the same reasons for being proud of England, for loving England, for defending England? Has she been 'greatly blessed' in England? History and biography when questioned would seem to show that her position in the home of freedom has been very different from her brother's. . . ." The Englishwoman will find, she continues, when she studies the matter, that she has very good reason to be indifferent to the defense of England: "She will find that she has no good reason to ask her brother to fight on her behalf to protect 'our' country. 'Our country,' she will say, 'throughout the greater part of its history has treated me as a slave; it has denied me education or any share in its possessions. . . ." *Three Guineas*, pp. 12, 124–25.

11. Anna Julia Cooper, *A Voice from the South* (Ohio: The Aldire Printing House, 1892), pp. 121–25; Joan Kelly, "The Double Vision of Feminist Theory," *Feminist Studies* (Spring 1979): 223–24.

12. See my "Feminism and Feminist Movements in the Middle East, A Preliminary Exploration: Turkey, Egypt, Algeria, People's Democratic Republic of Yemen," in Azizah al-Hibri, ed., *Women and Islam* (London: Pergamon Press, 1982).

14

Class Structure and Social Change in the Arab World: 1995

Samih K. Farsoun

The study of the class structure and dynamics of the Arab world is very difficult, given the diversity of the region, and given the spotty and uneven character of relevant data. Difficult as it is to draw a picture of the contemporary class structure and dynamics of the Arab world, it seems an almost impossible task to attempt a projection a decade into the future. Perhaps the best approach is to sketch out a synoptic view of major developments of social structure and state, then attempt to draw out in terms of these changes the derivative class formations and class dynamics. This in turn will enable us to make some commentary on the potential political directions internal to major Arab countries and in the region as a whole.[1]

Political Economy of the Arab World

The Arab world—divided into relatively distinct regions, the Mashriq and the Maghrib—has experienced three broad phases in its modern political economy. In the Mashriq, the first phase was characterized by an integrated precapitalist economy under the Ottomans.[2] The second was a period of European colonization which resulted in political, economic, and social fragmentation of the area. The third has been the post-World War II period of politically independent and Balkanized nation-states. Despite a period of radical political and economic nationalism during the 1960s, the Arab world in the 1970s and 1980s experienced accelerating integration into a new Western division of labor. This new division of labor is characterized by an international circulation of capital and labor. The oil-rich Mashriq countries export money capital along with oil and import labor power and vast varieties of commodities and consumer goods.[3] While exporting money capital to the West, the oil-rich nations import labor power from the oil-poor Arab countries, thus integrating the Mashriq as a region into the new international division of labor.

On the other hand, the Maghrib exports labor power to Europe and imports tourists/consumers from the north. The oil-poor Arab countries have become the locus for the reproduction of major supplies of labor power for European and oil-rich Arab states. In this sense these Arab countries have emerged as labor reserves for the labor-hungry nations of Europe and the oil-rich states.[4] Labor-exporting Arab countries import monetary remittances from expatriate labor.[5] The size of worker remittances as a percentage of total exports reached 28 percent for Egypt, 43 percent for Morocco, 198 percent for Jordan, and 5,897 percent for Yemen.[6]

The process of accelerated integration into the new international division of labor has had its consequences for both the individual Arab countries and the region as a whole. The Arab Mashriq is undergoing its own division of labor in response to regional dynamics and the more powerful dynamics of its linkage to Western capital. Elements of Arab Mashriq regional integration are the already-noted movement of labor and commodities accompanied by the equally massive counterflow of monetary capital. In addition to remittances from individuals, the capital counterflow includes bilateral state-to-state aid, joint Arab institutional aid, joint Arab investment capital, and direct private investment. The flow of such massive amounts of capital has energized the economic expansion of oil-poor Arab countries. The whole Mashriq has become one "oil economy," as Roger Owen argues,[7] while the Maghrib remains divided and unintegrated economically.

Paradoxically, increasing Mashriq regional integration has been taking place simultaneously with the process of greater consolidation of individual Arab countries' *national* economies, yet this seemingly contradictory development is in large part due to the fact that the processes working for the greater integration of the Arab Mashriq are weak by comparison to those integrating each of the Arab countries, *individually*, into the international division of labor.

Accompanying the region's accelerated integration into the world economy, a decline in subsistence production and other transformations have taken place.[8] Accordingly, massive occupational shifts from agricultural to industrial and service activities have occurred.[9] The agricultural sector in the various Arab nations has been undergoing increasing transformation, which is leading to class changes in the rural areas. This is not only forcing people off the land, but is also creating new rural social relations. There is, thus, a massive exodus of surplus agricultural labor, in particular poor, unskilled, and young farmers or peasants, to the urban conglomerations and to the oil-rich states. Two specific aspects of these developments are noteworthy: one is the marginalization of Arab women from production in those areas where commercial agriculture has taken root, and the second is the proletarianization of the young male migrant. One other derivative feature is of long-term consquence. *Infitah* (economic liberalization) policies of oil-poor nations have led to a process of economic denationalization and the increasing reprivatization of the economy, which allows the growth of new entrepreneurs and a new bourgeoisie in both rural and urban areas. However, the significance of the policies of *infitah* and reprivatization have differed in different Arab states. For example, these two policies were instituted earliest (in the early 1970s) and most extensively by Anwar al-Sadat in Egypt. In Sudan, North Yemen, Syria, and Iran, they were introduced later, in lesser scope and differently. Algeria, since Boumedienne, has become the latest of the radical nationalist states to quietly undertake a version of such policies. While Sadat announced the introduction of these policies with much political fanfare coupled with an exaggerated promise of well-being for all Egyptians, the leaders of the latter states introduced "liberalization" quietly, usually under an ideological rubric of reform. Of course, in the oil-rich countries, accelerated integration into the world economy produced a quantum leap of commercialization and the final destruction of the subsistence economy.

In the oil-poor Arab countries, and also Iraq, the previously radical nationalist regimes of the 1960s instituted extensive land reform which broke up the vast holdings of the feudal landlords and distributed some of the confiscated land to peasants and other small farmers. Their agrarian policy over the years created a new *kulak* class of landowners. This class, with the help of the state, increasingly rationalized its agricultural production and introduced scientific farming and rural wage labor in place of tenancy, sharecropping, and other precapitalist forms of relations of production. These developments stimulated further the rural-to-urban exodus. In oil-rich countries (but to a lesser extent in Libya than in the rest), settlement of nomads with the help of enormous state subsidies is also creating a rural landowning bourgeoisie which in Saudi Arabia is using expatriate wage labor.

Commercialization of agriculture in the Arab world has come to mean increasing dependency on state economic policy regarding infrastructure, financing, pricing, price supports, subsidies, and import policies concerning farm equipment, fertilizers, pesticides, warehousing, transport, and marketing. Thus, through the *infitah* policies of the 1970s, well-connected agrarian capitalists have increasingly gained the advantage over others in a process which has begun a more intensive concentration and capitalization of the countryside and a deeper structural change there. While this analytical description is general, research is needed to delineate and analyze country-specific transformations.

Arab industrial growth is very uneven[10] and generally has a weak financial base, except of course in oil-related industries in oil-rich states. Arab state industrialization is highly differentiated in both the depth and the level of industrial and technical development.[11] There seems to be a dual tendency of industrial centralization and concentration in oil-producing states and some decentralization and deconcentration in the labor-exporting oil-poor nations. Of course, Iraq and Algeria share aspects of both oil-poor and oil-rich states. Import substitution, textiles, and some high-technology and heavy industries are characteristic of the oil-poor states. The older industries, such as textile and steel (in Egypt, for example), are stagnating. The new high-tech industries have not taken solid root, and the transition from old, declining industries to new ones is not taking place rapidly or smoothly. It is problematic socially, politically, and economically.

In general, Arab industry has a weak competitive position both in the region and internationally (except, of course, for the extractive oil industry—but not for petrochemicals). This weakness, as well as the particular structure of the regional and individual state industries, is directly related to Arab state policy in regard to finance, subsidy, import regulation, and marketing. The status of the public, mixed, and private industrial sectors in individual Arab states needs detailed study. The Arab industrial bourgeoisies are weak, much too small and insecure to make a significant impact in the present Arab political economy. The local bourgeoisies cannot compete with Western capital and must either complement Western or state capital or enter into weak areas of business. While studies on and plans for pan-Arab economic—including industrial—development abound, few concrete results have materialized.

Industrial development, largely capital-intensive, has not absorbed very large numbers of the workers who have been displaced from the rural areas. Migrant Arab labor is employed mostly in services and construction. Hardly any Arab country has more than 15 percent of its labor force in industry.[12] Displaced villagers swell the urban mass of the unemployed and the underemployed in the oil-poor Arab states. The older and declining industries of the oil-poor countries, with their more skilled and unionized workers, are likely to suffer attrition in employment and worsening working conditions. The new high-tech industries will have such a diversified and unorganized group of workers that they will add to the variation and fragmentation of the various Arab countries' working classes. This, in addition to a growing internal differentiation of the working class, will have important future social and political implications. That is, an increasingly differentiated and fragmented working class will produce new and diverse and fragmented styles of political action in the future.

In the Arab world, real estate capital has assumed major significance by absorbing large amounts of private savings, bank capital, and in some states (principally the oil-producing ones) government subsidy. This investment pattern has reflected itself in the investments that Arab entrepreneurs have been making in Western industrial countries. In the Arab world, however, real estate investment is not restricted to the new rich or the wealthy. The small savings of many a returning labor migrant also have been invested in real estate.[13] The popularization of real estate investment is caused not only by housing shortages, but in part also by the security of such investments. Furthermore, real estate holdings do not interfere with other occupations and have become an important source of income to an increasing number of families.

Rent income, small business investment income, and possibly income from wages or other labor have emerged as key sources for an increasing number of multiple-income households. This pattern, which has been accelerating since the beginning of the oil decade, clearly blurs class lines, decreases the likelihood of class consciousness and class-based politics, and increases the chances for new styles of social and political action. What form this action will take in rich oil-producing states and in oil-poor, labor-exporting countries is difficult to predict. It will derive from the increasingly fragmented nature of Arab societies.

Perhaps of greatest significance in this structural fragmentation is the reproduction of Arab Mashriq societies of petty commodity producers and distributors (including services). This is the great mass of very small scale family enterprises and of self-employed merchants, manufacturers and artisans, repairmen, service and transport workers, and others in the rural areas.[14] Petty commodity producers and distributors form an especially large part of the "informal sector" (which includes women) or of the so-called "underground economy." Most of these petty economic activities are traditional in style of organization and social relations of work (patronage), that is, in the labor process. Such "old" petty commodity producers and distributors have been accompanied by "new" similar strata. These are modern, efficient, and competitive small- and medium-sized enterprises of entrepreneurs, designers, professionals, and subcontractors, specialized and technically very advanced or highly skilled. They operate domestically and regionally, sometimes even internationally, and may have a network of their own smaller subcontractors to whom they farm out work. The reproduction of the "old" and the emergence of the "new" petty commodity producers and services distributors have increased the internal differentiation and heterogeneity of this class as well as increased its size, contrary to conventional wisdom. The traditional sector is not declining in favor of the modern. Further, members of this latter sector often own stocks and bonds in Western stock markets, local land, or other real estate, and therefore have diversified investments and multiple incomes. Thus they increase internal differentiation and stratification, reinforcing the blurring of class lines and the social fragmentation and heterogeneity of these societies.

The reproduction and expansion, not diminution, of petty commodity producers and distributors have accompanied the development of typically state-promoted, large-scale, capital-intensive, and technologically-advanced industry. This seemingly contradictory dual development is directly linked to the role of the Arab world in the international division of labor, that is, to the nature of integration of the region into the European and American economies. In short, the reproduction and expansion of precapitalist forms and relations of production and distribution simultaneously accompany distorted capitalist growth and development in the region.

These transformations of interlocked and mutually reinforcing capitalist and precapitalist forms of production and labor processes have not caused an irrevocable rupture with the social relations, ideology, and culture associated with the previous "traditional" social formation. On the contrary, they helped reproduce those traditional social relations associated with the precapitalist social structure of economic activity, social values, kinship relations, and political behavior.

Patriarchy, patronage, and the mercantile spirit became intertwined with new capitalist social relations to produce a unique amalgam which manifests itself in the behavior and values of contemporary Arab society.[15] The resultant heterogeneous and fragmented class structure and heterogeneous and fragmented social forms produce fragmented and heterogeneous social views and social action. Less energized by nationalist issues than the previous generation, this fragmented urban mass is also less likely to engage in class organization. It is more likely to engage in social and political action based on kinship or on neighborhood, street, ethnic, sectarian, or religious organizing. This will be more so in the absence of socially conscious and relatively autonomous (from the government) political parties.

Class and Social Change

Accelerated integration of the Arab world into the capitalist world system, the collection of vast and unprecedented oil revenues, and the rapid economic growth of constituent states of the region have led to significant class transformation and social change.

To begin with, we noted that the massive labor migration of waves of people over the last decade has meant, among many other things, the externalized proletarianization (transformation into wage labor) of increasing numbers of former peasants and the subsequent repatriation of a fraction of these as members of the petite bourgeoisie. An agricultural villager exits a peasant, becomes employed as a wage worker, returns home with a small savings, and often establishes himself as a petty commodity producer and/or distributor. While externally-induced proletarianization and bourgeoisification are taking place, simultaneous large-scale internal subproletarianization also is proceeding. The rural/urban population ratio has been falling rapidly, and urbanization has been progressing explosively. This double process of externalized proletarianization/bourgeoisification and internal subproletarianization in association with some industrialization is producing growing differentiation and fragmentation in the working class of the varied oil-poor Arab countries and in mixed Arab communities of the oil-rich city-states.

While some of the repatriated workers often become petty bourgeois, a smaller number make large fortunes and return to join a rapidly expanding new bourgeoisie in their respective countries. This, along with the *infitah* in the oil-poor nations of the Arab world, has allowed the rapid accumulation of private capital and created in the process a powerful new grande bourgeoisie. In the oil-rich peninsula, the new bourgeoisie is largely a group of middlemen, merchants, brokers, and agents of and for Western economic interests, allowed—indeed encouraged—by the state to enrich themselves practically overnight. The activities of this new class quickly spilled into investments and ventures overseas in the Western world, primarily in real estate (hotels, office buildings, shopping malls, etc.), government securities, stock and bond trading, and mercantile activity. This class has helped integrate the Arab world into Western capital. While in the oil-rich countries this class is composed of members of the ruling dynasties and their relatives, close associates, and advisors, in the oil-poor nations it is constituted from among those repatriated from the oil areas and those who capitalized on their position in or access to the state to enrich themselves quickly. Corruption and patronage have been rampant. The officer corps of the military establishments of most of the Arab states have not been immune to this. Many an officer or ex-officer or a close relative has joined the ranks of the *nouveaux riches* by capitalizing on their position or connections in the state.

The state policies which helped produce the new bourgeoisie and expand the petite bourgeoisie also vastly expanded the white-collar strata employed in the state bureaucracy, its ministries, its coercive apparatuses, and its social and economic agencies. In many countries of the Arab world, the state is by far the largest single employer. In addition to those in the above state bureaucracies, the public sector employees also are subject directly to the state. In Jordan, for example, just over 50 percent of the labor force is employed by the state.[16] In Syria, the figure may be higher. For many of these state bureaucrats, after-hours employment or business[17] or real estate investment provides one or more additional sources of income. Here again, among the middle strata, multiple-income households are proliferating. As among many workers, increasing numbers of the middle strata occupy more than one class position, reinforcing further the process of the blurring of class lines and of increasing social heterogeneity and fragmentation.

The regional factors that generated the social class transformations are the very same ones responsible for a group of other social phenomena. The first is the steady rise in income and the rapid rise in the standard of living for vast sectors of the population of the Arab world. This *embourgeoisement* is reflected visibly not only in gross economic growth rates, but also in the rapid spread of consumerism,[18] especially of imported Western goods. In turn, this has helped to homogenize the Arab consumer lifestyle, many of whose aspects are mimetic of Western styles, first in consumer goods, but increasingly in behavior. This homogenization of consumer lifestyles among Arabs is paradoxically associated with social fragmentation and the resurgence of parochial identities including ethnic, sectarian, religious, regional, tribal, and clan consciousness. It is the processes of social fragmentation and corresponding fragmentation of social forms and views which allow the reproduction and reinforcement of patriarchal and parochial consciousness despite homogenized consumerism.

The second of these new social phenomena is the reproduction and expansion of inequalities[19] in the Arab world despite the clear overall bourgeoisification and visible rise in the standard of living. R. Paul Shaw analyzes three types of inequalities in the Arab Mashriq which have grown so rapidly that the phenomenon is quite unique in history. Shaw writes:

> Previous to . . . [1973/74], the absolute differential in GDP per capita between the two groups of countries [oil-producing and labor-exporting] was only $460 . . . By 1980, it had swollen to over $5,000 per capita and the ratio of per capita incomes in oil-rich versus oil-poor countries had more than doubled to 7.3.[20]

> Between 1976 and 1981, the oil-rich countries allocated an average of $36 billion per year for the implementation of their national development plans . . . This compares with an average of $14.5 billion per year for the oil-poor countries. On a per capita basis, the oil-rich countries invested an average of $1,360 per year versus only $115 for their oil-poor counterparts.[21]

The poorer Arab countries have significant trade balance deficits, staggering foreign debts, and huge debt service, in contrast to the oil-rich countries, which have substantial surpluses deployed overseas. These inter-regional inequalities are accompanied by inter-sectoral inequalities as well. Restricting the analysis to the contrast between agriculture and industry, Shaw writes: "Agriculture . . . employs no less than 50 percent of the total Arab labor force. Yet between 1976 and 1981, it received only 8.8 percent of total development funds. In contrast, urban-based manufacturing, with only 9 percent of the total Arab labor force, was slated for approximately 20.3 percent of the total development budget."[22]

Like development expenditures, per capita income of the agricultural labor force is a small fraction of that of the personnel in urban industrial and services establishments. Differences in per capita and/or household incomes are especially severe among the oil-poor countries. For example, in Egypt and Morocco 44 percent of rural families are below official poverty lines.[23] Within rural areas, continuing severe income discrepancies still exist despite ambitious land reform programs.

> In Egypt, an initial reduction in the concentration of landholders between 1958 and 1965 gave way to a subsequent rise in concentration because (1) land distribution was limited to previous tenants and small farmers, and (2) later reforms did not distribute land rights to the growing number of landless peasants.[24]

Increasing commercialization and capitalization of agriculture may have caused an arrest of land redistribution and/or caused reconcentration in land ownership.

> According to the latest round of agricultural censuses, large farms still hold disproportionate shares of arable land. For example, in Syria, 2.5 percent of the relatively large farms (say, in excess of 50 hectares) hold 29 percent of the arable land; in Algeria, 2.2 percent hold 47 percent; in Tunisia, 4.6 percent hold 46 percent; in Morocco, 2.5 percent hold 27 percent; in Kuwait, 3.1 percent hold 37 percent; and in Lebanon, 0.2 percent hold 15 percent. In Egypt, 12 percent of the land is still held by only 0.2 percent of the farms and, with 46 percent of the total land being rented, the reign of the absentee landlord may again be visible.[25]

While income distribution data[26] for the region and the aggregate data cited above include important exceptions, there is no doubt of the extremely wide inequalities between and within oil-rich and oil-poor countries of the

Arab world. These wide inequalities, along with those among the various economic sectors, have also increased substantially[27] over the "oil decade."

Inequalities in the region and within each country also contribute to the fragmentation and heterogeneity of the Arab social formation. The ability to make new wealth has been determined principally by the degree to which the middleman entrepreneur or merchant has a connection or access to the power centers of the state and not by innovative industrial or other productive development. Such patterns reinforce the patriarchal and patronage system of social relations, thus reinforcing fragmented social relations, views, and consciousness in Arab societies—that is, parochialism.

Arab intellectuals have not really addressed the above processes or derivative social/political issues. The majority of the intellectuals/activists of the 1950s and 1960s have been professionalized and absorbed into a bureaucratized apparatus, that is, institutionalized. Indeed, some of them have abandoned their socialist principles (even principles of Islamic social justice) and emerged as ideologues of the new bourgeoisified social order. These new ideologues propagate neo-liberal doctrines and a "born-again democracy" which objectively justify state postures that during the past oil decade brought about *infitah* policies characterized by a frantic rush for get-rich-quick schemes, by a predatory class of comprador bourgeoisie that has strongly influenced the development model of the region, and by further social fragmentation. These policies discouraged, at least in the oil-poor states, authentic attempts at socioeconomic development of the productive sectors. Instead, they reinforced service-based capitalist transformation of the region. They also linked organically the economic destiny of the region to the fate of Western economies. Thus, the status of Arab economic well-being is externally determined rather than domestically controlled by its own people.

The State, Class, and Political Change

Arab countries have syncretic states characterized by what James Petras calls "multiple states"—that is, three "states" in one.[28] The first is the "historic state," the traditional bureaucracy which functions as an instrument for political patronage and—as in Nasser's Egypt—the "employment agency of last resort." This "state" dispenses economic favors, positions of power, and employment. The ruling elite uses the system of patronage to consolidate its position and to gain solidarity and support from varied sectors of the population.

In the oil-rich countries, the system of patronage is a vehicle of co-optation which functions principally along kinship, clan, and tribal lines, but incorporates adjuncts, agents, friends, colleagues, handlers, and others. This historic state is subject and responsive to the political elites and their constituencies in the population. In the oil-poor countries, the "historic states" function in a similar manner, but are subject as well to claims from the leadership of the dominant political party or coalition of parties. It is this process of patronage which recruits into the top leadership kinsmen, relatives, and close members of the same clan or tribe or the same ethnic, sectarian, or class fragment, and gives the different Arab regimes the character of a narrow social base, as Hanna Batatu typically argues.[29]

This patronage system is associated with the second "state"—the "modern state"—a conglomerate of autonomous and semi-autonomous agencies and bureaucracies. This is the state of technocrats, often educated in the United States, and of the development-oriented sectors of the local bourgeoisie. It performs in the Arab nations two principal functions, the first of which is the planning, financing, and establishing of new economic enterprises and infrastructure.

The second function is the establishment, financing, and managing of the bureaucracies of the welfare state. In the oil-rich nations, the welfare state agencies serve to integrate the native into the nation-state and to legitimize the regime, especially the ruling elite. Above all, they serve to mobilize solidarity of the natives of the oil-rich states with one another and with the ruling elites against the ultimate threat of the more numerous resident migrant workers.

On the other hand, in the oil-poor countries, the welfare state programs, which include basic food subsidy, also function to defuse discontent and mobilize solidarity with the ruling elite. In Egypt, for example, the Sadat-instituted welfare program came to be known popularly as *"Ma'ash al-Sadat"* (the Sadat-provided salary).

The point of overlap between the "historic state" and the "modern state" is the patronage-based positions of power in the varied agencies of development and welfare. This linkage meshes effectively to legitimize the regime and mobilize support for it. In short, both modern and traditional leaderships have a vested interest in the survival and stability of the regimes of their respective states of the Arab world.

The third major "state" is the "repressive state." This is the self-contained caste that operates the repressive organs of the state which protect the ruling class, the elite, and the propertied classes. It often stands above society and above the law, and as often makes its own law. It is the proverbial stick to the welfare carrot of the Arab states. It can be as harsh as it pleases, and can violate the human and civil rights of the citizens without having to answer to anyone except its own caste leaders. Like the other bureaucracies, the "repressive state" is also an important employer of last resort and functions in its own right as a mobilizer of support and enforcer for the regime.

This syncretic "state-in-three" constitutes the contemporary state structure in the Arab world. However, the inter-penetration of the three states may lead to contradictory and conflicting processes within the state and within the society as a whole. In the short term, such contradictory processes may lead to some political instability, while for the long term they set the stage for a more profound transformation. One such example of the latter should suffice here.

The welfare programs and basic food subsidies that have been instituted by ruling elites to defuse popular discontent and to mobilize support for the regime will change over the years from being a grant of favor by the rulers to a political right of the citizen. Thus, any dismantling or severe constraint of the programs in the future will likely trigger movements of opposition against the regime. In short, unwittingly, all states of the Arab Mashriq are planting the seeds of an important political principle: that is, the citizen's political (not merely humanitarian) right to economic security.

This right may then emerge in the early twenty-first century as the central issue of domestic Arab politics. The issue may or may not be directly linked to the foreign policy of the respective states, as it already has been in Egypt. What will determine the nature of the linkage is the actual dynamics of domestic and regional politics in the last decade and a half of the twentieth century.

Two aspects of the contemporary fragmented and heterogeneous social structure of the Arab Mashriq will have a direct bearing on the future of Arab politics. The first is ideological, and the second is organizational. Leaders of the Arab regimes of both the oil-rich and the oil-poor states have come to be seen by their own compatriots as corrupt and with little legitimacy or popularity. However, with rapid embourgeoisement or, more correctly, the Arab individual's frantic rush to enrichment, especially in the Mashriq, cynicism has replaced much of the progressive (nationalist or leftist) and conservative (traditionally Islamic) ideology of the previously activist masses, groups, intellectuals, and individuals. This development may be one factor behind the rise of militant Islamic fundamentalism. The post-World War II great liberating Arab ideologies of freedom, independence, social justice, development, and citizen involvement have been replaced among the middle strata by a political culture of rampant consumerism, possessive individualism, and disenchanted political withdrawal; and among the working and poor strata, by religious revival and utopian idealism. A new security-conscious statism which imports the tools and social organization of repression has replaced the liberationist Arab nationalism with the pan-Arabism (or sub-regionalism) of repression. Social and political repression have become generalized and more intensive in most Arab societies. It is as if the patriarchal tyranny of the traditional Arab family has been generalized into a modern state-security apparatus and ideology which pervades everyday life.

Arab institutions of civil society have retained little legitimacy and efficacy. The formal mediating institutions, such as unions and parties, which previously linked the individual with the state have progressively lost their autonomy, their substance, and their legitimacy. They have become shells of their former selves and have been turned into ready tools with which the Arab states control their citizens. That is, instead of being the mechanism for mobilizing the people and acting as centers for checking the authority of the state, these mediating institutions have become a means of control of the people by the state. The fragmented social formation of Arab societies is at once a contributor to the destruction of these formal institutions of civil society and a product of their demise. Without civil society, the Arab individual is a subject, not a citizen of the state. Democracy in the sense of participation in the decisions affecting one's life and destiny is not possible without civil society.

Many an analyst has noted the impact of the new wealth in the oil decade on the demise or corruption of an indigenous Arab social revolution. The impact of *al-tharwa* (wealth) on *al-thawra* (revolution) is not merely a cliché. It is a capsule characterization of the rise of the new parasitical clans or classes that have enriched themselves on the staggering surpluses of oil revenues. As merchants, contractors, agents, technocrats, and others, they allied themselves with ruling oil dynasties or minority rulers to create a new political order and a new political culture.

This political culture articulates well with a new set of cultural mores which include the demise of the work ethic;[30] work is now hardly related to high income or success. It is one's connections or one's status which determines the patronage—the key to quick and assured wealth. The new Arab mores are characterized by rampant consumerism and conspicuous consumption; status distinction and snobbism; reinforcement of the ideology of patriarchy, hierarchy, and subordination; loss of cultural authenticity; the rise of mimetic (of the West) culture; and finally, the loss of indigenous folk culture associated with the rise of the consumption of American (and European) mass culture. Such new cultural mores are both a reflection of and a factor reinforcing the fractured character of Arab social formations. The consequences for the political culture of the Arab world have been devastating. The Arab collective sense has been atomized, and the progressive thrust has been reversed.

In the post-World War II era, the Arab struggle for political, economic, and social independence gave rise to state capitalism in several core countries. Arab state capitalism has an inner dynamic logic with a natural history that propels it from progressive social, economic, and foreign policies into counter-revolutionary ones;[31] witness the shifts from the 1960s to the 1970s and 1980s.

The structure and dynamics of Arab state capitalism are complex and demand serious detailed research. Suffice it here to say that Arab state capitalism produces not only parasitic, but also predatory, bourgeoisies and helps reproduce overdeveloped state structures and underdeveloped productive forces. The overbureaucratization, inefficiency, repression, corruption, patronage, and welfare of state capitalism in the context of general oil-related bourgeoisification have *not* produced wide-scale disaffection and organized opposition. Instead, this has produced "politics of resentment" laced in some states with ethnic/sectarian resentment over distribution of resources, over access to the state (which is lucrative), over discrimination, over the lack of civil and human rights, and, among some sectors, over social oppression.

Expression of resentment is fragmented, as are the social structure, social views, and social consciousness. The religious fundamentalist movement is itself fragmented and reflects its social base. Even anti-regime violence is fragmented and discontinuous.

On an individual level, the Arab states have experienced in the oil decade the rise of economic neo-liberalism, political repression, and social conservatism, whereas on a regional level, the Arab world suffered a loss of pan-Arab national identity, of independence, and of regional coordination in social, economic, or foreign policies.

Along with these changes, the *terrain of struggle* also has shifted away from the mobilized streets and relatively autonomous political institutions and movements into the courts and lobbies internal to the ruling dynasties or one-party regimes. Most of the Arab populace are more like political spectators than participants. This transformation is in part also responsible for the emergence of fragmented new styles of social and political action and of violence by small fragmented groups.

In conclusion, the heterogeneous and fragmented class structure makes possible a political order with higher levels of state repression. The commensurate destruction of civil society and democratic freedoms is in part a product of the greater integration of the Arab world into Western political economy. In short, dependency and repression go together in a natural union.

Conclusion

Major class transformations do not occur overnight. Ruling elites or regimes may come and go in the next decade, and class conflict within any given country, or even the Arab region, may escalate or subside, but broad class changes will move somewhat more slowly. Of course, this assumes that an overarching crisis resulting in a revolutionary takeover is not in the cards in the next decade. The structural processes of change which are in motion now will continue in the same direction, but perhaps at somewhat attenuated rates because of the decline in oil revenues and growth rates. The reasons for this, as should be clear by now, are to be found in the economic and social structure of each country separately and in the region as a whole.

Contemporary Arab economic and social structures have been set and the die has been cast, so to speak, over the last two decades, but especially in the 13 years since the oil boom started. Current economic policy and economic development plans of the major Arab states do not indicate the probability of any wrenching shifts from past policy. This is in part a consequence of the class character of the states in these Arab societies and of their sociopolitical role.

The states in almost every Arab country have expanded in scope, function, and power, particularly in the economic sphere, and therefore in shaping the class structure of their respective social formations. The states of the Mashriq countries have become so centralized, all-pervasive, and efficient that they have managed to neutralize all organized opposition and to mobilize the support of large sectors of their own population, who benefit, albeit differentially, from their policies. This is the case despite the fact that the regimes' social base is narrow—in clan, ethnic group, or economic stratum. This phenomenon may be capsulized by the following conception: *étatization* of Arab societies and privatization of the state.

It is this seemingly self-contradictory feature—expansion of structure and function but narrowness of base—which is responsible for the pattern of coercion and co-optation so typical of contemporary Arab states. This double capability is behind the relative political stability of the regimes (and to a lesser degree the rulers) of the Arab states. My contention, then, is that even with changes in regime, the expanded role of the contemporary state in the Arab region will likely produce similar socioeconomic policies in the short and medium terms. Thus, resultant social processes, class formations, and dynamics also will be reproduced substantially unchanged in the next decade.

This projection into the future is all the more tenable because of the nature of the social structure in which this contemporary state is operating. As I have argued above, the development of capitalism in conjunction with the reproduction and expansion of petty-commodity production and distribution since World War II has produced and continues to produce a heterogeneous and fractured social structure which reinforces fragmented and heterogeneous social consciousness and social-political action, and, therefore, dynamic, occasionally violent, immobilism.

These trends picked up momentum and a relentless drive in the years following the spectacular increase in oil revenues. The pace of change escalated dramatically during the "seven fat years" of the oil boom and has slowed down, but has neither reversed direction nor changed character in what currently appears to be a period of "seven lean years."

The downturn so far is not riven with severe crises. It is, however, taking place at an important socioeconomic conjuncture: vast numbers of youth coming of age for employment (in most Arab countries 50 percent of the population is under 20 years of age). The plight of vast masses of unskilled and unemployed youth in social conditions lacking hope and future is a perfect social formula for frustration, bitterness, and violence—both criminal and political. If this is coupled with severe repression, as is the case for the Palestinians under Israeli occupation in the West Bank and Gaza and for their brethren in Lebanon who face Lebanese hostility and repression, then the likelihood of political violence—individual or organized—increases dramatically. While the conditions of the Palestinians are the most dramatic, other peoples, the Egyptians for example, are not far behind. But it should be clear that among other peoples, the bases of organizing this violence and political militancy in general are more traditional (through the kin, the clan, the neighborhood, the street, the sect, the ethnic group, and so on), fragmented, and discontinuous.

In short, the economic, cultural, social, and political structures of the contemporary Arab world are the foundations of the societal and class systems not merely in 1995, but also into the twenty-first century. The logic of dependent service-based capitalism formally in articulation with precapitalist social forms and social relations will reproduce the contemporary society in the short and medium terms, but may be developing into a real crisis in the long term when oil is depleted and/or when labor is repatriated.

Broadly, then, the class structure in the next decade will be composed of a tiny grande bourgeoisie intimately integrated into Western capital and acting increasingly as an international bourgeoisie with international and diversified holdings. It is a dynamic bourgeoisie, but its dynamism rests essentially on the (rapid) accumulation of capital through service activity rather than through the exploitation of land or labor. This comprador mercantile-financial bourgeoisie (with extensive interests as well in construction and real estate holdings) is dominant and sets the parameters of Arab development, particularly in the Mashriq. Its service base does not augur well for future investment in the productive sectors of the Arab world. These are left for the states themselves, but their performance in the past decade leaves much to be desired.

The industrial bourgeoisie is the weakest segment of the bourgeoisie. Despite state capitalism, the industrial working class is and will remain very small (averaging 9 to 12 percent of the workforce throughout the Arab world), weak, and protective of privileges won over the years, especially in the face of a vast reserve army of unemployed or underemployed labor. In between exists and will continue to expand a broad and great mass of stratified petty bourgeoisie—old and new petty commodity producers and distributors (including the service professionals). Furthermore, an increasing number of these petty and middle commodity producers and distributors will continue to derive their income from varied sources leading to the important phenomenon of multiple-income families whose class position will be unclear and whose cross-cutting interests will encourage heterogeneous and fragmented consciousness and politics. At best, one will expect populist politics of varied styles, as this broad and unproductive mass of people can hardly be organized and mobilized at the point of production. The bases of organizing such a mass will by necessity be as heterogeneous as the mass itself.

Such a fragmented and heterogeneous social structure will allow dramatic mass movements in periods of overarching crisis, not unlike that of Khomeini's Islamic revolution in Iran. In other periods, diverse, uncoordinated, fragmented, discontinuously violent opposition will emerge. Widescale spontaneous and potentially violent upheavals may also emerge when threats to "bread and butter" interests materialize, especially among the poorer classes of the urban centers. These will not be significantly different than the "food" or "bread" riots that took place in the past decade in Egypt, Morocco, Tunisia, Sudan, and elsewhere. Otherwise, the centralized and disciplined military of both the republics and the monarchies will in alliance with mercantile, real estate, and money capital continue to rule an Arab world characterized by structural dynamic immobilism. Political change or large-scale instability, if it is to occur, will likely be a product of factional (fragmented) conflict within the pivotal military establishment or dynasty, or else the military will intervene in the context of crisis of governance, as it did in Sudan.

In short, the Arab world, long known for volatility and political instability, will actually be increasingly transformed into a cluster of societies which will be structurally fractured but relatively stable, albeit occasionally punctuated by dramatic violence.

This relative political stability—characterized by a low level of violence—is a form of domestic balance of forces. It is, however, contingent in part upon the regional balance of power. If the latter is seriously upset, either through full-scale war (not merely a border conflict) or through a political realignment between pivotal powers in which one of the regimes is replaced and the regional balance altered significantly, then the relatively stable domestic sociopolitical structure in related (linked) states could become very volatile.

The regional balance of power, dependent as it is on both regional and domestic relations, is also directly linked to the policies and activities of the superpowers. In conclusion, it is ironic that the very same external linkages (integration) which helped generate fragmented but relatively stable social structures in the states of the region may be, in the next decade, the cause of both regional and domestic political instability and change.

Notes

1. The approach of this paper is inspired by that of a paper given by James Petras at the International Conference on Social Classes, Social Change, and Economic Development in the Mediterranean, Foundation for Mediterranean Studies, May 3–6, 1984 (Athens, Greece).

2. See an analysis of its last phases by I. M. Smilianskaya, "From Subsistence to Market Economy, 1850s," in Charles Issawi, ed., *The Economic History of the Middle East, 1800-1914* (Chicago, IL: University of Chicago, 1966).

3. Estimates of the number of migrant workers in the oil-rich states of Arabia range from three to six million in a given year. These do not include the families of a substantial fraction of these workers. See J. S. Birks and C. A. Sinclair, *Arab Manpower* (New York: St. Martin's Press, 1980); and idem., *Migration and Development in the Arab World* (Geneva: International Labor Organization, 1980).

4. The Palestinian Arabs of the West Bank and Gaza are the labor reserves of both Israel and the oil-rich Arab states. See F. A. Gharaibeh, *The Economies of the West Bank and Gaza Strip* (Boulder, CO: Westview Press, 1985).

5. Estimates for Egypt are usually $3 billion. David Ottaway of *The Washington Post* reports a remittance income for Egypt of between $6 billion and $10 billion.

6. H. Askari, "Oil and Economic Development in the Middle East," lecture, 1985 (Washington, DC). See also M. Abdul Fadil, *Al-Naft wa-al-wihda al-'arabiyya* (Oil and Arab Unity) (Beirut: Centre for Arab Unity Studies, 1980), p. 57.

7. R. Owen, "The Arab Oil Economy: Present Structure and Future Prospects," in S. K. Farsoun, ed., *Arab Society: Continuity and Change* (London: Croom Helm, 1985).

8. See K. T. Ali, "Tatawwurat muqliqa li-awda' al-zira'a wa-al-ghitha' fi al-watan al-'arabi khilal al-sab'inat" (Disturbing Developments in the Conditions of Agriculture and Nutrition in the Arab Nation During the Seventies), in *Dirasat fi al-tanmiya wa-al-takamul al-iqtisadi al-'arabi* (Studies in Arab Economic Development and Integration) (Beirut: Centre for Arab Unity Studies, 1982), pp. 405–43.

9. See A. H. Brahimi, *Ab'ad al-indimaj al-iqtisadi al-'arabi wa-ihtimalat al-mustaqbal* (Implications of Arab Economic Integration and Expectations for the Future) (Beirut: Centre for Arab Unity Studies, 1980), especially pp. 51–125.

10. See A. H. Brahimi, *Ab'ad al-indimaj al-iqtisadi al-'arabi*; R. S. Basadah, "Al-Anmat al-'ama li-al-tanmiya al-sina'iyya fi al-watan al-'arabi, 1960–1975" (General Modes of Industrial Development in the Arab Nation, 1960–1975), in *Anmat al-tanmiya fi al-watan al-'arabi, 1960–1975* (Kuwait: Al-Ma'had al-'Arabi li-al-takhtit, 1980), pp. 165–210. See also A. Bourgey, et al., *Industrialisation et Changements Sociaux dans L'Orient Arabe* (Beirut: Centre d'Etudes et de Recherches sur le Moyen Orient Contemporain, 1982).

11. *Ibid.*

12. Lebanon has been an exception.

13. See, for example, C. B. Keely and B. Saket, "Jordanian Migrant Workers in the Arab Region: A Case Study of Consequences for Labor Supplying Countries," *Middle East Journal* 38, no. 4 (Autumn 1984): 695.

14. Statistics on this are very difficult to find. One indicator is the persistence and/or increase of artisanal and other small-scale productive and distributive establishments. For example, in Lebanon the number of establishments employing less than 10 workers increased from 7,149 in 1955 to 13,939 in 1971, while for Iraq the comparable figures are 21,733 in 1954 and 37,669 in 1976, and in East Jordan 2,140 in 1967 and 4,790 in 1977. See S. Nasr, "Les Travailleurs de L'Industrie Manufacturière au Machrek," in A. Bourgey, et al., *Industrialisation et Changements Sociaux*, p. 158. Rose Musleh reports that in 1978, 92.7 percent of the industrial workforce of East Jordan was working in establishments of one to nine individuals. R. Musleh, "Al-Sina'a fi sharq al-Urdun, 1967–1979" (Industry in Transjordan, 1967–1979), *Shu'un filistiniyya* no. 99 (February 1980): 10.

15. See H. Sharabi, "The Dialectics of Patriarchy in Arab Society," in S. K. Farsoun, ed., *Arab Society*.

16. *Al-Dustur*, March 20, 1985.

17. Employment in state bureaucracies usually ends at 1 or 2 p.m.

18. Y. A. Sayigh, "Al-Taklifa al-ijtima'iyya li-al-'aidat al-naftiyya" (Social Costs of the Oil Revenues), in *Dirasat fi al-tanmiya wa-al-takamul al-iqtisadi al-'arabi*, p. 357; Keeley and Saket, "Jordanian Migrant Workers in the Arab Region"; M. Abdul-Fadil, *Al-Naft wa-al-wihda al-'arabiyya*, pp. 60–86.

19. Y. A. Sayigh, "Al-Taklifa al-ijtima'iyya," p. 364.

20. R. Paul Shaw, "The Political Economy of Inequality in the Arab World," *Arab Studies Quarterly* 6, nos. 1 & 2 (Winter and Spring, 1984): 126–127.

21. *Ibid.*
22. *Ibid.*
23. *Ibid.*
24. *Ibid.*
25. *Ibid.*

26. M. Abdul-Fadil, "Anmat tawzi' al-dakhil fi al-watan al-'arabi (1960–1975)" (Modes of Income Distribution in the Arab Nation [1960–1975]), in *Anmat al-tanmiya fi al-watan al-'arabi*, Part II, pp. 243–90.

27. Y. A. Sayigh, "Al-Taklifa al-ijtima'iyya," p. 364.

28. J. Petras, paper delivered at the International Conference on Social Classes.

29. H. Batatu, "Political Power and Social Structure in Syria and Iraq," in S. K. Farsoun, *Arab Society*.

30. Y. A. Sayigh, "Al-Taklifa al-'arabiyya."

31. S. K. Farsoun and W. Carroll, "State Capitalism and Counterrevolution: A Thesis," in B. H. Kaplan, ed., *Social Change in the Capitalist World Economy* (Beverly Hills, CA: Sage, 1978).

PART SIX

The Arab-Israeli Conflict

15

Israel: The Political Economy of a Garrison State and Its Future

Joel Beinin

As a historian, I have no professional qualifications to engage in futuristic projections. My intellectual orientation as a historian makes me skeptical about the possibility of learning lessons from history that enable us to predict the future with any certainty. Nonetheless, I have agreed to attempt to undertake a discussion of Israel in the coming decade because I believe that it is vital that the nature of Israeli society be widely discussed in light of the enormous importance of the relationship between Israel and the United States for the peace and security of the Middle East and, ultimately, the world as a whole. In order not to overextend too greatly the bounds of my professional competence, I propose to frame this analysis in terms of forward projections from recent historical trends.

For this purpose it is most useful to emphasize trends which have become increasingly apparent since the 1967 and 1973 wars. The choice of this starting point is not meant to imply that there was a fundamental shift in the character of Israeli political, military, or economic practices after 1967. Nonetheless, the 1967 and 1973 wars define the beginning of a new period in Israeli history because certain tendencies in Israeli society and politics, which were always imminent in Zionist practice but subdominant in its public face and self-image, became increasingly apparent after these wars. These tendencies are a consequence of the historical conditions of existence of the Israeli state.

Because of the unremitting opposition of the Palestinian and other Arab peoples to the establishment of a Jewish state in Palestine, Israel had to become a garrison state in order to survive. The Israeli army—Israel Defense Forces (IDF)—has always been a central institution in Israeli society, as were the military organizations, especially those of the labor Zionist movement, the prestate *yishuv*. Nonetheless, since 1967, and even more since 1973, there has been a significant change in the role of the military in

Israeli society, and the economy has been massively reoriented toward military requirements. These developments have been noticed by Israeli social scientists of varying political orientations and others who have recently begun to analyze the emergence of an Israeli military-industrial complex and to discuss openly the dangers it poses for the future of Israeli society.[1]

Accompanying the increased militarization of Israeli society has been the political decline of "socialist-Zionism"—the dominant ideological ethos of the Zionist movement and Israeli society from the 1920s to the 1970s. The recent overt assertiveness of religious-nationalist politics is rooted in the increasing disparity between the ideals of socialist-Zionism and the practice of the Israeli state since 1967. The political values and self-image of many Israelis have shifted in response to the circumstances in which the country found itself. In recent years, political leaders, even those of the Labor Party, have frequently justified their actions in terms of purely military considerations or in terms of religious or openly national-chauvinist political values which would have been absolutely rejected by the overwhelming majority of the Zionist public several decades ago. The rise of the Likud, Tehiya, Morasha, Gush Emunim, and Meir Kahane's Kach and their aggressive religious-national chauvinism, racism, and anti-democratic orientation, and the consequences of these views for the Israeli-occupied territories and Lebanon, have recently received some public attention in the United States. These political expressions are not, however, as they are often characterized, simply aberrations with no connection to the mainstream of Israeli political thought. They are consistent with the general trajectory of Israel's development and rooted in changes which have occurred in the society since 1967. They are, therefore, likely to flourish in the future.

The militarization of Israeli society is also related to the role that Israel now plays in the maintenance of the imperial hegemony of the United States, not only in the Middle East, but throughout the world. The United States, as is well known, has to a significant degree financed the militarization of Israel and insulated Israel from international criticism of its "new look." It is important to understand why this has happened and why it is likely to continue.

The economic and political changes in post-1967 Israel represent the unfolding of the internal contradictions of a garrison state. In the coming decade, as these contradictions intensify, we can expect to see a series of crises in the Israeli economy, sharpening social and political conflict, a more aggressive stance toward the Arab world, and growing Israeli dependency on the United States. This analysis suggests a pessimistic assessment of the likelihood that any government which will come to power in the foreseeable future will seek to resolve the Arab–Israeli conflict on terms which will secure self-determination for the Palestinian people, although it does not preclude efforts to resolve the conflict on other than those terms. This pessimistic assessment must be tempered by an acknowledgment of the importance of the internal struggle in Israel to which these very developments have given rise. Although today those elements in Israel which oppose the militarization of the society and all that it entails are relatively weak, disunited, and ideologically disoriented, they should by no means be dismissed. In the absence of dramatic changes in the Arab world, it may well be that the internal struggle within Israel will be the most decisive arena for determining the outcome of the Arab–Israeli conflict.

Militarization of the Economy

The Israeli economy is currently in a deep crisis—not a downturn in the business cycle, but a structural crisis rooted in the effort to maintain an artificially high standard of living and high military expenditures simultaneously on a precariously weak industrial base. The most visible sign of this crisis has been the astronomical rate of inflation during the early 1980s, but this is merely a symptom of the problem. Economic growth has been minimal for nearly a decade: from 1975 to 1983 the gross national product (GNP) grew at an average annual rate of only 1.2 percent. The net national saving rate has been declining and was negative from 1981 to 1983. The rate of investment less depreciation has been in steady decline since 1974. Israel's foreign debt is now over $23 billion (which already represents the highest per capita rate of indebtedness in the world), and it could reach as much as $41 billion by 1988.[2] None of the measures taken by the Israeli government to resolve this crisis as of this writing have begun to address its fundamental causes, which are essentially political rather than economic.

Israeli economists generally agree that the origins of the current economic crisis are in the dramatic escalation of the burden of military expenditures after both the 1967 and 1973 wars. The global cost of this burden can be summarized as follows: in the years 1965–1974, gross capital formation in Israel was 33 percent of the GNP. In the decade 1974–84, gross capital formation was 22 percent of the GNP.[3] Before the 1967 war, the cost of military expenditures, including imports, was 10 percent of the GNP. Since 1967, military expenditures have averaged 24 percent of the GNP. (See Table 15.1 for a more detailed breakdown.) This means that since the 1967 war, military expenditures have been roughly equal to Israel's new capital formation.

These global figures make it clear that the cost of military expenditures is directly responsible for the sluggish growth of the Israeli economy in the last decade. As Table 15.1 indicates, the economic burden of Israeli military expenditures has been very substantial despite the high levels of U.S. aid. Moreover, even if military expenditures remain at current levels, the burden of military expenditures will increase over time as the cost of interest on previous loans begins to mount. The periods of grace for the first major American military loans have expired. According to a report prepared by the U.S. General Accounting Office (GAO), the annual cost of Israel's military debt repayment was $772 million in 1982, and this is projected to increase to $1.1 billion in 1992 due to accumulating terminations of grace periods.

TABLE 15.1
Israeli Military Expenditures as a Percentage of GNP

Year(s)	Total Expenditures	Excluding Military Grants[a]	Excluding All Grants[a]	Local	Local[b] and Foreign Currency and Debt Service
1964-66	10	10	9	6	--
1967	18	17	17	10	--
1968-69	19	19	19	12	--
1970	26	26	26	14	--
1971-72	22	20	19	13	--
1973-75	32	25	24	17	--
1976-78	26	21	17	14	19
1979-83	23	20	15	15	19
1979	21	16	10	14	17
1980	24	19	15	14	18
1981	26	23	19	15	18
1982	24	21	18	16	20
1983	21	20	14	16	20

[a]Includes grant equivalent of U.S. loans.
[b]Includes local currency expenditures, foreign currency expenditures other than those covered by U.S. military grants and loans, and principal and interest on U.S. loans.

Source: Bank of Israel, Annual Report, 1983 (Jerusalem: The Bank of Israel, 1984), p. 52.

The GAO report hinted that Israel receives Economic Support Funds in order to be able to service its military debt, although this is not their explicit purpose. But the report noted that the current levels of economic support would be inadequate to offset military debt service as the level of interest payments rises in the coming decade.

Faced with military expenses of this magnitude, Israel has two basic alternatives: to reduce dramatically its military expenditures or to press the United States for higher levels of aid. Israeli military planners have always assumed that the conflict with the Arab world would continue indefinitely. The conclusion of a peace treaty with Egypt has not altered this assumption. Within this frame of reference, it is impossible to consider major reductions in military expenditures. Consequently, Israel has consistently chosen the second alternative. The share of the Israeli military budget funded by the United States has been increasing, from one-third between fiscal years 1977/78 and 1981/82 to 37 percent in 1982/83. Israel put pressure on the United States to further increase military assistance for 1985/86, and such pressures are likely to intensify as the cost of debt repayment increases. According to the CIA, Israel expects that the United States will fund half of its military budget in the future.[4]

As a result of the French embargo on arms to Israel after the 1967 war and of temporary halts in military supplies from the United States due to minor political disagreements between Washington and Jerusalem, Israel has sought to insure itself against the possibility that political considerations might affect the flow of military aid. After 1967, Israel embarked on a major undertaking to achieve as high a level of self-sufficiency in weapons productions as possible. This has resulted, especially since 1973, in restructuring a major component of Israel's industrial economy around the requirements of the military. By the early 1980s military production had become the leading sector of the Israeli economy. Some 25 percent of the labor force is employed either directly or indirectly by the military, and half of all industrial workers are involved in military-related production.[5] The two largest industrial enterprises in Israel are the government-owned Israel Aircraft Industries, which employs about 20,000 workers, and Israel Military Industries, which employs about 15,000 workers. Together, these workers comprise nearly 30 percent of all Israel's workers in the electronics and metals industries. Several other major producers of military products are counted among Israel's largest industrial enterprises.

The development of such a large military production sector placed a great burden on Israel's capital resources. In an attempt partially to offset this burden, Israel aggressively sought to export its military products. As the military sector of the economy expanded, so did the export of military goods. The militarization of the industrial economy and the expansion of military exports seemed to provide a remedy both for the historic structural weakness of Israel's industrial sector and for the high cost of imported weapons and the potential political constraints to which imports were subject. Today it is clear that the production and export of arms is a major foundation block of the Israeli national economy and of Israel's international political orientation. I fully concur with Aharon Klieman's judgment that

> . . . as the mid-1980s approach, the export of arms has become a national strategic commitment rather than simply the tactical expedient of any single government coalition. Consequently, should present trends continue, the manufacture and export of arms will figure centrally in the Jewish state's quest for security, economic viability, and an independent course of diplomacy throughout this decade and, indeed, well into the 1990s.[6]

As military exports grew rapidly in the late 1970s, Israel's military and economic planners hoped that military exports would provide an important source of hard currency, offset the cost of military research and development, lower the unit cost of items purchased by the IDF from Israeli manufacturers, and serve as a factor overcoming Israel's diplomatic isolation. While none of these objectives has been fully achieved, this has not slowed the pace of military exports.

TABLE 15.2
Israel's Military Exports, 1972-1983

	1972	1975	1976	1977	1978	1979	1980	1981	1982	1983
As percentage of total exports	9.7	17.9	22.8	24.8	25.7	25.9	20.0	22.2	23.0	22.0
Value (in millions of dollars at current prices)	52.4	179	285	390	503	657	668	807	809	703

Note: While the authors do not specify it, the percentage figures appear to exclude the value of polished diamond exports. This exclusion is customary since raw diamonds are imported into Israel and only the value added is a net export.

Source: Yoram Peri and Amnon Neubach, The Military-Industrial Complex in Israel: A Pilot Study (Tel Aviv: International Center for Peace in the Middle East, 1985), p. 69.

The figures in Table 15.2 are the result of an important new research project on Israel's military-industrial complex being undertaken by the International Center for Peace in the Middle East in Tel Aviv. While they clearly indicate the trend toward the increasing importance of military exports in the Israeli economy, these figures represent extremely low estimates for the value of military exports in the most recent years. This is perhaps not surprising, since they are based on figures given in the IDF monthly magazine, *Maarachot*, a semi-official publication which may have an interest in concealing at least some military exports.[7]

By contrast, for example, in 1980 Israeli military exports totaled $1.2 billion according to the Stockholm International Peace Research Institute (SIPRI) and $1.3 billion according to the *New York Times*; while for 1981 the *Jerusalem Post* gave the figure of $1.3 billion in military exports.[8] In 1980 Israel's total exports were $5.292 billion, of which $1.41 billion consisted of polished diamonds. On the basis of the higher figures for military exports given by SIPRI and the *New York Times*, it can be calculated that in 1980 military exports were approximately 32 percent of all Israeli exports excluding polished diamonds. The figure would be even higher if exports to the occupied territories ($584 million in 1980) were excluded.[9] By the early 1980s, Israel's ratio of military exports to total exports had become the highest in the world and Israel had become the world's seventh largest arms exporter.[10]

After peaking in 1980 and 1981, military exports declined in 1982 and 1983. The reasons are partly the same as those which accounted for the weak performance of all Israeli industrial exports in these years: the international recession and the strong dollar. But the largest reason for the decline in military exports was the dramatic increase in purchases of local military manufactures by the Israeli government following the 1982 Lebanon war. However, the military sector of the economy remained strong and led the 3.5 percent increase in Israel's industrial product in 1983.[11]

Military production is therefore likely to continue to dominate Israel's industrial and export economy. The other traditionally strong export sectors of the Israeli economy—diamonds, textiles, and citrus fruits—have been weak performers in recent years, although diamonds have made a partial recovery. There have been recent efforts to build up high-technology exports in Israel, but the development of technology is often linked to military applications. The Israeli government has indicated a strong commitment to this orientation by allocating 46 percent of all of its research and development expenditures to military-related projects.[12] This level of investment ensures that military-industrial projects will retain a central place in the Israeli economy.

Politics and Society

Between 1949 and 1981, 640 colonels and generals retired from the IDF, of whom about 20 percent entered political careers, while the remainder went into business or accepted positions in the administration of the state or various Zionist institutions. These former commanders constitute a high proportion of senior management in Histadrut, state-owned, and private industry.[13] The names of some of the leading former generals who have been prominent in Israeli politics are well known. They include Moshe Dayan, Yigal Allon, Yisrael Galili, Yitzhak Rabin, Ezer Weizmann, and Ariel Sharon. Except for Ezer Weizmann, all of those named began their careers as members of the labor Zionist camp. Within the labor Zionist camp, however, they were prominent advocates of an "activist" military policy. Proponents of this policy favored massive retaliation against border incursions and preemptive strikes against perceived Arab military threats. They were also generally disinclined to seek diplomatic means to resolve the Arab–Israeli conflict, especially if this involved any perceived risk to Israeli military supremacy.[14] Under Mapai/Labor rule, the "activists" were responsible for the massive attacks on Qibya in 1953 and Gaza in 1955, the Anglo–French–Israeli aggression against Egypt in 1956, and the decision to launch a preemptive strike in 1967. The invasions of Lebanon in 1978 and 1982 under the rule of the Likud can be seen as a more extreme version of the military "activism" advocated by elements of the labor Zionist movement.

In alliance with leading civilian politicians, the most important of whom have been David Ben Gurion and Shimon Peres (who as director general of the Ministry of Defense in the 1950s was instrumental in developing Israel's military industries), these military activists have been a leading force in promoting the pragmatic, technocratic, and statist political values which have now largely replaced "socialist-Zionism" as the dominant Israeli ideology. This process began within Mapai (precursor of the Labor Party) itself in the mid-1960s. Historically, the military activists and their civilian allies were concentrated in two constituent components of the Labor Party—Rafi and Ahdut ha-Avoda. The Rafi group, led by Ben Gurion, Dayan, and Peres, split from Mapai in 1965. Ahdut ha-Avoda was a tendency within the labor

Zionist movement which was closely identified with the IDF and the prestate military organizations. In 1968 Mapai, Rafi, and Ahdut ha-Avoda united to form the Labor Party.

The campaign for the 1984 elections offered a good illustration of the extent to which labor Zionism has become discredited even within the Labor Party itself. The party jettisoned its historic image and adopted a "centrist" political stance. The abandonment of Labor's traditional social democratic orientation has been solidified by the ascendancy of former Rafi elements and former military commanders within the Labor Party—Shimon Peres, Yitzhak Rabin, Yitzhak Navon, Chaim Bar Lev, and Mota Gur. The ideological distance of this group from the traditional social democracy of the Labor Party is further highlighted by Ezer Weizmann's decision to join forces with Labor and Labor's subsequent dependence on Weizmann and Yigal Hurewitz—both of whom have historically been antagonistic to the nominal values of Labor—in order to form even a national unity government in 1984. (It must be noted that since the original writing of this chapter, Ezer Weizman has distinguished himself from most of his Labor allies and become the leading advocate of a peaceful settlement of the Arab–Israeli conflict, including possible negotiations with the PLO, in the cabinet.)

The personal and political ties of former Rafi elements and military commanders within the Labor Party constitute an important social bond within the military-industrial establishment. For example, the management of Israel Aircraft Industries historically has been dominated by a clique of friends and supporters of Rafi. Retired senior officers also have provided an important bridge between the political establishment and the military-industrial establishment. For example, former chief of staff Tzvi Tzur became head of Clal Industries. Major General Yishayahu Gavish took over management of the Histadrut-owned conglomerate Koor; former Air Force commander Benny Peled became director of Elbit; and another former Air Force commander, David Ivri, became the head of Israel Aircraft Industries. All of these firms are major military manufacturers. Former military commanders are also linked to American arms manufacturers; for example, former Air Force commander Mordechai Hod represents Northrop in Israel. Hod also appeared on Ezer Weizmann's list for the 1984 Knesset elections.[15]

The consequence of these developments is that there is an identifiable common bond of careers in or close to the Israeli military and a shared political outlook among the now-ascendant forces within the Labor Party, the IDF, and the top echelons of the military sector of the economy. The outlook shared by these elements, although somewhat more pragmatic, does not stand in fundamental opposition to the general perspective of the Likud. They are somewhat more inclined than the Likud to seek a negotiated settlement to the Arab–Israeli conflict based on an Israeli evacuation of part of the West Bank and Gaza Strip following negotiations with Jordan. In the absence of such negotiations, the areas of fundamental agreement between most of the leading elements of the Labor Party and the Likud (and more extreme rightwing elements) are salient. They include the propositions that

TABLE 15.3
Average Number of Knesset Members

Period	Labor Bloc	Nationalist/ Religious Bloc
1949-51	61.7	42.0
1961-69	57.7	46.6
1973-84	43.5	60.7

Source: Gershom Schocken, "Israel in Election Year 1984," Foreign Affairs 63, no. 1 (Fall 1984): 89.

there can be no full Israeli withdrawal from the territories occupied in 1967, no negotiations with the Palestine Liberation Organization, no recognition of the Palestinian people's right to self-determination, and no Palestinian state.

The decline of labor Zionism and the rise of the religious-nationalist right is unmistakable as a global trend in Israeli politics since 1967. This trend did not originate in 1967, but it accelerated rapidly after that date, and especially after 1973. The figures in Table 15.3, showing the average number of Knesset members in each bloc for three periods in Israeli history, demonstrate a steady erosion of the electoral support of the Labor bloc (including all of the historic components of the Labor Party and Mapam, Labor's former partner in the Alignment). The magnitude of the post-1973 swing is understated by Table 15.3, because before that year, the religious parties tended to be in the camp of the Labor Party, while they have tended to be in the camp of the Likud since then.

A clear political trend enduring over such a length of time is not accidental. It is a direct consequence of the garrison-state character of Israeli society. The values of socialist-Zionism have been steadily eroded by the realities of constant military confrontation and the attitudes and techniques they have engendered. This explains the dominance of the military activist and statist/technocratic trend within the Labor Party. As long as this confrontation persists, the traditional values of labor Zionism will be increasingly in contradiction with the political practice of the state.

The decline of labor Zionism and the strong likelihood that this trend will continue is confirmed by the electoral preferences of the youngest voters—those currently in the army. Table 15.4 compares the percentage of the vote that various electoral lists obtained in the 1984 elections from the Israeli population as a whole with the percentage of the army vote alone those lists received. (The army vote includes reservists temporarily on active duty and career soldiers—although not those soldiers on leave who voted in civilian polling stations—but it is preponderantly comprised of draftees aged 18 to 21.) The predominance of the right wing, or what

TABLE 15.4
Distribution of the 1984 Knesset Vote (by percentage)

Party	Total Population	Army Vote
Likud	31.9	36.0
Tehiya	4.0	12.0
Meir Kahane/Kach	1.2	2.5
Alignment	34.9	31.0
Shinui & CRM[a]	5.0	4.0
DFPE[b]	3.35	<1.0
PLP[c]	1.8	<1.0

[a] Citizens' Rights Movement.
[b] Democratic Front for Peace and Equality.
[c] Progressive List for Peace.

Source: Yediot Aharonot and Jerusalem Post, July 27, 1984; a-Aretz, August 1, 1984.

is euphemistically called the "national camp," within the army is clear. The relatively large army vote for Tehiya, which is more intransigent than the Likud on Arab–Israeli issues, was sufficient to change the overall distribution of Knesset seats and give Tehiya an additional seat while taking one seat away from the total the Alignment had before the military vote was added in. On the basis of the army vote alone, the Likud, together with Tehiya and the right-wing religious parties of Morasha and Shas and even without Meir Kahane's Kach, would have been able to form a coalition which would have been even more extreme than the Likud governments of 1977 and 1981.

The implications of the electoral preferences of the army for the future of the Arab–Israeli conflict are that younger Jewish Israelis are less inclined than their elders to abandon the occupation of the West Bank, the Gaza Strip, and the Golan Heights. A generation has now reached maturity which does not know an Israel without these territories. During the years of Likud rule, the Ministry of Education was controlled by the National Religious Party (NRP). The NRP undertook a major effort to alter curricula and instructional programs to reflect the religious-national chauvinist values of the government. This campaign has apparently borne fruit. The exceptional popularity of Tehiya within the army compared to the population as a whole may be due to the fact that former Chief of Staff Rafael Eitan became a leading member of this party immediately after his retirement from the IDF and is now one of its Knesset representatives.

Lest anyone conclude that the results of the army vote simply reflect youthful extremism, it should be noted that the leftist electoral lists—the Democratic Front for Peace and Equality and the Progressive List for Peace—that favor negotiation with the PLO would not have received a single Knesset seat on the basis of the army vote (as opposed to the four and two seats, respectively, which they did obtain). Shinui and the Citizens' Rights Movement, which are considered more accommodating toward the Palestinians than the Labor Party, also registered less support in the army than among the population as a whole.

The strengthening of the nationalist right wing within the Labor Party and within Israel more broadly has not gone unopposed. The 1984 Knesset elections also showed that the political forces favoring accommodation with the Palestinians have increased their strength. As a protest against the formation of a national unity government, Knesset member Yossi Sarid, an outspoken advocate of a negotiated settlement with the Palestinians, left the Labor Party and joined the Citizens' Rights Movement. Mapam, formerly Labor's junior partner in the Alignment, reluctantly dissolved the Alignment rather than sit in a government with the Likud. A group of discontented intellectuals left the Labor Party.

All of these forces have begun discussions on the formation of a new social democratic Zionist party. So far these discussions have been inconclusive. Whether they ultimately succeed or not, there must be a serious doubt about the ability of these forces to attract widespread popular support for an ideology which has already been rejected by a substantial portion of the Israeli public and whose premises are undercut by the economic and political realities of the garrison state. However, these forces may serve to encourage fundamental criticism of the prevailing political assumptions in Israel.

Both the left and the right have been gaining strength in Israel in recent years. Consequently, the clashes between them have intensified. However, in any national trial of strength the right-wing has generally been the preponderant force. The rapid political rehabilitation of Ariel Sharon and his return to prominence within the Likud is the result of his enormous popularity with a large number of Israelis. There is no sign that this balance of forces is likely to change dramatically in the near future, although the left will grow the more it becomes apparent that a peaceful settlement of the Palestinian question which does not threaten Israeli security is possible.

The American Connection

The extent of Israeli dependency on the United States makes it impossible to discuss the future of Israel without mentioning the role of the United States. Since the subject of American–Israeli relations is complex and difficult, it will not be possible to do more than outline briefly why the United States has supported and is likely to continue to support the developments in Israel which have been examined here. Since 1967, Israel has emerged as the major strategic ally of the United States in the Middle East. Israel's value in this regard was first demonstrated in the crisis of "Black September" 1970. This role was enhanced after the fall of the Shah of Iran in 1979. The Israeli failure to impose a new order on Lebanon has demonstrated that Israel's power is not without limits, but there has been no sign from Washington that this has led to a reevaluation of the relationship. It must be underscored that despite much protest by the Arab states, none of them has imposed a significant penalty on the United States for its policy of nearly unrestrained support for Israel in this period. This policy has therefore not incurred significant regional costs.

The United States is deeply involved in supporting the militarization of the Israeli economy. According to the 1983 GAO report: "Israel is heavily dependent on U.S. financial and technical support to achieve its own arms production capability . . . Almost every Israeli arms production effort includes a U.S. input."[16]

Even as the limits of Israeli power in the Middle East have become apparent, Israel has expanded its role as a source of military supply and expertise to pro-American states with which it has sometimes been uncomfortable for Washington to deal directly. The biggest customers for Israeli military exports have been South Africa and Argentina under the military dictatorship.[17] Israel supplied weapons to Iran under the Shah and collaborated closely with the Iranian security services. Taiwan has developed a close military supply relationship with Israel, and recently there have been reports of developing relations with South Korea and the Philippines. (It is unclear whether this will continue under the Aquino regime.) Israel has supplied weapons to nearly every Latin American dictatorship. The largest recipients, after Argentina, have been Nicaragua under Somoza, El Salvador, Honduras, Guatemala, and Chile. In order to circumvent congressional limits on aid to El Salvador, Israel "lent" El Salvador $21 million from U.S. aid funds it had been granted in 1981. There have been numerous reports that Israel has been aiding the Nicaraguan "contras" in Honduras and Costa Rica. Israel has sent military advisors to El Salvador, Costa Rica, and Honduras.

These examples make it clear that the Israeli contribution to the overall maintenance of America's power and influence in the Third World is significant. As long as the militarization of Israel continues to support and augment American power in the Third World in this manner, it is highly unlikely that it will be opposed by the United States government, even if Israel's aggressive and independent arms marketing programs have occasional undesirable side effects for perceived American interests. On the contrary, as long as there is considerable resistance to direct American intervention in the Third World in the Congress and among the American people, it is likely that Israel's military role in the Third World will increase.

There are two significant wild cards whose precise impact on future trends is difficult to factor into the analysis presented here: the economy and war. The economic crisis in Israel could easily get out of control, and a total economic collapse is not inconceivable. The resultant social conflict could do more to alter Israeli policy toward the Arab–Israeli conflict than any action by the Palestinians or the Arab states. A deep crisis in the American economy which would make it impossible for the United States to continue to support Israel at current and projected levels could have the same effect. The likelihood of another Arab–Israeli war is very high if there is no resolution to the conflict. Such a war, even though it is not likely that the Arabs would score a military victory, could cause a major political upheaval in Israel. In the case of either economic collapse or war, political polarization and contention within Israeli society would intensify, and their outcome is difficult to predict. Plausible scenarios range from a military coup of the right to the emergence of a realistic leadership prepared for coexistence with the Palestinian people on the basis of mutual recognition of the right of self-determination. In the absence of any major Palestinian or Arab political initiative, the internal conflict within Israel could emerge as one of the most important determinants of the future of the Arab–Israeli conflict.

Notes

1. See, for example, Yoram Peri, *Between Battles and Ballots: Israeli Military in Politics* (Cambridge: Cambridge University Press, 1983); Yoram Peri and Amnon Neubach, *The Military-Industrial Complex in Israel: A Pilot Study* (Tel Aviv: International Center for Peace in the Middle East, 1985); Aharon Klieman, *Israeli Arms Sales: Perspectives and Prospects* (Tel Aviv: Tel Aviv University, Jaffee Center for Strategic Studies, 1984). An entire issue of the *Journal of Strategic Studies* (Vol. 6, no. 3, September 1983) was devoted to the subject of "Israeli Society and Its Defense Establishment," and several of the authors (all of whom are Israelis) expressed concern for the future of Israeli society on the basis of current trends. Esther Howard, "Israel: The Sorcerer's Apprentice," *MERIP Reports*, no. 112 (February 1983), provides a concise survey of the militarization of the Israeli economy and its effects. I have earlier raised some of these issues briefly in "Challenge from Israel's Military," *MERIP Reports*, no. 92 (November–December 1980).

2. Figures are based on: Bank of Israel, *Annual Report 1983* (Jerusalem: The Bank of Israel, 1984), p. 20; Economist Intelligence Unit, *Quarterly Economic Review: Israel* (4th quarter 1982), pp. 9–10; U.S. Senate Foreign Relations Committee Staff Report, "The Economic Crisis in Israel," November 1984.

3. *Jerusalem Post Weekly*, November 3, 1984.

4. *U.S. Assistance to the State of Israel: Report by the Comptroller General of the United States Prepared by the U.S. General Accounting Office* (GAO/ID-83-51, June 24, 1983) and the uncensored draft version published by the American-Arab Anti-Discrimination Committee, which includes the CIA estimate as well as many other passages deleted from the official published version. *World Armament and Disarmament: SIPRI Yearbook 1984* (London: Taylor & Francis, 1985), pp. 105–106.

5. Alex Mintz, "The Military-Industrial Complex: The Israeli Case," *Journal of Strategic Studies* 6, no. 3 (September 1983): 108.

6. Klieman, *Israeli Arms Sales*, p. 3. Klieman's judgment merits particular consideration because in his study he uses lower figures than Mintz or Peri/Neubach to indicate the size of the military sector of the economy. His estimate of the value of

military exports is higher than that of Peri/Neubach, but apparently due to a mathematical error, his estimate of military exports as a percentage of total exports is far too low.

7. The low level of these estimates may also reflect the authors' desire to argue that militarization of the economy has not been cost-effective. However, Peri and Neubach seem somewhat careless in this regard, as their own internal evidence seems to indicate that a much higher proportion of military production is exported than they admit. For example, on p. 15 they declare that 25 percent of IAI's production is for export. But an appendix on p. 89, based on the annual reports of IAI, clearly shows that at no time since 1975 have IAI's exports been anywhere near that low. From 1980 to 1983 IAI's exports as a percentage of total production have been 53, 63, 42, and 38 percent, respectively.

8. *SIPRI Yearbook 1982*, p. 188; *New York Times*, March 15, 1981; *Jerusalem Post*, February 5, 1982.

9. Export figure based on Bank of Israel, *Annual Report 1983*, pp. 159–60.

10. Mintz, "The Military-Industrial Complex," p. 112; *SIPRI Yearbook 1982*.

11. Bank of Israel, *Annual Report 1983*, pp. 64, 88–89.

12. Mintz, "The Military-Industrial Complex."

13. Peri, *Battles and Ballots*, p. 105. On p. 108 Peri states that 700 generals and colonels retired as of 1977. Among generals alone, the proportion entering politics is one-third.

14. The activities and opinions of the "activists" are described in Livia Rokach, *Israel's Sacred Terrorism: A Study Based on Moshe Sharett's Personal Diary and Other Documents* (Belmont, MA: Association of Arab-American University Graduates, 1980).

15. Peri and Neubach, *The Military-Industrial Complex in Israel*, pp. 51–52.

16. *U.S. Assistance to the State of Israel*, pp. 42, 44.

17. Information about the recipients of Israeli military exports and advice is now becoming widely available. See Klieman, *Israeli Arms Sales*; the various *SIPRI Yearbooks*; Israel Shahak, *Israel's Global Role: Weapons for Repression* (Belmont, MA: Association of Arab-American University Graduates, 1982); Ronald Slaughter, "Israel Arms Trade: Cozying Up To Latin Armies," in *NACLA Report on the Americas* (January–February 1982), pp. 49–54; Clarence Lusane, "Israeli Arms in Central America," *Covert Action Information Bulletin*, no. 20 (Winter 1984): 34–37; James Adams, *Israel and South Africa: The Unnatural Alliance* (London: Quartet, 1984.)

16

Palestinian Impasse: Constraints and Opportunities

Naseer H. Aruri

This paper will attempt to shed some light on alternative futures for the Palestinian people. The prospects of reaching a peaceful settlement over the next decade which would grant the Palestinian people a sovereign existence in eastern Palestine (West Bank) and Gaza, in accordance with the Palestinian and Arab consensus agreements of the past ten years, will be central to our assessment.

At present, the Palestinian people have reached an impasse in their struggle to realize their minimal objective as defined by the Tenth Palestine National Council resolutions of 1977: in effect, a West Bank–Gaza state. Whatever hopes were pinned on the diplomacy of the 1970s have been shattered by Camp David, the Israeli invasion of Lebanon, and the subsequent departure of the Palestine Liberation Organization (PLO) from Lebanon, which was followed by a serious rift, if not fragmentation, of the Palestinian national movement. Israeli strategy during the past few years, irrespective of whether Likud or Labor was at the helm, revealed a capacity to initiate (while the Palestinians react)—diplomatically, by trying to de-emphasize the legitimacy of the PLO and the centrality of the Palestine question to Middle East peace and its relevance to regional stability; economically, through land confiscation, water deprivation, and the creation of facts which would render the *de facto* annexation of the occupied territories irrevocable; and politically, through the continuous search for alternative voices described euphemistically as "moderate" Palestinians, who would negotiate on the basis of limited autonomy, and in an adjunct role. The attempts to appoint Palestinian mayors under the guise of "improving the quality of life" in the West Bank is a case in point.

This assessment requires a brief survey of the conditions leading to the present impasse, as well as a description and analysis of the present environmental factors—the local, the regional, and the global—in order to determine the constraints which these factors impose on Palestinian prospects and/or the opportunities which they may afford.

The Diplomatic Imperative: 1974–82

It can be easily assumed that the PLO, given its organizational structure, ideological character, and regional relationships, as well as the nature of its enemy, has never developed an effective military option against Israel. During the largest portion of its 20-year existence, the PLO was engaged more in a diplomatic than in a military struggle against Israel. By the late 1960s, when the Palestinian armed struggle had reached its zenith, Israel was already in possession of a sophisticated military-industrial complex and a capacity to strike preemptively against any Palestinian armed presence in the Arab world. Such a capacity is, of course, no barrier to launching a successful guerrilla war, as the many wars of national liberation during the 1950s and 1960s demonstrate. The Palestinian movement, however, was hamstrung by certain constraints dictated by the manner in which it defined its relationship to its constituents and to the Arab environment in which it had to operate.

As the PLO grew dangerously dependent on external support and its future was inextricably linked to the changing interests of the Arab states, its effectiveness in trying to realize its own *raison d'être* of changing the status quo was seriously curtailed. The Arab state system simply would not tolerate any change in the status quo which ran counter to the interests of that system, as the experiences with Jordan and Syria demonstrated in 1970 and 1976. Defiance of any component of the inter-Arab system of states often brought punishments ranging from cutting off funds or denying sanctuary and arms, to playing one Palestinian group against another or acting as co-belligerent in inter-Palestinian conflicts.

Given these constraints, PLO behavior at times inevitably reflected inter-Arab policies more than Palestinian needs. The organization was in danger of becoming more answerable to the Arab state system than to its own constituents. By the mid-seventies, the PLO's strategy and demeanor began to resemble those of an Arab "progressive" regime rather than those of a revolutionary guerrilla movement. Therefore, Palestinian inability to engage in a sustained guerrilla war against Israel and to challenge the Arab status quo in pursuance of that objective compelled the PLO to embark, together with the Arab states, on a diplomatic campaign for the realization of its aims. That campaign, which was waged in earnest following the October 1973 Arab–Israeli war, did not bring the Palestinians nearer to achieving their goals. In fact, during the 1982 Israeli invasion of Lebanon, the diplomatic successes of the PLO during the 1970s weighed very little on the siege of Beirut or on the political outcome of the battle.

Between Two Assaults

The 1982 Israeli invasion of Lebanon, which resulted in the current impasse, was the second major blow to the Arab forces which had declared after World War II their intent to achieve political independence and socioeconomic transformations. The first critical assault of 1967 removed those forces from the forefront of Arab politics and set the stage for a resurgence of the American–Israeli counteroffensive against all remnants, offshoots, or accessories of radical Arab nationalism. In the era which followed, the United States and Israel confronted the revolutionary thrust in the region, sometimes using force and at other times using co-optation and accommodation.

This post-1967 era can be divided into three periods. The first, extending from 1967 to 1973, was characterized by the rise and fall of the revolutionary Arab current. The second, from 1973 to 1977, was marked by an ascendancy of Arab diplomatic efforts, fueled by oil wealth, and a rising Palestinian legitimacy, which in turn prompted Israeli isolation. The third, from 1977 to 1982, witnessed an Israeli counteroffensive, Arab paralysis, and Palestinian disorientation.

The First Period: 1967–73

The 1967 war produced two political currents in the Arab world: an accommodationist current led by the oil-rich states in the Gulf and a revolutionary current spearheaded by the Palestinian resistance movement. The war enabled the United States to promote an Arab political order that would seek integration into the world economy and state system. The accommodationist current, which was to be the pillar of that order, was therefore pitted against the revolutionary thrust, and a new Arab cold war[1] was provoked.

The Palestinian resistance collided with the Arab "confrontation" states, which endeavored to recover occupied territories by peaceful means. Between 1969 and 1976, the PLO fought a propaganda war with Egypt and a real war with Jordan, Lebanon, and Syria. The non-confrontation Arab states either acquiesced in the attacks on the PLO or contributed materially to them.

Egypt, which prior to 1967 was the vanguard of militant Arab nationalism, had to shelve its pan-Arab concerns and refocus attention and redirect its energies toward recovering occupied *Egyptian* land—hence its acceptance of the Rogers Plan in 1969,[2] and hence its first skirmish with the Palestinian resistance. Jordan, emboldened by Egypt's decision, preempted the PLO role and pursued the course of a diplomatic settlement for the recovery of the West Bank. The result was the Jordanian offensive against the Palestinian movement in September 1970. Syria under Hafiz al-Asad was the third Arab state to become occupied with recovering land and trying to "erase the consequences of the aggression."[3]

Thus, by 1970, the Arab world was torn between two tendencies: while the oil states, together with Egypt, Jordan, and Syria, would embark on accommodation as a means to restore Arab land and assure a stable political order, the Palestinian resistance movement, together with undifferentiated Arab masses, would topple that order. Those masses believed that a revolutionary situation, created by the 1967 war, would launch a post-Nasserite brand of Arab revolution that would not only liberate Palestine, but also confront Western domination and create a new, politically independent, socially and economically autonomous Arab society.

The potential role of the Palestinian resistance in this anticipated transformation was the main catalyst during the first phase of the post-1967 Arab cold war. The radical intelligentsia and the Arab left in general looked up to the Palestinian movement as the new vanguard on its way to becoming the new Arab revolution. That revolution was to have been produced by the objective conditions emanating from the 1967 war. The self-evident truths of the previous era would be reexamined against the empirical facts which the war supplied, and soon they would be exchanged for a more convincing set. A sampling of these truths which sustained the old order would readily show how tenuous that order was: that Israel could be defeated only by conventional warfare; that the liberation of Palestine was the responsibility of Arab armies, Arab diplomacy, and international goodwill; that the new middle class of professionals and soldiers ushered into power by the Egyptian revolution in 1952 was the redeemer that would eliminate the remnants of European colonialism and put an end to Western political and cultural intrusion into the Arab world.

These truths were shattered in six days of June 1967, during which Israel occupied Arab lands in three Arab states, forcing upon them an unconditional ceasefire along lines which resembled natural frontiers. It was not only a defeat of Arab regular armies, but also a defeat of Arab ideologies, political parties, and other institutions, upon which great hopes had been pinned since 1948. It was a failure of the Arab guardians and trustees who took upon themselves the task of emancipating the Palestinians and other Arabs from colonialism when it was presumed to be universally repudiated. Arab tutelage was to be terminated, and the Palestinians would take their destiny into their own hands. What loomed on the horizon for the post-1967 Arab order was an ominous sign, a substitutability of roles: the Palestinians could become guardians not only over Palestine but over the Arab world as well. The trend was a threat to the very existence of Arab regimes and to the designs of the United States and Israel for a complacent and obsequious Arab world. The two were inevitably on a collision course, which culminated in "Black September."

The Arab order was on the rebound by 1970, reasserting control and no longer feeling defensive about its incredible rout in 1967. In Black September and its aftermath, the expectations placed upon the Palestinian movement proved to have been too high, given the overwhelming odds against its success. The Jordanian army was not the only counter-revolutionary force fighting against the Palestinians. The U.S. Sixth Fleet was on the alert, the Israeli army was itching to intervene, and the commander of the Syrian air force denied air cover to the only Arab force that went to rescue the Palestinians. And when it was over, Jordan's performance was generously rewarded.[4] (In a later period, a second performance would be carried out by Syria, brokered by Jordan, and facilitated by the non-intervention of Israel and the United States. Not unlike the Jordanian attack, it would result in preservation of the dominant order, and it, too, would be seen by the Arab state system as a stabilization act worthy of political and financial support.)

The Arab order, which had been undermined during a three-year interlude, recovered from the shock of 1967 and between 1970 and 1973 proceeded to draw new perimeters for an Arab strategy. By 1973, the Arab populace, which had experienced the euphoria of the Palestinian armed struggle, was pacified by the new euphoria of the October War. The premise of those who hoped that the Arab order was doomed proved quite illusory. Equally illusive was the hope that the Palestinian resistance was the torchbearer of a brave new world. Far from creating that long-awaited revolutionary situation, the 1967 war was the first decisive strike which set the stage for what Samir Amin calls the "re-compradorization" of the Arab world.[5] It set the stage for a second phase of Palestinian–Arab relations in which cooperation and co-optation replaced the use of force.

The Second Period: 1973–77

The October war of 1973 ushered in a new order and a new era in Palestinian–Arab relations. The Palestinians, represented by the PLO, were to march together with the Arab state system to reap the benefits which a limited Arab–Israeli war would provide. It was a war of maneuver in which Syrian–Egyptian military power, in combination with the Saudi oil weapon, would be brought to bear on the diplomatic equation.

Ignored by the United States, which failed to recognize the centrality of the Palestine question to a negotiated settlement, the PLO sought the remedy through Arab diplomacy and in the corridors of the United Nations. A unified diplomatic strategy calling for a new accommodation and adjustment in Arab–Palestinian relations began to unfold in November 1973 at the Algiers Arab summit and in the following year at Rabat.

The 1974 Rabat summit conference created two frameworks for the Arab states, one on how to deal with the United States, and the other on how to handle the Palestinians. With regard to the United States, a pattern of collaboration was manifested in the Sinai accord of 1975 and in Syria's intervention in Lebanon. With regard to the Palestinians, the Rabat summit designated the PLO the sole legitimate representative of the Palestinian people. Implicit in that recognition was the obligation which the PLO must undertake in return: to enhance the broader common interest. That obligation included the incorporation of the PLO struggle for Palestine into the Arab diplomatic strategy for "erasing the consequences of the aggression." Otherwise the two might find themselves at cross purposes and might collide again. Initial PLO reservations about that formula were largely responsible for Arab acquiescence in the second major offensive against the PLO, which was administered by Syria in 1976.

Arab containment of Palestinian nationalism, whether in Jordan, in Lebanon, or in Rabat, had taken its toll; it forced the transformation of the PLO's revolutionary goal of a unitary, democratic, non-sectarian state in all of Palestine to the goal of a mini-Palestinian state in the West Bank and Gaza. That transformation, however, which represented a concession to the Arab state system, the United States, and Israel, was instrumental in the emergence of the global consensus on Palestinian rights. It produced political victories for the PLO which bolstered its already recognized status as a representative of a colonized people entitled to inalienable rights and the pursuit of independence "by all available means, including armed struggle."[6] The PLO was invited in 1974 by the United Nations General Assembly to attend that body's twenty-ninth session, and was subsequently admitted to the world organization as an observer.[7] The secretary-general was then formally requested to establish contact with the PLO on all matters concerning the question of Palestine. Significantly, Security Council resolution 242, which failed to recognize the national rights of the Palestinian people, was in effect pre-empted by this recognition, which reflected a broader segment of world opinion.

Concurrent with this startling political success of the PLO and the ascendancy of Arab diplomacy was a perceptible isolation of Israel in the world community. An exceedingly large number of Third World nations severed diplomatic ties with Israel for its relentless opposition to the global consensus. By the latter part of the 1970s there were more states that dealt with the PLO than with the state of Israel.

Israel was condemned by the world organization for violations of the 1949 Geneva accords on the status of occupied territories and for organized state terrorism. The Palestinians were seen as a disinherited people seeking to return home to reorganize their shattered society, not as Arabs threatening to throw Israel into the sea.

The great political victories of the PLO were traceable to the investment of economic and diplomatic resources by the Arab state system in its campaign to achieve a negotiated settlement. A resolution of the Palestine question was the only secure guarantor for the hegemony of the post-October Arab order. Thus the relationship between that order, which was largely accommodationist, and the supposedly confrontational Palestinian movement was characterized by antagonistic collaboration, whose common denominator was a political solution to the Palestine question. Ironically, however, while the revolutionary current (principally Palestinian) was effectively contained by the 1973 war, the question of Palestine remained the centerpiece of the Arab states' diplomatic agenda. An astute observer commented on this apparent paradox thus: "In one sense, the elevation of the Palestine question to such political prominence was the 'price' of containment of Arab social revolution."[8] It was an unwritten agreement whereby the PLO would diminish its revolutionary posture in return for Arab financial and diplomatic clout. The PLO would thus be enabled to "eliminate the consequences of the aggression," a more respectable and manageable endeavor than that of overthrowing the Arab order—hence the Arab offer to recognize the PLO as the "sole legitimate representative" in Rabat.

The Third Period: 1977–82

The success of the joint Arab–PLO strategy was contingent on U.S. cooperation and approval. The third and last phase, which began in 1977, was characterized by certain basic changes in the American and Israeli approaches to Middle East politics. After a period of vacillation on the ingredients of a negotiated settlement, the United States tried to keep things in order by building a special relationship with Israel while maintaining friendly relations with the so-called moderate Arab states. In 1978 President Carter godfathered the Camp David accords, setting the stage for a stronger relationship with Israel; President Reagan and former Secretary of State Alexander Haig developed the consensus of strategic concerns to enlist the Arab states and Israel in the new containment policy. The Carter Doctrine and Reagan Codicil expressed the American approach to the Middle East during the third phase.

A separate Israeli–Egyptian peace, coupled with the prospect of a truncated West Bank entity, was unfathomable to the Arab world; Arab acceptance of Camp David could only lead to increased antagonism and decreased collaboration with the PLO.

Meanwhile, the mounting internal problems in Israel were compounded by its isolation, which was caused by the Arab diplomatic offensive; and that, in turn, contributed to the victory of the Likud in the 1977 Israeli elections. The Likud government of Menachem Begin made abrasive the policies of the Labor government. It seemed as though Likud came to reverse the trends which were set in motion in 1973: to undo the diplomatic victory of the PLO and to undermine whatever goodwill the Arab states had been able to earn in Washington. The worldwide recognition of the PLO as the legitimate representative of the Palestinian people had disturbed the Likud leadership more than anything else, and led ultimately to the 1982 invasion of Lebanon. Prior to the invasion, however, Israel embarked on a three-pronged campaign to reverse the trend and to effect a foreclosure on the option of Palestinian independence, which was being carefully nurtured by the Arab states and the PLO. Specifically, Israel sought to achieve the foreclosure, first, diplomatically, by propagating the notion that the idea of a Palestinian state had negative implications for U.S. interests in the Middle East as well as for regional stability. Such a state was presented as irredentist, turbulent, unnecessary, and almost destined to become a Soviet power base.

Second, Israel attempted its foreclosure militarily by rapidly increasing the level of violence, bombing PLO military bases in Lebanon, and assassinating Palestinian leaders. The third approach was the application of the "iron fist" policy in the occupied territories and the *de facto* annexation of the West Bank through the escalation of settlement building and through integration into the Israeli economy.

These Likud attempts to undermine the international legitimacy of the PLO and reverse its diplomatic successes also included the Camp David agreement, which neutralized Egypt, weakened the Arab moderates, and arrested the American momentum for a peaceful resolution of the Palestine–Israel conflict.

Egypt's fateful decision to break with the Arab world and seek bilateral arrangements with Israel while Palestine and the Golan were under *de facto* Israeli sovereignty had a far-reaching impact on future developments in the Arab–Israeli conflict. It split the Arab world, then polarized it, and started the countdown to zero. When the Israeli invasion of Lebanon was mounted in June 1982, the Arab world was in total paralysis. The PLO, which had achieved a phenomenal diplomatic triumph during the 1970s, was lonely and disoriented. The imbalance created by the Camp David agreement made the Arab world so vulnerable to Israeli attack that their diplomatic and economic leverage was rendered ineffectual. Indeed, Israel delivered a number of critical punches to the Arab world in the aftermath of the Camp David negotiations: a full-scale invasion of southern Lebanon in the spring of 1978, a daring penetration of three Arab countries' airspace to bomb the Iraqi nuclear facility near Baghdad in 1981, a savage aerial raid on downtown Beirut in July 1981, and the annexation of the Golan Heights in December 1981, followed by the invasion of Lebanon in June 1982.

The Israeli invasion was met with total Arab inaction. Saudi Arabia, which had deployed the "oil weapon" in 1973 in support of Egyptian–Syrian military action, gave its assurance that economic reprisals were not contemplated. Egypt's commitment to the peace treaty with Israel was to hold firm, and the rest of the Arab world which recognized the PLO in the 1970s maintained silence.

The 1982 invasion was intended, among other things, to end the stalemate produced by Camp David and to create a new geopolitical reality in the Middle East. Israel was to be a junior partner in a *Pax Americana* which would undergird an Israeli hegemony of extensive dimensions. It was, in essence, the Israeli response to the strategic threat of Arab–American accommodation in the aftermath of the October War, to the mounting PLO legitimacy of the seventies, and to U.S. "vacillation."

The Palestine question was in effect removed from its central position on the Middle East peace agenda, and the PLO ceased to be considered sole legitimate representative of the Palestinian people.

The Framework for Common Action, known as the Amman accord of February 11, 1985, represents a substantial concession.[9] In the eyes of many Palestinians, it has already undermined the *raison d'être* of the PLO, as the sole representative of the Palestinian people seeking independence and statehood. Given that these elements were treated as an irreducible minimum in the joint Palestinian–Arab diplomatic campaign of the past decade, one must conclude that the Palestinian people are farther away today from their minimalist objectives than they were ten years ago. The question is whether the next ten years are likely to witness further erosion in the Palestinian position or a turning of the tide. The answer depends on the nature of the opportunities and constraints which local, regional, and global developments will entail.

Constraints on the Palestinians

The Local Environment

The chief local constraints on the Palestinian national movement are twofold—the fragmentation of the PLO and Israel's effective foreclosure of a viable territorial settlement which could offer the Palestinians a sovereign existence.

The presence of three distinct and hostile groupings within the PLO since the 1983 battles of Tripoli constitutes the chief constraint on the ability of the organization to pursue its goals coherently and autonomously.[10] Unless this conflict is settled within a context of inter-Arab harmony and cooperation, the Palestinians will be faced with a diktat. In the short term, neither Jordan nor Syria can promise the Palestinians fulfillment of their goals. Those Palestinians who have decided to cast their lot with Jordan stress the need to "save the land" and view their mission as a salvage operation in the face of steady Zionist colonization. From their perspective, the Mubarak regime has effectively shed Camp David. They welcomed Jordan's restoration of diplomatic relations with Egypt in October 1984 as a step toward settlement based on "land for peace." At the same time, though, none of these leaders anticipates that the Jordan connection can fulfill the irreducible minimum of Palestinian aspirations.

Those other Palestinians who have embraced Syria's position, or who have refused to endorse the Jordan connection, are convinced that their minimum redress is definitely excluded by the existing and prospective balance of forces. The alternative for them is to hold out for a more favorable regional balance of power that could only accrue from a sustained resistance to Israeli occupation and a reinvigorated campaign against U.S. interests in the region. They take inspiration from the success of the Lebanese resistance to Israeli occupation of South Lebanon and from Syria's stand against U.S. hegemony. And yet, the rapprochement between Jordan and Syria, which was emphasized by King Hussein's visit to Damascus in December 1985 and followed by Asad's visit to Amman in May 1986, as well as Hussein's closure of 25 Fateh offices in Jordan including that of Yasser Arafat on July 7, 1986, demonstrates the limitations and pitfalls of both Palestinian strategies. State relations in the Arab world have always taken priority over the Palestine question.

The Regional Environment

The regional situation is not less precarious for the future of Palestine. The milieu of Arab divisiveness and constraints will continue to retard any real opportunities for Palestinian redress. And as long as certain Arab states continue to have hidden forms of a special relationship with the United States, they will be unwilling or unable to confront the United States with regard to its unqualified support for Israeli policies. These Arab states are preoccupied with short-term security needs for regime protection and military purchases. The 1985 appearances of the Saudi king and the Egyptian president in Washington were related more to their countries' bilateral relations with the United States than to Palestine, despite the dominance of the Palestinian theme in the public portions of their U.S. visits. In fact, King Fahd's visit to Washington in February 1985 signified a further downgrading of Palestinian rights. He was silent on the questions of Jerusalem, Palestinian statehood, and the representative character of the PLO—the three crucial elements of the Rabat (1974) and Fez (1982) summit conferences. Unlike Israel, which treats U.S. aid as a premium on an insurance policy, the Arab states beg and plead; and they are occasionally reminded by Washington not to exaggerate their strategic value. Alexander Haig's consensus of strategic concern has never been more than a special relationship between the United States and Israel.[11]

Moreover, the general Arab expectation of a tougher U.S. stand against Israel during Reagan's second term is likely to be disappointed. There are no signs that Israel will cease to be treated as a strategic asset in Wasington. In fact, the special relationship was recently reinvigorated.[12] To confuse the importance of this determinant of U.S. mideast policy with that of the American Jewish vote is to misconstrue reality. What the Arab states fail to recognize is that they, not the United States, are the vulnerable party. The sharp decline of oil revenue, coupled with a decrease in U.S. dependence on Arab oil imports and a corresponding increase in Arab dependence on the United States for internal and external security needs, have already deprived the Arabs of any effective leverage that could be exercised on behalf of Palestinian rights. The "seven lean years" which Yitzhak Rabin said in 1975 Israel would have to endure came to an end in 1982; the Arab world had already forfeited its leverage during the last decade. There are no indications that the next decade will offer better opportunities.

Collective Arab lobbying in Washington, over the short and medium terms, for a new U.S. initiative in consonance with the global consensus, is, therefore, not likely to prove more successful than the pathetic efforts by a committee of Arab kings and presidents to sell the Fez plan in 1982, or the 1985 visits by King Fahd and President Mubarak. Not only did the Reagan administration defer discussion of Saudi Arabia's request for weapons purchases during the king's February 1985 visit to Washington; Reagan also told the king that the Arab case for a new American initiative was not very strong—i.e., that the American and Israeli conditions for a settlement had not been met despite the Hussein–Arafat agreement of February 11, 1985. The Arabs were told that although the agreement was a "step in the right direction," its lack of correctness and its "fuzzy framework"[13] meant it did not yet qualify for serious Israeli attention. Washington gratuitously urged the Arabs to stop the semantic maneuvering and negotiate directly with Israel. United States Assistant Secretary of State for Near Eastern and South Asian Affairs Richard Murphy issued the following warning to America's Arab clients:

> If 1985 is the year of opportunity, as Arab leaders say, then the Arab leaders themselves are going to have to make some hard decisions. One thing is certain: in 1985 no Israeli leader would be willing to sit at the bargaining table, either at an international conference or in bilateral negotiations, with avowed representatives of the PLO, nor would we ask Israel to do this. And without the Israelis present there is no negotiation and no opportunity to explore what the Israelis would be willing to trade for peace.[14]

This is a marked difference from the relationship between Washington and the Arab states during the Carter period. Washington is now asking the Arab regimes simply to abandon the PLO. Developments in the region leading to the *Achille Lauro* hijacking and other acts of violence throughout Europe seem to have enabled the United States to advance this argument in a vigorous and emphatic manner. The success of this strategy was revealed by the issuance of a stern warning to the PLO by President Mubarak and King Hussein. In December 1985, Mubarak served PLO chairman Yasser Arafat with an ultimatum: either accept, unequivocally, Resolution 242, or become what he calls "the big fat loser."

Hussein and Mubarak are asking Arafat to sign a document that considers the Palestinians merely as "refugees" and will not necessarily lead to restoration of occupied Palestinian land or to Palestinian sovereignty. Meanwhile, Hussein's ostentatious rapprochement with Syrian President Hafiz al-Asad in September 1985 was designed to enable Hussein to desert Arafat and to freeze the Amman accord of February 11, 1985, in a manner that would allow the king to rebut charges that he pursued a separate peace. In fact, when Hussein terminated the negotiations with Arafat on February 19, 1986, he laid the blame on the PLO, which he called an untrustworthy partner, despite the latter's agreement to recognize U.N. Resolution 242 in exchange for United States recognition of Palestinian self-determination and despite Arafat's declaration of November 1985 "condemning" and rejecting "terrorism."[15]

Not only was the PLO betrayed by Egypt and Jordan, which embraced Arafat after the Tripoli battle; it has also been forsaken by the so-called progressive Arab regimes that established the "Steadfastness and Confrontation Front" to oppose the Camp David peace. Iraq, which hosted the founding meeting in 1978, is now totally absorbed in its ever-continuing war against Iran. The impact of this war on the future of Palestine was underscored by Richard Murphy in the following manner: "On the Arab side, I think it significant that Iraq has publicly stated that it is prepared to endorse whatever agreement is acceptable to the Palestinians. This is a very different Iraq from the one which hosted the rejectionist gathering in Baghdad after Camp David."[16]

Iraq's war with Iran has not only drained Arab strategic resources, but has also created a dangerous sense of priorities by highlighting a "Persian threat" to the Arab patrimony. The significance of this phenomenon is crystallized by the growing segmentation of the Arab world. The Arabs of the Gulf region have begun to feel the "Shi'ite threat" weigh more heavily on their psyche than the Zionist threat. And so the Arab states, which agreed at the Baghdad summit of 1978 to isolate and punish Egypt for undermining Arab solidarity, decided, as the Iran–Iraq War continued, to rehabilitate Egypt and promote it as a bulwark against Iran. The PLO identified itself with that strategy and joined the shifting Arab realignment of the 1980s. Yet the PLO's concerns are not likely to be included on the agendas of the Gulf Cooperation Council for a long time to come.

Meanwhile, the Syrian regional strategy has been predicated in recent times on control of the PLO, and as long as the elusive Arafat remained at the helm, that objective would remain unfulfilled. Hence Syria gave a green light for the rebels' attack on Arafat's forces in Tripoli in November 1983 and for the Lebanese Amal militia's attacks on the Palestinian camps near Beirut in the summer of 1985.

The cumulative effect of all these factors on Palestinian prospects has been rather grim; the PLO has found itself drifting in the direction of Arab conservatives. It has, in effect, bought the Egyptian line, which hopelessly seeks an exchange of territory for peace, and found itself with no choice except the so-called Jordanian option, which has already proven to be no option.

The Global Environment

The global dimension of the Palestine–Israel conflict is not more promising than the regional dimension. Gone are the days when the Soviet Union was an active participant in the search for a negotiated settlement. Kissinger's shuttle diplomacy, which began in 1974, signaled the start of a process which deprived the Middle East of the normal superpower competition. Gradually, the Middle East has been on the way to becoming another Central America. The stillborn U.S.–U.S.S.R. communiqué of October 1, 1977, was an aberration which was negated by the Dayan–Carter Working Paper a few days later.

The Soviet Union has been effectively reduced to a spoiler and vetomaker, rather than a fully active partner in the search for peace. The Arab states' contribution to the Soviet ouster from the so-called peace process was clearly demonstrated by the semi-collective Arab decision to play by America's rules of the game. Not since 1977, when the Arabs lobbied the Carter administration for the convening of an international conference, has any serious attempt been made in that direction. Moreover, Egypt and Jordan have recently diluted the significance of that concept, which appeared in the resolutions of the seventeenth Palestine National Council (PNC) meeting and was reiterated in the Hussein–Arafat "Framework for Common Action."[17]

Even the Framework itself underplayed the significance of the international conference by using language which renders its role ceremonial rather than substantive. The agreement envisaged in the accord was to be reached not within the framework of an international conference, but only under its umbrella or in its "shadow." A genuine and substantive conference, which could reintroduce the Soviet Union into Middle East diplomacy, has no place on the agendas of the United States and Israel, both of which are in possession of a veto over the issues of war and peace in the region.

U.S. Secretary of State George Shultz coined the phrase "supportive international context" to ratify whatever is agreed upon in direct negotiations between Israel and Jordan, with the participation of acceptable Palestinians. On January 21, 1986, the U.S. position was defined thus: "When it is clearly on the public record that the PLO has accepted Resolutions 242 and 338, is prepared to negotiate peace with Israel, and has renounced terrorism, the U.S. accepts the fact that an invitation will be issued" to an international peace conference. That offer to a conference in name only was effectively rescinded on February 17, 1986, when the condition of Israeli agreement to the invitation was added.[18] The Arab world has understood this reality and ceased to challenge it seriously since Camp David. Hence the Soviet Union has had negligible influence during the last two Israeli invasions of Lebanon and their diplomatic follow-up. Also significant was the absence of the Middle East from the agenda of the Reagan–Gorbachev November 1985 summit in Geneva.

The Arab acceptance of U.S. parameters has been matched by a similar European acquiescence in an American diplomatic monopoly. The Venice declaration of June 1980 was the last European effort to repair the diplomatic imbalance in the Middle East. European willingness to stick to the sidelines while the United States forged ahead, together with Arab acceptance of the U.S. framework, have, in effect, kept the Soviet Union out of the picture.

Given these constraints on the local, regional, and global levels, the PLO has been left completely at the mercy of the United States and a pathetically helpless Arab world, which presently lacks the willingness to make autonomous decisions. The diplomatic game will likely continue to be on U.S. terms, which demand total Arab compliance. Those terms exclude the major Arab statements on Palestine of Rabat (1974) and Fez (1982) and the fundamental aspects of the global consensus. They include a face-saving formula designed to suit the narrow security interests of Arab regimes rather than Palestinian concerns about basic rights. A form of truncated West Bank–Gaza equation which allows for an Israeli–Jordanian condominium is the *maximum* expected result of future U.S. diplomacy.

The Jordanian Option: How Viable?

The Jordanian option, which was endorsed by the seventeenth PNC and formalized by the February 11, 1985, Amman accord was dictated by the constraints discussed above. But is it a real option? What is it likely to produce? And how is it perceived by the Israeli political establishment? We must recognize at the very outset that the original Allon plan of 1968, which was matched with King Hussein's United Kingdom plan of 1972, has been rendered inoperable by the demographic, territorial, economic, and political changes of the past 17 years.[19] Hence there is no Jordanian option as such; there is a Jordanian–Palestinian option, which translates as Camp David.

Although the "demographic imperative," as it is known in Zionist parlance, still weighs heavily in the ideological and strategic formulations of the Israeli political establishment, we are witnessing a perceptible shift away from the strict logic which used to dictate a Jordanian option. The Labor Party, which is the principal adherent to that logic, seems to be in search of a new consensus to accommodate the present demographic and territorial realities. Likud, on the other hand, has its own solutions for the "demographic problem," which include expulsion of Palestinian inhabitants in the interest of a more palatable demographic balance.

The politicians of Labor coalesce on what they term "functional compromise" rather than a territorial settlement; they disagree merely on the exact relationship of a truncated West Bank entity to Jordan and Israel. A functional compromise is one which is designed to leave the West Bank and Gaza under Israeli sovereignty. Not unlike the apartheid system in South Africa, its division of functions is based on inequality. Gadi Yatziv described this arrangement in *Al-Hamishmar* thus:

> We are talking here about separating the functions of the right to use force for internal and external security, which will remain in the hands of Israel while other functions will be transferred to the Palestinians or the Jordanians. . . . The actual borders of the state are the borders recognized for the use of force . . . our society will then be divided between citizens who are entitled to participate in the use of force and citizens who will not [have] this right. This is the "compromise" which would formalize the inferior status of the population of the territories which will be *de facto*, not *de jure* a part of the Israeli society.[20]

Yatziv goes on to distinguish between two types of autonomy: a "liberating" autonomy, which brings power centers closer to the reach of the people, such as the case in Spain involving the Basques; and a "restrictive autonomy," in which the people possess no role in the allocation of power relevant to their own destiny, as in the Bantustans of South Africa. He then concludes that the functional compromise of the Israeli Labor Party is "closer to the model of South Africa than the model of the Basque region," and that it is even less advanced than the concept of a Jordanian–Israeli condominium, which would be based on the principle of "functional cooperation" rather than the contemplated unequal "division of functions."[21] Abba Eban, a powerful voice on behalf of ethnic purity and usually a proponent of the Jordanian option, is now advocating a solution which excludes a territorial compromise. It calls, instead, for a "functional compromise" along the lines of the Benelux model, in which a relationship among Israel, Jordan, and Palestine will be patterned after the relationship among Belgium, the Netherlands, and Luxembourg.[22] Nadav Safran expressed that relationship this way:

> Palestine would, of course, be the Luxembourg; Jordan would be the Belgium; Israel would be the Netherlands . . . you would end up with the sovereign state of Israel, with its might, and the sovereign state of Jordan, with its might, and the sovereign state of Palestine, without might—but with all the other elements of sovereignty, with a flag and a legislature and stamps and whatnot.[23]

Eban's cosmetic shift from the orthodox Zionist view which characterized the Labor Party seems to have been decided, for the most part, by the existence of 114 colonial settlements stretching over more than 50 percent of the land in the West Bank. These settlements, with their own regional councils, court system, vigilante army, and powerful lobby, have imposed their permanence on the American–Israeli parameters of a negotiated settlement. The Reagan Plan as well as the Israeli Labor platform recognize their permanence. Eban's model accommodates the more than 100 Israeli colonies in the sense that "the boundaries become a painted line on a street, with little more significance than the Massachusetts–New Hampshire boundary."[24]

Labor Defense Minister Yitzhak Rabin speaks of cantonization and a settlement based on a Jordanian–Palestinian option, in which nearly 60 percent of the West Bank would be incorporated within Israel in a final settlement:

> There is no other solution than the one connected with Jordan . . . that will allow Israel to maintain a security border on the Jordan River for a period which I cannot for the moment set a term to, and [provide for] the return of parts of the West Bank and Gaza to form one entity with Jordan: one flag, one army, one capital—Amman. I would not object if Jordan and the Palestinians subsequently decided to establish cantons within one sovereign state, east and west of the Jordan. All this on condition that the peace agreement were signed between the State of Israel and one Jordanian–Palestinian State.[25]

An Israeli common denominator, given the present conditions and looking toward the next decade, is not likely to stray beyond the perimeters of the trilateral equation of Camp David (favored by Likud), the Allon–Rabin plan (favored by Labor), and the Reagan plan, which the United States would be expected to resurrect under optimal conditions. That "compromise" between Israeli factions is likely to focus not on the national rights of the Palestinians, not on the refugees' right of return, not on the status of Jerusalem, or the right of the PLO to represent the Palestinians; it will focus on whether Palestinian autonomy will be territorial or personal with the odds heavily favoring the latter, and on how much of the West Bank's water resources, labor, trade, and tourist resources are to be controlled by the autonomous regime. It will focus on the juridical relationship of Israel's colonial settlements to the "autonomous" regime and on the nature of the confederative links between Jordan and the "autonomous" regime. If and when these negotiations take place, Israel will play most of the cards against both Jordan and the Palestinians, while Jordan will produce cards of its own against the Palestinians, as has already been demonstrated since early 1983. Should the latter prove to be not sufficiently cooperative, Jordan would be able to call on its own Palestinians, who are well-represented in the present cabinet and are strategically situated in the West Bank. In fact, an unwritten agreement between Jordan and Israel to remove the PLO from the political equation seems to have been forged during the summer of 1986. The search by both parties for a more accommodating Palestinian leadership was evidenced in a series of moves taking place east and west of the Jordan River in coordination. Israeli efforts to replace military officers with Arab mayors in Ramallah, Bireh, and Hebron together with the crackdown on the pro-PLO press in the West Bank were deemed by the Israeli press as measures supportive of Jordan's dramatic closure of most of Fateh's offices and its unceremonious expulsion of the deputy commander of the PLO forces, Khalil al-Wazir.[26] Jordan's reactivation of so-called coordination committees for overseeing health and education affairs in the West Bank, together with its intent to issue Jordanian passports to the Gaza residents, as well as the highly publicized five-year development plan for the occupied territories are steps in the same direction. Jordan's economic support to the town of Dura, whose mayor is a member of the Village Leagues, signals a shift in policy. Members of the Leagues, an Israeli quisling, have been under a death sentence in Jordan.

The reincarnation of Camp David is expected to be Israel's best offer to the Palestinian people as long as the environmental constraints with which they have to deal remain: the lack of cohesion; the lack of a secure base; the lack of independent financial, military, and technological resources; and the inability to count on big-power support. Trying to enlist Egyptian support to gain leverage with Israel and the United States implies PLO acceptance of Mubarak's commitment to Camp David. Nor will Egypt be expected to deliver, given the mood in the U.S. Congress. The Jordanian card is even more ineffective, in addition to the fact that Jordanian suspicions of Palestinian nationalism are just as strong as those of Israel and the United States. In the meantime, neither Egypt, under the present regime, nor Jordan would be willing to risk war with Israel in the foreseeable future. Yet the Egyptian–Jordanian connection had only until September 1986 to deliver, before Yitzhak Shamir assumed the leadership of the national unity government. The Palestinians were faced then with more of the open-ended occupation and the state of no war, no peace.

That state would not be expected to last very long in view of the development of new demographic and consequent socioeconomic realities in the territories occupied since 1967. The Arab population of the West Bank and Gaza Strip has registered a 3.5 percent annual increase since

1983. According to the *1984 Statistical Abstracts* of Israel, this rate contrasts with an average of 2 percent annual increase between 1968 and 1983. The increase since 1983 can be attributed to the decline in employment opportunities in the Gulf States, to which a significant sector of Palestinian skilled workers had emigrated. According to the findings of the Bank of Israel's Research Department, from 1975 to 1980 emigration to the Arab states was about 17 per 1,000 inhabitants; in 1981 it decreased to 9, and in 1983 it decreased to 3 per 1,000.[27] The overwhelming majority of the 4,000 annual university graduates join the ranks of the unemployed.

This situation has been compounded by the economic crisis in Israel and its fallout in the occupied territories, where the GNP is not growing, local production is shrinking, and investments are coming to a virtual halt. The sociopolitical significance of these economic and demographic facts cannot be underestimated in view of the revolutionary potential of a rising mass of unemployed in the ranks of the intelligentsia as well as the manual workers. This trend will most likely be aggravated by worsening economic conditions in Israel and the Arab countries. It could cause an escalation of resistance activities among the Arab population which might, in turn, provide Israel with a pretext for a new war designed to reduce the Arab population to manageable proportions. An Israeli thrust in the direction of Amman could be Israel's response to a state of no war, no peace on the Jordanian front unless current cooperative efforts achieve some function, or a war against Syria would aim to realize the unfulfilled objectives of the 1982 invasion of Lebanon.[28]

Constraints on Israel

The future of the Palestinian situation has an Israeli dimension, which shows constraints of its own on the regional and domestic levels. On the regional level, Israeli "invincibility" has suffered a serious setback. For the past three and a half years, Israel has been trying to extricate itself from the war which was to establish its hegemony in Lebanon. Instead, most of its war gains have been erased and its armed forces have, in effect, retreated for the first time in front of Arab guerrillas.

On the domestic level, Israel is beset by political, moral, and economic crises. A mixture of xenophobic chauvinism and religious fundamentalism, fueled by endemic economic problems, has split Israeli society and caused a severe crisis of governance. The ascendancy of a militant rightwing movement, with an orientation toward brute force and terrorism and a protective umbrella provided by the religious, military, and political establishments, does not augur well for a society which has pretensions to democracy. Israeli intellectuals have been warning about the proximity of the right to the fascist conception of the state.[29]

This moral decadence is compounded by an economy plagued by quadruple-digit inflation, a colossal foreign debt which equals the GNP, a huge trade deficit, and a rapidly rising defense budget (from 10 percent of the

GNP in 1967 to 32 percent at present, compared to 7 percent for the United States, 4 percent for NATO countries, and 1 percent for Japan). Combating inflation, Israel's most publicly acknowledged problem, and even reducing military expenditure are not likely to give Israel a respite. As Lawrence Meyer wrote in the *The Washington Post*: "Israel will remain in serious economic trouble until it figures out how to climb out of its current stagnation, create productive jobs, export more than it imports, and pay its bills without massive handouts from abroad . . . what life-support systems are to medicine, American foreign aid has become to Israeli life . . . roughly 19 percent of the government's budget in 1985."[30]

The partially inhabited West Bank colonies, which are estimated to cost about $750 million per year ($100,000 for a family of four),[31] are raising some real questions about domestic priorities.

Israel's resort to repression and its proclivity for empire building have already proven to be morally corrosive and economically and politically untenable. And while the outcry for a reassessment is not likely to produce a short-term change in national policy, the days are gone when conflicts with the Arabs defused internal differences. These escalating crises of a society living beyond its means will have their impact on Palestinian options over the next decade. As Abba Eban wrote in *Harper's* magazine: "What is conventionally described as the Palestine problem is really the problem of Israel itself."[32]

Equally important for the future of Palestine are developments on the political scene in the United States. On the negative side, the United States is expected to continue its superpower monopoly of Mideast diplomacy, absent an alteration in the regional status quo. Meanwhile, the U.S.–Israeli special relationship seems to be getting stronger, and the American domestic consensus on Israel seems to be holding firm.

We must not underestimate, however, the serious setback which U.S. diplomacy has suffered in Lebanon. The crises of U.S. diplomacy constitute a constraint on Washington's ability to determine the future of the Middle East. They undermine U.S. credibility as a superpower and as an arbiter. Today's constraints might be tomorrow's opportunities for the Palestinians.

The Palestinian prospects will appear to be gloomy when analyzed in the context of the conventional wisdom about rules of the game defined by the United States and Israel and accepted uncritically by Arab regimes, whose short-term concerns about security needs take precedence over the future of Palestine. Hence the exchange of territory for peace, as if international politics were a real estate transaction, assumed a prominent place on the agenda. And hence the familiar outcries about the "last chance for peace," which have been heard with monotonous frequency since the occupation in 1967 of eastern Palestine and Gaza. Ironically, this regime insecurity, so eloquently demonstrated in the phrase "last chance for peace," has become the Arabs' most important leverage vis-à-vis the United States. The Arab regimes are, in effect, threatening Washington with their own downfall and the consequences of such developments for U.S. interests in the region.

The pursuit of a Jordanian option in 1985–86 was a pursuit of a nonexistent option. While Israel's Likud is opposed to it, its so-called doves question its feasibility. Meron Benvenisti's elaborate survey concludes that Israel's control of the West Bank and Gaza has now reached a "state of quasi-permanence": "There are strong indications that the critical point has passed and that therefore the whole political discussion, which is based on the premise that things are reversible, is irrelevant and has been overtaken by events."[33]

When Ezer Weizmann was pressed on March 3, 1985, by Sam Donaldson of ABC News to answer a question about Israel's willingness to make a territorial withdrawal, he said: "We can trade not land but sharing the governance process . . . direct talks, without mediator—bilateral with Egypt, with Jordan . . . There is no role for Arafat . . . only Hussein . . . Let us carry on what was achieved in 1978–79."[34] Meanwhile, Abba Eban and Yitzhak Rabin are talking about forms of cantonization bordering on *apartheid*.[35] And the United States has already ruled out Palestinian independence, PLO representation, and the international conference.

Surely, the Arab regimes must be aware that the so-called Jordanian option is doomed; and the only explanation for their tenacious adherence to it is self-preservation.

Alternative Futures

The preceding discussion focused on the trials and tribulations of the Palestinian past and present and the constraints which the political environment at three levels—local, regional, and international—impose on the pursuit of Palestinian options. The simple fact is that the Palestinian national movement suffers from serious structural problems. It lacks a viable and secure territorial base; independent financial, technological, and military resources; a rational connection between means and ends; and a firm structure of foreign alliances. It is also beset by a crisis of leadership, ideology, cohesion, and legitimacy. If these problems seem insurmountable, however, it is partly because the Palestinian struggle has been waged against exceedingly unfavorable odds—a primary antagonist which has managed to cynically transform its own image from that of a colonial settler-oppressor to that of an oppressed people, and whose Holocaust legacy has given it an impenetrable shield in the arena of public relations; an auxiliary antagonist which, besides having a near-monopoly of superpower influence in the region, has managed to play the role of chief conciliator simultaneously with a role as co-belligerent, which relegates any opponent of its hegemonic position to the status of terrorist; and a third antagonist which, while selling out Palestinian rights and waging wars against Palestinian refugee communities, has managed to retain its title as the Palestinians' guardian and chief attorney in international councils.

Such a combination of anomalies has rarely plagued national liberation movements during the twentieth century. Yet the Palestinians have vacillated between, on the one hand, conducting a revolution (*al-thawra al-filastiniyya*) and pursuing it until victory (*thawra hatta al-nasr*) and, on the other, engaging in a pseudo-diplomatic struggle anchored more in a misconceived notion of Arab power than in Palestinian readiness. And so, despite the ferocity of the enemies, the Palestinians need to take an inward look in order to determine their own responsibility for the debacle, to reexamine their priorities, to reassess their strategies, and to distinguish between vision and policy.

The past ten years have shown the futility of a diplomatic "option" pursued from a position of weakness. This fact has become widely known, not only among the anti-Arafat factions of the PLO but also among a Palestinian generation born around the time of the June 1967 war. Inside the West Bank and Gaza, this generation was impressed by the October 1973 war and the Israeli debacle in Lebanon. Outside Palestine, mainly in Lebanon, this generation was deeply affected by the massacres of Sabra and Shatila camps at the hands of Phalangists aided by Israel. The proclivity of this generation to a confrontationist posture toward Israel will undoubtedly please the latter, whose tactics are based on the attempt to retard negotiations while giving the appearance of pursuing them. The stepped-up level of violence in airports throughout Europe and inside the occupied territories will enable the Israeli government—Likud or Labor—to pursue aggressively the present campaign designed to completely exclude the PLO from any negotiations and to force Jordan to enter negotiations without the PLO, or else to find a pretext for a military campaign on the Jordanian and/or Syrian fronts.

The future possible courses for the PLO, it seems, are three: first, to continue on the present path of no war, no peace, hoping against hope to move the United States and Israel away from their intransigent posture. This would be disastrous for the movement, which is already in a state bordering on anomie. For as long as the PLO maintains its explicit refusal to accept UN Resolution 242, the Israeli Labor Party will continue prodding Hussein on toward their "functional compromise," the real content of the current Israeli "peace initiative," which excludes the PLO. This course is suicidal!

The second possibility is to surrender "Arafat's last card," recognition of Israel without Israeli reciprocation. Would such an action challenge Israel's refusal to consider the PLO a qualified negotiating partner, as some Israeli and U.S. commentators claim? While such an unequivocal recognition might strengthen Israeli "liberals" and proponents of the Jordan option, the anticipated shift it would create in the Israeli domestic political balance is not likely to be of a dimension that would have a substantive effect on Israeli policy. Nor would the preoccupation of the Arab states with particularistic concerns, which obviates the threat of a united Arab world against Israel, enhance the Israeli "peace camp's" argument for Israel's imperative to seek a political settlement in enlightened self-interest. Thus, at the present conjuncture of Israeli and Arab politics, the results of an historic Palestinian concession which brings no assurance of a Palestinian sovereignty are likely to be additional fragmentation and increased demoralization in the Palestinian community.

The third possible course is to shun the diplomatic charade of the past decade altogether, to rebuild the unity of the movement on the basis of the Aden–Algiers agreement of June 1984,[36] to restructure the movement's alliances and repair the damage created by the shifting alignments of the past decade, to develop an austerity program that would enable the movement to rationally seek and maintain independent financial resources, and to solve the legitimacy crises by creating real avenues for political participation and by dealing effectively and dispassionately with the leadership's inability to solve the mounting problems of Palestinian communities. The Palestinian psyche suffers from having lost that hopefulness of success which is so essential to the triumph of revolutionary movements. The restoration of that feeling can be obtained only through a rediscovery of abandoned values.

The Palestinian national movement cannot succeed on the basis of cooperation with an Arab state system whose very survival is considered a vital American interest. Nor can it succeed in isolation from Arab nationalism.

While it is fashionable for Western and Westernized Arab intellectuals to regard Arab nationalism as nonexistent, it is not inconceivable that the urge for Arab unity and for mobilization of Arab resources may surface vigorously again. After all, how long will the Arab populace tolerate the present state of dependency, which can only lead to a thorough-going American–Israeli penetration at the economic, political, and cultural levels in the region? And wouldn't the persistence of the Arab malaise encourage the rejectionist attitudes of Israel and the United States, which in turn would fuel the urge to challenge their omnipotence, which can only be done through the efforts of a coherent and progressive Arab national movement?

The uniquely Palestinian approach devised by the PLO almost two decades ago has not succeeded; and as recent history shows, Israel has not been a menace to the Palestinian people only, but to other Arabs who strive for strategic parity and who resist Israeli imperialism. Hence, there exists the need to rethink the facade of "independent decision" which in actuality placed the PLO in an adjunct role to the Arab state system as it embarked on a fruitless lobbying effort in Washington and some European capitals.

Nothing that the Palestinian movement can do will endear it to Washington: neither frequent reminders that the PLO was instrumental in preventing the Lebanese National Movement from holding several thousand Americans hostage in Beirut during the 1982 siege and in facilitating safe entry into and exit out of Lebanon in the 1970s, nor assertions that the PLO stands for stability and constitutes a wall against nihilism—not only in the Palestinian community but throughout the Arab world. Irrespective of any image transformation, the Palestinian movement can never be a viable candidate for the consensus of strategic concerns—not even if Arafat were to stand firmly behind Washington and offer unconditional support of its regional and international endeavors.

In the final analysis, Palestinian redress cannot emerge from the present constraints embedded in the local, regional, and international environments. When these restraints are overcome, however, they may be turned into opportunities. That process of converting restraints into opportunities can begin only when the Palestinian national movement decides to redraw the terms of discussion, to redefine the rules of the game, and to recapture the initiative which had placed it on the map of the region. It would be better to abandon the unseemly haste to secure a tangible achievement, which is not in the offing, in favor of a long-range investment for succeeding generations. In the final analysis, the current choice for the Palestinian people is between armed struggle and Camp David, stripped of its requirement of "full autonomy."

Notes

1. See Malcolm Kerr, *The Arab Cold War* (London: 1971).
2. See Seymour Hersch, *The Price of Power: Kissinger in the Nixon White House* (New York: Summit Books, 1983).
3. This was the euphemism which the Arab states used to describe their efforts to regain occupied territories on the basis of UN Resolution 242.
4. Hussein's performance in Black September was rewarded generously by the United States. The first installment of $5 million was advanced before the conclusion of the ceasefire, to be followed by another payment of $30 million during Hussein's visit to Washington in early December 1970. During the following April, and prior to the final confrontation of July, President Nixon asked Congress to appropriate $45 million for Jordan on the grounds that "a stable and viable Jordan is essential if that nation is to make a viable contribution toward working out an enduring peace settlement." See *The New York Times*, September 26, 1970 and April 8, 1971.
5. Samir Amin, "The Middle East Conflict in a World Context," *Contemporary Marxism*, no. 7 (Fall 1983).
6. United Nations General Assembly Resolution No. 2535, December 10, 1969; No. 2649, November 30, 1970; No. 2787, December 6, 1971; and No. 2792, December 6, 1971.
7. UN General Assembly Resolution No. 3210, October 14, 1974.
8. Khalil Abu-Rouwayda, "Pax Americana in the Middle East," unpublished manuscript (1984), p. 4.
9. Text of the "Framework" and analysis in *Shu'un Filastiniyya (Palestinian Affairs)*, no. 144 (March/April 1985): 116–24 and in *Palestine Perspectives*, no. 14 (March 1985): 6.
10. See Naseer Aruri, "The PLO and the Jordan Option," *Third World Quarterly*, Vol. 7, no. 4 (October 1985): 882–906.
11. See Naseer Aruri, et al., *Reagan and the Middle East* (Belmont, MA: Arab-American University Graduates Press, 1983), pp. 5–10.
12. The United States and Israel concluded a strategic accord in November 1983, a Free Trade Area Agreement in April 1985, and an agreement on joint research

on President Reagan's Strategic Defense Initiative (known as Star Wars). Secretary of State Shultz said at the American Israel Public Affairs Committee's (AIPAC) Annual Policy Conference in April 1984 that strategic cooperation with Israel "has become a formal institutionalized process." For more details, see Rex Wingerter, "Israel's Search for Strategic Interdependence," *American-Arab Affairs*, no. 14 (Fall 1985): 81–94; also Abbas Alnasrawi, "The American–Israeli Free Trade Area Agreements," *Mideast Monitor* (December 1985).

13. *The New York Times*, February 25, 1985.

14. Richard Murphy, "Maintaining Momentum in the Middle East Peace Negotiations," U.S. Department of State, Bureau of Public Affairs, *Current Policy*, no. 726 (June 27, 1985).

15. Text of the Cairo declaration in *Palestine Perspectives*, no. 20, (November/December 1985): 5.

16. Murphy, "Maintaining Momentum in the Middle East Peace Process."

17. Statements by Osama Al-Baz, Ismat Abdel-Maguid, and Taher al-Masri in *The Washington Post*, December 4, 1984; *The New York Times*, December 2 and 7, 1984.

18. See Godfrey Jensen, "Who Was Fooling Whom?" *Middle East International*, no. 270 (March 7, 1986): 4; also Naseer Aruri, "United States Opposition to an International Peace Conference in the Middle East, 1967–1985," *International Journal of Islamic and Arabic Studies*, Vol. 2, no. 1 (1985).

19. See Yigal Allon, "Israel: The Case for Defensible Borders," *Foreign Affairs*, Vol. 55, no. 1 (October 1976): 38–53; and *Al-Mamlaka al-'arabiyya al-muttahida* (Amman: Armed Forces Press, n.d.).

20. Gadi Yatziv, "Territorial Compromise or No Compromise," *Al-Hamishmar*, November 24, 1985. Translated in the *Shahak Papers*.

21. *Ibid*.

22. Nadav Safran, "The Jordanian Option," *Moment* (Boston, MA: November 1984).

23. *Ibid*.

24. *Ibid*.

25. *Yediot Aharonot*, June 5, 1984.

26. *Jerusalem Post*, July 9, 1986.

27. See Danny Rubinstein, "Economic Woes in the Territories," *Davar*, November 18, 1984; and Zio Rabi, "Demographic Update," *Ha'aretz*, November 28, 1984.

28. For an analysis of a possible Israeli war against Syria, see the following articles in the Israeli press: Levy Morav, "Good, Short, Strong and Elegant," *Al-Hamishmar*, March 18, 1986; Alex Fishman, "Change the Balance," *Al-Hamishmar*, February 25, 1986; Alex Fishman, "War Because of Political Isolation," *Al-Hamishmar*, March 3, 1986; Teddy Preuss, "High Probability-Low Budget," *Davar*, February 21, 1986; Ze'ev Schiff, "Do the Syrians Want War?" *Ha'aretz*, March 14, 1986; P. Sever, "X Theory: Perhaps It Was Not a Mistake," *Al-Hamishmar*, February 6, 1986; Ran Edelist, "The Artificial Short-Down," *Monitin*, February 1986.

29. See article by sociology professor Yoram Peri in *Davar*, May 11, 1984.

30. Lawrence Meyer, "Israel as Public Works Project," *The Washington Post*, December 15, 1985, p. C-1.

31. See article by Nehemiah Stressler (economic affairs editor), *Ha'aretz*, November 16, 1984; and Peter Demant, "Israeli Settlement Policy Today," *MERIP Reports*, July-August 1983, reprinted in Naseer Aruri, ed., *Occupation: Israel Over Palestine* (Belmont, MA: Arab-American University Graduates Press, 1983), p. 164. See also Ned Temko, "Israel's 190% Inflation Sparks Debate," *Christian Science Monitor*, March 12, 1984.

32. *Harper's* Magazine, December 1984.

33. *Christian Science Monitor*, April 25, 1984.
34. "David Brinkley This Week," ABC, Sunday, March 3, 1985.
35. Israeli satirist Ziva Yariv had the following to say about the so-called functional compromise: "What more can one say about this mongrel whose name is either 'one-sided autonomy' or 'increased jurisdiction,' or 'enlarged self-government'? Only one sentence more: We are prepared to give the Arabs full freedom, on the condition that they should always do what we want and shall never do what we do not want." *Yediot Aharonot*, February 12, 1986.
36. Excerpts in *Journal of Palestine Studies*, no. 53 (Fall 1984): 200–204.

17

The Implications of Current Trends in the Arab-Israeli Military Balance

Anthony H. Cordesman

It is one of the many ironies of the Arab–Israeli conflict that commentators and analysts always seem to be talking about peace and the participants always seem to be preparing for war. The Arab–Israeli conflict has virtually institutionalized a sequence in which prolonged arms races are followed by bursts of intense conventional combat, and the resulting Arab–Israeli conflicts have made the Levant the world's proving ground for new weapons and tactical technologies.

At the same time, the Arab–Israeli arms race is changing. As was the case in 1948, 1956, 1970, 1973, and 1982, the latest round of fighting has triggered a major process of rearmament and reorganization on both sides. "Peace for Galilee" may be one of history's classic misnomers, but it has led to changes in the Arab–Israeli balance. These changes are combining with the outcome of Camp David, and other political and economic forces, to change the way in which future wars are likely to occur. While it may be even more premature than usual to predict the future, certain key patterns seem to be emerging.

The Arab–Israeli conflict is increasingly an Israeli–Syrian conflict with occasional sideshows from the PLO and various ethnic movements in Lebanon. Whatever the full legacy of Camp David may be, the peace between Israel and Egypt seems likely to be stable for the next decade. This commitment to peace is steadily being reinforced by de facto cuts in Egyptian forces; Egypt's growing economic problems; a growing consciousness on the part of Egypt that it has nothing to achieve through military initiatives and is acutely vulnerable to conventional or nuclear attacks on its population and economy; and growing threats and instability in the Red Sea area, in Africa, and from Libya.

While Egypt's forces are still impressive on paper (453,000 active men and 360,000 reserves), Egypt has lacked the funds to give most of its manpower anything approaching the readiness it had in 1973. Despite its claims to have converted its Soviet-made equipment, or to have kept it operational, most of Egypt's Soviet-supplied fighters and surface-to-air missiles (SAMs) no longer are reliable and many no longer are operational. Egypt is acquiring a great deal of high-quality equipment from the United States and Europe and is absorbing it relatively well, but its true force size at the end of the 1990s will only be about 50 to 65 percent of its 1973 first-line operational strength.

At the same time, Jordan and Iraq—for very different reasons—have become the political enemies of Syria and show little interest in any military adventures. Jordan has no hope of achieving more than pyrrhic victories. It can lose lives, military forces, and key economic facilities, but it has no hope of regaining the West Bank by force—either alone or as part of any practical combination of Arab forces. Jordan has also lacked the resources and access to advanced weapons necessary to compete with the arms build-up in Syria and Israel. It can at best hope to protect itself against Syrian adventures and the backlash from future fighting between Israel and Syria. It will need the U.S. fighter aircraft and other improved defense equipment it has so far been denied to reach even this level of security.

Iraq's experience in the Iran–Iraq war has both moderated its attitude toward Israel and made it far more reluctant to engage in new military adventures. Its growing military forces should be able to secure its position in the Gulf, but they can aspire to damage Israel only at the cost of far greater damage to Iraq. Like Jordan, Iraq can at best hope for limited and largely pyrrhic tactical victories, and even this hope seems unrealistic.

As for Libya, it remains the world's largest, and loudest, military parking lot. It has 3,000 medium tanks, with more on order, and 510 combat aircraft, but a maximum of 76,000 men. Libya is having negligible success in translating its vast weapons holdings into an effective large-scale fighting force, and the limited capabilities it does have are becoming more of a threat to the Arab world than to Israel.

The arms race is shifting from force quantity to force quality. Syria is trying to cope with the situation through a hopeless search for military parity with Israel. It is buying force quantity at a time when it is force quality that really matters. (See Figures 17.1 and 17.2.) The 1982 fighting has led Israel virtually to halt its efforts to increase its force numbers and to shift to efforts to increase force quality. This is a major change from the period between 1956 and 1982, and it reflects military realities that Syria has little near-term prospect of being able to cope with.

While any full analysis of force numbers and force structures involves many complex factors, main battle tanks serve as a good example of the trends in force quantity. Israel increased its tank strength from 2,000 tanks in 1973 to 3,600 in 1982. It now has 3,650 main battle tanks and will probably drop back to 3,300 and convert its older tanks to the role of Mechanized Infantry Combat Vehicles (MICVs). Israel's priority is clearly to increase its number of Merkavas, rather than to increase its total tank forces.

Current Trends in the Arab-Israeli Military Balance   281

(Manpower shown in thousands of persons)

[Bar chart comparing Israel and Syria military capabilities]

- Manpower Active: Israel 149,000; Syria 392,500
- Manpower Total with reserves: Israel 703,000; Syria 592,500
- Tanks: Israel 3,660; Syria 4,200
- OAFVs*: Israel 6,300; Syria 3,400
- Artillery: Israel 1,800; Syria 3,800
- Combat Aircraft: Israel 629; Syria 483
- Helicopters Combat: Israel 58; Syria 100
- Helicopters Total: Israel 220; Syria 260

*Other armored fighting vehicles

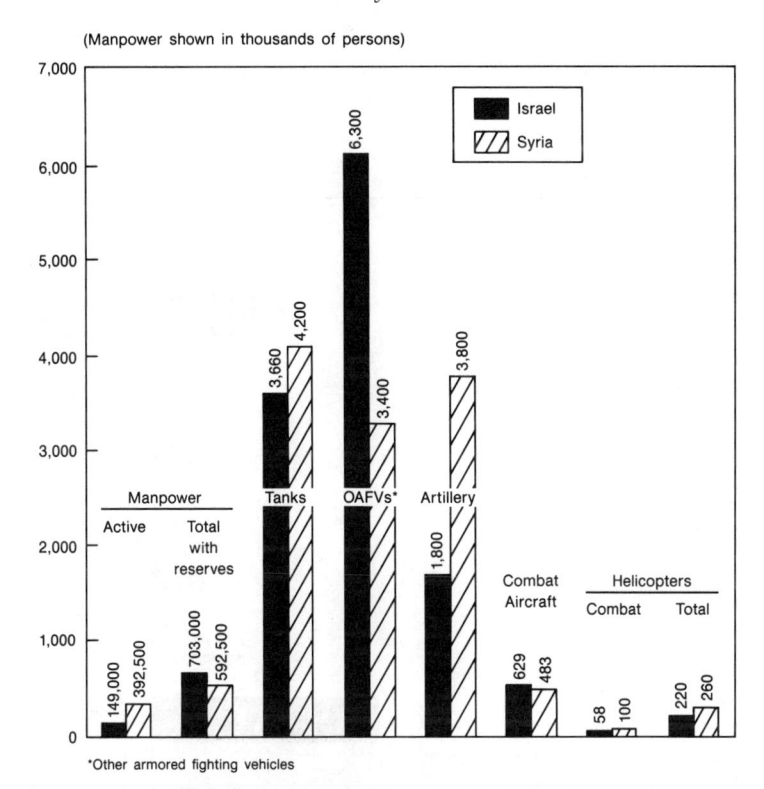

FIGURE 17.1. The Israeli-Syrian Balance, 1987. *Source:* Adapted from International Institute of Strategic Studies, *Military Balance, 1986–87* (London: The Institute, 1986).

The same is true of Israel's plans to improve its other fighting vehicles and artillery. Israel needs weapons with more mobility, survivability, and lethality. It does not need more mass—and may well have more equipment numbers than it can effectively man and deploy—but it does need to convert at least 60 to 70 percent of its inventory to new advanced types within the next seven to ten years.

Israel has also drawn the conclusion that it needs to improve the command, control, communications, and intelligence, or C^{3}I, capabilities of its forces. While it is still far from clear why the Israeli Defense Forces (IDF) often bogged down in Lebanon—and many of its problems can be laid to the inability properly to plan and execute an attack whose high-level objective was constantly being changed and expanded at the political level—Israel found that its present major combat units were too large and cumbersome to be effective.

Israel needs improved C^{3}I systems to be able to split up its combat elements and give them far more independence while still keeping them informed and maintaining overall cohesion. It also needs to maximize its use of technology in ways which reduce the exposure of its manpower, the

282

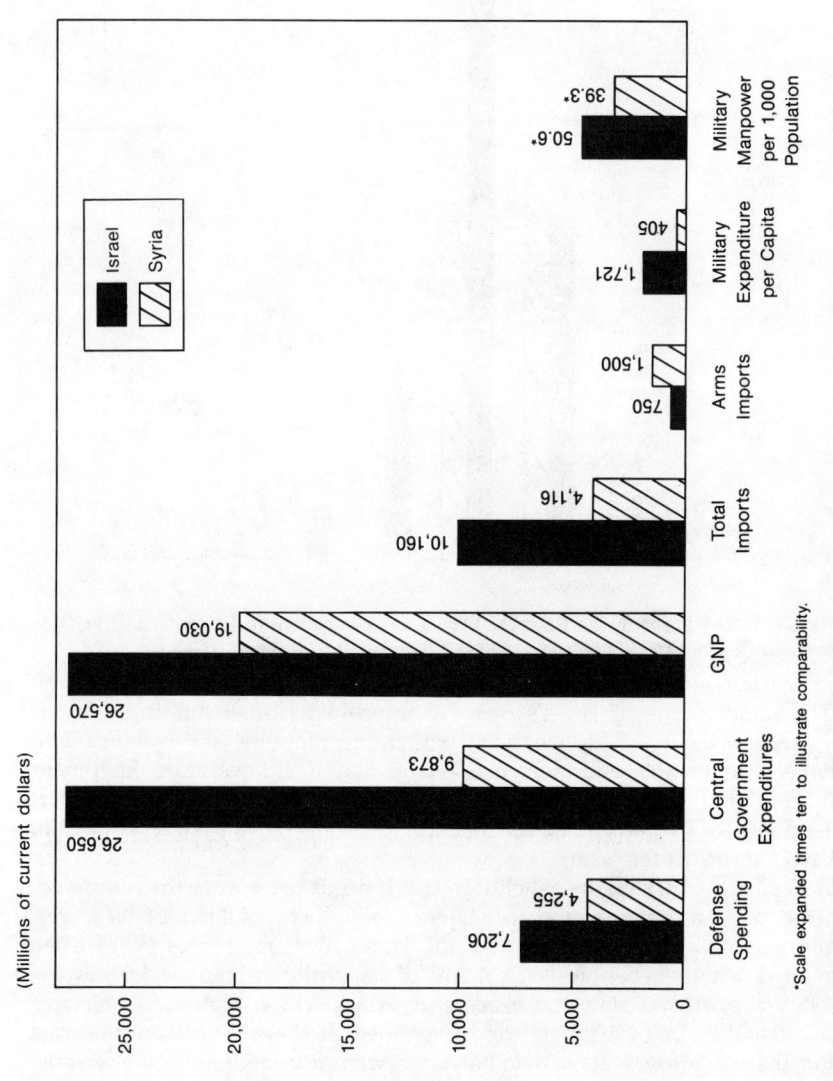

FIGURE 17.2. Israeli vs. Syrian Defense Effort, 1985. *Source:* Arms Control and Disarmament Agency, *World Military Expenditures and Arms Transfers* (Washington, DC: Government Printing Office, 1986).

cost of reserve and standing forces, and the risk of casualties. This means the IDF will have to slowly restructure its land forces and find new ways to improve the technical training of its reserves. It also means that the real Israeli defense budget spent on new equipment and investment will have to increase by 50 to 100 percent. Some of this increase can come from manpower cuts, but most must come from aid.

Syria faced far greater problems in using its existing equipment numbers in 1982. It is important to remember that the IDF's problems did not prevent it from decisively defeating Syrian forces whenever it was really prepared to engage them. Some individual Syrian units fought very well in defensive positions, but Israeli officers are probably correct in claiming that they could have decisively defeated the Syrian forces in Lebanon, and even those defending Damascus, if Israel had had the political support for such a war, and if it had carried out the planning and organization to make this one of its original objectives.

The problem Syria now faces, however, is that it is much easier for it to build up force quantity than force quality. It built up its tank strength from 1,600 tanks in 1973 to 1,700 tanks in 1978—long before Camp David indicated that it would probably face Israel alone. It then underwent a crash expansion to over 3,000 tanks in 1982. Syria has now reached a total of about 3,700 tanks, which gives it numerical superiority over Israel, and continues to expand its forces.

This is a far larger equipment pool than any Middle Eastern army can effectively absorb, and Syria's efforts to do so are now actually having the effect of reducing Syria's military capabilities rather than increasing them. Syria cannot afford to approach Israel's expenditures on manpower and operating costs, and Syrian training and pay standards remain far too low to provide the massive increases in high-quality manpower that Syria needs to go along with its new equipment.

The Syrian active forces are three times as large as those of Israel (300,000 compared to 130,000), but the personnel are now far less well trained in technical, maneuver, and C^3I capability than Israeli reserves. Syria's trained officers, noncommissioned officers, and technicians are spread far too thin, and the Soviet advisory effort in Syria is making very slow progress indeed. Syria's 350,000-man reserve forces outnumber Israel's 310,000-man reserves, but are of little military value except in static, well-prepared defensive positions dominated by infantry combat.

Syria's problems are further compounded by the high levels of politicization within the Syrian forces; the lack of a career structure that rewards military professionalism, honest intelligence, and integrity in reporting internal problems and shortcomings; and the lack of free access to high-quality Western military technology.

At the same time, Syria's search for military parity is producing sufficient numerical strength to arouse Israeli concern, stimulate Israel's side of the arms race, and provide a justification for more demands for U.S. aid. Neither military planners nor politicians are ever willing to rely on a qualitative advantage, no matter how real—and Syria is beginning to lead in mass. Syria now not only has more tanks than Israel, but has about 2,300 first-line artillery weapons while Israel has a little over 1,000. It is receiving about 50 percent more major weapons a year from the Soviet Union than Israel is getting from its own military industry and the United States. The visible side of the Syrian–Israeli arms race is almost designed to stimulate tension, if not actual conflict.

These trends are also apparent in the two air forces. Israel's total fighter strength climbed from about 340 main-line fighters in 1973 to about 760 in 1982, although many were in reserve or acting as trainers. Israel now has about 640 active main-line fighters. Syria, in contrast, increased its forces from about 290 fighters in 1973 to 535 in 1982. Syria now has about 650 fighters—a slight numerical superiority over Israel.

These totals are misleading in that Israel has about 470 very high-quality fighters in its forces while Syria has only 240 medium- to high-quality fighters. Israel has a superb training and operations research capability. Three years of Soviet aid since 1982 have improved Syria's capabilities in these areas, but only from awful to bad.

Israel has far superior air control and warning and C^{3}I capability, and both the 1982 fighting and other recent wars have shown that this is now more important than aircraft numbers or quality. Israel has very advanced air munitions and avionics and is steadily increasing their lethality. Syria is still getting third-rate munitions and export avionics from the Soviet Union.

Syria's SAM belt has had only limited improvement, even with the deployment of the SA-5 and SA-13. Its ground-based C^{3}I has improved, but scarcely enough to keep pace with Israel's postwar improvements in counter measures. The improved Hawk missile in Israeli forces is still far superior to the Soviet SAMs deployed to Syria, in part because Syria still does not have the upgrades to the SA-6 deployed to Warsaw Pact forces and is using obsolete SA-2s and SA-3s.

Israel will face major problems in finding the money it needs to pay for new equipment. It will probably need to double its military aid from the United States to an average annual level of $2 billion in real terms over the next decade. Even then, Israel can never hope to increase its edge of superiority to the point where it can invade Syria without major losses or recover the freedom of action it enjoyed in 1967.

Nevertheless, Israel probably will increase in military capability relative to Syria and any other Arab forces for the next decade. Syria too will need massive additional amounts of annual income to make its forces effective. Although it pays substantially less for most of its Soviet equipment than Israel pays for U.S. and Israeli equipment, Syria will need additional funding of over $2 billion annually to provide the manpower quality, infrastructure, C^{3}I equipment, and technology base needed to compete with Israel. It is highly unlikely to get such resources. It is equally unlikely to get the outside training and technology, or the improved internal organization and depoliticized command structure, that would be vital to success. Syria can get bigger, but its major problems are not in mass but in quality. Syria has few, if any, prospects of gaining the ability to acquire and use advanced military technology with the same skill and integration as Israel.

There is no easy way to prophesy whether these trends will lead to another war between Syria and Israel. Many political and military analysts currently feel that Israel suffered enough from its defeat in "Operation Peace for Galilee" so that it will be extremely reluctant to engage in combat. They feel that Israel also faces an increased risk of attacking Soviet advisers (some of whom it has already killed in air attacks on the Biqa' Valley). They feel, too, that Israel faces the practical dilemma that only a massive all-out attack can hope to be decisive enough to change Syrian behavior and justify the loss of technical and tactical secrets that is inevitable in any Israeli use of its "edge" in technology and training.

In contrast, a number of senior Israeli officers and strategists see a major war as almost inevitable. They feel that Israel cannot tolerate a Syrian drive toward military parity and will eventually have to act to defend its "edge" of military superiority. They agree, furthermore, that any major Israeli offensive, or even attack on Syria's air defenses and air power, would be justified only if it were far more intense and decisive than the 1982 fighting.

The military dynamics shaping any perceived Israeli need to attack Syria are at best confused. The Soviet Union has transferred at least $3 to $3.5 billion worth of major weapons to Syria since the 1982 fighting, but it has been grindingly slow in giving Syria large-scale transfers of advanced military technology. Moscow seems to want to avoid being embarrassed by any more easy Israeli victories, but it is confining its technology transfers to relatively simple items like the T-72 tank and SA-13 surface-to-air missiles; older generation C^3I systems, radars, and electronic warfare equipment; and "export" or stripped-down versions of current systems. It has provided some MiG-25s and at least some MiG-23s with more sophisticated avionics and munitions than the stripped-down MiG-23s that performed so poorly in 1982, but it has made only token deliveries of high-visibility systems like the SS-21 and SA-5 and still controls the maintenance and even operation of key technologies. The Soviet Union has improved its advisory effort, but there are strong indications that it regards Syrian progress as slow and has limited respect for the Syrian high command or Syrian organizational and training capabilities.

Syria, in turn, is experiencing growing external and internal problems in funding its defense build-up. Its improved field and exercise training has been partially offset by growing internal problems in the top command levels of its regular and security forces, and it is still hurt by a low-level succession crisis. Other Arab countries indicate that Syria has remarkable problems in applying its considerable scientific and engineering resources to improving its military forces, and Western European arms firms indicate that Syrian efforts to buy Western technology reflect both relatively unsophisticated planning and obvious problems in obtaining many items commonly deployed in Soviet forces.

If these dynamics continue to characterize the Syrian military build-up, they will reduce any Israeli military need to take preemptive action or escalate any clash with Syria. Nevertheless, one should not dismiss the feeling within the Israeli Defense Forces that another war is likely. Any sudden catalytic increase in Soviet technology transfers to Syria could be particularly important in triggering a new conflict, although the visible cause would undoubtedly be political.

In any case, the current Syrian build-up is creating a situation where Israel has a growing incentive to act either in a very limited manner or on a massive and decisive basis. The more Syria improves in qualitative terms, the more Israel will be forced to suddenly escalate to an all-out attack rather than risk exposing its tactics and technical secrets in a low-level conflict. Syria and probably the Soviet Union lack the sophistication to understand this, and this might well lead to major political and military miscalculations.

Some form of low-level guerrilla war seems likely to continue, but Israel may now be experiencing the worst phase of such conflict it is likely to experience for some years. The Lebanon problem has certainly been extremely costly for Israel, but it is far from clear that any major element in Lebanon will challenge Israel now that it has withdrawn to a narrow, primarily Christian-controlled, belt along its own border. As the United States has learned at great cost, first prize is staying out of Lebanon, second prize is having your opponent stay in Lebanon and suffer the consequences, and losing is getting involved in Lebanon. Neither the Shi'a nor the Druze seem likely to sustain attacks on Israel once they again control their own territory or can turn to trying to secure their own interests within Lebanon.

At the same time, the PLO's military elements remain wretchedly led and organized and the PLO shows no sign of rebuilding its regular military forces or of creating effective forces and tactics for guerrilla war. The PLO's forces now total about 17,000 men, but they are divided into twelve factions. The largest, Al-Fateh, has about 8,000 men but is the worst trained and led for the kind of low-level warfare that might succeed.

Another 8,000 to 17,000 men and women have some kind of training or organization for "freedom fighting" or "terrorist" military actions, but only about 200 seem to have the kind of advanced training that would allow them to act. These are virtually all outside Israel and the West Bank and too visible to avoid eventual detection or reprisals, and they lack a popular Arab base in Israel or the occupied territories. While Israel would have far more severe problems in dealing with any organized violence which was endemic to the West Bank, there seems to be little immediate prospect of such a conflict.

The irony of the PLO's attempts to use force is that these do far more to block any U.S. or moderate Israeli dialogue with the Palestinians and to block any movement toward a just peace than to force Israel to the conference table. Every low-level PLO success is worth millions to Israel in aid and is of vast political benefit to movements like the Likud, which favor repression and annexation. The one thing that all the elements in the Arab–Israeli conflict have in common is the ability to be their own worst enemy, but the PLO is more successful in this regard than most.

In broader terms, the shifts in the military balance increasingly constrain the kind of peace that can be achieved on the West Bank and Golan Heights. There are so many barriers to peace that the military build-up is often forgotten. Nevertheless, it is steadily contributing to the problem. Israel's problems of time and space inevitably increase with the range and lethality of the fighters, missiles, and artillery weapons in Arab hands. This makes Israeli access to or control of the West Bank and Golan Heights increasingly critical—particularly its control of key sensor and targeting locations and lines of advance for armor. It also increases the value of keeping any Arab armored, artillery, and missile forces out of the West Bank and Golan.

The arms build-up has not yet created military necessities which preclude a just peace, but it has created the necessity for far more Arab and Israeli understanding and flexibility than have yet been apparent. On the Arab side, these might take the form of leasing Israel the locations it needs for its sensors, keeping the West Bank and Golan free of Arab military forces, and possibly allowing limited Israeli military deployments. At the same time, Israel will need more flexibility and more realism in knowing what it can give up and in limiting any Israeli presence.

Fortunately, technology does offer hope for both sides. New airborne sensors like remotely piloted vehicles (RPVs) or the long-range surveillance and targeting sensor technology being developed for NATO will soon offer a superior alternative to stationary sensors. A dedicated satellite might offer Israel many of the same security features. As the ranges of Arab sensors and arms improve, Israel increasingly also will face a targeting and lethality problem that cannot be solved by control of the ground or "time and space." U.S. transfer of advanced technology to maintain Israel's "edge" in long-range strikes might substitute in part for control of territory.

These, however, are only ideas that might be able to change the current Israeli view. Israel's withdrawals in Lebanon show that it will trade space and key sensor locations for political and military security, but the Golan and West Bank involve far more sensitive issues. At present, the Israeli–Arab military build-up is yet another problem creating new "facts on the ground."

The arms race has no inherent reason to increase the risk of attacks on Arab or Israeli civilians but will certainly increase the lethality of such attacks if they occur. There is no doubt that the potential lethality of Israel's conventional and nuclear strike capabilities against Arab forces will steadily increase during the next five to ten years. So will Arab conventional capabilities against Israel, but the relative increase will be sharply affected by Israel's superior C^3I, targeting, and battle management capabilities. The growth in Israel's ability to damage Arab targets will greatly outpace similar increases in Arab capability.

It is still premature to predict the emergence of a visible Israeli nuclear deterrent, but *Aerospace Daily* has recently revealed a massive increase in

Israeli nuclear capabilities. Certainly, no Arab state can seriously talk about defeating Israel without considering the implications of a sheltered Israeli nuclear capability.

At the same time, improvements in conventional weapons, munitions, and technology will allow both Israel and its Arab opponents to be more selective in destroying military and civilian targets. Aircraft and missiles will steadily increase in range and payload. Remote sensors will improve targeting. The probable proliferation of gas warfare, improved cluster and Fuel Air Explosive munitions, "smart" bombs and minelets, and earth penetrators will increase lethality.

Hopefully, this will act to establish a process of mutual deterrence. Pragmatically, the impact of the steady increase in area, hard target, and point target killing capability will depend on politics and each side's understanding of the other's ability to escalate. Just as there are no "offensive" or "defensive" bullets, there are no "deterrent" or "aggressive" technologies. The ability to kill purely military targets without collateral damage will probably increase in direct proportion to the ability to kill civilians and destroy economic facilities with deliberate intent. No one can predict intent. The only thing that is certain is an increased ability to kill.

The socioeconomic dynamics of the Arab–Israeli arms race are equally complex. There is no question that this military build-up is imposing severe social and economic costs on Israel and Syria, and to a lesser extent on the Arab world. The questions for Israel are whether it can cope with the economic burden of substituting advanced technology for manpower and force size, whether it can regain its military freedom of action in the face of the political and social backlash from "Operation Peace for Galilee," and whether it can obtain massive long-term grants from the United States.

The issue for Syria is whether it can find equal or greater financial resources and some means of obtaining and absorbing high-technology weapons with far greater speed than it has in the past. As in the case of Israel, it is uncertain whether Syria's political, economic, and cultural structure can bear another decade of military competition at current levels, and whether it can obtain sufficient aid from other Arab states.

There are no easy answers to these questions, but it is obvious that both nations are on the edge of socioeconomic crisis because of the strains imposed by the arms race. This, unfortunately, is just as much a recipe for irrational or preemptive action or a military stalemate as it is for peace.

The stalemate option deserves particular consideration because it is now the most likely alternative to a sustained build-up. For all the occasional rhetoric, both sides have tremendous flexibility in making temporary reductions in their current arms expenditures and still maintaining the arms race. The chance of actual national bankruptcy on either side seems virtually negligible, and social strains and internal politics are likely to be the critical uncertainties. Unfortunately, there are very few examples of nations blundering into peace through exhaustion, and most of these historical examples are similar in duration and cost to the Hundred Years War.

Time is on no one's side. In summary, there is little prospect that the arms race will end. On the other hand, there is no inevitability about its leading to ungovernable levels of conflict. For all the occasional Israeli rhetoric about a massive unified Arab threat and Arab rhetoric about Arab unity, joint Arab action against Israel seems even less realistic in the near term than it has been since Camp David. If anything, the Arab–Israeli military struggle is likely to be contained to one between Israel and Syria with occasional Palestinian and Lebanese sideshows.

One conclusion can, however, be drawn from the current trends, and that is that time is on no one's side. Israel has no prospect of gaining enough military strength to provide security without some form of conflict and a constant social and economic struggle to feed its military machine. Syria has no hope of transforming its search for military parity into regaining the Golan or dominating the region, and runs the risk of triggering another war. Military action by the Palestinians or Lebanese can only make their respective situations worse.

The United States can only suffer if it continues to provide military aid to Israel without a more forceful search for peace. The Soviet Union has no real hope of expanding its present "spoiler role" to dominance over some Arab state, and runs an increasing risk of becoming involved in conflict or sustaining another blow to its tarnished reputation as a source of arms and military advice.

Whatever arms increases do to the Arab–Israeli military balance over the next decade, it is clear that they will make the current situation worse. There is no light at the end of this particular tunnel. There is only a gathering darkness.

PART SEVEN

Priorities for Arab Studies

18

Social Science Research and Arab Studies in the Coming Decade

John Waterbury

At a minimum, Arab studies are devoted to societies in which Arabic is spoken by the majority of the population, and which share in different measure some common sense of history, "national" origin, and perhaps religion. For my purposes, I wish both to narrow and to broaden these terms of reference. They will be narrowed by reducing Arab studies to consideration of social science research only, and broadened, at least by implication, to include all the Middle East.

The record of social science research in the Middle East and the nature of Middle Eastern studies are intimately and unhappily linked. By and large, social science research in the Arabic-, Turkish-, and Persian-speaking parts of the Middle East has failed to produce innovative or pathbreaking results. The record in Israel has been somewhat more distinguished. I will try to justify this assertion below, but for the moment I hope that it will be taken on faith.

The reason for the failure probably stems from the very process by which outsiders have acquired the skills to carry out research in the area. The entry fee is high. None of the dominant languages spoken in the region is readily accessible to non-natives. The amount of time invested in mastering any of the four major languages is enormous. But the supplicant cannot ignore European languages in which much of the contemporary social, economic, and political history of the region has been written. As a consequence, the Middle East may attract a peculiar kind of social science scholar: one who comes first to the area and only secondarily to the discipline (political science, sociology, anthropology, psychology) that structures the research. The outsider must have felt some pull of the region that predisposes him or her to fasten on what are perceived to be its unique cultural characteristics. Prolonged immersion in the language may tend to reinforce the preoccupation with the area *qua* area.

By contrast, one finds that area studies focusing on Latin America, Sub-Saharan Africa, and South Asia have been far more productive in generating findings and paradigms of relevance to their disciplines as a whole. This statement certainly needs qualification when one thinks of the vast but somewhat *sui generis* literature on Indian caste, but its basic thrust seems to me defensible. The difference in social science production stems from the greater accessibility of these areas to social scientists. Mastering the basic language of government and research is generally not difficult: French, Spanish, Portuguese, and English have not constituted formidable barriers to Western social scientists. Consequently, we tend to find scholars with strong social science interests at the outset, who then use an area as a venue for testing various propositions and hypotheses. Because they are not quite so caught up in the cultural uniqueness of the regions they work in, they tend also to have a greater sensitivity to issues of comparison across cultures.

It would be foolish to push this argument too far. There have been many social scientists who have come to Middle Eastern studies with their tool kit in hand, so to speak. One thinks of Morroe Berger, or Clifford Geertz, or Janet Abu Lughod, among several others. Each paid a price in coming late and perhaps superficially to the predominant language in the region. Other social scientists, like Daniel Lerner, have made no claims to linguistic competence and skimmed rapidly, although not unproductively, over the area. All in all, however, I would argue that the Middle East and the Sinitic cultures of the Far East have exacted a high price for entry and have tended to attract scholars whose devotion is to the area itself rather than to their disciplines, and that in consequence the contemporary social science scholarship dealing with them has tended to be imitative, occasionally deficient, and all too frequently uninteresting.

One should note also that comparison among cultural and linguistic segments of the Middle East itself has not been very frequent. The major figures that have attempted such bridging have been of the orientalist tradition, whether or not they accept that label. It has been rare for social scientists to attempt similar leaps: Leonard Binder and the thoroughly undisciplined Charles Issawi are notable but not unique exceptions. Indeed, Issawi should not even be mentioned here, as he was raised in one of the languages that the outsider must acquire painfully, late in life.

I find this general state of affairs distressing. First, it may well be that the Middle East *is* unique and that much that transpires within its social confines is explicable mainly or only by reference to itself. I do not share that view, but it would be sustainable only if its proponents were thoroughly conversant with explanatory frameworks developed for other cultural areas. An example may be in order here. Is political corporatism a common feature of contemporary Middle East politics, and if so does it take on a peculiar cast due to the region's cultural makeup? Some Latin Americanists, such as Howard Wiarda and Alfred Stepan, have seen Latin American corporatism as rooted in the region's cultural and political heritage from the Catholic

Church and traditions of Roman law. In areas where this heritage is meaningless, is corporatism of a different nature, or not corporatism at all? Or could it be that Wiarda and Stepan have misunderstood the social conditions giving rise to corporatism? One has to be familiar with their cultural referents before one can apply their constructs to Middle Eastern society. Not so parenthetically, I would note that Robert Bianchi's recent book on Turkish interest groups manifests consistently a fine sense of what is peculiar to Turkey in its corporatist experiments, and what is not.

What is at stake, of course, is the rather hoary question of the rationale for area studies. The leading departments of economics in the United States and elsewhere have resolved the issue for their discipline; there is no justification for an area focus. Economics is economics regardless of culture, race, or creed. One need not and should not go so far. Still, after three or more decades of study funded and guided by area institutes of one kind or another, we are not any nearer to making an explicit, social scientific rationale for carving out one chunk of humanity and treating it in some broad sense as a unit. Do we do it out of convenience or out of intellectual necessity? For my part it is the former, not the latter, that has underlain my own Middle East research.

Having said that, I immediately want to retreat. The Iranian revolution and the more general phenomenon of a militant and politicized Islam cry out for some cultural analysis. The sheer outpouring of literature on the subject in recent years indicates broad-based concern, but it is not at all apparent that we have in hand generalizations and propositions that explain much of what is going on, distinguish among regional variants, or attempt to compare Islamic militancy in some rigorous fashion to say, Protestant militancy in Ireland, or militant Hinduism in India.

The issue of religion and politics is only one among several that call out for careful analysis in terms of regional and cultural specificity, and of basic causality. When is it that we are dealing with factors of style, the garb in which more profound and perhaps not very unique social processes cloak themselves, and when with patterns of individual and group behavior that in fact determine in significant ways the outcomes of these processes? Thus, in the coming decade, I would hope that the old question of "Why Arab or Middle Eastern studies" will be raised and addressed in a systematic way. Part of that systematic way should involve concerted efforts to compare broad social phenomena across cultures—at a minimum within the major subregions of the Middle East, and maximally with reference to other developing societies. The prototypes that come to mind are few and far between: Robert E. Ward and Dankwart A. Rustow's *Political Modernization in Japan and Turkey*, Clifford Geertz's *Islam Observed*, and Ellen Trimberger's *Revolution from Above*, while in no way definitive studies, certainly point in the right intellectual direction.

A partial remedy to the social science problem I have outlined may lie in the relatively new generations of Arab and other Middle Eastern social scientists. Just as the *khawajat* have for the last three or four decades been acquiring language and area experience, so too have the scholars of the region itself been acquiring the training and skills associated with social science inquiry. Comparative advantage in the long run must surely lie with them. Their entry fee into the social sciences is lower than that of the outsider social scientists for language acquisition. Indigenous scholars are born into the language of their society and research. They need some methodological tools that are not too difficult to pick up.

Until recently, the major obstacle has been mastery of English—and for North Africans, French and English—as languages of scholarly discourse. North American universities are liberally sprinkled with Middle Eastern scholars who have successfully mastered English, social science inquiry, and field situations in the Middle East. They are too numerous to cite individually. For an older generation, peopled with the likes of Albert Hourani, Charles Issawi, Majid Khadduri, among many others, the intellectual preoccupation was not so much with social science inquiry as it was with dialogue with the Western orientalists. The focus was on intellectual history and the development of political and economic institutions. Most of this earlier generation came from elite educational institutions and stood at some distance from their own societies. Nonetheless, one should not forget the few figures like the Egyptian sociologist Sayyid Oweiss, trained in the 1950s in the United States in sociology, who wrote his dissertation on a comparison of juvenile delinquency in South Boston and Bulaq, Cairo. He had few imitators among his peers.

The post-war and post-independence generation is much more numerous and considerably more exposed to social science methodologies, but, in many instances, far less at ease in Western cultures and languages. They came to teach in the rapidly expanding universities of their countries and presided over a process in which large numbers of students were superficially introduced to social science issues and techniques. Many, of course, wound up in universities outside the Middle East altogether.

It is to this generation, including Arabs at the beginning and at the end of their academic careers, that the social science future belongs or should belong. It is from them that one reasonably expects the kind of development of indigenous schools of inquiry which Latin Americans have accomplished in all the social sciences. Increasingly, one would expect them to formulate their own set of research priorities. Moreover, as much of the advanced training is now locally administered, one would expect to find, for the first time, the emergence of social science discourse in the languages of the region. In this discourse, the audience will be largely other Arabic-, Turkish-, or Persian-speaking intellectuals. They will be reacting to or trying to stimulate research that has been defined locally and for local consumption. My impression is that something along these lines has already developed in Turkey in the past few decades, and that there is now a considerable body of periodical and book-length research written by Turks in Turkish and addressed, for obvious reasons, to other Turks.

This has not occurred yet in the Arab world. There are beginnings, some more promising than others. Kuwait and the Arab Gulf in general have spawned an important periodical literature in Arabic, devoted to history and contemporary social issues. The Centre for Arab Unity Studies, through its remarkable periodical, *Al-Mustaqbal al-'arabi* fostered social science research in Arabic of the highest order. The Arab League through its specialized agencies has published extensive technical reports to which social scientists have contributed and which they can certainly use in their own research. Specific countries or institutions have, for more or less extensive periods of time, published regularly in the social sciences; there are the long-established journal of the Center for Criminological and Sociological Research at Imbaba, Cairo, and the *Bulletin Economique et Social du Maroc*, now paralleled by a political science journal published by the Law Faculty at Mohammed V University. These and other journals, like the *Journal of Palestine Studies*, are published in English or French and Arabic. Perhaps *L'Egypte Contemporaine* was the pioneer in this respect. The point is that these diverse publications and the institutions that sponsor and fund them may constitute the nuclei for an indigenous, inward-looking Arab social science. Techniques may be borrowed. That is readily apparent in the limited attempts at survey research (in which the American University of Beirut and the American University in Cairo have played leading roles) and the more widespread efforts in demographic analysis. There is something faintly pejorative, perhaps implying escapism, about the term "inward-looking." I think that to look inward may be a good thing at this time, corresponding in some measure to a general mood among the Arab intelligentsia as well as establishing habits of intra-Arab intellectual discourse outside the areas of history, law, and literature, where they have always prevailed.

It may be, but this is much less sure, that the center of gravity for social science research will shift physically from Western institutions to the Arab world itself. After all, through the weight of numbers, most practicing social scientists specializing in the Arab world will be Arab and in the Arab world. One hopes that the institutional infrastructure to support them will follow. It is not really there yet. Kuwait, as it fulfills its 20th-century role as a commercial city-state, may finance an Arab renaissance in the arts and sciences. It is much less clear that Saudi Arabia is ready to do much more than provide physical infrastructure for similar efforts. Iraq and Algeria have the wherewithal and ambition to institute major university systems, but it is likely that the research agenda will be so carefully controlled and censored in both countries that the social sciences will continue to suffer as they do now. At least one traditional center of Western social science inquiry, the American University of Beirut, can barely sustain itself as a functioning seat of learning, much less promote social science research in a near-stateless society.

Egyptian institutions continue to pour forth vast quantities of low-quality research with occasional exceptions. Egypt certainly has the capacity in terms of personnel and institutions to establish a vibrant community of social scientists, but the combination of high salaries in other markets, the lack of any clear policy for higher education, and considerable residual constraints on free and open research may lead to the continual stripping of the Egyptian system of its best and brightest. Similarly, it is more than saddening to watch the precipitous decline of Sudanese universities that in the past provided a reasonably secure home for a small but outstanding group of Arab social scientists.

Thus while the numbers may lie in the Arab world, it is not at all certain that the best research will be undertaken there. My own impression is that in general the political constraints on social science research have never been stronger. Indeed, even in Turkey, which had moved the furthest in establishing an autonomous social science tradition, the last five years' military rule and repression have sapped the morale of intellectuals and driven many into jail or mental torpor, or out of the country. One is hard put to discern any liberalizing trends in the Arab university world, except perhaps in Egypt. It is significant that the recent founding of the Arab Political Science Association took place in Cyprus; the association is in fact the offspring of the conference on "The Crisis of Democracy in the Arab World," held in Cyprus in November 1983. Something substantial will have changed when this, or any other professional association in the social sciences, can hold its meetings openly and without political interference in a major Arab capital. I do not believe that that day is close at hand. Consequently, I tend to think that Arab social science research that attracts favorable attention will continue to be done "offshore."

I hope I am wrong. What might dissipate some of my pessimism would be the strengthening or creation of financially autonomous research centers, affiliated where possible to universities. This is the model followed in Latin America, with remarkable results in countries like Chile, Peru, Mexico, and Argentina. The centers have attracted outside funding over the years from foundations such as Ford or the Federal German foundations. They have never been fully insulated from the political traumas of their societies, but they have endured and provided a beacon, albeit flickering, for academic freedom. They have also fostered some fine indigenous scholarship and problematics that have traveled fairly well to other developing countries. The Arab world could certainly use some beacons of that kind.

Whether or not the major centers of Arab Middle Eastern research in the West are eclipsed by the growth of such centers in the Middle East, there is another kind of eclipse taking place to which "old hands," both Arab and non-Arab, have not paid sufficient heed. Much of the best research within the social sciences, or at least speaking directly to the social sciences, has not been carried out within the context of regional centers or even universities at all, but rather within the context of technical assistance and foreign and regional aid. Much of the research is commissioned, and a good bit of it is never made fully public. Nonetheless, it is there and it is important. Those who are carrying it out occasionally come from within our own ranks, causing some of us considerable misgivings about the propriety of doing applied research for the aid and technical assistance arms of major Western powers. Some similar research is carried out for the major Arab development funds. I myself have participated in such research and do not have grave misgivings about it—as I would about research sponsored and funded by intelligence-gathering bodies. The kinds of questions that are addressed in this research are crucial to the social sciences including economics.

Let me outline some of these questions through reference to specific research projects known to me. Much of the most interesting applied research has focused on the rural world. Colorado State, for instance, has carried out extensive micro-surveys of on-field water use in Egypt, a subject astonishingly neglected by anthropologists heretofore. Rick Huntington and Sohair Mehanna, among others, have begun to remedy that situation. The World Bank in Sudan, through its multi-volume study for rehabilitating the Gezira scheme, has produced probably the most extensive analysis extant of that project. In a number of countries, studies have been conducted for the reorganization of rural credit systems, cooperative boards, and local development finance. Other projects have produced studies on range management, cattle-marketing, rural labor markets, off-farm employment, and so on down a very long list. Urban studies have focused on low-cost housing, public transport, waste disposal, potable water, and sewage. Entire industrial sectors have been studied from the point of view of their management, financial accounting, marketing, labor relations, and product lines.

In many ways this type of research constitutes base-line studies that speak directly to core concerns of the area specialist: cultivator behavior, calculation of risk, class formation, state capacity, and so forth. The problem is that it is carried out parallel to the research undertaken by area experts, and it is frequently conducted by persons with little area expertise. That is not always the case. Many indigenous scholars have participated in these projects as consultants either to their governments or to the project itself. A number of foreign experts also have participated in them. In my view there has not been enough systematic communication between university-based research and project-generated research. The pay-offs of such communication may be not only significant but sometimes unexpected.

I am reminded of the U.S. agricultural expert on animal husbandry who knew nothing of Moroccan culture or social organization, but who noted that Moroccan sheep have poor herding instincts. He guessed that that fact would have direct implications for the division of labor in Moroccan villages, and that cross-breeding with Spanish sheep, whose herding instincts are more pronounced, might lead to far-reaching redeployment in village labor. I cannot of course comment on the accuracy of his views; but what is clear is that he came to the subject with a very different eye than that of an anthropologist and immediately fastened on to a phenomenon of potentially great significance.

In our own professional gatherings, it may behoove us to seek out and include in our proceedings the non-area experts, or senior investigators in applied research projects that bear directly or indirectly on major social science issues in the Arab world or the Middle East. This now happens on a hit-or-miss basis. Many scholars of the Middle East have strong reservations about such research in the first place. I think that is a question that should be debated, although I doubt that it can be resolved to everyone's satisfaction. But it appears to me absurd to deny ourselves access to an increasingly vast body of research findings, the result of access to data and people which such projects assure but which is not often available to the academic researcher, and which provides information that bears directly and usefully on our own concerns.

Is there a future for the non-native Middle Eastern expert in all this? The answer is, of course, yes, but the role will be different in several respects. If there is in fact a substantial growth in the body of literature in Middle Eastern languages dealing with the social sciences, not to mention history and the arts, then it will be important that we continue to have non-natives who can understand and absorb that literature and communicate it to wider audiences of social scientists and students. One hopes that there will continue to be room for individual non-native scholars to carry out their own research in the area, but questions of affiliation to local institutions and collaboration with local scholars will rightly take on greater importance.

Finally, I still firmly believe that it is important to see through the outsider's eye. The outsider does not necessarily accept the givens inherited by the insider; he or she deals frequently with a different set of research priorities and may be more effective in communicating with audiences outside the Middle East itself. Indeed, by the same token, I hope that we will finally see Arab and other scholars from the developing countries who study societies other than their own. It is understandable that Middle Eastern scholars, or African scholars, or Asian scholars, study their own societies to the exclusion of all others. After all, their comparative advantage lies in such studies. But too often they deny themselves the analytic insights provided by systematic cross-cultural and cross-system research.

The United States awaits its Middle Eastern de Tocqueville, and when he or she comes I hope it will not be alone. There is an Upper Voltaic anthropologist who has lived among and published a book in French on the Eskimo. He is pictured on the cover with his black face wreathed in an enormous fur parka. Whether he intended it or not, he has made a dramatic disciplinary point. Western or any other societies should be open to scholars of the Middle East, and if they avail themselves of the opportunities for cross-cultural research, they will sharpen and enrich their research on the area that most concerns them.

When we talk of the social sciences, we have in mind, inevitably and without apology, an epistemology that is rooted in a Western tradition of scientific investigation and discourse. The approaches have of course never been the preserve of the West, nor has the West always honored the precepts of this discourse. Flat-earthers and creationists of various sorts have been abundant and continue to abound in Western society. Perhaps the age of reason, enlightenment, and positivism will amount to no more than an interesting anomaly in the course of human affairs. In his 1975 book *The*

Human Prospect, Robert Heilbroner speculated rather gloomily on the future of post-industrial societies in these terms.

> It is therefore possible that post-industrial society would also turn in the direction of many pre-industrial societies—toward the exploration of inner states of experience rather than the outer world of fact and material accomplishment. Tradition and ritual, the pillars of life in virtually all societies other than those of an industrial character, would probably once again assert their ancient claims as the guide to and solace for life. The struggle for individual achievement, especially for material ends, is likely to give way to the acceptance of communally organized and ordained roles. (p. 140)

If Heilbroner is at all right, then the philosophical underpinnings of contemporary social science research may gradually erode in post-industrial societies before they have even rooted themselves in pre-industrial and industrializing societies. Certainly there is good reason to fear that the intellectual mood is such that the social sciences will never really be given a chance.

The growing quest for cultural purity, authenticity, and the reassertion of basic religious truths does not produce an atmosphere in which social science methods are granted legitimacy. Whatever else we may understand by social science methods, at a minimum we must agree that any question can be asked, any hypothesis formulated, and evidence selected as much as possible in a way that would allow for the rejection of the hypothesis. We must accept the conclusions of carefully conducted research no matter how distasteful they may seem. A social scientist cannot intellectually accept that any question is off limits, and it is in the nature of his or her approach that disagreeable questions, dealing with social and political pathology, will be asked.

An earlier generation of Middle Eastern political leadership did not deny the premises of social science research, but rather sought to guide it, censor it, and turn it to their own purposes. Most of these leaders, typified by Gamal Abdel-Nasser, might have preferred that such research not take place at all, but they were, no matter how authoritarian and repressive, comfortable with the presumed rationalist, positivist, and objective attributes of that kind of research. These men were, after all, leaders of a generation that believed in central planning and allocation of resources, the efficacy of bureaucracies, technocratic management, optimization in policy selection, social engineering, mass secular education, and mass participation in the development effort. C. S. Sulzberger once nicely captured the mental image these leaders summoned up when he referred to Nasser as a "Saladdin in a grey flannel suit."

Many observers of the contemporary Arab world, such as Philip Khoury, Fouad Ajami, and myself, have argued that this generation and its spiritual legatees in Syria and Iraq have had their chance and in many ways lost it. As they die out, fall from power, or change their skins, the Western positivism that they accepted so long as they could put it to their own purposes will itself come under direct challenge. A new era of flat-earthism may emerge in the Middle East in which the epistemology underlying social science inquiry may well be rejected as a culturally alien importation, a tool of the devil, or at the very least, a tool of the adversaries of Arabs and Islam. If the gates of social scientific *ijtihad* are closed, the closing will not take place everywhere at the same pace or with the same conclusiveness.

Perhaps we shall see at most the manipulation of social science by new orthodoxies to their own purposes, and the crisis of conscience for the social scientist who plays their game will be no more wrenching than that of the social scientists who played the Shah's game. But I suspect the matter will not be so simple. For to whom would these manipulated studies be addressed—to Western audiences outside the area, whose respect is not of particular concern to religious fundamentalists or to those in search of authenticity? To their own intelligentsia, whom they regard with profound suspicion anyway? To the "popular masses," who have been the objects of but never the audience for social science research? To the new elites, who can see no justification, academic or divine, for this kind of intellectual démarche? Probably none of the above.

If social science research is to survive in an increasingly hostile environment, it will be because the state will still engage in planning, resource allocation, and human engineering. If the social scientist can be of use in helping understand savings behavior under Islamic banking, in redesigning school curricula, or in determining the characteristics of the draft-age population, then social science methodology may survive. But certain questions will not be asked, not merely because they are politically sensitive but because they are potentially blasphemous.

Positivists make lousy martyrs; it is in some sense unreasonable to die for reason. So if and when the gates begin to close, there will not be much of a fight on the part of those who would like to see them remain open. What there will be in the coming decade and after is a search for space, an intellectual ground for compromise where faith and science need not threaten or confront each other. The search for authenticity, with its emphasis on the cultural as much as the religious, may come to delineate that ground. The search for what it is that is authentically Arab in terms of basic values, social organization, or economic practices will require use of social scientific tools, and, if the gates do not slam all the way shut, will lead to the development of an authentically Arab research agenda. To conclude in a burst of social science jargon, the excitement that this prospect stirs in me is inversely related to its chances for success.

19

In Search of a New Identity of the Social Sciences in the Arab World: Discourse, Paradigm, and Strategy

El Sayed Yassin

The basic challenge of Arab social science in the eighties can be characterized as the search for a new paradigm after the fall of the ancient one. This is a very complicated process which needs to be objectively understood through the adoption of a global approach in which the particular is studied in the light of the whole. Technical jargon should not replace the epistemological discourse which is necessary for understanding the present course and future developments.

Our approach to the problem is based on three principles. First, discussions of the present position of social science in the Arab world or predictions of its future development can be of value only if they are based on critical analysis of the intensive ideological debate which is going on in the Arab world. Hence, the adoption of a technical approach in proposing a research agenda for the Arab world without putting it in the wider sociopolitical context is worthless.

Second, an epistemological critique of the theoretical and applied practices of Arab social science in the past and the present should be done as a necessary step toward understanding its problems and planning for its future.

Such a critique should concentrate on the analysis of the conflicting Arab discourses and on the debate about the prerequisites and conditions of the new paradigm of Arab social science after the fall of the old one. We have in this context three basic controversies: the Marxist versus the functional; the Arab versus the Western; and the Islamic versus the non-Islamic (whether this non-Islamic is described as Western, foreign, positivist, or alien).

Third, the classification and analysis of the conflicting Arab discourses and the epistemological critique are not sufficient to elaborate a futuristic outlook about the development of Arab science. An alternative concept of strategy should be formulated to be applied in the Arab world. This concept would have the basic function, among other functions, of conditioning the theoretical and applied practices in Arab sciences and, more important, would set out the research agenda.

The Conflicting Discourses in the Arab World

There are several ways of "reading" ideologies. One may assert that the analysis of text, or of the discourse which reveals a specific ideology, has developed as an area of research in the last three decades. Structuralism, semiology, and structural Marxism are basic schools of thought which enriched the study of ideology. The names of Roland Barthes, Althusser, Michel Foucault, Derrida, and Kristeva are the most representative of scholars whose works are the sources of new concepts, approaches, and theories.

The analysis of discourses used by the French philosopher Michel Foucault is one to analyze ideology. By discourses Foucault meant "organized bodies of knowledge and practice in their spatiotemporal articulation." Certain discourses may reveal the existence of a specific *episteme* (a term used by Foucault to indicate the existence of a more intricate set of relations).

The terms discourse and *episteme* are frequently regarded as idiosyncratic expressions for the more common terms "discipline" and "world view," but Foucault stresses that these terms refer to a different classificatory scheme. What is important for us is that Foucault's definition of "discourse" combines the analysis of ideas and that of practices. If we are studying, for example, the "liberal discourse" in the Arab world, we should study not only the basic ideas incorporated in this discourse over time and the changes in them, but also the practice of these ideas.

This is a basic methodological principle which is often ignored in the heated ideological debate in the Arab world. Ideologies are defended or criticized as if they were mere ideas, without referring to the historical experience and the practice of these ideas. Thus analysis of the Islamic discourse stresses the basic ideas in Islam, referring to a certain corpus of texts which may differ according to the religious doctrine of the speaker, but it is only rarely that any systematic study of Islamic practice in the past is done. The same criticism may be applied to analyses of the "liberal discourse" or to the "socialist discourse."

The analysis of discourse has been used by the Moroccan philosopher Muhammad Abed El Gabry to present a critical study of the "contemporary Arab discourse," in a book by that name published in 1982. El Gabry appears from his introduction to be very aware of the centrality of the problem of method. He states clearly his choice: he will not limit himself with the conditions specified by certain authors about the application of their techniques or methods. Thus he may not necessarily use the concepts of "discourse" or *"episteme"* as Foucault has used them. That is why in studying the contemporary Arab discourse he focused his attention on the contradictions in the various discourses and rarely referred to practice. He was interested more in measuring internal consistency than in evaluating the living experience.

He divides the Arab discourse into four major parts:

1) The renaissance discourse, which deals mainly with questions related to the reasons for underdevelopment and the conditions for renaissance of the Arab world and with the basic problem of authenticity and modernity.
2) The political discourse, which deals with the problem of religion and the state and the question of democracy.
3) The national discourse, which deals with the questions of Arab unity and socialism and the liberation of Palestine.
4) The philosophical discourse, which deals with establishing the roots of the philosophy of the past and advocating a contemporary Arab philosophy.

I will not discuss in detail this highly intelligent book of El Gabry, which was the introduction to his recent seminal work, *The Critique of the Arab Mind*. Nevertheless, a few critical remarks should be stressed.

Because he has limited himself to a very narrow definition of "discourse," El Gabry seems in his study to be ahistorical (he never studies the historical conditions of the emergence of a certain type of discourse) and also asocial (he is not interested in the conditions for the failure or success of a certain discourse). He is not interested, for example, in the study of the wide popularity of the "Islamic discourse" in the Arab world now. This dialectic between thought and existence, which is basic to any sociology of knowledge, is totally absent from his analysis. To be fair to El Gabry, one should consider his reply: "I am not a sociologist of knowledge; I am studying the discourse from the epistemological point of view."

If we accept El Gabry's classification of the Arab discourse, we may raise some questions, some of them formulated as research problems.

- First of all, is it possible to "impute" (a concept proposed by Karl Mannheim) each discourse to the social groups which adopt it?
- How can the goals of cultural authenticity, Arab unity, social justice, democracy, and the formulation of an independent Arab paradigm be achieved?
- What are the similarities or the differences between competing Arab discourses concerning these goals? What is the likelihood of arriving at a national consensus?

The Fall of the Ancient Paradigm and the Problematic of the Emerging New Paradigm

As an observer of the scene of Arab social science in the last 30 years, I may assert that the ancient paradigm has fallen, and that we are now in the process of creating a new paradigm, a process which is characterized by extreme difference of opinions among Arab social scientists regarding the coming paradigm. It is at the same time a process and a battle of ideas which can be linked to the conflict between the competing Arab discourses.

Before entering into the discussion, let me define what I mean by a paradigm, as well as the characteristics of the ancient paradigm.

We use the term "paradigm" as defined by T.S. Kuhn in his *Structure of Scientific Revolutions*. Kuhn's talk of a paradigm is meant to direct our attention to these common factors, reference to which is required in explaining the behavior of scientists. The question here is, what do the members of the scientific community share that accounts for the communication and relative unanimity of their professional judgments?

Through the notion of a paradigm, Kuhn wishes to isolate several elements.

Shared symbolic generalizations. This meant to cover the basic theoretical assumptions held in common which are deployed without question.

Models. Agreement on models may be agreement either that a particular analogy provides a fruitful heuristic method to guide research, or that certain connections should be treated as identities.

Values. Kuhn takes it that the members of the scientific community will agree that theories ought as far as possible to be accurate, consistent, wide in scope, simple, and fruitful.

Metaphysical Principles. A scientific community will agree on certain untestable assumptions which play an important role in determining the direction of research.

Exemplars or Concrete Problem Situations. What Kuhn has in mind is the agreement one finds within a scientific community on what constitutes the problems in the field and on what constitutes their solution.

It is well known that Kuhn's notion of paradigms has been shown to be systematically ambiguous, but nevertheless, one may use the notion because paradigms, or *disciplinary matrices*, as Kuhn later calls them, do have identifiable characteristics.

The question now is, if we accept in its very general sense the notion of the paradigm, how can we characterize the ancient paradigm of Arab social science?

From my point of view, this is a combination of shared symbolic generalizations, models, values, metaphysical principles, and concrete problem situations. Without undertaking any systematic study, I will highlight some of the basic shared ideas.

- Social science is a Western phenomenon. This idea is related to a basic postulate, accepted by philosophers, historians, and sociologists of science, that science in its origin as well as in its classical modernity (seventeenth century) is essentially Western. This postulate, asserts the well-known Egyptian historian of science R. Rashed of the Centre National de la Recherche Scientifique at Paris, whose influence in such disciplines is considerable, is still conditioning contemporary scientific ideologies. For social science, the story is similar. Sociology was created as a discipline by Auguste Comte, we learn from Western references. It is seldom that Ibn Khaldun is mentioned. The contributions of scholars from non-Western countries are cited infrequently in textbooks tracing the emergence and development of social sciences. In particular, the contributions of the Arabs, the Indians, and the Chinese, are rarely mentioned.

- The idea of a value-free social science has been widely accepted, under the impact of the French school of sociology.
- Empiricism, sometimes in its vulgar forms, has been accepted under the impact of American sociology as the equivalent of "good science."
- A belief in a clear-cut difference between science and ideology has been adopted. The idea that science, especially social science, can be mixed with ideology was never accepted until the 1960s, under the impact of some basic books about the sociology of knowledge.
- Functional analysis has been adopted by political scientists without awareness of its *raison d'être* and function in the context of American political science.
- The ahistorical approach in the practice of sociology led to the involvement of sociologists in empirical studies without paying enough attention to social history.
- A negative attitude, perhaps implicit, toward religion led to the exclusion of religious problems in all their verities from the research agenda. (The sociology of religion in the Arab world is very underdeveloped.)
- The definition of social problems as presented by Western sociology has been adopted without serious critique.
- The commitment of the researcher to a certain political ideology will affect his objectivity.

These are some of the basic features of the ancient paradigm of social science in the Arab world which came under fire starting in the late sixties (I am speaking here mainly about Egypt).

Toward a New Paradigm

The critique of the ancient paradigm was launched under the impact of some basic writings about the rise of the Western sociological theory. Zeitlin's *Ideology and Sociological Theory* was widely read by Egyptian sociologists. Unlike books written about the history of sociology, which applied a traditional approach to the history of ideas, Zeitlin's book presented for the first time the history of sociology as a battle between two competing paradigms: the conservative, defended by Durkheim, Weber, and Pareto, and the radical, defended by Karl Marx. For the first time the true story of the emergence of sociology as a discipline whose function was mainly to defend the status quo, i.e., the capitalist system, was revealed.

From this beginning a series of epistemological questions has been raised. First of all, doubts have emerged concerning the validity of the belief in a value-free social science. In addition, the claim of researcher neutrality toward a research problem has been proven to be a myth. On the contrary, the commitment of the researcher was stressed, and more attention has been paid to the theoretical framework of any research, in which the stand and position of the researcher should be clear.

More importantly, many questions have been raised concerning the appropriateness of postulates, concepts, and models drawn from Western sociology. The Egyptian political scientist Bahgat Korany, in an excellent study on *Underdevelopment and Political Theory: The Case of Foreign Policy Analysis*, quotes a Moroccan scholar, Abdel Baki Hermassi, who stated that these postulates, concepts, and models ". . . represent extrapolations of discrete [European] experiences and that attempts to universalize them beyond the time and place from which they emerged are likely to undermine their plausibility. This is as true of yesterday's Malthusian theory of population, the Marxist theory of the increasing misery of the masses, and the Keynesian theory of unemployment as it is of today's social scientific models of military-civilian relations, political formation, patterns of growth, nuclear family, democratic association, and the like."[1]

The process of formulating a new paradigm has taken at least three major directions: The first is an attempt to build a Marxist paradigm to replace the positivist and functional paradigms. A group of Egyptian sociologists tried to apply a Marxist framework in their dissertations for the M.A. and Ph.D., as well as other works. One non-academic writer (Ahmed Sadek Saad, an old Egyptian Marxist) wrote a history of the Egyptian mode of production applying the Marxist theory of the Asiatic mode of production, which aroused a heated debate about the validity of the framework as being applied to Egyptian realities.

Second, very recently a movement toward the establishment of an Arab sociology began. Evidence of this movement is to be found in some writings and conferences. Representative of these writings is a very important article written by the Tunisian sociologist Abdel Khader Zagal about "Western Schools of Thought and the Social Structures of the Middle East."[2] Zagal tried in this article to use the basic argument by Bryan Turner in his important book *Marx and the End of Orientalism*[3] to criticize the application of both the Marxist and Weberian approaches in studies about the Middle East. He ends his article by referring to Ibn Khaldun, calling for an Arab effort to build an Arab paradigm which may be more appropriate for the study of Arab society.

On the other hand a very important seminar was held in Abu Dhabi in April 1983, organized by the Arab Regional Centre for Research and

Documentation in Social Sciences in Cairo. The basic theme of the seminar is revealing: toward an Arab social science. Of the papers delivered at the conference, the most important was the one written by Nahed Saleh, director of the National Center for Social and Criminological Research. In her paper, "Toward An Arab Social Science: A Study of the Sociology of Methodology," she presents brilliantly the case for the establishment of this science.

It was very indicative that Ahmed Khalifa, who has been the director of the National Center in Egypt for more than 20 years, stated in his opening remarks that after 25 years of experiences in the practice of social research in the Arab world we should ask ourselves: Are we taking the right direction, or have we just relied upon Western theories and imported methodologies, which have not helped us to understand our social problems in depth?

But what is meant by an Arab social science? Dr. Saleh, summarizing the discussion of the seminar, stated that it is an Arab science by its intellectual orientations stemming from our own social history, by its subject matter which is Arab society as the central topic, by its tackling the basic issues in Arab society and not the marginal topics, and by its direction toward serving the interests of ordinary individuals and not of specific social classes, institutions, or limited interests.

The third direction in the process of formulating a new paradigm is presenting the Islamic model to replace the Western, or foreign, or alien models.

We have here several contributions coming from different sources. First of all there are many contributions by eminent Shi'i scholars, like 'Ali Shari'ati, Bani-Sadr, Talkani, and Baker Al-Sadr. On the other hand, there are important writings by Sunni scholars, like Sayyid Qutb, A. 'Awda, and Al-Mawdudi.

Finally, there is a very interesting selection of highly sophisticated Islamic writings by some Pakistani scholars who are fully aware of the concepts and models of Western theory. For example, Sardar, in his important book, *The Future of Islamic Civilization*, applies the systems analysis approach to Islamic civilization. Also Kalim Saddiki applies Kuhn's notion of paradigm to contemporary Islam in order to compare the Islamic and Western models.

These three directions are competing in the process of formulating a new Arab paradigm. And this competition is linked organically to the conflict between Arab discourses.

Toward the Formation of a Strategy of Arab Social Science

As we have said in the beginning, any discussion of the present position of Arab social science, or of predicting its future development, cannot be of any value if not based on the critical analysis of the intensive debate going on in the Arab world. In other words, the struggle over the basic direction of Arab society will affect the theory and practice of the social science, if it is perceived as it should be—as not isolated from society.

The analysis of the conflicting discourses, of the epistemological critique of the ancient paradigm, or of the emerging paradigms are but one task of the Arab social scientists. More important, if we look to the future, is the elaboration of strategy for the social sciences in the Arab world.

In this context we need first to revise the Western concept of strategy to broaden its scope to cover areas which are not dealt with in this concept. Traditionally, defense and national security are the chief preoccupation of strategic studies. But are these also the concerns of the Third World countries?

In an excellent article, a Bangladesh scholar, Abdur Rob Khan, raises this basic question and specifies a general catalogue of problems faced by the Third World countries.[4] These are the following:

- Threats to security.
- Lack of national integration.
- Lack of national consensus.
- Low levels of political development.
- Lack of legitimacy of the state apparatus.
- Unresolved conflicts and colonial legacy.
- Poverty, low level of development, and resource scarcity.

Given the problems and issues of the Third World as outlined above, one may assert that the content of strategic theorizing in the Third World is different from that of the developed West.

Several problems from this catalogue exist in the Arab world. The broadening of the concept of strategy may help in adding these important problems to the research agenda.

Finally, what will be the role of Arab social scientists in the future, in light of the existence of conflict among Arab discourses and the process of formulating a new paradigm?

Here again we agree totally with Khan about the decisive role of building up a national consensus. Social sciences could take a twofold approach in this respect.

First is providing a forum for different shades of opinion and different interest groups, including the policy planners, civil and military bureaucracy, and academic and political leaders. A continuous series of dialogues could be initiated, and the outcomes should be carefully analyzed and fed.

Second, in-depth analyses of national problems and specific policy proposals could be put forward to the policy makers for necessary action. Then comes the question of national security against both internal and external threats.

Taking all these proposals into consideration, it is worthwhile mentioning that a steady movement toward the attainment of the goals of this strategy is going on in some Arab countries. In Morocco there is the Club for Dialogue, which has held several seminars about vital questions, like problems of democracy in the Arab world and the problem of elaborating an Arab cultural project.

In Egypt a Forum for Democratic Thought has been established to discuss the basic elements of a cultural national project, which, as specified in its program, are cultural authenticity, democracy, national independence, social justice, independent development, and the popular struggle against Zionist aggression in the area.

In Jordan also there is a forum for dialogue whose members are businessmen and intellectuals.

Over and above all these tasks the primary goal for Arab intellectuals is to practice a double-edged critique *vis à vis* both the negative aspects in our cultural heritage and all foreign ideologies of domination.

Finally, in the face of a real threat of a free-hand Israel, our major responsibility is to prepare our nation to defend itself and be ready for the confrontation in this protracted conflict.

Notes

1. Bahgat Korany, *Underdevelopment and Political Theory: The Case of Foreign Policy Analysis* (1979), p. 12.

2. Abdel Khader Zagal, "Western Schools of Thought of the Social Structure and the Middle East," *Al-Mustaqbal al-'arabi* 37, no. 3 (1982): 6–25.

3. Bryan Turner, *Marx and the End of Orientalism* (London: G. Allen & Unwin, 1978).

4. Abdur Rob Khan, "Strategic Studies in the Third World: A Suggested Approach," *Biiis Journal* 5, no. 3 (April 1984): 117–35.

20

Middle East Studies in the United States: The Coming Decade

Judith E. Tucker

Middle East Studies in the United States: 1975

The history of Middle East studies in the United States informs the present state of the field as well as the shape of its future. In 1975, while still a graduate student in Middle East history, I worked with a colleague on a survey of the state of the field for *MERIP Reports* which attempted to identify the major institutions and figures in Middle East studies, the sources of research funding, the various uses to which Middle East scholarship had been put, and the dominant epistemological trends.[1] The resulting article was clearly imbued with our own frustrations and even a sense of outrage at the limitations of the field in both an intellectual and a political sense. Nevertheless, despite some oversimplifications and a certain crudeness in our identification of the "power brokers" in the field (both individuals and institutions, to whom, I feel in retrospect, we ascribed far too much consciousness of their aims and means in shaping Middle East studies), three of our major conclusions about the state of affairs in 1975 have stood the test of time.

We found, first, that the field of Middle East studies in 1975 was actually two rather poorly integrated fields. On the one side stood the hoary discipline of orientalism, which had dominated the teaching of Middle East languages, cultures, and history in North American universities ever since the early 19th-century expansion of "oriental" studies. Often ensconced in departments of Semitic languages, orientalist scholars worked with a now well-understood focus on the Islamic "essence" of the Middle East past and applied a methodology centered on textual exegesis. The contours and history of orientalism were subsequently traced, and the consciousness of an entire generation of scholars of the Middle East heightened as a result, by the 1978 publication of Edward Said's *Orientalism*.[2]

Alongside the orientalist discipline had arisen, however, a Middle East specialty in the various social science fields: in political science, economics, sociology, and anthropology, scholars applied the standard approaches and methodologies of their disciplines to the study of the Middle East. In marked contrast to the orientalists, the new breed was not necessarily well trained in the language or culture of the area, but rather stressed the applicability of sophisticated and "scientific" disciplinary tools, developed elsewhere, to the study of the Middle East.

By 1975, these two quite different approaches had been coexisting for over a decade in an often uneasy proximity in the centers for Middle East area studies scattered across the country. Communication between the two groups was poor; mutual comprehension was minimal. Students found themselves in a field without overall coherence; they were liable to graduate as the patchwork products of orientalist-style training in language and culture and social science training in their chosen discipline.

While lacking in internal coherence, the activities of area studies centers did reflect, by and large, the second major feature of the field—its pronounced policy orientation. The various area studies centers—East Asian, Russian, and Latin American, as well as Middle Eastern—were originally established and funded by federal mandate in the late 1950s and 1960s to fill the perceived gap in American knowledge of other cultures of importance to U.S. foreign policy in the postwar period. Most research in the field was funded either by government agencies directly, or by foundations which often received some government funds.[3]

The resulting tendency for research projects with policy relevance to receive funding was only natural: the 1950s Cold War drive to study radical ideologies and the attraction of left-wing movements gave way, during the more sophisticated 1970s, to a more general concern with understanding and documenting the process of social change in the area. The instrumentalist orientation of research in the field, heightened by the limited number of sources for research funds, still meant, for example, that political science research by the early 1970s was focused on the behavior of political elites in the region, a direct and short-term interest of U.S. foreign-policy makers.

Policy-oriented funding intensified the third critical feature of the field: its epistemological backwardness. In a period when Latin American, East Asian, and African studies were undergoing internal critiques of the dominant paradigms in the field, and indeed, in the case of Latin American studies, even charting a new theoretical course with the rise of the dependency school, Middle East studies appeared to be the Rip Van Winkle of the regional studies scene. The standard texts in the field and much of the ongoing research remained imbued with the orientalist emphasis on Islamic essence or the modernization concern with formal political institutions and elites, or both. At the Middle East Studies Association (MESA) annual meeting in 1975, orientalist or modernization approaches dominated most panels. Two or three panels did raise, however, generally for the first time, questions about the study of women, the working class, and alternative paradigms. Still, as of 1975, most of the discourse in Middle East studies in the United States disregarded major theoretical developments in other circles: the physical and intellectual isolation of the field had bred theoretical impoverishment as well as a pervasive malaise especially marked among graduate students. Change of some sort was on the agenda.

Middle East Studies in the United States: 1985

The past ten years have indeed brought significant change to the field. First, the tension between the orientalist and social scientist approaches has diminished appreciably. To some extent, this greater sense of harmony is due to the fact that the social scientists now clearly dominate the field. The weight of Middle East studies in terms of conference themes and published books has clearly swung toward political science, economics, anthropology, and history of a kind that increasingly uses social science methodology. The demands for relevance, enforced by the exigencies of the marketplace, have effected the final transition.

We have also seen in the past ten years or so, however, a certain convergence of the orientalist and social science traditions. Students who received training on both fronts—orientalist language training and social science disciplinary training—have become the new hybrid scholars. Armed with strong language skills geared to textual exegesis, they are able to interrogate textual sources in new ways. Basim Musallam's *Sex and Society in Islam*, for example, is very much a product of the ability to work with texts in the classical Islamic tradition on the one hand, coupled with a firm grasp of the problems and methods of social history on the other.[4]

His method, a fine reading of Islamic juristic texts, owes much to orientalism, but his use of this material to understand the social practice of birth control would appear quite foreign to an orientalist scholar. The techniques of orientalism have thus been harnessed to different ends, a development which continues to lend greater coherence to the field as a whole. As more and more students of the region combine within themselves orientalist and social science training, we can expect this convergence to continue. Ten years hence, the old orientalist/social science division will no longer be a significant issue.

When we turn to the second issue, policy-oriented research, change has not been so significant nor results so net. Funding structures have remained much the same: the U.S. government and a small number of foundations still play the key role in awarding research monies. While the Fulbright program and the Social Science Research Council (SSRC) underwrite much of the research in the field, there has been a visible effort to expand selection committees to include representatives from the younger generation of scholars who, ten years back, were very much on the fringes of the field.

Even more significant, perhaps, has been a change in attitude among people in Middle East studies. We now find a much greater awareness of funding structures and a consciousness of the sensitivity of this issue as witnessed by the activities of the MESA Ethics Committee. Under its mandate from MESA, the committee has been investigating the Defense Intelligence Agency's (DIA) forays into the funding of research and specific projects in Middle East studies.[5] The wisdom of allowing an intelligence agency to set research priorities as well as the question of how such funding looks to people in the Middle East have been raised by MESA members as major issues. MESA also went on record, at its annual meeting in November 1985, as deploring the activities of Nadav Safran, the director of Harvard's Center for Middle Eastern Studies. Safran had organized a conference at Harvard on Islamic fundamentalism, using Central Intelligence Agency (CIA) funding, but neglected to inform the invited participants of CIA involvement. The entire Safran case, which also involved public disclosure that his own research on Saudi Arabia had been funded heavily by the CIA, occasioned a number of newspaper stories, protests from other Harvard faculty, widespread criticism in academic circles, and Safran's forced resignation as director.[6] Such government intervention in the field is certainly not new, but the open and ongoing debate about it is very much a product of the last decade.

If funding structures are little changed, is research still as obviously policy-oriented as it was ten years ago? In the early 1970s, the policy orientation of the field was unmistakable. Of 24 SSRC grants awarded over a two-year period (1972–73), six funded studies of the behavior of elites, both current and historical, in Egypt, Israel, Algeria, Afghanistan, and finally Iran, where the researcher proposed to take on the enviable task of studying the "private life style of Iranian elites."[7] In addition to studies of elite behavior, which jibed very nicely with the policy imperative of understanding those in power, the SSRC also awarded three grants for studies of the process of modernization in Tunisia, Turkey, and Morocco and two grants for the study of women which proposed to focus only on female attitudes toward family planning. Almost half of the SSRC's awards in this two-year period, then, carried direct policy relevance. During the same years, the specialized conferences held in the field also tended toward the practical and policy-oriented end of scholarship; conferences on the development of arid zones, on applications of science and technology in the region, and on prospects for the use of behavioral science were the ones that received support.

Ten years later, in the early 1980s, many of these policy concerns seemed no longer relevant. In the two-year period 1980–81, the SSRC funded 24 individual projects. Among the 24, we find not a single elite study, and nary a mention of modernization. There are studies of women, but none are clearly linked to policy concerns. Certainly some new policy-related themes have emerged, such as the impact of agricultural development in Sudan or a special concern with the formation of Islamic nationalism. Overall, however, we find that the range of research topics has broadened considerably and bears less of the imprint of stringent policy demands.

Topics which reflect a new breadth of interest, such as the history of blindness and the blind in medieval Islam or the political culture of Egyptian workers, also have entered the lists. The broadening of research scope should not suggest, of course, that policy orientation is now absent from funding. Specialized conferences still tend to reflect issues of concern to policy makers. In the early 1980s, the questions of religion and politics and the role of minorities in the Middle East emerged as the two major conference themes as the United States government dealt with Iran and Lebanon. Still, on balance we find a certain expansion and deepening of research topics in this period. The constraints of ten years ago are nowhere so obvious; although research on the region is certainly not entirely free of the test of relevance to policy concerns, the scope of topics funded is much greater, reflecting a growing diversity in both the composition of selection boards and the aims of major funding sources.

The events of the last ten years have been far more dramatic on the epistemological level, where we have seen what approaches a revolution in the use of theoretical frameworks. The old choice between orientalism and some form of modernization theory gave way in the face of sustained critiques and the articulation of alternative approaches. By the late 1970s, the standard paradigms employed in Middle East studies had become the focus of intellectual discontent. First, Said's book on orientalism and Bryan Turner's *Marx and the End of Orientalism* sparked discussion and argument, all of which placed critical consciousness of the orientalist paradigm at the center of the field.[8] Orientalism, as a world view and as an epistemology, never recovered its former innocence. The average graduate student in Middle East studies today is, at a minimum, conversant with the essentialist assumptions of the orientalist paradigm and aware of the arguments about its limitations.

Secondly, modernization theory, which had informed so many of the social science studies of the Middle East, also drew critical comment in the early 1970s. The first major set of critiques came from the "Hull group," an informal association of younger Middle East scholars based in England but followed closely by North American students, who shared a sense of dissatisfaction with prevailing paradigms. Their efforts, collected in several numbers of the *Review of Middle East Studies* published between 1975 and 1978, focused on systematic critiques of the dominant books in the field. The use of modernization theory, as well as orientalism, was attacked as a static, elitist approach which failed to take into account the basic problems of economic relations, social class, and the colonial heritage in Middle Eastern society.[9] The capstone to this critical assault on modernization theory came with the recent publication of Irene Gendzier's book, *Managing Political Change: Social Scientists and the Third World*.[10]

As old paradigms were being reassessed, scholars in the field also undertook the construction of other approaches. The emergence of a number of alternative forums aided this project immeasurably at a time when the boards and pages of journals in the field appeared impervious to change.

The Middle East Research and Information Project, which actually began publication of its *MERIP Reports* in 1971, increasingly drew its authors from the ranks of students in the field in the late 1970s. Issues devoted to labor history, women, and the nature of class formation in the region reflected the new range of methodological and political concerns.

In 1977, a number of professors and graduate students established the Alternative Middle East Studies Seminar (AMESS), a loosely organized body which aimed at providing an intellectual and political alternative to MESA. After a successful national conference on Middle East women held in New York in 1979 in response to the convening of the MESA annual meeting of that year in Utah, a non-ERA state, AMESS functioned primarily as a series of locally based discussion groups in Boston, New York, Washington, Ann Arbor, Austin, and Los Angeles. In 1979, the Association of Arab–American University Graduates and the Institute of Arab Studies in Belmont, Massachusetts, decided to publish a new journal, the *Arab Studies Quarterly*, which from its inception followed an editorial policy of encouraging theoretical creativity. By the late 1970s, then, organizations and journals, albeit with limited resources, had arisen to support the development of different paradigms and the sense of a new political agenda in the field.

What, then, comprised the epistemological revolution in the field? In broadest terms, students of the Middle East began to employ a "political economy" paradigm as outlined in Peter Gran's seminal article published in 1980.[11] In practice, many ways of doing political economy emerged: authors might draw on Marxian class analysis, a mode of production focus, or the dependency perspective. In the course of the last decade, however, the basic political economy approach has received wide acceptance in the field and assumed an ever more sophisticated form. As a first and basic step in this process, a number of broad historical studies of various Middle Eastern countries have appeared: Hanna Batatu on Iraq, Ervand Abrahamian on Iran, Berch Berberoglu on Turkey, and Pamela Smith on Palestine all contributed overview historical studies of the modern period which drew on a basic understanding of economic and social relations.[12] Much of the elementary work still remains to be done, for we lack, for instance, broad studies of the political economy of Syria and Egypt. Still, both the utility and the techniques of the paradigm are now clearly understood and well practiced.

Alongside a general acceptance of the political economy approach, the last decade saw the arrival of the dependency perspective. In its widest definition, dependency analysis inspired studies of the region which sought to situate the Middle East within its global context, to analyze the ways in which the Middle East participated in the evolution of a world capitalist system. In Middle East studies, as in other fields, much work has combined understanding of the broad sweep of global integration and of the specificities of internal class development: authors have been concerned with the intersection and interaction of these two processes. Among the monographs particularly sensitive to the study of this interaction, we mention Peter

Gran's book on the cultural revival in late 18th-century Egypt, Eric Davis' study of Bank Misr, and Suraiya Faroqhi's work on 16th- and 17th-century Anatolia.[13] Roger Owen also has contributed an overview of the Middle East in the nineteenth century, tracing the evolution of the region in response to world market integration.[14] While not all of these authors are North Americans, their work has had great influence here.

The new paradigms have also encouraged scholars to pay more attention to categories of gender and class in the analysis of Middle Eastern society. Scholarship on women, long absent altogether from the field, established a foothold only in the past decade. Progress, however, has been dramatic; at the 1984 MESA annual meeting, one saw an explosion of interest in research on women, demonstrated by the large number of panels devoted to women's economic, social, and political conditions. Written studies which grapple with the question of the meaning of gender in the region have also begun to appear. The pioneering collection of articles on women edited by Lois Beck and Nikki Keddie and the collection of primary sources by Basima Bezirgan and Elizabeth Fernea have been joined by a growing number of monographs on women, including those of Vanessa Maher and Susan Schaefer Davis on women in Morocco.[15] The impressive quantity and diversity of current research on women is amply demonstrated in the selections found in the most recent collection, Elizabeth Fernea's *Women and the Family in the Middle East.*[16]

Social classes which had previously been very little studied also have begun to enter the field. The seminal historical work on artisan and merchant classes, André Raymond's two-volume study of Cairo, stimulated interest in the study of the non-elite groups in the population.[17] More recently, a beginning has been made in the study of the formation of the working class. Donald Quataert's research on working-class movements in the late Ottoman Empire[18] and the forthcoming studies by Joel Beinin and Zachary Lockman on the Egyptian working class mark the commencement of serious Middle East labor history in this country.[18] One could multiply the examples of current research on women, workers, and peasants, for the social categories which had been so strikingly absent in standard works on the region are now finding a place in the lexicon of Middle East studies.

The Future of the Field

At least three developments in the field of Middle East studies can be expected to shape the discipline in the coming decade. First, the opening of the field to diverse theoretical approaches, and particularly to the political economy paradigm, has liberated the study of the Middle East from its former myopia. The acquisition of theoretical consciousness is irreversible. Because no one paradigm holds uncontested sway at present, we should expect ongoing debate and a certain openness to theoretical experimentation to prevail. The relevance of work in other fields, in other area studies in particular, is now obvious, and the old insularity of Middle East studies seems quite out of date: greater contact with others and theoretical cross-fertilization appears a given for the future.

Second, in the coming decade, we should witness the coming of age of a generation of scholars who combine disciplinary training with long residence in Middle East countries. Armed with good language skills and sound cultural acquaintance along with the tools and theories of their disciplines, these scholars, who were the graduate students of the last decade, should begin to make their contributions. As a result, we can expect that the concerns of the last ten years with political economy, class, and gender will be reflected in the books of the next ten.

Third, contact between North American scholars of the Middle East and their Middle Eastern counterparts will continue to grow. Increasingly, American conferences are truly international and almost always include participants from the region itself. Many American scholars are now in close touch with their counterparts in the region. Scholars resident in the Middle East will thus have a greater impact on the shape of the field in this country, as their interests and concerns are better communicated and understood. It is too soon to calculate all the effects, but we may expect, for instance, that their greater sensitivity to the political uses and abuses of scholarship will help keep this issue on the agenda.

Will these developments change the field significantly? Certainly we will continue to confront the thorny issue of who, precisely, should set research priorities. The uneasiness surrounding the role played by the U.S. government in funding decisions will not disappear; the entire question of how research in the field should be funded is very much unresolved. The situation in Middle East studies reflects a more general confusion surrounding the proper relationship between the state and academe, a confusion that reaches its zenith in such an historically policy-oriented field.

On an intellectual level, the coming decade should see a further refinement of the political economy paradigm, with particular emphasis on the ways in which one can link the different levels of analysis, that is, integrate the broad sweep of dependency with the fine brush of class analysis. There is little doubt that the future will multiply the number of studies of the political economy of the region, both past and present. One also perceives a growing awareness, however, that the traditional concerns of political economy with the economic, social, and political systems of the region have, by and large, led to neglect of the cultural sphere. Most of the dramatic changes in the field have not affected the ways in which we understand Islam or the broader cultural and ideological dimensions of life. While the orientalist vision of a monolithic and all-determinant cultural essence has been generally rejected, we lack an articulated alternative framework for the study of culture in Middle Eastern society. This question, perhaps above all others, will help define the agenda for Middle East studies research in the coming decade.

Notes

1. See Peter Johnson and Judith Tucker, "Middle East Studies Network in the U.S.," *MERIP Reports* 38 (June 1975): 3–20.
2. Edward Said, *Orientalism* (New York: Vintage, 1978).
3. The lion's share of grants to U.S. scholars for research in the Middle East came from two sources: the U.S. government Fulbright-Hays program, administered by the U.S. Department of Health, Education and Welfare, and the Social Science Research Council, which in turn received an important part of its funding from U.S. government agencies and departments as well as private foundations. For details of funding patterns, see listings in the *Middle East Studies Association Bulletins*, 1971 to 1975. For SSRC funding, see the Social Science Research Council *Annual Reports* for the same years.
4. Basim Musallam, *Sex and Society in Islam* (Cambridge: Cambridge University Press, 1983).
5. *MESA Newsletter*, Winter 1985.
6. *MERIP Reports* 136–37 (October–December 1985): 33–34; *MERIP Middle East Report* 138 (January–February 1986): 38.
7. For these and other listings of SSRC grants, see the SSRC *Annual Reports* for the years concerned.
8. Bryan Turner, *Marx and the End of Orientalism* (London: Allen and Unwin, 1978).
9. See, for example, Joanna de Groot, "Empty Elites or the Perils of Political Science," *Review of Middle East Studies* 3 (1978): 105–119.
10. Irene Gendzier, *Managing Political Change: Social Scientists and the Third World* (Boulder, CO: Westview Press, 1985).
11. Peter Gran, "Political Economy as a Paradigm for the Study of Islamic History," *International Journal of Middle East Studies* 11 (1980): 511–26.
12. Hanna Batatu, *The Old Social Classes and the Revolutionary Movements of Iraq: A Study of Iraq's Old Landed and Commercial Classes and of Its Communists, Ba'thists, and Free Officers* (Princeton, NJ: Princeton University Press, 1978); Ervand Abrahamian, *Iran Between Two Revolutions* (Princeton: Princeton University Press, 1982); Berch Berberoglu, *Turkey in Crisis: From State Capitalism to Neo-Colonialism* (London: Zed Press, 1982); Pamela Ann Smith, *Palestine and the Palestinians, 1876-1983* (New York: St. Martin's Press, 1984).
13. Peter Gran, *Islamic Roots of Capitalism: Egypt 1760-1840* (Austin, TX: University of Texas Press, 1979); Eric Davis, *Challenging Colonialism: Bank Misr and Egyptian Industrialization, 1920-1941* (Princeton, NJ: Princeton University Press, 1983); Suraiya Faroqhi, *Towns and Townsmen of Ottoman Anatolia: Trade, Crafts, and Food Production in an Urban Setting, 1520-1650* (Cambridge: Cambridge University Press, 1984).
14. Roger Owen, *The Middle East in the World Economy, 1840-1914* (London: Methuen, 1981).
15. Lois Beck and Nikki Keddie, eds., *Women in the Muslim World* (Cambridge, MA: Harvard University Press, 1978); Basima Bezirgan and Elizabeth Warnock Fernea, eds., *Middle Eastern Muslim Women Speak* (Austin, TX: University of Texas Press, 1977); Vanessa Maher, *Women and Property in Morocco: Their Changing Relation to the Process of Social Stratification* (Cambridge: Cambridge University Press, 1974); Susan Schaefer Davis, *Patience and Power: Women's Lives in a Moroccan Village* (Cambridge, MA: Schenkman, 1983).
16. Elizabeth Fernea, ed., *Women and Family in the Middle East* (Austin, TX: University of Texas Press, 1985).

17. André Raymond, *Artisans et commerçants au Caire au XVIIIe siècle* (Damascus: Institut Français de Damas, 1974).

18. Donald Quataert, *Social Disintegration and Popular Resistance in the Ottoman Empire, 1881–1908: Reactions to European Economic Penetration* (New York: New York University Press, 1983).

19. Joel Beinin and Zachary Lockman, *Class and Nation: Workers and Politics in Egypt, 1899-1954* (Princeton, NJ: Princeton University Press, forthcoming).

21

Futurology and the Study of the Arab World

Elia T. Zureik

It is customary to divide the evolution of Arab social science into three phases. The first was a colonial, pre-independence phase, in which orientalism and cultural ethnocentrism shaped most of what passed as Middle East "scholarship"; central to this tradition were the works of anthropologists, historians, and philologists whose mission consisted mainly of interpreting indigenous cultures in order to advance the policies of the colonial powers of the day. Next came a post-colonial phase, which emphasized the need to decolonize Arab social science by adopting critical approaches which questioned the basic premises of Western social science regarding the core values of pre-industrial societies in general. This in turn has led to what I shall call, for the lack of a better term, a contemporary social science intended to reflect the maturity of independent colonial states and to make use of the sophisticated methodologies associated with advanced industrial societies.

My fear is that the lingering influence of colonialism at both the cultural and economic levels is now being extended and in a sense strengthened by the importation of an empiricist research tradition that has the appearance of science, with its utilization of computers, prediction techniques, policy analysis, and the like, but whose premises remain entrenched in Western intellectual experience. It seems that the critical post-colonial interlude, which has seen numerous attempts at incorporating on a large scale variations of Marxism from the Eastern and Western blocs, has not led to the development of an indigenous social science capable of addressing the issues at hand. What is needed, I believe, is a revival of the debates that ensued in the post-colonial phase in order to assess what prevented the development of an authentic social science. I hope that this presentation will provide a contribution to the formulation of what I shall call emancipatory methodological considerations for the study of the Arab world.

The Arab world's development problems clearly remain unsolved. Its experiments with both capitalist and socialist models have been resounding failures; the notion of representative government of any kind still eludes every contemporary Arab regime. Furthermore, it is unlikely that the current much-publicized flirtations with religious fundamentalism will bring the Arab world any closer to workable participatory democracy than they did in Iran. On the contrary, the spread throughout the Middle East of primordial politics rooted in religion, ethnicity, and close kinship structure is bound to exacerbate endemic cleavages and conflict, the price of which will be paid by the Arab societies themselves.

The Arab world is a conglomeration of rich and poor states, where the annual per capita income ranges from a high of $16,000 in the oil-rich Gulf states to a low of $200–$300 in countries such as Sudan and both Yemens. It is a world in which the most affluent states rely on foreign expertise to define their needs and execute the so-called development plans; it is a world which is at the mercy of the East and West to supply it with military needs; it is a world which, except for rare cases, treats its women as second-class citizens. In short, the Arab world is really many worlds—worlds which are at odds with each other. And the various institutions which were established to forge some semblance of unity and integration have remained ineffective and fractured, thus mirroring the Arab world itself.

My reading of indigenous and external social science about the Arab world is that, on the one hand, we have the ideologues of the left who have adopted a mechanistic, outmoded brand of Marxist, ruling-class theory of the world, in which history appears to be a series of conspiracies machinated by an omnipotent elite, and in which the masses are portrayed as the dupes of their own false consciousness. At the other extreme, we have the positivists who abstract from the complex world around us a highly simplified version of reality which fits neatly the latest modeling techniques of the day as advanced by systems analysts. In both cases, the human agency as an intelligible and intelligent entity seems to have been sacrificed at the altar of fashionable social science and methodological conveniences.

Let me offer two examples in order to demonstrate my point. First, not too long ago, I had the opportunity to examine a Ph.D. thesis in sociology submitted to a major Canadian university. The thesis dealt with the healthcare delivery system on the West Bank in the context of Israeli occupation. The major finding of the thesis was that Israeli occupation has created economic and political dependency of the West Bank on Israel, which in turn has contributed to a backward health-care delivery system, as measured in terms of per capita physicians, specialists, hospital beds, and other essential health provisions deemed necessary in a normal environment. This finding is useful, but hardly unexpected. No one would have anticipated that an occupying force would be in the business of furthering the well-being of its subject population, particularly when the force represents a country like Israel, which has been busy all along trying to deplete the size of the Palestinian population under its control. It is no coincidence that the current size of the population on the West Bank is almost identical to that which existed in 1967, the year Israel occupied the territories after the Six Day War. Meron Benvenisti, the previous deputy mayor of Jerusalem, demonstrated in his recently released *The West Bank Data Project* that economic stagnation, underdevelopment, land confiscation, and sheer suppression of political rights have led to a large-scale emigration of Palestinians, particularly male professionals, which in turn has contributed to a drastic decline in marriage and birth rates, with population growth on the West Bank standing at near zero.[1]

What I found strikingly missing from this and other similar works in the tradition of dependency theory is a delineation of the cognitive map and world view of the average Palestinian under occupation. In other words, it is terribly important to find out how the average Palestinian copes in his/her day-to-day encounters with oppressive circumstances. How do people living in oppressive circumstances, which are found throughout the Arab world in varying degrees, make sense of the world around them? The dependency school, though useful in highlighting distorted forms of urbanization and economic development, has next to nothing to say about the role of the individual in effecting change. Indeed, when I asked the Ph.D. candidate in question to describe in concrete terms how the average Palestinian patient and his family cope with inadequate health services and how Palestinian medical authorities deal with the constant harassment and obstacles put before them by the occupying forces, the response was silence and bewilderment at such a question.

The genre within which this approach is anchored, namely dependency theory, sees the Arab world (as it does the rest of the Third World) as being constantly molded by a world capitalist system. According to this logic, the Arab world constitutes a periphery to an aggressive capitalist economic order centered in Western Europe and North America. The economic and political retardation of the Arab world is laid squarely at the doors of imperialism and neocolonialism. Whether commentators cite 400 years of Turkish rule or more than a century of European domination, the cause of the Arab predicament as well as its solution is sought solely in external factors. Real or imaginary, imperialism is blamed for the ills of Arab society. But at the same time as the so-called revolutionary Arab regimes are busy condemning the West, they are also frantically attempting to copy and emulate Western technology and know-how—though, I must say, with little success and without the usual anti-imperialist rhetoric.

The second example, which is my main concern here, is drawn from a wider and more established tradition of pluralist and positivist social science. It is this tradition that has made significant inroads in studies about the Third World in general and the Arab world in particular. Systems analysis and structural functionalism have been incorporated into the works of Gabriel Almond, I. William Zartman, Daniel Lerner, David McClelland, and others, to name a few of the founding fathers of comparative politics and sociology. Here a unilinear stage theory of history has been advanced to account for the underdeveloped nature of the Arab world, with the Western experience being considered as the prototype.

While the spread of survey-type research on the Middle East in the writings of established comparative analysts has been hampered due to language, distance, and other cultural factors, a new generation of Middle Eastern social scientists trained in the West is now coming of age and is beginning to apply quantification techniques in the study of their societies. I must say that this fascination with survey research is, on the whole, not making significant contributions to our knowledge about the Arab world, though in certain instances it is highlighting some well-known generalizations about political alienation and the lack of citizen trust in the dominant political institutions and practices of Arab regimes. A great deal of this type of research seems to be carried out in the spirit of what C. Wright Mills calls "abstracted empiricism," i.e., the application of quantification techniques in the study of social facts without situating either the methodology or the findings in a proper historical perspective.

Far from resolving the important issues raised by survey research, positivist social science in and about the Arab world is now pitched at an even higher plateau of abstraction, where simulation techniques, multivariate and factor analysis, and the various versions of forecasting and modeling are being deployed to predict the course of events in the Arab world.

Of the two contending brands, empiricist and positivist social science commands more legitimacy and attention in planning and academic circles, here as well as in the Middle East. I shall consider in this paper the relevance of one influential brand of positivist social science, namely systems analysis and by implication its associated specialty known as futurology (which incorporates simulation techniques, operations research, prospective analysis, conditional forecasting, and other variations), which seems to be making headway in current Arab social science. Positivist social science, which provides the intellectual basis for much of this work and which has come under scrutiny in the West, seems to be gaining ground in Arab intellectual and research circles and appears to be immune to the kinds of criticisms leveled against it by its Western originators and practitioners.

One subject dominated by the futurologists' methods is the study of Middle Eastern elites. In a recent collection of articles in this area edited by Zartman,[2] one author writing very much in the tradition of "abstracted empiricism" singled out no less than 90 analytic and background variables linked to one another in a maze of crisscrossing, reciprocal relationships. The result is more a heuristic exercise intended to test the computer's CPU (Central Processing Unit) and its ability to handle the latest statistical software packages than any genuine contribution to understanding elite behavior either in the Middle East or elsewhere. Consider the following quotation from the same study concerning the relevance of futurology to the study of Palestinian elite behavior:

> At present, the most crucial issue in the Middle East requiring a future study is the Palestine–Israel conflict. Among the Palestinians, the questions range from identification of elites, including the composition of existing groups and the potential for emergence of new elite groups, to the analysis of the whole

range of background, educational, religious, socioeconomic, political, and ideological characteristics and the relations between these and the consequences for society leadership, policies, decision making, political and military action.[3]

A similar approach, though anchored in social psychology and psychiatry, is adopted by, among others, S. Cohen and H. Kelman.[4] In it, the future is viewed as the outcome of a progressive activity, so it comprises the study over time of the personal interaction process among contending parties. Here the Palestine–Israel conflict is reduced to studying the mutual perceptions of *proxy* protagonists (usually Israeli and Palestinian college students and/or academics) examined through laboratory settings, in which simulated encounters are used as the basis from which to extrapolate possible clues as to how political negotiations in real life are likely to progress. Thus, one of the world's most intractable conflicts is abstracted from its historical and *realpolitik* context and is presented in terms of psychological gratifications and personality needs.

It is important to recall that systems analysis and its offshoot, futurology, arose to meet the needs of the (U.S.) military, of bureaucratic apparatuses of the state, and of private mega-organizations. These were basically administrative needs which had to do with the administration of people and things in the context of a bourgeois industrial order. I am using the concept of administration in Foucault's sense,[5] namely, a centralized deployment of power, discipline, and surveillance over people. In other words, this brand of intellectual technology, futurology, is a sophisticated form of social control used by elites and decision-makers in their administrative capacity.

Abstract modeling, to the extent that it is effective (and there are serious questions about its predictive and explanatory power, even in stable political environments), serves the interests of those in control. In the case of the Arab world this means giving more illegitimate power to those who already have it. Whether the result is intended or not, this brand of social science becomes an exercise in furthering the cause of illegitimacy, of unrepresentative political regimes. In its place I suggest a social science approach which helps us understand the way the average Arab citizen copes with her/his social world. This is the world of domination, alien sociopolitical forces, and an international system that is hostile to the Arab people. I am going to suggest, if you will, a critical-interpretative approach which helps us understand not the world of the self-selected member of the elite or the nebulous multilayered structure of social formations but the socially constructed world of the average person. What we need is a social science from the bottom up, so to speak, which would reveal to us the methods of negotiating and coping devised by people in their daily struggles with odd circumstances and unresponsive political environments, and ways to make these coping methods more effective in transforming the social reality to one in which the average person feels that he or she can affect the course of events in society.[6]

It is true that there are those futurologists who reject the claim advanced here that to study the future necessarily implies positing a single preferred outcome. Rather, what makes futurology promising, they claim, is that it enables one to project various conditional scenarios and then apply sophisticated cybernetic feedback analysis in which each possible scenario is weighed in the light of different inputs and outputs, whose patterns of change are monitored over time.[7]

Be that as it may, my point is that the macro-approaches, whether they be of mainstream social science or of the radical types, have a purpose to serve. And this purpose, I believe, centers around defining the general contours of the issues at hand through adopting premises and values of decision-makers imposed from above; because of their ideological basis, these scenarios have little utility in effecting social change at the grassroots level, and for this reason they must be supplemented by micro-studies of the narrative kind in which the human agency is left to tell his or her story.

At the risk of sounding simplistic, let me suggest a revival of the case-study approach with one important qualification, namely, that the starting point of the analysis must be located in a dissolution of the object/subject dichotomy which characterizes a great deal of the positivist case-study research. Instead, it is imperative to adopt a research agenda in which issues and methodological considerations are left to unfold and be defined in the context of the immediate needs of those who are likely to be affected by such research. Here there is room to carry out interesting, innovative, interventionist research through the use of affordable new technologies. Yes, computers can be put at the disposal of peasants, refugees, and community workers in order to tackle the issues of illiteracy and cultural survival and, through two-way interactive systems, to enhance the sharing of experiences by people who face similar oppressive circumstances. Think about it: a personal computer linked via satellite (which would put the Arab satellite in the sky now into good use) to other computers and data banks should be able to provide cheap and accessible information about irrigation, agriculture, health, distance education, and so on. The immediate task is to design the new technology in such a way as to reflect the needs of users in deprived political circumstances. No technology is neutral. Embedded in any technology there are certain social and cultural assumptions, and these affect the design and deployment of any technology with serious repercussions, including the new information and communication technology. In order to ensure that the imported new technology is not grafted onto an unreceptive culture and used to extend the system of control over the citizenry, an input on the level of the user becomes essential. It is here that social scientists can make significant contributions by studying human-machine interaction in an Arab environment with a view to maximizing the benefits to potential users.

It is important to note, in conclusion, that I am not denying *sui generis* the utility of empirical research to the study of Arab or any other social reality. Far from it. My point is rather simple: high-level methodological abstractions have low priority on the agenda of emancipatory social science, since they are of little use to those who are removed from the power nexus in society and who are groping with the pressing issues of democracy, political participation, and economic dependence, which I take to be pivotal for a better understanding of the Arab world.

Notes

1. Meron Benvenisti, *The West Bank Data Project* (Washington, DC: American Enterprise Institute, 1984).
2. I. William Zartman, *Elites in the Middle East* (New York: Praeger Publishers, 1982).
3. Russell Stone, "The Impact of Elites and their Future Study," in Zartman, *Elites in the Middle East*, pp. 196–218.
4. Stephen P. Cohen and H.C. Kelman, "Evolving Intergroup Techniques for Conflict Resolution: An Israeli–Palestinian Workshop," *Journal of Social Issues* 33, no. 1 (1977): 165–89.
5. Michel Foucault, *Discipline and Punish* (New York: Vintage Books, 1979).
6. An excellent representation of what I call emancipatory social science is the work of the sociologist Rosemary Sayigh; see her *Palestinians: From Peasants to Revolutionaries* (London: Zed Press, 1979).
7. It remains to be seen whether the recent attempt by the Beirut-based Centre for Arab Unity Studies to engage in creative scenario construction will yield fruitful results. See *General Theoretical Framework for Prospective Analysis of the Arab World* (mimeographed, ca. 1983) (In Arabic).

About the Contributors

George T. Abed received a Ph.D. in economics from the University of California at Berkeley. He has written and published numerous analytical studies on energy, development, and international finance. Now director general of the Palestine Welfare Association, a Geneva-based development assistance foundation, he was most recently division chief in the International Monetary Fund's Middle Eastern department. Dr. Abed is currently working on a book of essays on the economic development of the occupied areas of Palestine.

Kamal Abu-Deeb is a noted poet and literary critic. He earned a Ph.D. in literature at Oxford University. Currently a professor of comparative literature at San‘a University, previously he served as chairman of Yarmouk University's Department of Arabic. Dr. Deeb is the author of *Min Marathi Armiya*, a collection of his poetry, as well as a number of important works on literary theory and criticism, including *Al-Jurjani's Theory of Poetic Imagery* and *Jadaliyyat al-Khafa' wa-al-Tajalli*. In addition, he translated Edward Said's seminal work, *Orientalism*, into Arabic (*Al-Istishraq*).

Leila Ahmed holds a Ph.D. from the University of Cambridge, England. Currently an associate professor at the University of Massachusetts at Amherst, she recently conducted research as a Bunting Fellow at the Bunting Institute, Radcliffe College, for a book on women in Middle East history. Her publications include a book on E. W. Lane and British ideas of the Middle East in the nineteenth century, and numerous articles on Middle Eastern women published in such journals as *Signs*, *Feminist Studies*, and the *International Journal of Women's Studies*.

Naseer H. Aruri obtained a Ph.D. in political science from the University of Massachusetts at Amherst. His publications include *Occupation: Israel Over Palestine, Enemy of the Sun: Poems of Palestinian Resistance*, and *Middle East Crucible: Studies on the Arab–Israeli Confrontation of 1973* (editor) as well as numerous articles dealing with such issues as human rights, the Palestine question, Lebanon, Islam, and U.S. policy in the Middle East. A professor of political science at Southeastern Massachusetts University, Dr. Aruri is also a former president of the Association of Arab–American University Graduates, editor of *Mideast Monitor*, consulting editor of *Arab Studies Quarterly*, and a founding member of the Arab Organization of Human Rights.

Joel Beinin is assistant professor of history at Stanford University. He is also a member of the editorial committee of *MERIP: Middle East Report*, to which he has contributed numerous articles, including "Marching Toward Civil War," "The Cold Peace," "Likud's New Economic Policy," and "Challenge from Israel's Military." Dr. Beinin received his doctorate in history from the University of Michigan. His book (co-authored with Zachary Lockman), *Class and Nation: Workers and Politics in Egypt, 1936–1954*, is forthcoming from Princeton University Press.

Issa J. Boullata received his Ph.D. in Arabic literature from the University of London. He is the author of over eight books, 29 articles, and many translations, including *Al-Rumantiqiyya wa-ma'alimuha fi al-shi'r al-'arabi al-hadith* (Outlines of Romanticism in Modern Arabic Poetry), *Badr Shakir al-Sayyib: Hayatuh wa-shi'ruh* (Badr Shakir al-Sayyab: His Life and Poetry), *Critical Perspectives on Modern Arabic Literature* (editor), and "Contemporary Arab Writers and the Literary Heritage." Dr. Boullata serves on the editorial boards of *The Muslim World* and *Oral Tradition*, is co-editor of *Mundus Arabicus*, and is a member of the board of the Project of Translation from Arabic. He is also a professor of Arabic language and literature at the Institute of Islamic Studies at McGill University in Montreal.

Anthony H. Cordesman is the Washington vice president of the Analytical Assessments Center, the Eaton Corporation, and an adjunct professor at Georgetown University. He has served in senior posts in the Office of the Secretary of Defense, the State Department, and the Department of Energy. Dr. Cordesman has published extensively on the Middle East and the Gulf; the military balance; strategic issues; defense planning; and large-scale planning, programming, and budgeting systems. His most recent publications on Middle Eastern military affairs include *Jordan and the Middle East Balance* and *The Gulf and the Search for Strategic Stability*. At present, he is completing a study for the Hoover Institution on the Iran–Iraq war and is writing a new series on Middle Eastern military forces for the Royal United Services Institute in London.

Samih K. Farsoun is an associate professor of sociology at the American University. He earned his doctorate from the University of Connecticut. Dr. Farsoun is editor of *Arab Society* (London: Croom Helm, 1985), has contributed chapters to many books, and has written a number of articles for such journals as *Monthly Review, Contemporary Society, Journal of Palestine Studies, Palestine Studies, American–Arab Affairs, MERIP Reports*, and *Middle East Journal*. His research interests include economic and social development, the sociology of the family, and political sociology.

Nadia W. Hijab earned an M.A. in English literature from the American University of Beirut. Previously editor-in-chief of *The Middle East* magazine (London), Ms. Hijab is currently a freelance journalist and information consultant, and comments regularly on Arab affairs on the British Broadcasting Corporation and to independent radio and television. In 1986 she completed a book *Arab Women at Work*, which was commissioned by Cambridge University Press.

Michael C. Hudson is the director of the Center for Contemporary Arab Studies and the Seif Ghobash Professor of Government and International

Relations at Georgetown University. He received his Ph.D. in political science from Yale University. Dr. Hudson is the author of several books, including *Arab Politics: The Search for Legitimacy*, and his 1968 study of Lebanese politics, *The Precarious Republic: Political Modernization in Lebanon*, was reissued by Westview Press in 1985. Dr. Hudson is a member of the editorial boards of the *Journal of Arab Affairs* and the *International Journal of Middle East Studies*. He was president of the Middle East Studies Association in 1986–87.

Ibrahim Ibrahim received his Ph.D. from Oxford University and is currently a research professor of Arab studies at the Center for Contemporary Arab Studies. Among his research interests are the politics of the Gulf states, political theory, and Arab political thought. Dr. Ibrahim's publications include *Arab Resources: The Transformation of a Society* (editor), "The Impact of Arab Expatriates on Social and Political Developments in the Gulf States," "Islam's Struggle Toward the Modern Age," and "The Quest for Scientific Culture in Modern Egypt."

Saad Eddin Ibrahim obtained his doctorate from the University of Washington. He is head of the Arab Affairs Unit of the Al Ahram Center for Political and Strategic Studies and professor of sociology at the American University in Cairo. Currently he is the secretary general of the Arab Thought Forum (Amman, Jordan). Dr. Ibrahim has published extensively in the areas of Middle Eastern sociology and politics, and urbanization in the Arab world. Some of his more recent articles include "A Message from Inside Sabra and Shatila," "What is Happening to the Islamic City," "The July Revolution: Lessons of Failure and Success" (all in Arabic), and "Egypt in the Eighties: A Sociological Profile," and *The New Arab Social Order* (1982) (in English).

Rashid I. Khalidi is an associate professor of history at Columbia University. He received his D.Phil. in modern history from Oxford University. His publications include *British Policy Towards Syria and Palestine 1906–1914: The Antecedents of the Hussein–McMahon Correspondence, The Sykes–Picot Agreements and the Balfour Declaration, P.L.O. Decision-making During the 1982 War*, and *Palestine and the Gulf* (editor) as well as such articles as "The Role of the Press in the Early Arab Reaction to Zionism" and "Social Factors in the Rise of the Arab Movement in Syria."

Bahgat Korany is a professor of political science and director of the Arab studies program at the University of Montreal. He is the senior author of *The Foreign Policies of Arab States* (Westview, 1984) and *How Foreign Policy Decisions Are Made in the Third World* (Westview, 1986). Dr. Korany's book, *Social Change, Charisma and International Behavior* (1976), was awarded the Hauchman Prize for 1976.

Alan R. Richards received his Ph.D. in economics from the University of Wisconsin. He has taught at Harvard University, the University of Wisconsin, and the University of California at Santa Cruz, where currently he teaches and serves on the Board of Studies in Economics. Dr. Richards is the author of many articles which have appeared in journals such as the

Journal of Economic History, MERIP Reports, and the *International Journal of Middle East Studies.* He has also written *Egypt's Agricultural Development: Technical and Social Change, 1890-1980* and *Migration, Mechanization, and Farm Labor in Egypt: Essays in Third World Socioeconomic Change.*

Hisham Sharabi earned a Ph.D. in the history of culture at the University of Chicago. He is a professor of history at Georgetown University and has taught at the American University of Beirut. At present, he is also editor of the *Journal of Palestine Studies.* Dr. Sharabi has written extensively on the Arab world; among his works are *Nationalism and Revolution in the Arab World, Palestine and Israel: The Lethal Dilemma,* and *Arab Intellectuals and the West.*

Michael J. Simpson received his Ph.D. in sociology from Princeton University, where he also served as a lecturer in sociology. He holds degrees from Oxford University and the American University of Beirut. Dr. Simpson was a visiting scholar at the Center for Contemporary Arab Studies at Georgetown University during 1984-86, where he conducted research and analysis on the introduction of modern technology into the Arab world. His other research interests include social stratification and political sociology.

Ismail A. Sirageldin is a professor of population dynamics and political economy at the Johns Hopkins University and visiting professor of international economics at the Johns Hopkins University School for Advanced International Studies. Dr. Sirageldin received his doctorate from the University of Michigan. His major research and professional interests are in the areas of human resource development, economic development and planning, international migration, and population and agricultural development. He is the author of *Population Policies and Development in the 80s: Issues and Puzzles, Saudis in Transition: The Challenge of a Changing Labor Market,* and *Evaluating Population Programs: International Experience.* Dr. Sirageldin is the series editor for *Research on Human Capital and Development,* published annually by JAI Press.

Judith Tucker is an assistant professor with the Georgetown University History Department. She received her Ph.D. in history and Middle Eastern studies from Harvard University, where she completed her thesis, "Women and the Family in Egypt, 1800-1860." Her book *Women in Nineteenth Century Egypt* was recently published by Cambridge University Press. Dr. Tucker's many articles include "Insurrecting Women," "Women and the State in 19th Century Egypt," "Women and the Middle East," and "Women as Male Property: Slaves and Prostitutes in Egypt, 1800-1860." Currently she is working on a study of women in Nablus, the West Bank during 1720-1858.

John Waterbury received his Ph.D. in political science from Columbia University and is currently William Stuart Todd Professor of Politics and International Relations at Princeton University's Woodrow Wilson School. A prolific writer, he has published *The Egypt of Nasser and Sadat: The Political Economy of Two Regimes, The Middle East in the Coming Decade,* "The Implications of Infitah for U.S.-Egyptian Relations," and "Riverains and Lacustrines: Toward International Cooperation in the Nile Basin."

About the Contributors

El Sayed Yassin is director of the Center for Political and Strategic Studies at the Al Ahram Foundation in Cairo. He is also editor-in-chief of *The Arab Strategic Report* and principal investigator on a project on the social history of Egypt conducted under the auspices of the National Center for Social Research in Cairo. Dr. Yassin also teaches on a part-time basis at Ain Shams University, Cairo University, and the American University in Cairo. He obtained his LL.B. from Alexandria University. Among his publications are *Analysis of Arab National Thought, The Arab Personality, Man, Society, and Law,* and *Rich and Poor States in the Middle East: Egypt and the New Social Order.*

Elia T. Zureik is a professor of sociology at Queen's University, Kingston, Ontario, Canada. He is a frequent media commentator on the Middle East. His works have been published in such scholarly periodicals as *The Sociological Review, British Journal of Sociology, Third World Quarterly, British Journal of Political Science,* and *Political Studies.* Dr. Zureik is the author of *The Palestinians in Israel: A Study in Internal Colonialism* and co-editor of *Sociology of the Palestinians* and *International Public Opinion and the Palestine Question.* He earned his doctorate from Essex University, England.

Index

'Abd al-'Arwi, Allah, 152
'Abd al-Da'im, 'Abd Allah, 151
'Abd al-Kabir al-Khatibi, 171
'Abd al-Malik, Anwar, 152, 153
'Abd al-Sabur, 162
Abrahamian, Ervand, 317
Abu Dhabi, 24
Abu Nuwas, 172
Achille Lauro incident, 265
Adab, Al-, 166
Adelman, M. A., 198
Aden-Algiers agreement, 275
Adnan, Etel, 215
Adonis ('Ali Ahmad Sa'id), 152, 162, 168, 173, 175
Afghanistan, 119, 315
Agriculture, 71, 81(table), 107–128, 194, 200(table), 222, 228
  commercialization of, 223, 228
  investment in, 115–116, 120–123
  irrigation, 122–123
  oil revenues and, 115–116, 124–125
  prices, 117, 118, 120, 123–124, 128(n42)
  productivity, 110(table), 111–112, 116, 122, 125, 126(n13)
  shortfalls, 107, 108, 115, 116, 120, 235. *See also* Food dependency
Ahmed, Muhammad Sid, 17
AI. *See* Amnesty International
Ait-Laoussine, Nordine, 98
Ajami, Fouad, 301
ALECSO. *See* Arab League, Educational, Cultural, and Scientific Organization
Alf layla wa laylatan (al-Rahib), 176
Algeria, 24, 26, 29, 55, 57, 76, 99, 113, 134, 137, 143(n2), 197, 207(n25), 223, 297, 315
  agriculture in, 115, 121, 228
  debt, 74, 86(table), 87(table)
  economic policies, 223
  Moroccan dispute, 57
  oil revenues, 92
  Soviet relations, 73
  stability of, 27
  trade patterns, 72
  U.S. relations, 57
  women in, 47
'Alim, al-, Mahmud Amin, 152
Allon, Yigal, 247
Allon plan, 268
Almond, Gabriel, 324
Alternative Middle East Studies Seminar (AMESS), 317
Althusser, Louis, 304
American University (Beirut), 297
American University (Cairo), 297
AMESS. *See* Alternative Middle East Studies Seminar
Amin, Ahmad, 17
Amin, Galal, 193
Amin, Qasim, 210
Amin, Samir, 1, 7, 152, 192, 193, 194, 198, 259
Amman accord. *See* Framework for Common Action
Amnesty International (AI), 39
AOAD. *See* Arab Organization for Agricultural Development
AOHR. *See* Arab Organization for Human Rights
Aquino, Corazon, 252
Arab Association of Political Scientists, 7
Arab Association of Sociologists, 7
Arab awakening, 1, 7
Arab Development: Present, Possible, and the Future, 194
Arabism, 26, 34. *See also* Pan-Arabism
Arab League, 297

Educational, Cultural, and Scientific Organization (ALECSO), 156
Arab nationalism, 61, 154–155, 231, 275. *See also* Arab unity
Arab Organization for Agricultural Development (AOAD), 71
Arab Organization for Human Rights (AOHR), 39, 43, 44
Arab Political Science Association, 298
Arab Socialist Union, 17
Arab Studies Quarterly, 317
Arab Thought Forum, 43
Arab unity, 2, 5, 15. *See also* Arab nationalism
Arab Women's Association, 7
Arafat, Yasser, 263, 264, 265, 266, 273, 274, 276
Argentina, 119, 252, 298
Arms transfers, 73, 280. *See also* Dependency, military
Art, 172, 180. *See also* Culture
Asad, al-, Hafiz, 33, 67, 257, 263, 265
Asad, Talal, 216
Aslan, Ibrahim, 177
Association of Arab-American University Graduates, 317
Association of Arab Economists, 7
Atatürk, 210
Australia, 71
Authoritarianism, 23, 25–26, 34. *See also* Political systems
Autumn of Fury: The Assassination of Sadat (Heikal), 65–66
'Awda, A., 309

Badayia, al-, Bahithat, 213
Bahrain, 24, 32, 92, 95, 207(n25)
Ba'labakki, Layla, 215
Balance of power, 279–289
Balfour Declaration, 69
Bani-Sadr, 309
Barakat, Halim, 216
Barthes, Roland, 171, 304
Batatu, Hanna, 230, 317
Bayyati, al-, 162
Beck, Lois, 318
Begin, Menachem, 261
Beinin, Joel, 318
Beirut University College, 49

Belgium, 269
Benelux, 269
Ben Gurion, David, 70, 247
Benvenisti, Meron, 273, 324
Berberoglu, Berch, 317
Berger, Morroe, 294
Bezirgan, Basima, 318
Bianchi, Robert, 295
Bimodalism, 113–114, 116
Binder, Leonard, 294
Birth rates, 186, 187(table), 188(fig.), 192–193, 195, 203
Black September, 258, 276(n4)
Boullata, Kamal, 173
Boumedienne, Houari, 223
Bourgeoisie. *See* Middle class
Bourguiba, Habib ben Ali, 33, 47, 67
Brain drain, 139–140
Brazil, 105(n7), 114(table), 118, 127(n35), 134, 139, 142
Brecher, Michael, 69
Bretton Woods system, 75
Bulletin Economique et Social du Maroc, 297

Camp David Accords, 119, 255, 261, 262, 263, 265, 267, 268, 269, 270, 276, 279
Canada, 71, 99
Capital
  accumulation, 226
  flight, 131–132, 224
  in real estate, 224
  state, 232, 234, 235
  world, 324
  See also Investment
Capitalism
  state, 232, 234, 235
  world, 324
Carter, Jimmy, 261, 265, 266
Carter Doctrine, 261
CAUS. *See* Centre for Arab Unity Studies
Centre for Arab Unity Studies (CAUS), 43, 156, 193, 297, 328(n7)
Centre for Criminological and Sociological Research, 297
Chile, 114(table), 252, 298
CIA. *See* United States, Central Intelligence Agency

Civil rights, 4–5, 18. *See also* Human rights
Class
  structures, 221–238
  struggle, 152, 179, 218
  transformation, 226–229, 233
  See also Demographic transitions; Middle class
Club for Dialogue, 310
Cohen, S., 326
Cold War, 66, 313. *See also* Superpower relations
Colombia, 105(n7), 114(table)
Colonialization, 197
Colonial period, 113, 169–170, 221, 322
Comte, Auguste, 307
Confucius, 190
Consumerism, 227, 231, 232. *See also* Capitalism
Consumption patterns, 199
Cooper, Anna, 217
Costa Rica, 252
Critique of the Arab Mind, The (El Gabry), 305
Cultural dependency, 74, 78
Culture
  art and literature, 160–181
  authenticity, 147–159, 232
  colonialization and, 169–171
  fragmentation of, 161–163, 166–167, 169, 179–181
  as heritage, 148–149, 152
  Islamic, 149, 150, 154, 161, 167, 168, 171–174, 180. *See also* Islam
  state intervention in, 165–166
  synthesis of, 179–181
  western influence, 149–150, 151–152, 161, 166–167, 171, 209–211, 217–218, 232
Cyprus, 166

Darwish, Mahmoud, 170, 180
Davis, Eric, 318
Davis, Susan Schaefer, 318
Dayan, Moshe, 247, 266
Debt
  foreign, 50, 74–75, 86(table), 87(table), 201(table), 202
  inter-Arab, 74
  private, 94

Defense spending, 84–85(table)
Democracy, 323
Democratization, 43, 44
Demographic transitions, 185–186, 187(&table), 188(fig.), 194, 195, 196(fig.), 198, 202, 203–204
Deng, Francis M., 14
Dependency, 2, 3, 65, 67–68, 193, 194, 198, 204
  cultural, 74, 78
  food, 70–72, 81(table), 107, 108, 112, 116–120, 122, 123, 124, 125, 200(table), 202, 235
  military, 73, 74, 78, 83(tables), 283, 284, 287, 289, 323
  security, 264
  stability and, 25, 32
  structural, 70–75
  technological, 131, 136
  theory, 317–318, 324
Derrida, Jacques, 304
Development, 228, 322
  agricultural, 71
  demographic transition and, 186
  instability and, 48
  oil revenues and, 93, 95, 101
  pan-Arab, 93, 103
  paradigms, 193–202, 203–204
  political modernization and, 28, 102–103
  strategies, 101–104
  studies, 190, 191–192
  women and, 48–51
DIA. *See* United States, Defense Intelligence Agency
Discourse, 304–305
Dissidents. *See* Opposition activity
Divorce, 46
Domestic politics, 22–37
Donaldson, Sam, 273
Drought, 112–113
Dubai, 24
Dunqul, Amal, 175
Durkheim, 308

Eban, Abba, 268, 269, 272, 273
Economics, 295. *See also* Political economy paradigm
Economies
  efficiency of, 196
  fragmentation of, 223–226

inequalities among, 227–229
integration of, 103–104, 221–222, 225, 257
irrationality of, 5
liberalization of, 222–223
oil and, 92–94, 100, 101
reform, 33–34
reprivatization of, 222–223
underground, 225
world system, 192, 196(fig.), 196–202
See also Development
Ecuador, 99
Education, 95
  abroad, 75, 87(table)
  technological development and, 130–131, 136, 137, 138(table), 139
  of women, 49, 214–215, 218
  See also Literacy
EEC. *See* European Economic Community
Egypt, 24, 26, 33, 35, 55, 57, 58, 109, 113, 175, 187, 195, 199, 202, 209, 210, 223, 230, 231, 234, 235, 258, 297–298, 299, 307, 311, 315
  agriculture in, 114(&table), 115, 116, 123, 124, 126(n13), 128(n42), 228
  Arab relations, 13, 14, 18, 19–20, 262, 263, 266
  debt, 12, 74, 86(table), 87(table)
  demographics, 11, 16
  dependency of, 12–13
  economy, 16, 59, 93, 94–95, 115, 203, 222, 223, 228
  education in, 139
  food shortages in, 70
  human rights in, 40, 43–44
  infrastructure, 12
  inter-Arab relations and, 56, 59–62
  Israeli relations, 19, 59–61, 244, 261, 262, 263, 270, 273, 279. *See also* Camp David Accords
  judicial system, 43–44
  land reform in, 228
  military strength, 279–280
  modernization, 17
  oil production, 105(n7)
  oil revenues, 92
  PLO and, 257, 259, 265
  political system, 16–17, 18, 19, 39–40, 42, 43

resources, 11, 18
  Soviet relations, 73
  stability of, 16, 27, 29, 32, 34
  technological development in, 131, 132, 134, 137, 139, 140
  U.S. relations, 12, 33, 57, 59, 60–61, 65, 72, 74, 118, 120, 280
  women in, 46, 47, 50
Egyptian Feminist Union, 213
Eitan, Rafael, 250
El Gabry, Muhammad Abed, 304–305
Elites
  political, 4–6, 33, 34, 229
  study of, 325–326
  technocratic, 30, 31
  technological development and, 132, 134–135
  See also Stability
El Salvador, 252
Embourgeoisement, 226, 227, 231
Emmanuel, Arghiri, 192
Engels, Friedrich, 153
Environment, 122–123
Ethiopia, 29
European Economic Community (EEC), 118

Fahd bin 'Abd al-'Aziz Al Saud, 264
Family, 46–47, 209
Fanon, Franz, 169
Faroqhi, Suraiya, 318
Farouk (king of Egypt), 17
Faysal (king of Saudi Arabia), 56, 67
Faysal bin 'Abd al-'Aziz, 33
Federal German Foundation, 298
Federal Republic of Germany, 73
Feminism, 213, 217. *See also* Women
Fergani, Nader, 193, 194, 206(n21)
Fernea, Elizabeth, 318
Fez summit, 264, 267
Food dependency, 70–72, 81(table), 107, 108, 112, 116–120, 122, 123, 124, 125, 200(table), 202, 235
Ford Foundation, 298
Foreign aid, 32. *See also* Dependency; United States, aid from
Foreign assets, 93
Foreign exchange, 115, 116, 117
Foreign relations. *See* Inter-Arab relations; Soviet Union; United States

Forum for Democratic Thought, 311
Foucault, Michel, 304, 326
Framework for Common Action, 262, 265, 266–267
France, 68, 73, 197, 245
Fundamentalism. *See* Islam, fundamentalist
Fusul, 166
Future of Islamic Civilization, The (Sardar), 309
Futurology, 325, 326–327

Gabon, 99
Galili, Yisrael, 247
Garang, John, 13
Gavish, Yishayahu, 248
GCC. *See* Gulf Cooperation Council
Geertz, Clifford, 294, 295
Gendzier, Irene, 316
Germany, 66. *See also* Federal Republic of Germany
Gezira scheme, 299
Ghazali, al-, Zeinab, 211, 212–213
Ghitani, al-, Jamal, 170
Gnostic Gospels (Pagels), 216
Goldmann, Lucien, 177
Goldmann, Nahum, 69, 70
Gorbachev, Mikhail, 267
Gramsci, Antonio, 165
Gran, Peter, 317–318
Great Britain, 68, 69, 73, 77, 197, 198, 203, 220(n10)
Greater Syria, 15
Guatemala, 252
Gulf Cooperation Council (GCC), 20, 73, 103, 266
Gur, Mota, 248

Habibi, Emile, 170, 173
Hafez, Salah, 66
Haig, Alexander, 261, 264
Hallaj, al-, 173, 174
Halpern, Manfred, 34
Hassan II (king of Morocco), 44
Hawi, 162
Health care, 95, 135, 136
Heikal, 65–66
Heilbroner, Robert, 301
Hermassi, Abdel Baki, 308
Hijazi, 162
Hitler, Adolf, 69

Hod, Mordechai, 248
Homans, G., 75
Honduras, 252
Hong Kong, 139
Hossain, Adel, 203
Hourani, Albert, 296
Hudson, Michael, 17
"Hull group," 316
Human Prospect, The (Heilbroner), 301
Human rights, 4–5, 7, 38–44, 45–52
Huntington, Rick, 299
Huntington, Samuel, 26, 34
Hurewitz, Yigal, 248
Husayn, al-, 173, 174
Husri, al-, Sati', 151
Hussein (king of Jordan), 33, 264, 265, 266, 268, 273, 274, 276(n4)

Ibrahim, Saad Eddin, 211, 216
ICJ. *See* International Commission of Jurists
Ideologies, 304
Ideology and Sociological Theory (Zeitlin), 307
IDF. *See* Israel Defense Forces
Income distribution, 190–191, 192, 200(table), 224–225, 227, 228–229, 323
India, 75, 102, 105(n7), 114(table), 134, 139, 295
Individualism, 51
Indonesia, 99
Industrialization, 51, 115, 116, 140–141, 204(n1), 222, 223–224
 investment in, 131, 140, 141
 population growth and, 195, 203
 technology and, 135–136
Infitah. *See* Economies, liberalization of
Information revolution, 204
Instability. *See* Stability
Institute for Women's Studies in the Arab World, 49
Institute of Arab Studies, 317
Intelligentsia, 7
Inter-Arab relations, 55–63, 263–264
 Lebanonization of, 64
 oil and, 94, 103–104
Interdependence, 72, 75. *See also* Economies, integration of
International Commission of Jurists (ICJ), 39

Index

International Covenant on Civil and Political Rights, 39
International Monetary Fund, 33
Investment, 197, 222
  in agriculture, 115–116, 120–123
  in industry, 131, 140, 141
  in technology, 130, 131, 132–134
  in United States, 77
  in Western countries, 224
Iran, 5, 16, 27, 29, 56, 59, 96, 113, 315, 316, 323
  agriculture in, 112, 114(table)
  economic policies, 223
  inter-Arab relations and, 58, 61, 266
  Israeli relations, 252
  oil production, 99, 100, 105(n5)
  revolution, 34, 35, 193, 235, 252, 295
  security systems, 34
  women in, 214
Iran-Iraq war, 5, 6, 35, 50, 57, 59, 73, 94, 99, 100, 111, 198, 265, 266, 280
Iraq, 24, 26, 29, 55, 56, 57, 61, 96, 113, 172, 175, 197, 207(n25), 237(n14), 297, 301
  agriculture in, 115
  debt, 74, 86(table)
  defense spending, 73, 84–85(table)
  economy, 94
  education in, 139
  Israeli bombing of, 60, 262
  land reform in, 223
  oil production, 99, 100, 105(n5)
  oil revenues, 92
  Palestinians and, 265
  political system, 40
  stability of, 25, 27, 34
  technology development in, 132, 134, 137
  U.S. relations, 57, 94
Ireland, 295
Irrigation, 122–123. *See also* Water
Islam, 314
  cultural impact of, 149, 150, 154, 161, 167, 168, 171–174, 180
  discourse of, 304–305
  fundamentalist, 1, 5, 6, 7, 231, 232–233, 295, 323
  human rights and, 38, 40–41, 47
  inter-Arab relations and, 61
  political, 26
  resurgence of, 34–35, 154–155, 168–169, 180, 181, 231
  women and, 210–214, 215–216, 218–219, 219–220(n2)
Islam Observed (Geertz), 295
Ismail (khedive), 16
Isma'il (Adonis), 175–176
Israel, 6, 7, 12, 27, 77, 154, 161, 163, 164, 167, 170, 178, 234, 236(n4), 260, 275, 293, 311, 315, 323
  anti-PLO policies, 60, 248, 249, 255, 256, 262, 263, 265, 270, 273, 274
  Arab emigration from, 270–271
  conflict with, 33, 56, 58, 59, 61, 68–69, 73, 78, 242, 247, 248, 250, 253, 256–257, 258, 259, 262, 274, 279, 285–289, 324, 325–326
  constraints on, 271–273
  debt, 243–244, 244(table), 271
  domestic politics, 247–251, 271
  economy, 242–247, 272
  Egyptian relations, 19, 59–61, 244, 261, 262, 263, 270, 273, 279. *See also* Camp David Accords
  extraterritoriality of, 69–70, 255, 261, 262, 269
  inter-Arab relations and, 69, 259, 267
  isolation of, 260, 261
  Jordanian option, 266, 267–271, 273, 274
  militarization of, 242–247, 248, 249–251, 252, 253–254(nn 6, 7), 256, 271–272, 280–281, 281(fig.), 282(fig.), 283–286, 287–289
  nuclear capability, 287–288
  political parties in, 247–248, 249(table), 250(&table), 251, 261
  recognition of, 274
  U.S. support for, 12, 242, 243–245, 251–253, 257, 261, 262, 264, 272, 274, 276–277(n12), 284
Israel Aircraft Industries, 245, 248
Israel Defense Forces (IDF), 241, 245, 281, 283, 286
Israel Military Industries, 245
Issawi, Charles, 294, 296
Italy, 73, 197

Ivri, David, 248

Jahiz, al-, 170
Japan, 66, 68, 77, 102, 157, 272
Jayyusi, al-, Salma, 215
Jesus, 174
Johnson, Lyndon B., 68
Jordan, 24, 27, 29, 57, 58, 60, 77, 78, 92, 109, 137, 141, 143(n8), 202, 209, 227, 237(n14), 276(n4), 311
  agriculture in, 124
  debt, 74, 86(table), 87(table)
  economy, 93, 95
  Israeli relations, 248, 267–271
  military strength, 280
  PLO and, 256, 257, 258–259, 260, 263, 264, 265, 266, 268, 270, 274
  political system, 43, 44
  remittances to, 22
  stability of, 32
  U.S. relations, 33
  women in, 50
Jordanian option, 266, 267–271, 273, 274
Joseph, Suad, 216
Journal of Palestine Studies, 297
Judicial systems, 40, 43–44

Kahane, Meir, 242, 250
Kalimat, 166
Karammita movement, 218, 219
Keddie, Nikki, 318
Kelly, Joan, 217
Kelman, H., 326
Kenya, 114(table)
Kerr, Malcolm, 58
Khadduri, Majid, 296
Khail, Al-, Abu, 77
Khaldi, Nabil, 112
Khaldun, Ibn, 307, 308
Khalid, Fawziyya Abu, 215
Khalifa, Ahmed, 309
Khalik, Abdel-, 193
Khan, Abdur Rob, 310
Khattab, al-, 'Umar bin, 173
Khomeini, Ruhollah (Ayatollah), 26, 235
Khoury, Philip, 301
Kissinger, Henry, 198, 266
Klieman, Aharon, 245
Korany, Bahgat, 308

Kristeva, Julia, 304
Kuhn, T. S., 306, 309
Kuwait, 24, 29, 35, 55, 77, 78, 96, 99, 137, 143(n8), 207(n25), 296, 297
  agriculture in, 228
  defense spending, 73, 84–85(table)
  oil production, 100
  oil revenues, 92, 94
  political system, 43, 165

Labor, 109
  agricultural, 228
  expatriate, 57, 58, 109, 111, 197, 199, 202, 221–222, 223
  female, 49, 51
  force strength, 190–191, 192, 195, 199
  international division of, 221, 225
  migration of, 50, 199, 202, 207(n31), 224, 226, 236(n3)
  productivity, 190
  remittances from, 109, 111, 125(n8), 141, 201(table), 202, 222
  technological development and, 130, 136–140
Land
  distribution of, 126(n21)
  reform, 114–115, 223, 228
  tenure, 113, 115, 121, 126(n19)
  See also Agriculture
Language, 293–294, 296–297
League of Arab States, 5
Lebanese National Movement, 275
Lebanon, 24, 26–27, 57, 58, 62, 137, 141, 143(n8), 175, 187, 234, 237(n14), 259, 272, 286, 316
  agriculture in, 228
  art and literature in, 162–163
  civil war in, 42, 50, 56
  instability of, 33
  Israeli conflict, 43, 56–57, 60, 234, 242, 246, 247, 255, 256, 261, 262, 263, 267, 271, 274, 281, 287
  PLO and, 257, 260, 266
  political system, 39–40
  Syrian forces in, 283
Legitimacy, 23, 25, 26, 27–29, 35, 36–37, 326
L'Egypte Contemporaine, 297
Lenin, V. I., 66, 192

Index

Lerner, Daniel, 294, 324
Lev, Chaim Bar, 248
Liberalism, 193–194. *See also* Economies, liberalization of
Libya, 24, 26, 56, 58, 72, 99, 197, 207(n25), 223, 279
  agriculture in, 123
  economy, 94
  Egyptian relations, 13, 14, 18, 19–20
  human rights in, 40
  military build-up, 280
  oil revenues, 92, 94
  political system, 18, 40
  Soviet relations, 73
  stability of, 14–15, 19, 27, 34
Life expectancy, 141
Literacy, 109, 125(n5)
Literature, 162–163, 166, 170, 172, 173–177, 180. *See also* Culture
Living standards, 227
Lockman, Zachary, 318
Lughod, Janet Abu, 294
Lukacs, Georg, 4
Luxemburg, Rosa, 192, 269

Ma'arri, Al-, 172, 173
Mabro, Robert, 198
McClelland, David, 324
Mahd, Al-, 166
Maher, Vanessa, 318
Mahmud, Zaki Najib, 151
Mala'ika, al, Nazik, 214, 215
Malik al-Hazin (Aslan), 177
Malraux, André, 177
Malthus, Thomas, 190–191
Managing Political Change: Social Scientists and the Third World (Gendzier), 316
Manakh, Al-, stock market, 94
Mannheim, Karl, 305
Manufacturing sector, 228. *See also* Industrialization
Marriage, 46
Marx, Karl, 153, 177, 190, 308
Marx and the End of Orientalism (Turner), 308, 316
Marxism, 152–153, 193–194, 308, 323
Matar, M. 'Afifi, 175
Mawaqif, 166
Mawdudi, Al-, 309

Mehanna, Sohair, 299
MERIP. *See* Middle East Research and Information Project
Mernissi, Fatima, 215
MESA. *See* Middle East Studies Association
Mexico, 99, 114(table), 118, 122, 298
Meyer, Lawrence, 272
Middle class, 24, 28
  creation of, 226–227
  culture and, 152
  industrial, 224, 235
  landowning, 223
  stability and, 30–31
  technology development and, 131
Middle East Research and Information Project (MERIP), 317
Middle East Studies Association (MESA), 313, 315, 317
Mikha'il, Hanan, 215
Military
  dependency, 73–74
  force balance, 279–289
Mills, C. Wright, 325
Modeling, 326
Modernity, 3, 7
Modernization, 6, 34, 95
  culture and, 147, 150, 151, 155–157, 161, 163, 167–168, 169
  political, 28, 102–103
  stability and, 29
  theory, 313, 316
Mohammed V University, 297
Mohsen, Safia, 212
Morocco, 14, 24, 26, 29, 33, 92, 109, 117–118, 141, 172, 202, 235, 299, 310, 315
  agriculture in, 113–114, 114(table), 122, 228
  Algerian dispute, 57
  debt, 74, 86(table), 87(table), 127(n35)
  economy, 228
  food shortages in, 70
  political system, 39–40, 43, 44
  remittances to, 222
  stability, 27, 34
  U.S. relations, 33, 118
Mortality rates, 186, 187(table), 188(fig.), 203
M'Rabet, Fadela, 215

Mu'awiya (caliph), 38
Mubarak, Hosni, 12, 17, 60, 66, 263, 264, 265, 270
Muhammad (prophet), 38, 150, 174
Murphy, Richard, 265
Muruwwa, Husayn, 152
Musallam, Basim, 314
Muslim Brothers, 18, 41, 42, 150
Muslim Women's Association, 212, 213
Mustaqbal, Al-, al-'arabi, 297
Mutanabbi, al-, 178

Nahda. *See* Arab awakening
Nassef, Malak Hifni, 213
Nasser, Gamal Abdel-, 2, 14, 15, 17, 19, 26, 33, 65, 66, 162, 193, 203, 229, 301
National security, 42
NATO. *See* North Atlantic Treaty Organization
Navron, Yitzhak, 248
Neo-imperialism, 35
Neopatriarchy, 2-4, 7
Netherlands, 119, 198, 269
New International Economic Order (NIEO), 76
Nicaragua, 252
Nicholson, Harold, 66
NIEO. *See* New International Economic Order
Nigeria, 76, 99
Nixon, Richard, 276(n4)
Nomads, 223
North Atlantic Treaty Organization (NATO), 69, 287
North Yemen. *See* Yemen Arab Republic
Numayri, Jaafar, 13, 16, 40-41, 44
Nuwayhi, al-, Muhammad, 151

OAPEC. *See* Organization of Arab Petroleum Exporting Countries
O'Donnell, G., 25, 26
OECD. *See* Organization for Economic Cooperation and Development
Oil, 2, 72
  Arab consumption of, 97, 99
  arms transfers and, 73
  development and, 197-198, 199
  embargo, 66, 67, 75, 92-93, 95
  glut, 76, 77
  markets, 93-94, 96-97, 98(table), 99, 100, 102-103, 105(n2)
  prices, 92-93, 96-97, 98, 116, 117, 124, 198
  production policies, 102, 105(n6)
  production rates, 98-99, 105(n4)
  revenues, 32-33, 50, 74, 76, 77, 91-95, 96, 98, 100, 101, 102, 109, 111, 115-116, 124, 131, 136, 199, 232
  stability and, 57-58
  technological development and, 131, 136, 140
Olayan, Suleiman, 77
Oman, 24, 92, 95, 207(n25)
OPEC. *See* Organization of Petroleum Exporting Countries
"Operation Peace for Galilee," 285, 288
Opposition activity, 30, 31, 32, 34, 35, 36, 40-41, 233
Oppression, 4-5, 15-16, 164-166, 230, 231-232
Organization for Economic Cooperation and Development (OECD), 116, 118
Organization of Arab Petroleum Exporting Countries (OAPEC), 76
Organization of Petroleum Exporting Countries (OPEC), 76, 77, 91, 93, 94, 96, 97, 98(&table), 99, 100, 105(nn2-6), 189, 197
Orientalism, 312, 313, 314, 316, 322
Orientalism (Said), 312, 316
Ottoman Empire, 7, 169, 197, 221
Oweiss, Sayyid, 296
Owen, Roger, 222, 318

Pagels, Elaine, 216
Pahlavi, Mohammed Riza, 16, 252
Pakistan, 29, 114(table)
Palestine Liberation Organization (PLO), 267, 279, 286-287
  Arab relations, 256, 257-259, 260-261, 262, 265, 266, 275
  fragmentation of, 263, 273, 274, 275
  Israeli conflict, 60, 248, 249, 255, 256, 262, 263, 265, 270, 273, 274

Jordanian conflict, 256, 257, 258–259, 260, 263, 264, 265, 266, 268, 270, 274
  recognition of, 259, 260, 261, 274
  support for, 256
  Syria and, 256, 257, 258, 259, 263, 266, 274
  U.S. and, 259, 260, 261, 267
Palestine National Council (PNC), 266
Palestinians, 2, 5, 6, 24, 27, 29, 33, 50, 56, 57, 61, 62, 163, 170, 180, 234, 236(n4), 241, 249, 251, 253, 255–278, 289, 323–324, 325–326
Pan-Arabism, 231, 257–258. *See also* Arab unity
Paradigms, 306
Pareto, Vilfredo, 308
Parra, Francisco R., 98
Patriarchy. *See* Neopatriarchy
Patronage, 229–230
Peled, Benny, 248
People's Democratic Republic of Yemen, 5, 24, 32, 55, 57, 58, 72, 92, 141, 143(n18), 222, 323
  agriculture in, 126(n10)
  economy, 93, 95
  Soviet relations, 73
  stability of, 27, 32, 34
  women in, 46, 47
People's Republic of China, 60, 77, 102, 139, 189, 194
Peres, Shimon, 247, 248
Personal status codes, 46
Peru, 114(table), 298
Petras, James, 229
Petrochemical industry, 140–141. *See also* Oil
Philippines, 252
PLO. *See* Palestine Liberation Organization
PNC. *See* Palestine National Council
Political economy paradigm, 317, 319
Political Modernization in Japan and Turkey (Ward), 295
Political participation, 34
Political parties, 40
Political systems, 23, 28–29, 39–40
  bureaucratic, 25–26, 27, 35
  change factors, 27–29, 32–36
  human rights and, 39–40

opposition. *See* Opposition activity
  women and, 50, 52
Politics, 22–37
Population, 108–109, 110(table), 126(n9), 186–187, 189, 190–191, 194, 195, 202, 203, 206(n21)
Positivism, 323, 325
Power
  absolute, 39, 41–42, 43
  transfers, 24, 26
  See also Balance of power
Praetorianism, 26
Prayer in a Deserted Temple, 174
Professional unions, 43
Proletarianization, 222, 226
Property rights, 113. *See also* Land
Public Faces (Nicholson), 66

Qadhafi, Muammar, 14, 15, 26, 40
Qa'id, al-, Yusuf, 175
Qasim, A. H., 175
Qatar, 24, 92, 99, 137, 207(n25)
Quataert, Donald, 318
Qutb, Sayyid, 150, 309

Rabat summit, 259, 264, 267
Rabin, Yitzhak, 247, 248, 264, 269, 273
Radicalism, 5, 6. *See also* Islam, fundamentalist
Rahib, al-, Hani, 175, 176
Rahman, Fazlur, 216
Rashed, R., 307
Raymond, André, 318
Reagan, Ronald, 12, 68, 261, 264, 267, 277(n12)
Reagan Codicil, 261
Reagan Plan, 269
Religion, 295. *See also* Islam
Repression. *See* Human rights; Oppression
Republic of Korea, 114(table), 118, 134, 139, 142, 252
Research and Development, 132, 133(table), 134, 137, 204, 293–302, 303–311, 312–321, 322–328. *See also* Technology
Resources
  human, 198–199
  technological development and, 140–141

Revolution, 6–7, 16
Revolution from Above (Trimberger), 295
Robinson, Joan, 190
Rogers Plan, 257
Ruling class. *See* Elites, political; Legitimacy
Rustow, Dankwart A., 295
Rutherford, Ernest, 67

Saad, Ahmed Sadek, 308
Sabra massacre, 274
Sadat, al-, Anwar, 34, 40, 44, 57, 60, 61, 64, 65, 66, 67, 167, 193, 203, 223, 230
Sa'dawi, al-, Nawal, 214, 215
Saddiki, Kalim, 309
Sadr, Al-, Baker, 309
Safran, Nadav, 269, 315
Sa'id, 'Ali Ahmad. *See* Adonis
Sa'id, Amina, 215
Said, Edward, 172, 312, 316
Saleh, Nahed, 309
Salem, Elie, 56
Salih, Saniyya, 215
Sam'an, Ghada, 215
Sardar, 309
Sarid, Yossi, 251
Sa'udi, Muna, 215
Saudi Arabia, 20, 24, 32, 55, 56, 77, 96, 99, 137, 143(n2), 207(n25), 297, 315
  agriculture in, 71, 116, 121, 123, 124
  defense spending, 73, 74, 84–85(table)
  Israel policies, 262
  middle class in, 223
  oil production, 100
  oil revenues, 92, 94, 102–103
  PLO and, 259, 264
  political system, 40
  regional status, 62
  stability of, 27, 34
  U.S. relations, 33
Sayegh, May, 215
Sayegh, Yusuf, 198
Sayyab, al-, 162
Sayyid Marsot, al-, Afaf Lutfi, 210, 216
Seale, Patrick, 62

Secularization, 7
Security forces, 6, 30, 32, 34
Senegal, 114(table)
Sex and Society in Islam (Musallam), 314
Shamir, Yitzhak, 270
Sharabi, Hisham, 216
Sha'rawi, al-, Huda, 213
Shari'a. *See* Islam
Shari'ati, 'Ali, 309
Sharon, Ariel, 247
Shatila massacre, 274
Shaw, R. Paul, 227–228
Shi'ism, 266
Shi'r Mawaqif, 166
Shukri, Ibrahim, 17
Shultz, George, 267, 277(n12)
Sid-Ahmed, Suleiman, 71
Smith, Adam, 77
Smith, Pamela, 317
Social science research, 293–302, 303–311, 312–321, 322–328
Social structures, 2–7, 221–238. *See also* Class; Demographic transitions
Somalia, 73
Somoza Debayle, Anastasio, 252
South Africa, 252, 268
South Yemen. *See* People's Democratic Republic of Yemen
Soviet Union, 12, 56, 57, 58–59, 60, 65, 66, 68, 71, 117, 119, 266, 267, 283, 289
  arms transfers by, 284, 285, 286
  military dependence on, 73, 78, 83(tables)
  regional influence, 68–69, 72, 73, 78
  See also Superpower relations
Spain, 268
SSRC. *See* United States, Social Science Research Council
Stability, 23–29, 30–32, 33, 34, 35–36, 236
  economy and, 32–33
  inter-Arab relations and, 56, 57–58
  oil and, 57–58
  regional, 31–32
  See also Iran-Iraq war; Israel, conflict with
State structure, 229–234

Steadfastness and Confrontation
   Front, 265
Stephan, Alfred, 294–295
Structure of Scientific Revolutions
   (Kuhn), 306
Struggle for Syria, The (Seale), 62
Sudan, 24, 34, 35, 55, 57, 58, 62,
     109, 117, 137, 141, 143(n18), 195,
     202, 235, 236, 299, 315, 323
   agriculture in, 112–113, 115,
     126(n10)
   debt, 74, 86(table), 87(table),
     127(n35)
   economy, 19, 223
   Egyptian relations, 13, 18–20
   food shortages in, 70
   human rights in, 40–41, 44
   political system, 18, 39–41, 43
   resources, 13, 140
   stability of, 13–14, 16, 19, 27, 34
   trade, 127(n34)
Sudanese People's Liberation Army,
   13
Suez Canal crisis, 68
Sufism, 218, 219
Sulzberger, C. S., 301
Superpower relations, 12, 19, 58–59,
     66, 154, 236, 266, 267, 313. *See
     also* Dependency
Syria, 14, 24, 26, 56, 57, 58, 60, 61,
     113, 141, 172, 175, 199, 227, 271,
     301
   agriculture in, 113, 114(table), 123,
     124, 128(n39), 228
   Ba'th in, 15
   debt, 74, 86(table), 87(table)
   economy, 95, 223
   education in, 139
   Egyptian relations, 19
   Israeli relations, 279–289
   military strength, 280, 281(fig.),
     282(fig.), 283–286, 288
   oil revenues, 92
   PLO and, 256, 257, 258, 259, 263,
     266, 274
   political system, 40
   regional influence, 62
   Soviet relations, 73
   stability of, 25, 27, 34
Systems analysis, 325–326

Taiwan, 114(table), 118, 252

Tajalliyat (al-Ghitani), 170
Talkani, 309
Tawil, Raymonda, 215
Technocrats, 36, 230
Technology, 204–205(n2), 206–
     207(n24), 324, 327
   culture and, 167, 168
   development of, 129–144
   education and, 130–131, 136, 137,
     138(table), 139
   foreign, 131, 132, 136
   investment in, 130, 131, 132–134
   military, 288. *See also* Arms
     transfers
   product markets, 142
   of security, 34, 35
   social change and, 185
   state-organized, 134
Thaqafa, Al-, al-jadida, 166
Third World Forum, 43
Thought and Dialogue Forum, 43
Tizini, Tayyib, 152
Tocqueville, Alexis de, 300
Tradables, 127(n30)
Trade, 72, 81(table), 82(tables), 93,
     101, 115–116, 118, 131–132, 200–
     201(table)
Trade unions, 43
Tradition. *See* Culture
Traditionalism, 150–151, 161, 163–164,
     167–168, 171, 172–174, 225
Trimberger, Ellen, 295
Truman, Harry S, 68, 69
Tucker, Judith, 216
Tunisia, 14, 24, 26, 29, 33, 57, 58,
     67, 75, 109, 114(table), 117–118,
     134, 137, 141, 235, 315
   agriculture in, 122, 123, 228
   debt, 74, 86(table), 87(table)
   education in, 139
   food shortages in, 70
   political system, 39–40, 43, 44
   stability of, 27, 33
   U.S. relations, 33
   women in, 46, 47
Tuqan, Fadwa, 215
Turkey, 29, 114(table), 118, 127(n27),
     295, 298, 315
Turner, Bryan, 308, 316
Tzur, Tzui, 248

UAE. *See* United Arab Emirates

Underdevelopment and Political Theory: The Case of Foreign Policy Analysis (Korany), 308
Underground economy, 225
Unequal exchange. *See* Dependency
UNESCO, 48
United Arab Emirates (UAE), 77, 92, 96, 99, 100, 207(n25)
United Nations, 66, 259, 260
  Anti-Torture Declaration, 39
  Universal Declaration of Human Rights, 39, 45–46
United States, 6, 57, 59, 61, 65, 68–69, 77, 78, 99, 117, 118, 127(n33), 166, 259, 272, 286
  aid from, 12, 13, 70–71, 73, 74–75, 119, 127(n27)
  Central Intelligence Agency (CIA), 315
  Defense Intelligence Agency (DIA), 315
  Egyptian relations, 12, 33, 57, 59, 60–61, 65, 72, 74, 118, 120, 286
  inter-Arab relations and, 61
  Israel and, 12, 242, 243–245, 251–253, 257, 261, 262, 264, 272, 274, 276–277(n12), 284
  Middle East studies in, 312–321
  military dependence on, 73, 74, 280, 283, 284, 287, 289
  oil dependency of, 68, 264
  PLO and, 259, 260, 261, 267, 275–276
  regional influence, 32, 33, 36, 257, 258, 259, 261, 263, 264–265, 266–267, 269, 272, 275
  Social Science Research Council (SSRC), 314, 315
  stability and, 32, 33, 36
  trade with, 72, 119, 120(&table)
  women in, 209
  See also Superpower relations
Urban bias, 113, 116
Urbanization, 47–48, 51, 226

Value systems, 51
Veil, 208–212, 213–214
Venezuela, 99
Vietnam War, 66
Von Neumann, 191

Wannus, Sa'dallah, 173

Ward, al-, Arwa bint, 173
Ward, Robert E., 295
"Washing Off Disgrace" (al-Mala'ika), 215
Water, 77, 112–113. *See also* Agriculture, irrigation
Wazir, al-, Khalil, 270
Weber, 308
Weizmann, Ezer, 247, 248, 273
Welfare, 230, 231
West Bank Data Project, The (Benvenisti), 324
Westernization, 149–150, 151–152, 161, 166–167, 171, 209–211, 217–218, 232
Wiarda, Howard, 294–295
Women, 208–220, 315, 317, 318, 323
  in agriculture, 222
  change and, 45–52
  development and, 48–51
  education of, 49, 214–215, 218
  Islam and, 210–214, 215–216, 218–219, 219–220(n2)
  in labor force, 49, 51
  life-expectancy, 141
  literacy among, 109, 125(n5)
  status of, 45–52, 169
Women and the Family in the Middle East (Fernea), 318
Women's organizations, 43
Woolf, Virginia, 216
World War I, 66
World War II, 66
World Zionist Organization, 69

Yalta Conference, 67
YAR. *See* Yemen Arab Republic
Yariv, Ziva, 278(n35)
Yassin, El Sayed, 58
Yatziv, Gadi, 268
Yazid (son of Mu'awiya), 38
Yemen Arab Republic, 24, 29, 32, 55, 57, 58, 92, 109, 124, 141, 143(n18), 222, 323
  agriculture in, 126(n10)
  debt, 74, 86(table), 87(table)
  economy, 93, 95, 223
  oil production, 105(n7)
  remittances to, 109
  Soviet relations, 73
  stability of, 27, 32, 34

Yusuf, Sa'di, 175

Zagal, Abdel Khader, 308
Zahlan, A. B., 134–135, 139
Zaini, Al-, Barakat (al-Ghitani), 170

Zaki, Ramzi, 193, 194
Zartman, I. William, 324, 325
Zeitlin, 307
Zionists, 241, 242, 247, 249, 266
Zurayq, Qustantin, 151